Exploring African Life and Literature

Novel Guides to Promote Socially Responsive Learning

Jacqueline N. Glasgow
Linda J. Rice

EDITORS

INTERNATIONAL
Reading Association
800 BARKSDALE ROAD, PO BOX 8139
NEWARK, DE 19714-8139, USA
www.reading.org

The International Reading Association attempts, through its publications, to provide a forum for a wide spectrum of opinions on reading. This policy permits divergent viewpoints without implying the endorsement of the Association.

Executive Editor, Books   Corinne M. Mooney
Developmental Editor   Charlene M. Nichols
Developmental Editor   Tori Mello Bachman
Developmental Editor   Stacey Lynn Sharp
Editorial Production Manager   Shannon T. Fortner
Production Manager   Iona Muscella
Supervisor, Electronic Publishing   Anette Schuetz

Project Editors   Stacey Lynn Sharp and Cynthia L. Held

Cover   Design, Linda Steere; Photographs, JupiterImages/Photos.com

Library of Congress Cataloging-in-Publication Data
Exploring African life and literature : novel guides to promote socially responsive learning / Jacqueline N. Glasgow & Linda J. Rice, editors.
    p. cm.
  Includes bibliographical references and index.
  ISBN-13: 978-0-87207-609-9
  1. African literature (English)--Study and teaching. 2. Africa--Civilization--Study and teaching. 3. Social justice--Study and teaching. 4. Human rights--Study and teaching. 5. Africa--In literature. I. Glasgow, Jacqueline, 1941- II. Rice, Linda J.
  PR9340.A53E97 2007
  820.9'96--dc22   2007016101

To all our students who learned to teach English in order to create justice

"Waking Dreams of Justice"

I woke from dreams in cold distress
With images of the dispossessed,
The hungry, the outcast, the powerless.

In the dark, and in despair, I cried.
"I have neither strength enough nor time."
"Who'll go into the world, instead?" I sighed.

I then remembered those who would teach
Stories, poetry, and verse,
And all the younger lives they'd reach.

In class I taught them "If?" and "How?"
While with their work
They said, "Yes!" and "Now!"

With each story I made my plea,
"Who will go and speak?" I asked.
"I will!" they said. "Send me, send me!"

So from dreams that disturbed my night
Of pain and loss from unbridled might,
They created dreams of things made right.

—by Jacqueline N. Glasgow & Stephen W. Spencer

CONTENTS

Part I
Getting Started

Part II
Novel Guides to Explore the Arab World in Northern Africa

Part V

Resources to Explore Africa Through Film, Children's Literature, and the Oral Tradition

ABOUT THE EDITORS

Jacqueline N. Glasgow is Professor of English Education at Ohio University, Athens, USA. She teaches methods courses for the Integrated Language Arts Education (grades 7–12) teaching license along with survey courses on young adult literature and children's literature. Her passion is to open the doors to literacy for everyone by providing rich experiences in multicultural literature, nurturing multiple intelligences, and actively participating in Making-A-Difference Projects such as the ones included in this book to have an impact on social justice issues.

Jackie began her teaching career after graduating from Miami University, Oxford, Ohio. She taught French and English in nine different school districts throughout the state of Ohio before acquiring her PhD in literacy education from Kent State University, Ohio. A secondary English teacher and university professor, Jackie is an active presenter at local, state, national, and international professional meetings and conferences such as the Ohio Council of Teachers of Language Arts (OCTELA), National Council of Teachers of English (NCTE), and International Federation of Teachers of English (IFTE). She works with secondary teachers in Ohio on implementing state standards and assessment, reading instruction, curriculum development, and teacher research.

Jackie was named Outstanding High School Language Arts Educator by OCTELA in 1998. She was the recipient of the Education Press Association of America's Distinguished Achievement Award for Excellence in Educational Journalism for "Accommodating Learning Styles in Prison Writing Classes" *Journal of Reading* (November 1994, Vol. 38, No. 3, pp. 188–195). She is past president of OCTELA and now serves on the Board of Trustees. Teaching for Success: The International Teaching for Success Program awarded Jackie a Certificate of Appreciation for Sharing Ideas on Improving College Teaching.

Jackie is editor of *Strategies for Engaging Young Adult Readers: A Social Themes Approach* (Christopher-Gordon, 2005), *Using Young Adult Literature: Thematic Activities Based on Gardner's Multiple Intelligences* (Christopher-Gordon, 2002), and *Standards-Based Activities With Scoring Rubrics: Middle and High School English* (Volumes I and II; Eye on Education, 2002). Her numerous articles have appeared in *English Journal* and *Journal of Adolescent & Adult Literacy* as well as in a variety of other research journals. Jackie's research and teaching interests are focused on pedagogy, curriculum development, and performance-based assessments for secondary English; social justice issues in children's and young adult literature; and reading intervention strategies for at-risk readers and writers in secondary English classes.

Linda J. Rice was awarded the distinction University Professor for English by the Center for Teaching Excellence at Ohio University for 2006–2007. As Assistant Professor in the Department of English at Ohio University in Athens, Ohio, USA, Linda teaches Integrated Language Arts methods courses, courses in young adult literature, and a variety of other courses such as Women and Writing, Writing and Research in English Studies, and Critical Approaches to Fiction. Beyond the classroom, Linda enjoys working with students as the faculty advisor of the Ohio University student affiliate of the National Council of Teachers of English (OU NCTE). Linda has worked on special projects with the Ohio Department of Education and regularly presents at state and national conferences. She serves on two executive boards, including Ohio Council of Teachers of Language Arts (OCTELA) and the College English Association of Ohio.

Linda earned a bachelor of arts degree from Grove City College, Pennsylvania, in 1992 with majors in Communication Arts and Literature. While teaching developmental writing and Advanced Placement English at Mercer High School, Pennsylvania, Linda earned a Master of Education in Administration from Westminster College in New Wilmington, Pennsylvania, in 1995. She then moved to Ohio to teach junior and senior English at Lakeview High School in Cortland, Ohio, and pursue a PhD in Curriculum and Instruction at Kent State University, Ohio. During that time, Linda spent summers at the University of New Hampshire's Summer Writing Program and Harvard University's Graduate School of Education Institute on the Media and American Democracy through a scholarship from the John F. Kennedy School of Government and Joan Shorenstein Center on the Press, Politics, and Public Policy. Linda taught middle and high school English for 10 years before earning her doctorate and moving to Athens to teach at Ohio University. She was named Outstanding High School English Language Arts Educator by OCTELA in 1998 and became a National Board Certified Teacher in 2001.

Beyond African literature and teaching methods, Linda's research and professional interests include young adult literature; literary theory for high school teachers; recruiting and retaining high-quality teachers; and promoting teacher creativity, confidence, and efficacy to combat anxiety related to standards and assessment. Linda is the author of *What Was It Like? Teaching History and Culture Through Young Adult Literature* (Teachers College Press, 2006) as well as numerous articles and chapters in edited books.

CONTRIBUTORS

Allison L. Baer
Assistant Professor of Literacy Studies
Western Michigan University
Kalamazoo, Michigan, USA

Jacqueline N. Glasgow
Professor, English Education
Ohio University
Athens, Ohio, USA

Kara Haas
English Teacher
Aurora High School
Aurora, Ohio, USA

Ruth McClain
Instructor of English
Ohio University–Chillicothe
Chillicothe, Ohio, USA

Linda J. Rice
Assistant Professor, Department of English
Ohio University
Athens, Ohio, USA

Alexa L. Sandmann
Associate Professor of Literacy
Department of Teaching, Leadership,
   and Curriculum Studies
Kent State University
Kent, Ohio, USA

FOREWORD

To be conscious in the 21st century is to be aware of an array of challenges facing various regions in Africa. Researchers provide a wealth of data and analysis on infection rates ranging from HIV to malaria, population migrations due to famine and armed conflict, and the economic consequences of foreign control of natural resources and Western agricultural tariffs. Meanwhile, news media inundate the developed world with images of refugee camps and children in the death throes of AIDS and starvation. The research data and analysis provide the intellectual framework for public policy discussions; the media images create visual shocks to complacency.

Despite this, sustaining the global attention necessary to provoke political engagement and cooperation remains difficult. Prior to the Internet and the saturation of electronic media, developed countries lived in relative ignorance of the depth of suffering in the developing world. Today, many turn away for the opposite reason: information overload.

One problem is that news analysis and reports are unable to provide the rich emotional context of everyday life and relationships. As a result, their human subjects are reduced to statistics and visual props. Portrayed as numbers, pixels, and sound bites, they too easily become the "Other" to many Western cultures.

Literature has an important role to play in breaking down this barrier to empathy. Its focus on the human condition links contemporary issues to timeless themes, opening within us unique portals to understanding. How? By getting under our skin. By becoming a part of us—of the way we think and feel.

Throughout history, stories have transported people across time and space through the power of imagination. They take us into other lives, lands, and centuries, connecting us with the experiences of individuals and communities affected by circumstances quite different from our own. As we are moved by the joys and ordeals of stories' protagonists, we grow to see the Other in ourselves and ourselves in the Other. Once we make that leap, we are changed forever, sometimes with extraordinary social consequence. For example, Victorian readers internalized and ended the horrors of their child sweatshops in large measure due to the novels of Charles Dickens. The works of James Baldwin confronted U.S. citizens on a personal level with the brutality of racism, helping to fuel the Civil Rights movement, while the fiction of Alexander Solzenitzen

Exploring African Life and Literature: Novel Guides to Promote Socially Responsive Learning edited by Jacqueline N. Glasgow and Linda J. Rice. © 2007 by the International Reading Association.

brought readers inside a totalitarian world and shook the foundations of the Soviet gulag.

That is why this book is such an important resource for educators. It provides insight into a body of literature that illuminates issues within Africa by creating emotional connections and bonds between the reader and the Other. In so doing, it provides educators with tools to become agents of profound social change.

Allan Stratton

 Allan Stratton is an internationally award-winning author and playwright. His novel *Chanda's Secrets* (2004) won the Children's Africana Award, Best Book for the Older Reader from the African Studies Association, the Printz Honor Book Award from the American Library Association, *Booklist*'s "Editor's Choice," and an International Reading Association Notable Book for a Global Society citation, among other honors. It is published and taught around the world. His new novel *Chanda's Wars* will be published by HarperCollins in spring 2008. For more information, you can visit his website at www.allanstratton.com.

Teaching Human Rights in the Era of Globalization

Jacqueline N. Glasgow and Linda J. Rice

Africa—not a country, but a vast continent—is composed of 54 distinct countries, with Sudan being the largest geographically and Nigeria, Egypt, and Ethiopia the largest by population. To many around the globe, Africa is a large, mysterious continent that comprises huge deserts, wild animals, and primitive tribal cultures. Not enough people visualize skyscrapers, busy city streets, and men and women wearing business suits, never mind interesting stories, art, sculpture, music, and traditional literature. Africa is the second largest continent, with over three times the land area of the United States. One in every 10 persons on the globe lives in Africa, and yet the literature of Africa is still underused and relatively unknown in the Western educational curriculum and educational curricula throughout the developed world (in this book we adhere to the traditional definition of *Western* meaning "of or relating to the noncommunist countries of Europe and America"; Merriam-Webster, n.d.).

The purpose of this book is to support educators by giving access to quality literature that would enable a better education for all. The book highlights the significance of the African people, history, and culture, including serious human rights issues that raise global consciousness. A study of African society through literature also provides understanding of universal themes such as governance by consensus, the importance of social relationships, respect for elders, and strong family ties. African literature can enrich Western education as it demonstrates the union of man, God, and nature in African thought. This book is a guide for those who have an abiding interest in teaching critical literacy using quality, multicultural literature that addresses social justice and diversity issues in a global context. Encountering African culture through literature challenges readers to new levels of understanding and tolerance toward new ideas and encourages an examination of injustices within their own cultures. By

Exploring African Life and Literature: Novel Guides to Promote Socially Responsive Learning edited by Jacqueline N. Glasgow and Linda J. Rice. © 2007 by the International Reading Association.

learning to respect the rights and freedoms of others as portrayed in the literature, readers can acquire a global perspective of awareness and tolerance for others. If we believe in teaching tolerance and empowering our students to take their rightful places in the global community, then we must know more, do more, and be more than we are at present. As we become thoughtful world citizens, we can have the satisfaction of knowing we have made productive contributions to society.

Who Should Read This Book

This book is designed for use in high school English language arts and social studies classrooms and for use in university-level African studies programs, world literature courses, and methods courses for the preparation of future teachers. It is particularly suited to classrooms with integrated English–social studies curricula, an approach that is already popular at the elementary school level and gaining popularity at the high school level. We wrote the book for teachers interested in examining diversity, equity, and human rights issues in their classrooms, and we use children's, young adult, and traditional African literature as the mode for exploring these issues.

The academic reader can move easily through the chapters, either looking for answers to a particular question (e.g., how to talk about female circumcision) or simply browsing to find new ideas to transform classroom instruction. This book provides guidance in addressing sensitive issues, such as female circumcision, with the understanding that when teachers have more information on a topic, they will hopefully feel more comfortable teaching the books where such topics are key to understanding the text and integral to the culture being described. Professional development consultants will find many ideas that can be adapted for workshops and short courses on Africa and global change. Educators also will discover materials useful for enriching their curriculum with global issues and multicultural literature. Teachers in the International Baccalaureate Program may implement innovative instructional strategies for required African literature. Nonacademic readers may look to the chapters for interesting reading materials to enrich their understanding of the wider world in which they must inevitably take their place.

How This Project Was Conceived

The editors, Jacqueline Glasgow and Linda Rice, have been working with a group of experienced Ohio Council of Teachers of English Language Arts (OCTELA) members who teach either in an intermediate school, high school, or university. Our project was initially funded by the Ohio Resource Center, a subsidiary of the Ohio Department of Education, which asked us to develop integrated instructional units for English and social studies classrooms that deal with human rights and global education. Outraged by the recent genocide at Darfur in the Sudan, our group of educators chose an area that concerned us the most—the struggle for human rights as portrayed in African young adult and classical literature. What started as a summer project has blossomed into this book manuscript as a group of teachers decided that they wanted to continue exploring and writing about African life and literature so that its culture and conflicts could become more accessible to students and thus position them to make a difference.

About the Contributors

While none of the high school and university teachers contributing to this book are Africanists—specialists in African affairs, cultures, or languages—per se, each is a master teacher and each has personal reasons for assigning the novel(s) they teach. For example, Jacqueline Glasgow's expertise in teaching social justice issues in young adult literature resulted in her desire to expose racial discrimination, confront human rights violations, and give voice to the issues in this manuscript. She worked with high school teachers Michelle Stoutamire and Annette McCorvey, who teach a pedagogy of empowerment to students in an urban high school to enable them to draw strength from their roots in Africa. Linda Rice has maintained regular correspondence with South African friends for over 20 years, spent a summer traveling throughout South Africa, and took the recommendation of a native South African friend to teach the novels of Nadine Gordimer, Alan Paton, and Dalene Matthee to convey some of the trials, conflicts, and change in the apartheid structure of the country and the history of the Knysna Forest region. Alexa Sandmann has met and worked with author Jane Kurtz and shared her passion to connect the lives of people across Western and African societies and find their places in both societies. Due to Kara Haas's passion for women's rights, she directed her teaching of 12th graders to focus on gender inequities found in various novels written by African authors. Ruth McClain lived a number of years in Papua New Guinea as a missionary and delights in challenging her students to confront media images to examine how they stereotype or liberate a culture. Allison Baer's dedication to global literacy and multicultural literature led her to incorporate children's picture books into her classes and workshops to examine critical themes and setting. Together, we have collaborated in the writing and field-testing of the Novel Guides that comprise this book.

How This Book Is Organized

The novels selected for this book represent well-known authors and award-winning 20th-century African traditional, young adult, and children's literature drawn from across the African continent. For example, Nadine Gordimer, author of *July's People* (Viking Press, 1981), won the Nobel Prize for Literature in 1991. Nancy Farmer won the Newbery Honor award for *A Girl Named Disaster* (Orchard Books, 1996). Beverley Naidoo won an American Language Association Best Book for Young Adults award in 1990 for *Chain of Fire* (Lippincott, 1989), and her book *No Turning Back: A Novel of South Africa* (HarperCollins, 1992) was named a Notable Children's Trade Book in Social Studies. We selected other authors such as Bessie Head, Flora Nwapa, and Mariama Bâ, who were published in the Heinemann's African Writers Series. The selections include a variety of genres (memoir, fiction, nonfiction, film, folk tales, short stories, and children's picture books) representing literature from various countries and geographical regions. For the purposes of this book, the continent is divided into three regions: the Arab world of northern Africa, the eastern and western countries located in the central region, and the countries located in the southern part of the continent known as sub-Saharan Africa. All of the books, anthologies, and media are readily available from local bookstores and Internet sites.

This book of 16 chapters is organized into five parts. Part I: Getting Started (chapters 1–2) provides a framework for teaching global perspectives through African literature. Parts II, III, and IV include Novel Guides featuring literary texts from three regions of the African continent. Part II: Novel Guides to Explore the Arab World in Northern Africa (chapters 3–4) looks particularly at child slave trade in Sudan and women's struggle to lead self-determining lives. Part III: Novel Guides to Explore the Life and Culture of People in Central Regions of Africa (chapters 5–8) explores voices that defy colonial rule in Nigeria, conflicts in politics in Kenya, movements from Ethiopia to the United States, and rites of passage for young girls living in the countries located in the central region of Africa. Part IV: Novel Guides to Explore the Life and Culture of People in Sub-Saharan Africa (chapters 9–13) focuses on the exploitation of people and resources, struggles with racial injustice and human rights, the pandemic of HIV/AIDS, and the changing lives and opportunities for men and women in pre- and post-colonial African countries. Part V: Resources to Explore Africa Through Film, Children's Literature, and the Oral Tradition (chapters 14–16), rather than focusing on specific novels, includes rich resources found in films, collections of children's literature, and folklore. (For more in-depth summaries of individual chapters, see pages 16–21 in chapter 1.)

How to Use the Novel Guides

This book is not a work of literary criticism, nor is it about African novels as such; instead, it is a hands-on approach to literature from teachers who use these novels in their classrooms. This volume demonstrates how a number of committed educators bring African issues and topics into their classrooms, breaking down stereotypical notions and expanding global awareness about the continent with a variety of engaging instructional strategies. The Novel Guides, which have all been field-tested in intermediate, secondary, and university classrooms, can help make reading and talking about these books more relevant, interesting, and meaningful. Educators have the option of teaching the African novels as a whole-class activity or dividing the students into literature circle groups according to their interests.

While these special features are meant to help readers easily implement the use of African novels in the curriculum, it is important to note that the Novel Guides are just what their name suggests: guides. Designed with professional preservice and inservice teachers in mind, the instructional strategies of this book should not be seen as a checklist to complete but rather as a range of ideas from which to choose—ideas that may be modified to meet the unique needs of various student groups or adapted to other literary texts. Designed to make the African literature and serious issues the literature addresses quickly accessible and practical for teachers, the Novel Guides in chapters 3–13 include the following features.

Novels, Activities, and Curricular Standards for English Language Arts and Social Studies

Each of the Novel Guide chapters (chapters 3–13) begins with an overview of curricular standards, providing a quick snapshot of the authors and books of the unit and how the Novel Guide activities are aligned with standards. Because the classroom assignments involved in the Novel Guides are designed to engage students in critical reading and writing, in discussions that foster making cross-cultural connections, and ultimately, in social action through a Making-A-Difference Project (for more information, see the description of the Making-A-Difference Project on page xxi), these activities, by nature, meet national curricular standards. The overview, therefore, aligns the novels, Cross-Curricular Activities, and Making-A-Difference Project involved in each Novel Guide with the applicable guidelines in *Standards for the English Language Arts* (International Reading Association [IRA] & National Council of Teachers of English [NCTE], 1996) and *Expectations of Excellence: Curriculum Standards for Social Studies* (National Council for the Social Studies [NCSS], 1994).

Social and Historical Context

This section provides information on the main issues addressed by the literary texts featured in the chapters. Where relevant, social and historical background materials are included to help establish a clearer context for particular conflicts or issues in the novels. Similarly, this section may include statistics and other pertinent research with the aim of helping teachers assist their students in approaching and getting the most from the literary texts, while deepening their understanding of African life and culture.

Information on the Novels

About the Author. All of the chapters include brief biographies of the authors of the featured texts. Like the Social and Historical Context section, this piece is intended to further contextualize the literary study and, in some cases, link the authors' own lives and personal experiences with the aspects of African life, ritual, or cultural elements addressed in their writing.

Summary. Because this book includes so many literary texts, chapter authors have included a summary within each Novel Guide to help teachers efficiently gain a basic knowledge of the books. Subsequently, teachers can make decisions about which books will best suit their instructional purposes without having to read each one first or use outside sources to grasp the basic story elements of character, plot, setting, and conflict.

Making Connections

This is a crucial instructional tool for teachers to use after the basic social and historical, author, and summary information are in place. Each Making Connections section includes three question sets that help students link the literary texts featured in each chapter with their own lives (text-to-self), other texts (text-to-text), and the world around them (text-to-world). While the lists of questions are by no means exhaustive, they are particular to the novels and should be a great time saver for teachers looking to launch literary study efficiently. A sample student response to one of the Making Connections questions is included in each chapter.

Critical Exploration of Themes

This section provides some of the most critical–analytical thinking in the book and, in concise form, performs the work of the literary scholar. The critical analysis of themes is designed to build teachers' background knowledge and show how, when there are multiple books in a Novel Guide, those books can be synthesized through thematic analysis. While certainly helpful to teachers who may not have time to conduct this kind of research and synthesis, this section may also be shared with students to model literary scholarship.

Teacher Talk

While the questions in the Making Connections section help teachers and students make connections between the featured novels and self, other texts, and world, the Teacher Talk section also includes questions, but ones that exemplify different questioning strategies, some involving literary criticism, others involving convergent and divergent thinking. In all, 13 different research-based questioning strategies are included in the Novel Guides. The questioning strategies modeled in any chapter can be modified and related to other chapters featuring different novels and aspects of African life and culture.

Cross-Curricular Activities

This section includes a range of suggested activities, many supported by examples of student work, that teachers can use to engage students with the literature and to provide them with extended opportunities to reflect on and respond to the aspects of African life and culture addressed by the featured novels. Though each chapter features a different set of Cross-Curricular Activities, all are adaptable for the exploration of other literary texts and issues.

Making-A-Difference Project

As its name implies, this section of the unit offers teachers ideas for how to bridge the issues explored in the featured novels with projects that aim to make a difference. Many of the issues addressed by the featured texts are quite serious and have significant social justice and human rights implications, yet this book's stance aims always to be a positive one. Therefore, while not shying away from difficult issues, the Making-A-Difference Project in each Novel Guide points toward hope. A fundamental aim of global education is increasing social consciousness for the purpose of taking positive actions in the world around us. In effect, the Making-A-Difference Projects invite students to become socially responsive learners by engaging in social inquiry and taking active citizenship roles through productive contributions to society as they respond to important, universally relevant issues facing the world today—notably health and human rights in the areas of HIV/AIDS and child slave trade, environmental concerns, cultural and social stereotyping, changing gender roles, intergenerational relations, class conflicts, and spiritual connections. Highlighting conflicts in the featured African countries is necessary to this book's purpose of educating students in hopes of spreading cultural awareness and enacting social change.

Acknowledgments

As Alexander Graham Bell once said, "Great discoveries and improvements invariably involve the cooperation of many minds." We are indebted to the many minds that worked together to discover and produce this book of Novel Guides to explore the life and literature of Africa. First, our gratitude goes to the contributors to this book, who worked faithfully and diligently to write their chapters in such a strict time frame. These contributors, Allison Baer, Kara Haas, Ruth McClain, and Alexa Sandmann, are not only master teachers with creative minds but also friends, colleagues, and mentors. We have learned so much from them and have enjoyed the fellowship of working together to learn, write, and teach what works best.

This book comes not only from the result of discoveries and improvements by teachers but also from the many minds of their students. We thank the preservice teachers who enrolled in our literature, writing, and teaching methods courses at Ohio University, Athens. These students created many of the fine models for the cross-curricular activities that appear throughout this book.

Many more thanks go to the minds and reviewers at the International Reading Association. Thanks to Corinne Mooney for so graciously supporting our ideas for the book and to her talented staff who worked so creatively in producing this book. Stacey Sharp's close, careful attention to details strengthened the manuscript. Anette Schuetz used her artistic talent in formatting the text. Thanks to the reviewers who offered scaffolding to make the content meaningful for teachers and students. Thanks to all the staff at IRA who worked behind the scenes to make this book such a success.

Jacqueline N. Glasgow

A trip to the Republic of South Africa (RSA) became a reality that enhanced the manuscript, thanks to the sponsorship of the International Reading Association and the Colorado Writing Project under the leadership of Judy Casey. The program "Alive With Possibility: Engaging Collaboratively for Literacy" enabled me to meet, share, and discuss the book project with South African authors, elementary and secondary teachers, and educators from the University of Cape Town. Thanks to the following Ohio University administrators: Benjamin Ogles, Dean of the College of Arts and Sciences; David Descutner,

Dean of the University College; Stephen Howard, Director of African Studies; and Joseph McLaughlin, Chair of the Department of English Language and Literature, for financial support that made the trip possible

This book of Novel Guides for African literature would not have been possible without my husband, Stephen Spencer, who shares my passion for language and justice and has supported me throughout. Special thanks also goes to Allison Baer for her careful proofreading as the work progressed.

Additional thanks go to the many other cooperating minds such as Rena Allen, Director, South Regional Professional Development Center, who planned for the Ohio Summer Institute for Reading Intervention Workshops, and the middle school teachers who attended them and field-tested these activities. These teachers helped me understand the characteristics of their students that drove our search for activities for higher levels of critical thinking.

Linda J. Rice

I am grateful for the support of the many fine colleagues at Ohio University who make working in the Department of English Language and Literature so rich and rewarding. Particularly, I extend thanks to those who attended the colloquium in which I was seeking early feedback on draft chapters for this book—your challenges and critiques have sharpened my scholarship and research. I would also like to thank Ohio University Provost Kathy Krendl for sharing her professional journey, offering sound advice about leadership and service, and guiding my quest to find a healthy balance between teaching and publishing. I greatly respect your hard work, perseverance, and optimism—keep on shining!

Heartfelt appreciation goes to Elmo Davie of the Republic of South Africa for introducing me to the riches of his country, personally escorting me on a summer tour, and always remembering to call on my birthday. Our transcontinental friendship has thrived for more than 20 years, and I feel very blessed to know this exemplary RSA citizen. I also extend gratitude to Kenyan friend and colleague Evan Mwangi, who piqued my interest in the writings of Ngugi wa Thiong'o and shared many personal stories, from his childhood in rural Kenya to his university experience in Nairobi, to familiarize me with Kenyan culture, politics, and rites of passage. I will always treasure the hours we spent talking about life and literature, relationships and faith.

I am also very thankful for the friendship of Carolynn Orr—one who, through the good times and bad, has remained ever close. And I wish all the best to my godchildren Robert and Mailé Orr—what a great file of memories you, your mom, and I have shared! Cheers also go to Lakeview High School Media Specialist Christine Daubenspeck—you have my highest professional regard for being one of the most open, enthusiastic, and supportive colleagues

I have ever known, especially when it comes to exploring new ideas and literature for the classroom. Catherine Howard shares those qualities and will forever hold a place in my heart as a dear friend, kindred spirit, and "sister." I also wish to recognize Sam Scott for being tireless when it comes to listening and understanding—having you in my life as a loving neighbor and friend sharing the academic journey toward tenure has been priceless. Thanks also to my friends at Celebrate Recovery and Athens Community Church: Your warm embraces, encouraging words, and prayers have played a significant role in my professional progress.

I am also grateful for the ongoing foundational support of my beloved family members: Amy, Dave, Colleen, Kenny, and Daniel Young and Susan, Jeff, Nathan, Jennifer, and Andrew Colborn. Although we are not in touch daily, I know our closeness by heart and trust in your abiding presence to lift me up whenever I'm in need. Finally, and most of all, I wish to thank my wonderful parents, Charles and Janet Rice, whose lives and conversation have always demonstrated that knowing what is going on in the world and having compassion for all people are essential to good citizenship. Our years of eating dinner as a family, watching the evening news, and talking about politics, religion, education, and work have proven immensely valuable in giving me voice, causing me to think deeply, challenge ideas, and ask important questions that involve looking inward and outward. You have been the best role models any daughter could ask for, and I love you very much.

REFERENCES

International Reading Association & National Council of Teachers of English. (1996). *Standards for the English language arts*. Newark, DE; Urbana, IL: Authors.

Merriam-Webster. (n.d.). Western. *Merriam-Webster Online Dictionary*. Retrieved March 2, 2007, from http://www.m-w.com/dictionary/western

National Council for the Social Studies. (1994). *Expectations of excellence: Curriculum standards for social studies*. Silver Spring, MD: Author.

PART I

Getting Started

Rationale for Using Novel Guides to Explore African Life and Culture Through Literature

Jacqueline N. Glasgow and Linda J. Rice

"Peace on earth depends on our ability to secure our living environment. Maathai stands at the front of the fight to promote ecologically viable social, economic and cultural development in Kenya and in Africa. She has taken a holistic approach to sustainable development that embraces democracy, human rights, and women's rights in particular."

—OLE DANBOLT MJØS, CHAIR OF THE NORWEGIAN NOBEL COMMITTEE (2004, ¶ 3)

For the first time in history, the Norwegian Nobel Committee recognized that forests are a natural resource that sustains life in Africa and that deforestation leads to poverty, ethnic conflicts, and needless human suffering. Hence, the Nobel Committee selected Kenyan environmental activist, Wangari Maathai, as the winner of the Nobel Peace Prize in 2004 (Ahmad, 2005). In Kenya in 1977, Maathai founded the Green Belt Movement, a voluntary organization dedicated to environmental preservation, women's rights, and community development. These women have planted more than 10 million trees to prevent soil erosion and to provide firewood for cooking, nutritional fruits, and clean air. Maathai (2003) wrote that "because Kenya is an underdeveloped country with limited resources, trees are a vital natural resource that can sustain the traditional Kenyan way of life" (p. 17).

Maathai also believes that schools should teach students to take an active role in the protection of community resources such as trees and the environment. Hence, Maathai's Green Belt Movement introduced the tree-planting

Exploring African Life and Literature: Novel Guides to Promote Socially Responsive Learning edited by Jacqueline N. Glasgow and Linda J. Rice. © 2007 by the International Reading Association.

project to 3,000 schools (Breton, 1998). An average of 500 children per school worked on the project, culminating in more than 1 million children participating in the tree-planting campaign, and Maathai's Green Belt Movement gained support from groups around the world.

Maathai's positive influence worldwide through the Green Belt Movement is an example of the kind of global interconnectedness and consciousness we hope to raise through the Novel Guides presented in this book. Maathai's program established a connection between civic education and social activism at home and abroad that provides a model for educators to emulate. With African literature as the foundation, the Novel Guides are designed to encourage that type of global education in the classroom by addressing the serious issues facing various countries in Africa, to increase global consciousness, and to move students toward the kind of engaged social activism that strives for justice.

This chapter first explains what is meant by *global education* and then establishes a four-part conceptual framework for teaching global perspectives through African literature. This framework is the research-based core of the book and therefore is an integral part of understanding why we believe it is important to teach students about African life and culture and to use literature as the means for doing so. The last element of the framework concerns pedagogy and therefore segues naturally to an overview of several instructional strategies that appear throughout the book. The chapter closes with a concise chapter-by-chapter description of the book's remaining content, offering a quick look at what authors, literary works, and key issues are addressed in the Novel Guides.

Global Education

In today's global village, educational excellence depends on our ability not only to understand and contribute to the human condition at home but also to contribute to improving quality of life through active participation in the world community. A key to achieving this excellence is through educating and reinforcing global perspectives for teachers and students at all levels of education. While earlier models of global education were expressed as "perspective consciousness" and "planet awareness" (Kniep, 1986), more recent approaches have included social action in addition to awareness and understanding. Merryfield, Jarchow, and Pickert (1997), scholars of global education at the Ohio State University, defined global education in a way that gives a clear image of a proactive perspective:

> Global education develops the knowledge, skills, and attitudes that are necessary for decision-making and effective participation in a world characterized by interconnectedness, cultural pluralism, and increasing competition for resources. (p. 4)

This definition reflects the more modern concerns of the 21st century in that it includes student preparation for becoming knowledgeable, caring, and active citizens who work together to make the world society more just and humane.

This definition also correlates with the definition of global education found in the *Expectations of Excellence: Curriculum Standards for Social Studies* (National Council for the Social Studies [NCSS], 1994). Standard IX, Global Connections, states that "Social studies programs should include experiences that provide for the study of global connections and interdependence" (p. 29). This definition of global education also correlates with the *Standards for the English Language Arts* (International Reading Association [IRA] & National Council of Teachers of English [NCTE], 1996). The global perspective is voiced in Standard 2, which states that "Students read a wide range of literature from many periods in many genres to build an understanding of the many dimensions (e.g., philosophical, ethical, aesthetic) of human experience" (p. 3) and in Standard 11, which states that "Students participate as knowledgeable, reflective, creative, and critical members of a variety of literacy communities" (p. 3).

Global education builds on the principles of multicultural education but applies the concepts to the world community by emphasizing concerns for the planet, the welfare of its people, and the conservation of its natural resources. While global education and multicultural education share many commonalities, they also have different emphases. Both involve a process whereby individuals develop knowledge, skills, attitudes, and behaviors for participating effectively in a culturally diverse society. While multicultural education stresses the individuals and cultural groups within their local and national society (Banks, 1996; Nieto, 2000), global education emphasizes world problems and interconnections within the global context. When combined, multicultural education and global education can be seen as two parts of the same theme of how individuals, groups, and institutions can work together to build a better world locally, nationally, and internationally (Freire, 1998; Sleeter & McLaren, 1995).

As our focal point for exploring global education that examines world problems and interconnectedness, we have chosen the literature of Africa, particularly literature that highlights the struggle for human rights. While 13% of the world's population resides in Africa, a proportionally small amount of literature represents the African continent, its people, cultures, triumphs, and conflicts (Nations Online, 2007). Western schools teach very little about the African continent, let alone its 54 independent nations. For this reason, we have chosen literature from various African nations as the centerpiece for global education explored in this book. We can think of no better way for students to envision not only diverse cultures but also how, through our diversity, we are ultimately connected—connected and concerned for the well-being of people all over the world. African literature, as presented in the Novel Guides, exposes students to a wide range of human experiences and helps readers to expand not only their concept of global issues and awareness of what is at stake when various kinds of injustice are ignored but also how they may become activists on the global scene, people who can make a positive difference in the world.

A Global Perspectives Framework for Teaching African Literature With Novel Guides

If we are ready to commit to global education, then we need a framework to develop curricula based on the previously mentioned concepts and standards. In 1997, Merryfield and her colleagues developed a framework for teaching global perspectives. This framework includes four elements that undergird the Novel Guides in this book and help educators to (1) conceptualize global education, (2) acquire global content, (3) experience cross-cultural learning, and (4) develop a pedagogy for teaching and assessing global perspectives based on content knowledge and cultural experiences (Merryfield, Jarchow, & Pickert, 1997). This framework also calls for collaboration among administrators, faculty, and colleagues in schools, on and across campuses and overseas, to endorse global education. Adapting this basic framework from Merryfield and her colleagues' work with teacher educators to our work in developing global perspectives for a literature-based curriculum allows us the opportunity to develop a rationale to explore the life and literature of Africa through Novel Guides.

Conceptualizing Global Education

Merryfield and colleagues (1997) asked us to consider how we will conceptualize global education and provide a rationale for our program. In this book, the Novel Guides are used to create a conceptualization of global education that moves beyond stereotypes and misunderstandings of Africa and into the realm of hope. The Novel Guides do not shy away from the serious issues that face various countries in Africa; rather, through rich studies in African life and literature, they serve to increase social awareness regarding injustice and help teachers and students envision ways to get involved and support positive change where it is needed most.

Fred Mednick, president and founder of Teachers Without Borders, asserted that while Africa has long suffered the indignity of stereotype and cynicism, a hopeful story is emerging: "These 54 countries and 800 million citizens have made significant—even miraculous—progress since independence movements began more than forty years ago" (Mednick, 2003, ¶ 2). Mednick then explained the ways that the African Union is a strong network of information, communications technology, and health and human services and how the government is gaining momentum in improving these areas. In spite of the drought and disease of unimaginable proportions that ravage Africa's population, there is still potential for hope. Mednick feels the tipping point is education. He explained that the need for education is the most vital task. For example, he touted Nigeria as a country in which teachers are mobilized. "Teachers Without Borders (TWB) was contacted by several Nigerians, who in a short time, have mobilized a 144,000 teacher campaign for national renewal" (Mednick, 2003, ¶ 6). Mednick further stated that Ministry of Education and the Ministry of Health and Welfare officials in River State on the west coast of Nigeria have endorsed and encouraged several TWB conferences that have addressed community education, early childhood education, education of girls, safety, HIV/AIDS, literacy, corruption, and teacher professional development.

Through reading and responding to literature, teachers and students can aid in the progress and development not only of cultures like Nigeria's, as described by Mednick (2003), but in other African countries as well. Appropriate content is one of the major elements of a critical and transformative education that can prepare students to examine conflicting knowledge claims and perspectives (Banks, 1996). Literature, a major carrier of content, is a powerful medium for understanding the world. Through literature, we can introduce our students to global issues and problems such the pandemic of HIV/AIDS and the competition for resources such as oil. We can discuss human rights issues that include rights of women and children, cultural genocide, race, poverty, and education. Through literature, we can celebrate the oral tradition of folklore and the visual beauty of children's picture books. By bringing quality literature from the post-colonial period of the 1960s to the present, students can explore the life and literature of this part of the world, namely various countries that compose the continent of Africa. The Novel Guides found in this volume serve as navigational tools through the wealth of literature that is available to us.

Acquiring Global Content

In considering acquisition of global content, Merryfield and colleagues (1997) invited us to develop ways teachers will be able to acquire the knowledge of the world and its people necessary for teaching global perspectives. In the case of acquiring content pertaining to various African countries, the Novel Guides provided in this book facilitate this process. The book is constructed in five parts, with three parts organized according to major geographical regions of the African continent: Northern Africa, to explore the life and literature of the Arab world; central regions of east and west Africa, to explore the life and literature of post-colonial rule in Nigeria and Kenya; and sub-Saharan Africa, to explore the life and literature of South Africa, Botswana, and Zimbabwe. We are particularly concerned with how the novels representing these various regions and countries of the African continent address serious social issues, help readers understand the struggle for human rights, and increase global consciousness.

The structure of each chapter is designed to provide teachers with a historical and social knowledge base of the predominant global and human rights issues in the featured novels. For instance, in the Novel Guides for exploring life and literature in Sudan (see chapter 3), the Social and Historical Context section provides background knowledge for approaching the issue of child slave trade in Sudan. In the chapter exploring the struggle of Arab women to lead self-determining lives (see chapter 4), the Social and Historical Context section provides the teacher with background knowledge on the lives of women in the Arab world. Each chapter also features biographical information about each author to further contextualize and facilitate teachers' understanding of the texts. Biographical information helps provide a context for the time, genre, and social and political issues the authors presented in their writings. Following the author information, a summary of each novel familiarizes teachers with basic story and plot lines of the suggested novels. The Making Connections section in each chapter assists teachers and students in making connections to their own lives (text-to-self), other texts (text-to-text), and the world around them (text-to-world), thus supporting the acquisition of global content (Keene & Zimmerman, 1997). Evidence of how the questions in the Making Connections section aid in students' acquisition of global content appears in each chapter through various models of actual students' responses. Chapters 3, 6, 8, and 9 offer text-to-self examples written by students; chapters 10, 11, 12, and 13 offer text-to-text examples; and chapters 4, 5, and 7 offer text-to-world examples.

Assuming that some teachers might need support in designing questions to draw out the major themes for each novel, especially if they are unfamiliar with the work, each chapter also contains a Teacher Talk section with questions that may be used to explore the themes and concepts in the texts. Each chapter introduces a different type of questioning strategy to model ways to lead students to higher levels of thinking and critical analysis. The open-ended nature of these questions pushes students to engage in high-order critical thinking, effectively deepening their understanding through the process of negotiation, interpretation, and discussion (Wiggins & McTighe, 2005). Students' deliberation over the essential questions increases their readiness to complete a range of activities and inquiry projects linked to the novels. To further facilitate teacher preparation in regard to culturally responsive pedagogy, each chapter includes Cross-Curricular Activities designed to help students meet the standards by making global connections and realizing global interdependence. And finally, to help students build the "knowledge, skills, and attitudes that are necessary for decision-making and effective participation" (Merryfield et al. 1997, p. 4), each chapter contains a Making-A-Difference Project that engages them in active citizenship in the global community.

Experiencing Cross-Cultural Learning

For this component of education in global perspectives, Merryfield and colleagues (1997) invited teachers to consider how they will experience, participate in, and learn to live with cultures different than their own. They strongly advocate real-world cross-cultural experiences as essential for preparing teachers to instruct students of diverse cultural backgrounds, languages, and worldviews.

While we view cross-cultural experiences as ideal teacher preparation, another way to engage in cross-cultural experiences is vicariously through reading. Through reading quality history and literature, we can begin to understand many things even though we have not experienced them personally. At its best, literature, through its powerful artistry, can be a catalyst for engaging students in critical discussion and for eliciting multiple perspectives and multiple voices in pursuit of understanding other cultures. It is important to note that real change is beyond the purview of reading and responding to texts, even the best literature, for literature is an art form, not an instrument of indoctrination. However, according to Maxine Greene (1995), "engagement with literature can summon to visibility experiences and perceptions never noted before" (p. 84). These "experiences and perceptions" can educate readers about issues outside of their known, thus promoting inner change. While literature cannot be expected to carry the full responsibility for transforming the world, it can be a platform for envisioning a more just world.

Through the novels explored in this book, we want to support teachers in their effort to engage students with these serious social issues and increase their global consciousness and to equip them with strategies to make a positive difference through social activism. In particular, the Novel Guides presented in this book address serious conflicts involving injustices that have buffeted various countries in Africa. Rather than ignoring these injustices, this book looks directly at issues such as the Rwandan genocide, the AIDS pandemic, child labor, environmental exploitation, animal poaching, apartheid, colonial rule, and women's rights. Literature has the power to transport us into new cultures and new worlds, and to discover new selves. Our experiences, or lack thereof, do not preclude enjoyment and critical appreciation of such literature. We are moved by the artistry of literature and drawn into the "imaginative dimension" that is characteristic of all good literature by which we find ourselves affected (Scholes, 1989).

By reading the memoirs of Mende Nazer and Francis Bok (see chapter 3) we can begin to know something of what it means to be a child abducted into slavery. By reading novels by Mariama Bâ, and Andrée Chedid (see chapter 4), we can empathize with women resisting the patriarchy. We can more deeply consider the effect of cultural genocide, often euphemized as "ethnic cleansing," by viewing *Hotel Rwanda*, a film about the real-life experiences of Paul Rusesabagina who provided refuge for the Tutsis from the Hutu militia (see chapter 14). By identifying with the experiences of the protagonist, we are exposed to and begin to relate to the consequences of apartheid in the South African literature (see chapters 10 and 11). By being open to the vicarious experience literature offers, we are able to personalize learning, increase understanding, develop a concern for others that goes far beyond the classroom, and begin to understand what it is like to be of another sex, or of another race, or born to a different place and time (Adams & Hamm; Gregory & Chapman, 2002; Meyers and Jones, 1993; Rice, 2006). Through the authors' vivid description and our mind's eye, we can also begin to appreciate the beauty of the land, art, culture, and rich traditions of diverse cultures.

Pedagogy for a Global Perspective

This final element of the global perspectives teaching framework looks directly at pedagogy and explains what is meant by the social action approach to pedagogy. In considering pedagogy for a global perspective, Merryfield and colleagues (1997) suggest we examine the methods of teaching and learning, as well as construction of assessment that would be appropriate for fostering global perspectives. This pedagogy must help students build the knowledge, skills, and attitudes that support cultural diversity and social justice by making global connections and realizing our interdependence in global issues. For this, we suggest combining a cultural response approach with a social action approach to explore the life and literature of Africa that includes various types of discussion strategies that evoke critical thinking.

Cultural Response Approach. While many educators and researchers were initially influenced by Rosenblatt's (1938/1996) reader response theory, which encourages readers to make personal associations and connections to literature, others have found limitations to this pedagogy. According to Purves and Jordan (1993), personal responses for readers who are unfamiliar with the culture of the text may not necessarily lead them to an understanding of the culture. Further, some researchers argue that responding to literature entails more than simply reacting to a text. According to McGinley and colleagues (1997), responding to literature also entails a range of life-transforming functions in which students are invited to construct alternative versions to reality and self. Central to this transformation is an awareness of how one's own ideological stance shapes the meaning of one's experience with literature.

While many readers of this book will certainly be working with students who are well-versed in multicultural literature, others may have students who not only lack exposure but even resist it. Beach (1997) was particularly concerned about white students who resisted engagement with multicultural literature, either seeing "little reason for caring about the plight of characters or react[ing] defensively to challenges to their own sense of white privilege" (p. 88). In this or any case where students resist multicultural study, the teacher's challenge is to help students reflect on their backgrounds, understand the limitations of their personal response, and move beyond resistance to become engaged in a text that represents a different culture than their own. Or, as Enciso (1997) suggested, as we mediate this literature with students, we might go so far as to invite them to "talk back to constructions of difference found in literature" (p. 36). As such, the idea of cultural response as a theoretical frame challenges students' preconceived notions about another culture and helps them navigate toward a deeper understanding of culture and difference and explore the historical, social, and cultural context of the works. In the end, we strive to take our students to the critical literacy described by Shor (1999) that "questions the way things are and imagines alternatives, so that the word and the world may yet install a dream of social justice, bringing life to what Paulo Freire called the power not yet in power" (p. 24). In other words, by taking this cultural approach to multicultural literature, teachers can lead students into greater self-knowledge, knowledge of the perspectives of others, and knowledge of the world. With this new worldview, students can make informed decisions about their participation in local, national, and international affairs as they take their places in the global community.

Social Action Approach. The pedagogy for a global perspective that we suggest combines the cultural response approach with a social action approach. Although multicultural education advocates disagree about the types of curriculum approaches being used in the field, most see the approaches in some sort of progression from superficial contributions to in-depth restructuring of the curriculum (Banks, 1994; Grant & Sleeter, 1998). James Banks (1994) describes four levels of curriculum restructuring: (1) the Contributions Approach, offering token references to holidays and events outside the curriculum; (2) the Additive Approach, adding content, concepts, issues, and perspectives without changing the basic structure or perspective of the curriculum; (3) the Transformative Approach, changing the basic curriculum to view content, concepts, and issues from the perspectives of the diverse cultural groups; and (4) the Social Action Approach, going beyond the curriculum to make decisions and take actions to help solve important social issues. The different approaches are like steps toward taking a greater commitment to understanding and involvement in global issues. With the Social Action Approach, teachers can help students to become "social critics who can make reflective decisions and implement their decisions in effective personal, social, political and economic action" (Banks, 1994, p. 152). As informed citizens of the classroom, school, local community, and world, students then work for personal and societal change.

Having explored the four components of the global perspectives framework for teaching African literature with the Novel Guides in this book, the next section of this chapter presents specific pedagogical strategies for examining the literature and related serious issues that increase global consciousness and ideally move students toward the kind of social action that will enable them to make a positive difference in the world.

Novel Guide Pedagogical Strategies

Each of the Novel Guides presented in this book reflects different questioning strategies to provoke critical thinking, meaningful and personal discussion, and inquiry into new ideas. The questions generated for each novel unit can be used in various formats to include teacher-led discussions, student-generated discussions, and literature circles. In each case, students must prepare for the discussion by keeping a reader response log as the tool for learning different ways of thinking about literature (see Table 1.1 for a list of students' requirements in creating a reader response log). The reader response log encourages students to develop a set of strategies for pursuing their insights and questions and to develop the stance of competent and insightful readers. Because

---

Table 1.1. Reader Response Log Requirements

1. Divide each page of your journal or notebook with a vertical line down the center.

2. On the left side of each page, record a significant passage from the novel, noting the page number so you can find it again. Write a minimum of 10 entries for each novel.

3. On the right side, across from each passage, do any or all of the following: (a) ask questions that would help you understand the passage better, (b) give your personal response to the passage, (c) give your personal evaluation of the passage, or (d) think of a possible interpretation.

4. Choose a quote from the book (a quote or powerful passage that captures one of the main themes) and write a one-page reflective entry that explains the rationale for your choice.

many students have been conditioned to answer questions rather than ask them, they may need to be taught different kinds of questions to ask.

Teacher-Led Discussions

Because discussion has such a central place in good classroom teaching, and because the quality of those discussions in many ways determines the extent and quality of students' learning, teachers are encouraged to lead their students in thoughtful discussions about each novel. The better the discussion with respect to its intellectual demand and objective, the better the students' thinking is, and the more permanent their learning is. Table 1.2 shows the teacher-led questioning strategies utilized throughout this book, organized according to the

Table 1.2. Teacher-Led Questioning Strategies

Chapter	Novel Guide	Questioning Strategy	Types of Questions
3	*Slave: My True Story* (2003) by Mende Nazer *Escape From Slavery* (2003) by Francis Bok	Herber's (1978) Three Levels of Comprehension	Literal, Interpretive, Applied Levels of Questioning
4	*So Long a Letter* (1989) by Mariama Bâ *From Sleep Unbound* (1976/1983) by Andrée Chedid	Questioning Circles by Christenbury and Kelly (1983, 1994)	Knowledge of the Matter, Personal Reality, and External Reality
5	*Things Fall Apart* (1959/1994) by Chinua Achebe *Efuru* (1966/1978) by Flora Nwapa *The Joys of Motherhood* (1979/2003) by Buchi Emecheta	Angelo Ciardiello's (1998) Model of Questioning	Memory, Convergent Thinking, Divergent Thinking, Evaluative Thinking
6	*The River Between* (1965) by Ngugi wa Thiong'o *Weep Not, Child* (1964) by Ngugi wa Thiong'o	Focus on Literary Theories (Lynn, 2005)	Formalism/New Criticism, Feminism/Gender Criticism, Marxism/Economic Criticism, Reader Response Criticism, Deconstructive Criticism, Historical/Biographical Criticism, Freudian/Psychological Criticism *(continued)*

Table 1.2. Teacher-Led Questioning Strategies *(continued)*

Chapter	Novel Guide	Questioning Strategy	Types of Questions
7	*Our Secret, Siri Aang* (2004) by Cristina Kessler *No Laughter Here* (2004) by Rita Williams-Garcia	Shared Inquiry Discussion (Great Books Foundation, 2006)	Factual, Interpretive, Evaluative Questions
8	*Jakarta Missing* (2001) by Jane Kurtz *Memories of Sun: Stories of Africa and America* (2004) by Jane Kurtz	Ryder & Graves (2003)	Before, During, and After Reading
9	*Fiela's Child* (1986) by Dalene Matthee *Circles in a Forest* (1984) by Dalene Matthee	Socratic Seminar (Rice, 2006)	Opening, Core, and Closing Questions
10	*Cry, the Beloved Country* (1948/1987) by Alan Paton *July's People* (1981) by Nadine Gordimer	Wilhelm's (1997) Reflective Dimension	Considering Significance, Recognizing Literary Conventions, Recognizing Reading as a Transaction, Evaluating an Author, and the Self as a Reader
11	*Journey to Jo'Burg* (1988) by Beverley Naidoo *Chain of Fire* (1989) by Beverley Naidoo *Waiting for the Rain* (1987) by Sheila Gordon *Chanda's Secrets* (2004) by Allan Stratton	Bloom's Taxonomy (Learning Skills, 2003)	Memory, Comprehension, Application, Synthesis, Evaluation questions
12	*When Rain Clouds Gather* (1969) by Bessie Head The No. 1 Ladies' Detective Agency series (1998–2004) by Alexander McCall Smith	Wiggins & McTighe (2005)	Open-Ended Questions
13	*Nervous Conditions* (1988) by Tsitsi Dangarembga *A Girl Named Disaster* (1996) by Nancy Farmer	Question–Answer relationships (Raphael, 1986)	Right-There Questions, Think-and-Search Questions, Author-and-Me Questions, On My Own Questions

chapter and Novel Guide in which each questioning strategy appears (specific detail about each is described in the Teacher Talk section within each chapter).

Student-Generated Discussions

Another approach is to teach students how to generate their own questions for whole-class discussions of literature. Some teachers do take this approach regularly in their classrooms, particularly at the college level. Students could take from any of the above questioning strategies, but it is important to teach them how to ask open-ended and sincere questions rather than assessment questions with only one correct answer (Harvey, 1998). The purpose is to give students authority in their approach to reading and responding to literature. When given this opportunity, students often ask questions that result in compelling discussions conducted entirely by the students. (See Table 1.3 for instructions to students for the student-generated discussion assignment.)

Literature Circles

Yet another way of getting students to talk in exploratory ways is to have them discuss literature through literature circles (Daniels, 2002). The teacher plays a less directive role in these settings than in the student-led whole-class discussions. Literature circles are small, temporary discussion groups in which the group members have chosen to read the same work of literature (i.e., one of the suggested books listed in the text set for a particular novel unit). Each member of the group is responsible for completing a task that will facilitate the discussion of the text—for example, discussion director, summarizer, word wizard, or illustrator (Daniels, 2002). These responsibilities rotate for each meeting of the literature circle. After students have completed the reading and discussed

---

Table 1.3. Student-Generated Discussion Assignment

1. Divide class members into groups of four or five, depending on the chapters in the book, so that each group is responsible for leading a discussion of two chapters from the novel. Each group will use one full class period to discuss the assigned chapters.

2. Each group member should take roughly an equal part in leading the discussion.

3. The questions should not ask for factual information unless those facts help explore open-ended questions.

4. The questions should include (a) inferences about characters or events within the text, (b) generalizations from the text to society at large, (c) global connections and interconnectivity, (d) literary form or author techniques, (e) evaluations of the literature, (f) students' emotional responses, and (g) personal connections and associations.

the text, they plan how to share their reading experiences with the class as a literature celebration. The goal of the celebration is to interest other students in reading the book. Students present movies, skits, monologues, multimedia, or other types of presentations. The ultimate goal is for the student-led discussion in the literature circles to replace teacher-led discussion as a way of examining literature in class.

Chapter Content: The Literature and Issues

The following section offers a brief overview of the book's remaining chapter content as a quick reference to the Novel Guides and other instructional materials. Teachers may use this as a snapshot of the authors, literary works, and issues explored through the Novel Guides so that they may easily select the content that appeals to them.

Chapter 2: Building Students' Background Knowledge of African Life and Culture

Chapter 2 is designed to provide background knowledge on the countries of Africa and their cultures so that students can enrich their understanding of the literature. To understand the literature more fully, students will identify geographical features, important cities, peoples, languages, resources, birth rates, death rates, infant mortality rates, education levels, and gross domestic products of various African countries. Students will also gain an understanding about coming-of-age rituals such as male and female circumcision ceremonies. They will explore food groups, recipes, and tasting parties and will participate in activities that will help them appreciate artistic expressions of mask-making, sculpture, music, and dance.

Chapter 3: Life in Sudan: From Slavery to Freedom

Chapter 3 confronts the human rights issue of the forced slavery of children in the Sudan through Mende Nazer's *Slave: My True Story* (2003) and Francis Bok's *Escape From Slavery: The True Story of My Ten Years in Captivity—And My Journey to Freedom in America* (2003). After reading these harrowing memoirs, students will enhance their understanding of the major themes of this literature by participating in a Story Impressions activity, creating a Culture Notebook, and creating storyboarding scenes of the Nuba Mountains. The Making-A-Difference Project for this chapter is writing persuasive letters to influential officials in the position to adopt legislation against child slave trade in the Sudan.

Chapter 4: The Struggle of Arab Women to Lead Self-Determining Lives

The Novel Guides for this chapter include Andrée Chedid's *From Sleep Unbound* (1976/1983) and Mariama Bâ's *So Long a Letter* (1989). Through Prediction Card Word Sort and Sketchbook Journals, students find themselves relating to and empathizing with women, men, girls, and boys from different African cultures. Through text and film, students have the opportunity to discover not only the inequalities that African women face but also the larger theme of identity and its connection to family, heritage, religion, and culture. The Making-A-Difference Project is a reflective essay on cultural conflicts of women and society.

Chapter 5: Voices Resisting Colonial Rule in Nigeria

This chapter features Nigerian classical works such as Chinua Achebe's *Things Fall Apart* (1959/1994), Flora Nwapa's *Efuru* (1966/1978), and Buchi Emecheta's *The Joys of Motherhood* (1979/2003). The major themes focus on Igbo religion, culture, and social traditions including female circumcision, bride price, and the breakdown of polygyny. The Novel Guides provide opportunities for students to immerse themselves in the Igbo culture by creating an Igbo Visual Dictionary and attending to the African oral tradition. Students come to understand the protagonists' personal anguish under a corrupt military government and patriarchal culture through class discussion. For the Making-A-Difference Project, students act as photojournalists to create a documentary of the lives of Nigerian Igbo women.

Chapter 6: Conflicts in Rituals and Politics in Kenya

The two works featured in this chapter, *The River Between* (1965) and *Weep Not, Child* (1964) by Ngugi wa Thiong'o, are common reading for young adults in Kenya. Both novels depict outside influences on children and societies and show how those influences can inspire or diminish hope. This chapter includes a background of the Mau Mau War, the conflict between the African natives and the British colonial rulers, and some of the rituals that deeply divide the Kenyan people to this day. In addition to creative writing activities for students and outside resources linked with Ngugi's novels, this chapter includes a Microsoft PowerPoint project through which students can educate themselves and others about some of the crucial struggles of Kenya. The Cross-Curricular Activities for this chapter are designed to highlight the role of gender and economics in the Kenyan society, while also engaging students in creative writing and literary analysis. The Making-A-Difference Project involves students in researching the World Free Press Institute and the USAID Program and in supporting their efforts to build a democratic and economically prosperous Kenya.

Chapter 7: Rites of Passage for Young Girls in the Central Regions of Africa

This chapter features Novel Guides for *Our Secret, Siri Aang* (2004) and *No Condition Is Permanent* (2000) by Cristina Kessler, *The Fattening Hut* (2005) by Pat Lowery Collins, and *No Laughter Here* (2004) by Rita Williams-Garcia. All four are coming-of-age books in which female circumcision is either addressed directly or alluded to as an initiation or rite of passage. *Our Secret, Siri Aang* also deals with environmental issues regarding the survival of the Maasai and the Black Rhino as related to the protagonist's rites of passage. Students will complete Mind's Eye Predictions and respond to animal rights issues in a Q-Sort, an activity to help them rank or prioritize valuable, complex, and partially overlapping ideas. They will also explore coming-of-age-rituals through an Anticipation Guide, which will assess the class's prior knowledge of themes and issues before reading the novels. The Making-A-Difference Project is a multigenre research paper advocating for change in cultural practices or environmental issues.

Chapter 8: Connections and Communication Across the Continents: From Ethiopia to the United States

Writer Jane Kurtz, who was a child of missionary parents, lived primarily in Ethiopia from age 3 through high school. This experience, coupled with numerous trips back, has influenced her writing greatly. The poignancy of "living in two worlds" is reflected in her novel for middle graders, *Jakarta Missing* (2001). Content knowledge about Ethiopia, drawn especially from her picture books, is shared. Her edited volume, *Memories of Sun: Stories of Africa and America* (2004), provides further means for middle graders to find common ground, as revealed in the stories. Students will compare and contrast the American and African cultures and acculturation process. The Making-A-Difference Project for this chapter involves students in educating others about literacy needs in Ethiopia and raising funds to support its libraries.

Chapter 9: Exploitation Through Child Labor and Animal Poaching in 19th-Century South Africa

Focused on Kenya's forest region of southern Africa, Dalene Matthee's *Circles in a Forest* (1984) and *Fiela's Child* (1986) highlight the cruelty to animals and children in connection with the timber industry. Among the hardships reflected in Matthee's writing are child labor, the separation of children from loved ones, and the hunting of elephants for ivory. Composing a song, writing a Readers Theatre script, and making a storyboard are activities to help students explore the central characters and conflicts. The Making-A-Difference Project in this chapter is a Slideshow Documentary linking a key issue from the novel with current research related to adoption, child labor, or animal poaching.

Chapter 10: Racial Tensions, Injustice, and Harmony in South African Literature

This chapter features Alan Paton's *Cry, the Beloved Country* (1948/1987) and Nobel Prize winner Nadine Gordimer's *July's People* (1981). In addition to background information on the books, authors, and apartheid history of South Africa, this chapter includes related writings by U.S. Civil War President Abraham Lincoln and a film documentary about Nelson Mandela, who was a political prisoner in South Africa for 27 years and then elected as the nation's first black president, and his predecessor, F.W. de Klerk, under whose presidency the South African government disbanded apartheid and released Mandela, with corresponding student activities. The Making-A-Difference Project is a Reading Feast Day in which students share authentic South African cuisine and promote black South African writers through their creation of trifold presentations and handouts based on books read in literature circles.

Chapter 11: The Struggles for Human Rights in the Young Adult Literature of South Africa

After Beverley Naidoo's release from prison for her resistance to apartheid and her eventual asylum in England, she began to write novels such as *Journey to Jo'Burg: A South African Story* (1988), *Chain of Fire* (1989), and *No Turning Back* (1995) to show the courage of others to resist racism. These books, along with Sheila Gordon's *Waiting for the Rain: A Novel of South Africa* (1987), portray adolescents defying the grip of South African apartheid. Allan Stratton's *Chanda's Secrets* (2004) is a Printz Honor Book that explores HIV/AIDS in sub-Saharan Africa. The Making-A-Difference Project for this book is a process drama on HIV/AIDS in South Africa focusing on "What needs to happen?"

Chapter 12: Life and Literature in Botswana: Resolving Cultural Conflicts to Create a Better World

To explore literature from Botswana, readers can enjoy either Bessie Head's *When Rain Clouds Gather* (1969) or a delightful series of six titles in The No. 1 Ladies' Detective Agency series (1998–2004) by Alexander McCall Smith. In Head's novel, students confront the effects of apartheid as the protagonist escapes the tyrannies of South Africa by migrating to a more ideal life in Botswana and working on an agricultural project. In McCall Smith's novels, through intuition, wit, and practical wisdom, the protagonist deftly handles domestic issues typical of life in Botswana. Mma Ramotswe does not want Africa to change, to become thoroughly modern, but some aspects of traditional African culture trouble her. Students will investigate ways she regards the traditional African attitude toward women, marriage, family duty, and witchcraft and compare them to modern perspectives. For the Making-A-Difference Project, students create a zine (a noncommercial magazine) to explore cultural, environmental, and social issues in Botswana.

Chapter 13: Cultural Conflicts and Choices for Education of Young Women in Pre- and Post-Colonial Zimbabwe

In Tsitsi Dangarembga's *Nervous Conditions* (1988), cultural conflicts reside in the lives of the four female characters due to their education or lack thereof. At a time when women had little access to education, which kept them in domestic roles, the protagonist flourishes in a missionary school, but this puts her at odds with her family and culture. In Nancy Farmer's *A Girl Named Disaster* (1996), another protagonist resists unfair domestic roles by leaving her traditional culture and seeking an education in a different country. By completing the Cross-Curricular Activities students will focus on the consequences of resisting post-colonial patriarchy and explore possible career choices for educated women. The Making-A-Difference Project is an I-Search Paper on women's issues, cultural conflicts, and choices regarding education and leading a self-determining life. The I-Search paper is a type of research paper that gets students involved in firsthand searching through interviews and surveys and also requires them to keep track of their process and progress as investigators of a topic.

Chapter 14: Using Film Media as Visual Text for Studying the Rwandan Genocide

This chapter offers an overview of 12 films set in various African countries with a wide range of stories and conflicts. The chapter then models an instructional unit based on the film *Hotel Rwanda* (George, 2004). Between April 1994 and June 1994, about 800,000 Rwandan citizens were killed during a campaign of ethnic genocide. Centering on the film *Hotel Rwanda*, this chapter focuses on how using film in the classroom helps educators increase students' awareness of genocide and international responses to tragedy. For the Making-A-Difference Project, students sponsor an Empty Bowls Luncheon where students collect money to feed the poor and contribute the proceeds to the Hotel Rwanda Rusesabagina Foundation to support the orphans in Rwanda. Rusesabagina was the hotel manager who provided refuge for the Tutsis whom the Hutu militia sought to kill.

Chapter 15: Children's Literature as a Means of Exploring African Life

While contemporary South African children's picture books reflect the complexity of the geographic and cultural diversity, they also provide an opportunity to examine race relations before, during, and after apartheid. Along with thematic text sets, including detailed annotated bibliographies, this chapter provides meaningful story extension activities that encourage students to think critically about racial inequities both in their own country and abroad. Themes included are Picture Books That Give an Overview of Africa, Gender Issues in Children's Literature of Africa, Comparing and Contrasting City and Village Life, and the Effects of Poverty. The text sets in this chapter can be used easily to support the teaching of themes in the novels featured in this book. In addition, a bibliography of other pertinent children's books is included. The Making-A-Difference Project has students create their own picture book on a self-chosen theme with an African country of their choice as the setting.

Chapter 16: Exploring the African Oral Tradition: From Proverbs to Folk Tales

This chapter provides students with the opportunity to read collections of fables, myths, and folk tales published in Africa and compare them with ones published in the United States. Students will examine the literary devices and themes of the tales and then write and illustrate a folk tale to share with the class. The Making-A-Difference Project is a celebration of culture and art as students participate in henna hand painting and attend a Nigerian New Yam Festival with African storytelling performances.

Conclusion

Exploring African life and culture through literature, much of which takes a serious look at issues facing various countries in the continent, raises global consciousness and subsequently addresses the goals for global education. The Novel Guides included in this book are designed to help students examine and effectively advocate for human rights, economic and social well-being, environmental conservation, and democratic participation for all of the world's people. We begin this journey by building their background knowledge and leading students through well thought out and significant discussions of the varied global themes and concepts addressed in the literature of Africa.

REFERENCES

Adams, D., & Hamm, M. (1994). *New designs for teaching and learning: Promoting active learning in tomorrow's schools.* San Francisco: Jossey-Bass.

Ahmad, I. (2005). Nobel peace laureate Wangari Maathai: Connecting trees, civic education, and peace. *Social Education, 69*(1), pp. 18–22.

Banks, J.E. (1994). *Multiethnic education: Theory and practice* (3rd ed.). Boston: Allyn & Bacon.

Banks, J.E. (Ed.). (1996). *Multicultural education, transformative knowledge, and action: Historical and contemporary perspectives.* New York: Teachers College Press.

Beach, R. (1997). Students' resistance to engagement with multicultural literature. In T. Rogers & A.O. Soter (Eds.), *Reading across cultures: Teaching literature in a diverse society* (pp. 69–94). New York: Teachers College Press.

Breton, M.J. (1998). *Women pioneers for the environment.* Boston: Northeastern University Press.

Christenbury, L.(1994). *Making the journey: Being and becoming a teacher of English language arts.* Portsmouth, NH: Boynton Cook/Heinemann.

Christenbury, L. & Kelly, P.P. (1983). *Questioning: A path to critical thinking.* Urbana: IL: National Council of Teachers of English.

Ciardiello, A.V. (1998). Did you ask a good question today? Alternative cognitive and metacognitive strategies. *Journal of Adolescent & Adult Literacy, 42,* 210–219.

Daniels, H. (2002). *Literature circles: Voice and choice in book clubs and reading groups* (2nd ed.). Portland, ME: Stenhouse.

Enciso, P. (1997). Negotiating the meaning of difference: Talking back to multicultural literature. In T. Rogers & A.O. Soter (Eds.), *Reading across cultures: Teaching literature in a diverse society* (pp. 13–41). New York: Teachers College Press.

Freire, P. (1998). *Teachers as cultural workers: Letter to those who dare teach.* Boulder, CO: Westview Press.

Grant, C.A., & Sleeter, C.E. (1998). *Turning on learning: Five approaches for multicultural teaching plans for race, class, gender, and disability* (2nd ed.). New York: Macmillan.

Great Books Foundation. (2006). *Philosophy: Great books discussions and shared inquiry.* Retrieved February 3, 2006, from http://www.greatbooks.org/typ/index.php?id=gbphilosophy

Greene, M. (1995). *Releasing the imagination: Essays on education, the arts, and social change.* San Francisco: Jossey-Bass.

Gregory, C. & Chapman, C. (2002). *Differentiated instructional strategies: One size doesn't fit all.* Thousand Oaks, CA: Corwin Press.

Harvey, S. (1998). *Nonfiction matters: Reading, writing, and research in grades 3–8.* York, ME: Stenhouse.

Herber, H.L. (1978). *Teaching reading in the content areas* (2nd ed.). New York: Prentice Hall.

International Reading Association & National Council of Teachers of English. (1996). *Standards for the English language arts.* Newark, DE; Urbana, IL: Authors.

Keene, E.O., & Zimmermann, S. (1997). *Mosaic of thought: Teaching comprehension in a reader's workshop.* Portsmouth, NH: Heinemann.

Kniep, W.M. (1986). Defining a global education by its content. *Social Education, 50,* 437–446.

Learning Skills Program (2003). Bloom's taxonomy. Retrieved August 20, 2005 from http://www.coun.uvic.ca/learn/program/hndouts/bloom.html

Lynn, S. (2005). *Texts and contexts: Writing about literature with critical theory.* New York: Pearson.

Maathai, W. (2003). *The Green Belt Movement: Sharing the approach and the experience.* New York: Lantern Books.

McGinley, W., Kamberelis, G., Mahoney, T., Madigan, D., Rybicki, V., & Oliver, J. (1997). Revisioning reading and teaching literature through the lens of narrative theory. In T. Rogers & A.O. Soter (Eds.), *Reading across cultures: Teaching literature in a diverse society* (pp. 42–68). New York: Teachers College Press.

Mednick, F. (2003). *Africa: An educational renaissance has begun.* Retrieved January 10, 2006, from http://www.newhorizons.org/strategies/multicultural/mednick.htm

Merryfield, M.M., Jarchow, E., & Pickert, S. (Eds.). (1997). *Preparing teachers to teach global perspectives: A handbook for teacher educators.* Thousand Oaks, CA: Corwin Press.

Meyers, C. & Jones, T. (1993). *Promoting active learning: Strategies for the college classroom.* San Fancisco: Jossey-Bass.

Mjøs, O.D. (2004). *The Nobel peace prize for 2004.* Retrieved March 20, 2006, from the Nobel Foundation at http://www.nobel.no/eng_lect_2004a.html

National Council for the Social Studies. (1994). *Expectations of excellence: Curriculum standards for social studies.* Silver Spring, MD: Author.

Nations Online (2007). Retrieved January 12, 2007, from http://www.nationsonline.org/oneworld/world_population.htm

Nieto, S. (2000). *Affirming diversity: The sociopolitical context of multicultural education* (3rd ed.). New York: Longman.

Purves, A.C., & Jordan, S. (1993). *Issues in the responses of students to culturally diverse texts: A preliminary study* (Rep. Series 7.3).Albany: NY: National Research Center on Literature Teaching and Learning, University at Albany. (ERIC Document Reproduction Service No. ED361701)

Raphael, T.E. (1986). Teaching question-answer relationships, revisited. *The Reading Teacher, 39,* 516-622.

Rice, L.J. (2006). *What was it like? Teaching history and culture through young adult literature.* New York: Teachers College Press.

Rosenblatt, L. (1996). *Literature as exploration* (5th ed.). New York: Modern Language Association of America. (Original work published 1938)

Russell, D.E.H., & Van de Ven, N. (Eds.). (1976) *The proceedings of the international tribunal on crimes against women.* Millbrae, CA: Les Femmes.

Ryder, R.J., & Graves, M. (2003). *Reading and learning in content areas* (3rd ed.) New York: John Wiley & Sons, Inc.

Scholes, R. (1989). *Protocols of reading.* New Haven, CT: Yale University Press.

Shor, I. (1999). What is critical literacy? In I. Shor & C. Pari, *Critical literacy in action: Writing words, changing worlds* (pp. 1–30). Portsmouth, NH: Boynton/Cook.

Sleeter, C.E., & McLaren, P.L. (1995). Introduction: Exploring connections to build a critical multiculturalism. In C.E. Sleeter & P.L. McLaren (Eds.), *Multicultural education, critical pedagogy, and the politics of difference* (pp. 5–32). Albany: State University of New York Press.

Wiggins, G.P., & McTighe, J. (2005). *Understanding by design* (2nd ed.). Alexandria, VA: Association for Supervision and Curriculum Development.

Wilhelm, J.D. (1997). *"You gotta BE the book": Teaching engaged and reflective reading with adolescents.* New York: Teachers College Press/NCTE.

LITERATURE CITED

Achebe, C. (1994). *Things fall apart.* New York: Anchor Books. (Original work published 1959)

Bâ, M. (1989). *So long a letter.* Johannesburg, South Africa: Heinemann.

Bok, F., with Tivnan, E. (2003). *Escape from slavery: The true story of my ten years in captivity— And my journey to freedom in America.* New York: St. Martin's Press.

Chedid, A. (1983). *From sleep unbound* (S. Spencer, Trans.). Athens: Swallow Press/Ohio University Press. (Original work published 1976)

Collins, P.L. (2003). *The fattening hut.* New York: Houghton Mifflin.

Dangarembga, T. (1988). *Nervous conditions: A novel.* London: Women's Press.

Emecheta, B. (2003). *The joys of motherhood.* New York: George Braziller. (Original work published 1979)

Farmer, N. (1996). *A girl named disaster.* New York: Puffin Books.

Gordimer, N. (1981). *July's people.* London: Penguin.

Gordon, S. (1987). *Waiting for the rain: A novel of South Africa.* New York: Orchard Books.

Head, B. (1968). *When rain clouds gather.* London: Heinemann.

Kessler, C. (2000). *No condition is permanent.* New York: Philomel Books.

Kessler, C. (2004). *Our secret: Siri Aang.* New York: Philomel Books.

Kurtz, J. (2001). *Jakarta missing.* New York: Greenwillow Books.

Kurtz, J. (2004). *Memories of sun: Stories of Africa and America.* New York: Greenwillow Books.

Matthee, D. (1984). *Circles in a forest.* London: Penguin.

Matthee, D. (1986). *Fiela's child.* London: Penguin.

McCall Smith, A. (1998). *The no. 1 ladies' detective agency.* New York: Anchor Books.

McCall Smith, A. (2001). *Morality for beautiful girls* (The No. 1 Ladies' Detective Agency series). New York: Anchor Books.

McCall Smith, A. (2002). *The kalahari typing school for men* (The No. 1 Ladies' Detective Agency series). New York: Pantheon Books.

McCall Smith, A. (2002). *Tears of the giraffe* (The No. 1 Ladies' Detective Agency series). New York: Anchor Books.

McCall Smith, A. (2003). *The full cupboard of life* (The No. 1 Ladies' Detective Agency series). New York: Pantheon Books.

McCall Smith, A. (2004). *In the company of cheerful ladies* (The No. 1 Ladies' Detective Agency series). New York: Pantheon Books.

Naidoo, B. (1988). *Journey to Jo'Burg: A South African story* (E. Velasquez, Ill.). New York: HarperTrophy.

Naidoo, B. (1989). *Chain of fire.* New York: HarperTrophy.

Naidoo, B. (1995). *No turning back: A novel of South Africa*. London: Penguin.

Nazer, M., with Lewis, D. (2003). *Slave: My true story*. New York: Public Affairs.

Nwapa, F. (1978). *Efuru*. London: Heinemann. (Original work published 1966)

Paton, A. (1987). *Cry, the beloved country*. New York: Macmillan. (Original work published 1948)

Stratton, A. (2004). *Chanda's secrets*. New York: Annick Press.

wa Thiong'o, N. (1964). *Weep not, child*. Portsmouth, NH: Heinemann.

wa Thiong'o, N. (1965). *The river between*. Portsmouth, NH: Heinemann.

Williams-Garcia, R. (2004). *No laughter here*. New York: HarperCollins.

FILM CITED

George, T. (Director). (2004). *Hotel Rwanda* [Motion picture]. United States: MGM Home Entertainment.

CHAPTER 2

Building Students' Background Knowledge of African Life and Culture

Jacqueline N. Glasgow and Linda J. Rice

Maps reprinted from *The World Factbook 2007* by the Central Intelligence Agency, http://www.cia.gov/cia/publications/factbook.

Exploring African Life and Literature: Novel Guides to Promote Socially Responsive Learning edited by Jacqueline N. Glasgow and Linda J. Rice. © 2007 by the International Reading Association.

"For Africa to me...is more than a glamorous fact. It is a historical truth. No man can know where he is going unless he knows exactly where he has been and exactly how he arrived at his present place."

—Maya Angelou (BrainyQuote.com, 2006)

Exploring life and culture of Africa with Westerners can be both a daunting task and a humbling experience. The tendency of many students is to treat Africa as a monolithic country, not as a continent comprising over 50 nations, with people speaking many languages and representing many different cultures. Such diminution of Africa is one of the challenges facing educators. This chapter is designed to provide strategies to help students access prior background knowledge and consequently build a foundation of cultural knowledge in preparation for reading the novels featured in this book.

First, this chapter will explain the use of semantic mapping as a strategy to find out students' existing knowledge of the African continent. Second, this chapter establishes a purpose for studying Africa, as students explore their own presuppositions and associations with the continent. Next, the chapter goes more in depth in exploring Africa through the creation of K-W-L (Blachowicz & Ogle, 2001) posters and also provides specific criteria for conducting interviews that will result in more information on Africa. This is followed by an extensive discussion exploring body modifications, including the controversy surrounding male and female circumcision as a rite of passage—and it is essential to provide students with background knowledge in this area before having them read literature that includes these themes. The chapter closes with two hands-on, creative projects to immerse students in African culture, specifically African cuisine and masks. Although the activities provided in the chapter are suggested for use as an introduction to African life and culture, the activities can be used at any point in any of the Novel Guide units.

Semantic Mapping

As the first strategy for building background knowledge for exploring African life and culture, students will create a semantic map (Vacca et al., 2005). A semantic map begins with a key word or concept phrase in the middle, then students link other ideas to it to visually show related categories or subdivisions of the idea. Begin this activity by brainstorming (either during individual freewriting or as a small-group or whole-group discussion) what students already know about the continent of Africa. What stereotypes do they share?

What do they know about the diversity of cultures and languages? Can they locate any of the countries? Do they know any political leaders? What do they know of Africa's history? What religions are prominent in Africa? Have they read any literature or can they name any books? After getting some of their initial reactions, divide students into groups of four or five and ask them to construct a concept map based on the term *Africa*. Groups should place the word *Africa* in the center of a large sheet of newsprint paper or easel pad and make links to anything they know about Africa. Permit students to categorize the results of their brainstorming using any schematic approach that is familiar or comfortable to them.

As a final step, ask students to summarize their thoughts in a short paragraph or two. Typical response items include jungles, deserts, refugees, wild animals, safaris, pygmies, extreme heat, HIV/AIDS, famine, and other images that sometimes reflect their viewing of popular films, documentaries, and news reports.

Establishing a Purpose: Why Study Africa?

After students have completed the semantic map, the next strategy to help them build background knowledge begins with a question. Ask the students, "Why study Africa?" After freewriting for five minutes, many students will begin to acknowledge their ethnocentric views and entertain the idea that studying other cultures might be beneficial. For example, see the freewriting excerpt about Africa by university student Laura Patrone in Figure 2.1. Laura's response pinpoints the misconceptions of many Westerners, who often still see Africans living in tribes and fail to see that Africa is a part of the global community. Students often think of Africa as so underdeveloped that they find it difficult to visualize the many thousands of miles of railroad and paved highways or the numerous modern airports. They sometimes view Africans as ridden by superstition, rather than enjoying the rich oral tradition of folklore and ethnic myth.

Figure 2.1. Excerpt of University Student's Freewriting About Africa

The main reason to study the life and literature of Africa is because it is so largely unknown to our society. We have referred to Africa as "the dark continent" for years, implying that Africa is an uncultured and unsophisticated continent with nothing but trouble to offer. In reality, I think we will find out that Africa is rich with culture and tradition, worthy of study and enjoyment. Africa seems to be largely misunderstood by our society and studying it can change the misunderstandings we have of the African people. By reading African novels, we can break down the barriers and see a person's soul, which enables us to have more compassion for other human beings.

Often, they imagine the average African to be somewhat bewildered by modernity, rather than finding out the reality through reading children's and young adult literature along with classical literature.

According to Murphy and Stein (1973), "all these stereotypes, and many more, remain in our minds because our ancestors depicted the African as something less than human in order to try and avoid the moral dilemma that the slave trade aroused" (p. 12). These stereotypes were then reinforced and strengthened in the late 19th century in an effort to justify the European conquest and colonial partition of Africa. Fortunately, through the increase of travel to and from Africa in recent years, visitors are discovering that many of their previous perceptions were erroneous. Educators can further weaken these misconceptions by engaging students in pursuits of truth and knowledge in a literature-based curriculum.

Exploring the Continent: K-W-L Posters of African Countries

After students have confronted the stereotypes and established a purpose for further investigation, this strategy focuses on ways to strengthen their background knowledge and break down their stereotypical notions. Using the K-W-L strategy (What do I **K**now? What do I **W**ant to know? What did I **L**earn?) (Blachowicz & Ogle, 2001), students will select an African country and create an informational poster representing their understanding of national and cultural facts.

This K-W-L poster project can be completed individually or collaboratively. Either way, students must select a country for their trifold poster. Selection of countries can be assigned or student selected. Students can study the country that provides background for the literature they will be reading either in reading groups or as whole-group instruction.

The first section of the trifold should represent the knowledge students already have about their chosen or assigned African country. On this first section (K: what students **k**now), students should draw or trace a map of the country. Then they should make a list or identify places and things they already know about the country on the map. Under the middle section (W: what students **w**ant to know), students should brainstorm a list of what they would like to learn about the country.

For the remaining section (L: what students have **l**earned), students should research their country and report their findings on the poster, putting as much information as possible on a map. Information might include the following:

- important geographical features (landforms, climates, vegetation)
- major cities and historical sites
- agriculture and natural resources
- religions
- famous authors, artists, entertainers in the culture
- ways to make a living
- means of transportation
- languages
- birth rates, death rates, infant mortality, education levels
- economics (import, export, gross domestic product)

After students have completed their projects, they should present the trifold posters to the rest of the class. The posters should be assessed according to visual presentation (use of color, pictures, graphics, text), content (relevance and depth of the information), and oral presentation (clear delivery and articulation of ideas). See Figure 2.2 for an example of a K-W-L poster for Botswana.

Figure 2.2. K-W-L Poster for Botswana

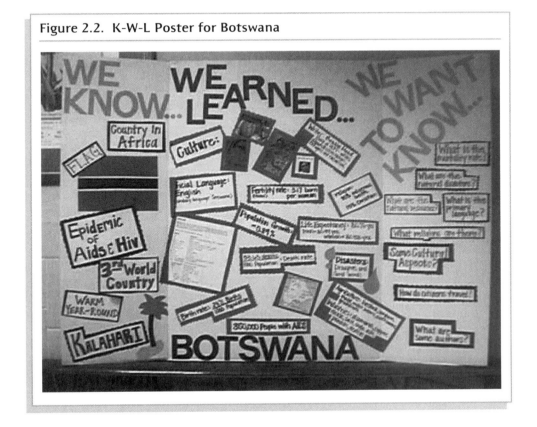

In general, it often surprises students to find out that Africa is more than three times the size of the continental United States and that it spans seven times zones. It takes longer to travel from Dakar, Senegal, in the western part of the continent to Nairobi, Kenya, in the east than to fly from New York to London. Many students are also surprised to find out that there are no tigers in Africa and that most African children have never seen a wild animal—they go to the zoo to see such animals for the first time. Through the interdisciplinary exploration of Africa through the K-W-L poster activity, a class can raise the larger questions concerning political, economic, agricultural, ecological, historical, and cultural issues as well as pursue investigations of class, gender, and ethnicity that will be raised in the African novels they choose to read.

Exploring African Culture Through Interviews

The next strategy to help students build background knowledge of African life and culture involves interviewing someone who was born in Africa or who has lived in Africa. Interviewing enables students to gain knowledge about African life and culture from someone who has experienced it firsthand. In the event that students have difficulty finding someone to interview, teachers may arrange for a guest to come speak to the entire class.

First, ask students to develop appropriate interview questions. These questions may be about daily life, work, family, cultural traditions, the country's history, or particular conflicts. See, for example, Figure 2.3 for a list of interview questions developed by university student Lacie Lessard.

Figure 2.3. Sample Interview Questions

1. Where in Africa did you live and what brought you to the United States?
2. What aspects about life in the United States do you like?
3. What aspects of life in the United States make your adjustment difficult?
4. What was your schooling like in Africa?
5. What kind of social freedoms do younger people have?
6. What are the gender issues in your country?
7. Is there an equivalent in your country to our pop culture?
8. What are the major cultural differences?
9. What are the major leisure activities in your country?
10. What special foods do you miss or have difficulty finding in the United States?
11. What kind of social issues does your country have?
12. Does your country have preconceived stereotypes about America?
13. Do you feel welcome here?
14. What are personal relationships like in your country? Marriages?
15. What are some of the positive experiences you have had here? Negative ones?

After the interview is complete, ask students to either write an essay or create a poster based on the interview. The essay should include a summary of the questions and the answers as well as reflections about what they have learned. If opting to create a poster, the students should use images from magazines or the Internet to represent the interviewee's experiences in Africa and in their current country of residence. Students should use quotes and labels to identify and explicate the graphics. Students can then share the results of their interviews in the whole-group setting and discuss some of the cultural differences.

Exploring African Cuisine: Connections Between Earth and Kitchen

Having examined some of their own presuppositions about the African continent through semantic mapping, K-W-L posters, and interviewing, students will next engage in hands-on activities that put them in touch with African culture. Providing students with an understanding of African environmental history familiarizes them in crucial ways with how Africans have interacted with their environments in the past. One cannot expect students to comprehend the significance of agricultural practices and politics when they have not stepped into a field, nor can they understand the significance of the cassava in the history of the Congo basin if they do not know what the tuber looks like and how it grows. Therefore, this activity is designed to acquaint them with the origins of agriculture and the basics of the African diet. Further, because food is often mentioned in the literature students are about to read, it aids in comprehension of the novels if they can experience firsthand what some of the African dishes contain. See Table 2.1 for five staple foods in African countries.

Adapted from Giles-Vernick (1999), this activity involves students researching one of the food staples and preparing an accompanying dish. Divide the class into five groups and ask each group to research the history and uses of one of these foods. Ask them to find a recipe, buy the ingredients, and prepare the food (or, provide the ingredients for them). On the designated date, groups give their presentations and serve their prepared foods to the rest of the class and perhaps other invited guests. Eating these foods—these contemporary embodiments of historical relationships between Africa and land—helps many students connect in small but meaningful ways to activities that Africans undertake in providing for their families and is essential for understanding daily life and culture as they appear in many of the books explored through the Novel Guides.

> ### Table 2.1. Five Staple Foods in African Countries
>
> 1. **Palm oil**—The oil palm tree is a tropical plant that commonly grows in warm climates and originates from the Gulf of Guinea in West Africa. This tree produces one of the most popular edible oils in the world—a versatile oil of superb nutritional value. The oil is extracted from the fruit, which is reddish and about the size of a large plum and grows in large bunches. (Carrere, n.d.)
>
> 2. **Millet**—Millet is one of the oldest foods known to humans and possibly the first cereal grain to be used for domestic purposes. It is mentioned in the Bible and was used during those times to make bread. Today, millet ranks as the sixth most important grain in the world, sustaining fully one third of the world's population (Railey, n.d.).
>
> 3. **Teff**—Teff is an intriguing grain, ancient, minute in size, and packed with nutrition. Teff is believed to have originated in Ethiopia between 4000 and 1000 BC. Teff is grown primarily as a cereal crop in Ethiopia, where it is ground into flour, fermented for three days, and then made into "enjera," a sourdough-type flat bread. It is also eaten as porridge and used as an ingredient of home-brewed alcoholic drinks (Railey, n.d.).
>
> 4. **Cassava**—Cassava is grown for its enlarged starch-filled roots, which contain nearly the maximum theoretical concentration of starch on a dry weight basis among food crops. Fresh roots contain about 30% starch and very little protein. Roots are prepared much like a potato. They can be peeled and boiled, baked, or fried. In Africa, roots are processed in several different ways. They may be first fermented in water. Then they are either sun-dried for storage or grated and made into dough that is cooked. Alcoholic beverages can be made from the roots (O'Hair, 1995).
>
> 5. **Yams**—The true yam is the tuber of a tropical vine and is not even distantly related to the sweet potato. It is generally sweeter than the sweet potato, and this tuber can grow over 7 feet in length. The word *yam* comes from African words *njam*, *nyami*, or *djambi*, meaning 'to eat.' The yam tuber has a brown or black skin that resembles the bark of a tree and off-white, purple, or red flesh, depending on the variety. Yams are at home growing in tropical climates, primarily in South America, Africa, and the Caribbean. Yams contain more natural sugar than sweet potatoes and a higher moisture content (Congo Cookbook, 2005).

Exploring African Culture and Literary Themes Through Mask-Making

As cuisine varies from culture to culture, so do handcrafts. Masks have fulfilled a variety of important cultural functions in many societies from the earliest times. The mask was traditionally used in Africa in the majority of ceremonies: fertility or initiation rites, religious or funeral celebrations, crop harvesting, and also in theatrical or comic performances that were often linked to the deepest ethnic myths. These complex ceremonial events expressed important social, religious, and moral values for the whole community. Wearing the mask is still a spiritual experience in that many Africans believe that the spirit of an ancestor possesses the person wearing the mask during the dance and song of the celebration. African masks are made from different materials such as wood, bronze, brass, copper, ivory, terra cotta, glazed pottery, raffia, and textiles. They are often decorated with cowrie shells, colored beads, bone, animal skins, and vegetable fiber. However, most African masks are made of wood because trees are plentiful, and carvers believe the tree has a spiritual soul and its wood is the most natural home for the spirit in the mask (Artyfactory.com, 2005).

For this project, students create masks using the symbolism, style, and naturalism used in the masks of Africa—exaggerations, animal features, geometric shapes, protrusions, ornaments, and natural fibers—to express their feelings and expressions. If students are doing this mask project before reading a novel, ask them to make a mask representing an ancestor, a ritual, or power figure from their own culture. Students can also represent a character from an African novel they are reading. In either case, the mask should emphasize the person's major characteristics, challenges in life, and themes in life or in the novel.

In order to make personal meaning, ask students to describe their experiences with wearing a mask in their society. Have they worn one to a Halloween party, Mardi Gras celebration, circus parade, play, or other costume party? Have they ever worn a bike rider's helmet, football player's mask and helmet, or fencer's or welder's mask? Have they seen a dentist's or surgeon's mask? Could wearing fashionable glasses be a type of mask? Have students share occasions when they have seen masks directly painted on people's faces or times when they have had their faces painted. What story can a mask tell? Ask students to recall what they felt when they saw various masks. Discuss the role masks play in our society and then continue by exploring the customs in Africa.

Introduce African mask-making by reading a children's book, *The African Mask* (Rupert, 1994). This is a story set 900 years ago in the area of Africa that is now Nigeria. It takes place in the city-state of Ife where Layo, a 12-year-old Yoruba girl, knows that she has a gift for working with clay because she comes from a village of potters. She longs to be freed from the menial tasks that young women perform and work with her grandmother in creating a death mask of terra cotta. However, when a Yoruba girl marries, she must learn whatever work is done in her husband's household. In Layo's case, a forthcoming betrothal may prevent her from achieving her dreams. This book will help build students' background knowledge about the important place of the mask-maker in the Nigerian culture.

Slideshow Collection of African Masks

After reading the introductory story, ask students to search the Internet for collections of African masks and then to create a slideshow presentation of African masks they find online (using software such as Microsoft PowerPoint).

Table 2.2. Websites of Collections of African Masks

The Art of the African Mask
http://cti.itc.virginia.edu/~bcr/African_Mask.html

Magical Faces of Africa
http://www.culturekiosque.com/art/exhibiti/index_me.htm

African Mask History
http://www.rebirth.co.za/African_mask_history_and_meaning.htm

Introduction to Basic Mask Forms
http://www.rebirth.co.za/african_mask_basic%20forms.htm

African Studies Center/Face Masks
http://www.sas.upenn.edu/African_Studies/Face_Masks/menu_Face_Mask.html

African Masks and the Quest for Transcendence
http://sprott.physics.wisc.edu/pickover/mask.htm

Faces of Africa Collection
http://members.aol.com/jandrea555/collect.htm

African Mask Information, Design, Examples, and Quiz
http://www.artyfactory.com/africanmasks

Each mask should be given a title and reference to the tribe, celebration, or explanation of the meaning of the mask. Table 2.2 provides a list of suggested websites for collections of African masks.

After sharing their slideshow presentations, students should write a reflective paper concerning their mask collection. What do these masks have in common? How are they different? What cultural and historical background information did they obtain? Who wore the mask? What materials and techniques were used by the artist? What colors were used on the masks? What was the purpose in making the mask? How was the mask used?

Masks: The Face Tells the Story

Once students have gained the necessary background information on the purposes and styles of African masks, you may assign students their own mask-making project. The following is a list of suggested themes to use with students for their mask-making project, and you can either allow students to choose one of the following themes or choose a theme for all students to use for their mask.

The Me I'd Like to Be—Create a mask that reveals your ideal self.

A Ritual From My Culture—Create a mask that portrays contemporary rituals such as a pregame pep rally, high school dances, the process of getting ready for school in the morning, or a march around the neighborhood on Halloween.

Power—Create a mask that shows either superiority or inferiority.

Figures in My Culture—Create a mask that symbolizes heroes in sports, law enforcement, entertainment, religion, politics, and so forth.

A View From My Culture—Create a mask that shows a typical individual from your present surroundings.

Reaching Out to the Past—Create a mask using imagery that relates to a person from the past: a relative, historical figure, or mythological figure to whom you relate.

Students can choose the media they prefer for making the mask. Table 2.3 provides a list of suggested websites to use for guidance on mask-making with various media.

African Mask Project for a Character in a Novel

Another possibility for mask-making it to have students create a mask in order to gain valuable insight into a character of their choosing from one of the African novels they have been reading in class. The assignment is as follows:

- Choose a character from the book that you would like to represent in your mask.
- Using everything you know about the character, construct a mask to represent the character or to be used by the character.

Table 2.3. Websites With Mask-Making Instructions for Various Media

Papier-Mâché
http://www.my-ecoach.com/resources/masks/maskmaking.html

Three-Dimensional Paper Mask
http://www.princetonol.com/groups/iad/lessons/elem/papermask.htm

Plaster Craft
http://www.ket.org/artonair/artists/alexanderguide.htm

Linoleum Prints
http://www.internet-at-work.com/hos_mcgrane/masks/mask_arnaud.html

---

- Use the media of your choice, such as papier-mâché, construction paper, plaster, or clay to construct the mask.
- When you bring your mask to class, be prepared to explain why you chose your character, what the mask represents in conjunction with the character, and how you created your mask.
- Write a brief rationale for your choices in creating the project. Who was your character, and what were you trying to represent?

Figure 2.4 illustrates a mask and rationale for the mask created by university student Laura Williams for Mma Ramotswe's cousin in Alexander McCall Smith's *The No. 1 Ladies' Detective Agency* (1998). Laura made her mask using papier-mâché. In another example, Figure 2.5 presents a mask and rationale for the mask created by university student Kristine Phillips as a representation of the character Dumi in Beverley Naidoo's *Journey to Jo'burg: A South African Story* (1988). The mask was made using the instructions for a creating a three-dimensional mask with construction paper.

Figure 2.4. Student Mask Project for "Mma Ramotswe's Cousin"

I have constructed a mask in relation to the character of Precious Ramotswe's cousin. The cousin looked after Precious as a small child and was her primary mother figure. As the cousin was unable to conceive, she was abandoned by her husband and ostracized by her community. The cousin took great joy in helping to raise Precious, as this task was her primary means of enjoying any kind of motherhood and helped her to feel useful and needed. This mask itself is a plea for fertility, and constructed to be worn as a call to the spirits to reinstate the cousin's womanhood. The features are "womanly," in hopes of allowing the cousin to once again feel like a woman, as her infertility caused her to feel stripped of her femininity. The small, white dots are used to represent the rounding of the belly in a pregnant woman, and are also egg-like to symbolize the process of fertilization. This mask conceals the cousin's fears of no longer being considered a woman or at the very least a contributing member of society, and displays her earlier hopes of one day being able to conceive.

Figure 2.5. Student's Mask Project for "Dumi"

My African mask is a representation of Dumi, the character who was taken from his family for standing up for what he believed in during apartheid. I focused on three symbolic colors: black, red, and white. Black, the color of Dumi's skin, and white signify the dominance of race. Red symbolizes the bloodshed of the many blacks, including innocent children, who were shot and killed in the streets. To represent the protest, I also included the shape of Africa with the word "death" written over it and a picture of a man with a gun. The word "family" appears at the top of the mask, split and divided by a red line to signify the division of families caused by the racial discrimination. "War" and "poverty" also appear to convey the tension and division between the whites and the blacks who struggled to get by. Naledi's family and so many other black families couldn't even afford food or medicine, and it was this inequality that led to the protest of blacks such as Dumi.

Celebrations

Through the incorporation of these cross-cultural projects into the curriculum, students will strengthen their background knowledge of specific African countries, cultures, and traditions. These projects should be shared with a larger audience through exhibition and celebration. Exhibit the masks in a showcase for all the students to view. Sponsor a family night at school featuring the masks and K-W-L posters as part of a larger celebration with African food, henna painting, music, or storytelling. After the celebration, find a library, local museum, or senior citizens facility that would exhibit the masks, perhaps for a special occasion. Students might also exhibit their masks during local ethnic and cultural festivals. Of course, the masks could be shared with other schools that are also involved in studying other cultures. These activities will help build and strengthen students' prior knowledge and connections with the rich literature of Africa and provide them with the necessary background knowledge for approaching the literature of the Novel Guides.

Exploring Body Modifications: Building a Context to Teach About Circumcision

While learning about the celebratory aspects of African culture, such as food and mask-making, is essentially part of the global education approach and critical exploration of African life and culture, it is equally necessary to delve into some of the more serious sociocultural issues. Most of the literature, in some way, includes themes of struggle, conflict, and controversy, one of the most significant being body modification and circumcision. Because so many of the Novel Guides examine literature that discusses body modification and male and female circumcision, among other serious topics, it is essential that students, particularly high school students, develop solid background knowledge on this complex topic.

Therefore, before delving into such controversial issues as male and female circumcision as practiced in coming-of-age ceremonies in Africa, it is important to first engage students in a discussion of Western concepts of body image and body modifications. In Western society, body image dissatisfaction is so epidemic that it is almost considered normal. Recent studies show that preschoolers are already exposed to hearing that certain types of foods, especially sugar, might make them fat. Children as early as third grade are concerned about their weight (Griffin, 2006; Kater, 2006; Natenshon, 2006). Girls are overly concerned about weight and body shape. They strive for the perfect body and judge themselves and others by their looks, appearance, and size (Peel Public Health, 2005). But boys do not escape either. They are concerned with the size and strength of their body (Peel Public Health, 2005) and live in a culture that showcases males as glamorous macho figures who have to be tough, build muscles, and sculpt their bodies—if they want to fit in. There is a lot of pressure to succeed and fit in for both girls and boys, and part of this is the pressure to have the perfect body. In order to address these issues of body image with your students, begin the discussion with such questions as the following:

- Which of you in the room is content with your body exactly the way it is?
- Which of you would like to make changes?
- What changes would you like to make?
- What changes have you already made?
- What changes would you never make?
- When is the body improved and when is it mutilated?

First of all, it is rare that students claim in front of a class that they are perfectly satisfied. Most people will admit to such superficial changes involving very little discomfort or pain such as plucking eyebrows, shaving body hair, and wearing contact lenses. It is not long before students are sharing stories about wearing braces to straighten their teeth, showing off their body tattoos, and discussing body piercings (ears, belly, nose, tongue, eyebrows, and even genitals). Of course, these modifications involve quite a bit more pain and discomfort, but they are generally considered to be worth it. The conversation may then move to a discussion of appropriate and inappropriate dieting and exercise programs. Many students know at least one friend or classmate who carried this practice too far, ending up bulimic or anorexic. When asked what other body modifications they know about, students sometimes mention abnormal elongations of lips, earlobes, and necks. Some responses deal with extreme measures for weight reduction such as liposuction, stomach stapling, and jaw wiring. Reflecting on what movie stars have done, students may mention face lifts, breast reduction or enhancement (silicone implants), depilation of other body areas, and extreme diet and exercise regimes. It becomes clear that Western conceptions of female beauty, in particular, encourage women to undergo a wide range of painful, medically unnecessary, and potentially damaging processes, such as those listed above.

Situating male and female circumcision in this larger context of body modification helps students to see that objections to the procedure are not driven solely by concerns of physical suffering but speak to culturally rooted messages about what it means to be beautiful or even acceptable. Without a clear understanding of the various facts, practices, and viewpoints surrounding circumcision, some teachers may be reluctant to teach novels that deal with this controversial issue as a rite of passage, such as it appears in chapter 6 through Ngugi wa Thiong'o's *The River Between* (1965) or in chapter 7 through Cristina Kessler's *Our Secret, Siri Aaang* (2004) and Rita Williams-Garcia's *No Laughter Here* (2004). For this reason, a more extensive discussion of circumcision follows.

Understanding Western Practices of Circumcision

In many Western societies, male circumcision is a cultural norm. According to research published by the American Medical Association (AMA; 2005), "ritual circumcision is common in the Jewish and Islamic faiths"—though it is "uncommon altogether in Asia, South and Central America, and most of Europe" (¶ 4). In the United States, routine male circumcision is particularly common. However, routine female circumcision is quite uncommon in the United States and other Western cultures. Though female genital surgery and female circumcision are not unheard of in the United States, the number of these procedures—both documented and undocumented—are not large enough for this practice to be considered common or routine, particularly in a way that is comparable to the number of routine infant male circumcisions. Therefore, because there is a history of routine infant male circumcision, as referenced throughout the section that follows, research on Western practices of circumcision will focus specifically on the infant male.

According to the AMA's report on neonatal circumcision conducted in 1999 and updated in 2005, the major factors in parental decision making in favor of circumcision are "the father's circumcision status, opinions of family members and friends, a desire for conformity in their son's appearance, and the belief that the circumcised penis is easier to care for with respect to local hygiene" (¶ 30). While these factors are considered to be highly influential, with 61% to 65% of male infants circumcised in the United States between 1987 and 1995, the AMA supports the general principles of the 1999 Circumcision Policy Statement of the American Academy of Pediatrics, which reads as follows:

> Existing scientific evidence demonstrates potential medical benefits of newborn male circumcision; however, these data are not sufficient to recommend routine neonatal circumcision. In circumstances in which there are potential benefits and risks, yet the procedure is not essential to the child's current well-being, parents should determine what is in the best interest of the child. To make an informed choice, parents of all male infants should be given accurate and unbiased information and be provided the opportunity to discuss this decision. If a decision for circumcision is made, procedural analgesia should be provided. (AMA, 2005, ¶ 34)

According to the American Academy of Family Physicians Reference Manual, even in the context of sterile hospital conditions, "current medical literature regarding neonatal circumcision is controversial and conflicting" (AMA, 2005, ¶ 8). The controversy surrounding routine circumcision of infant males, "a surgical procedure with concomitant pain," centers on whether the potential health benefits medically justify the risks associated with the procedure (¶ 8). The medical benefits suggested to accrue from circumcision, according to the AMA, are reduced incidence of urinary tract infection in infant males, decreased incidence of penile cancer in adult males, and possibly decreased susceptibility to certain sexually transmissible diseases, such as HIV. For the detailed Risk-Benefit Analysis of Circumcision by the AMA, consult Report 10 of the Council on Scientific Affairs (I-99)—full text available online at www.ama-assn.org/ama/pub/category/13585.html.

Understanding African Practices of Circumcision

In many African countries, male and female circumcision are cultural norms. "About 70 percent of men are circumcised at birth or during rite-of-passage ceremonies in early puberty" (Russell, 2005, ¶ 6), and an estimated 50 percent of females have undergone some type of circumcision (Kouba & Muasher, 1985, p. 99). Although complications can exist for both genders, the circumcision of males, while potentially very painful, is a comparatively far less dangerous procedure involving the "removal of the foreskin" (Russell, 2005, ¶ 6), similar to what infant males undergo in some Western cultures, as previously described. However, female circumcision as practiced during coming-of-age rituals is potentially much more dangerous and harmful than male circumcision, and because this issue is the focus of several of the Novel Guides in this book, female circumcision will be the topic of emphasis in this section examining African practices of circumcision.

Whether called female circumcision, female genital mutilation (FGM), genital cutting, genital operation, or genital or body modification, the practice emerges from many different sociocultural practices and beliefs found in different African countries. Culturally speaking, uncircumcised females are thought to be unclean, unmarriageable, and sexually promiscuous, thus bringing disgrace to their families (Althaus, 1997). There is also a common belief that "a woman's clitoris is deadly to touch, and if it is touched by a man during intercourse or by the baby during birth, it will prove immediately fatal to them" (Close, Farney, & Ortman, n.d., ¶ 3). With these culturally based views and beliefs in place, an estimated 90 to 100 million women and girls living in various African countries today have had some form of female circumcision (Lane & Rubinstein, 1996). There are differences in the age of those concerned, ranging from a few days old among the Yoruba in Nigeria, to 6 to 8 years old in much of Mali and Sudan, to early teens in various communities in Kenya and Sierra Leone. While we believe it is important for teachers to understand the various types of female circumcision, they should use their discretion—based on knowing their students—in determining how much of this graphic detail is appropriate to share with their students, particularly with younger high school students. As described in Daly (1990), the three operations generally distinguished are as follows:

1. Sunna Circumcision: Removal of the tip of the clitoris.
2. Excision or Clitoridectomy: Excision of the entire clitoris with the labia minora and some or most of the external genitalia.
3. Excision and Infulation: Excision of the entire clitoris, labia minora and parts of the labia majora. The two sides of the vulva are then fastened together typically with thorns or sewing with catgut and only a small opening is left for urine and later for menstrual blood. (p. 463)

As reported by the World Health Organization (2000), the health risks associated with female genital mutilation vary according to the type and severity of the procedure performed. "In the conditions under which female circumcision is generally performed in Africa, even the less extensive types of genital cutting can lead to potentially fatal complications such as hemorrhage, infection and shock" (Althaus, 1997, ¶ 15). The World Health Organization (2000) lists the following as Health Consequences of FGM:

> Immediate complications include severe pain, shock, hemorrhage, urine retention, ulceration of the genital region and injury to adjacent tissue. Hemorrhage and infection can cause death.
>
> Possible transmission of the human immunodeficiency virus (HIV) due to the use of one instrument in multiple operations.
>
> Long-term consequences include cysts and abscesses, scar formation, damage to the urethra resulting in urinary incontinence, painful sexual intercourse, and difficulties with childbirth.
>
> Genital mutilation also affects the psychosexual and psychological health of women. Women who have undergone FGM may suffer feelings of incompleteness, anxiety and depression. (¶ 4–7)

While these risk factors may be astonishing, the practice of female circumcision is embedded in broader context that reflects the culture's view of a woman's identity, morality, maturity, and capability for motherhood and therefore continues to be pervasive.

Critical Examination of the Circumcision Controversy

As evidenced by the previously mentioned research and also the African literature students will read, the most straightforward objection to the ritual of circumcision is that it is a painful procedure, imposed on young boys and girls and performed in conditions that could lead to permanent damage. As a rite of passage for girls in many African nations, circumcision typically occurs between the ages of 10 and 12. "The 'surgical instrument' may be as crude as a broken glass or a kitchen knife" (Daly, 1990, p. 471). The dangers in this procedure are inherent in the words of a woman from Guinea who testified before the International Tribunal on Crimes Against Women. In the passage from Russell and Van de Ven (1976) that follows, this woman described what she saw as six women held down her friend for the ritual, which was performed without anesthetic and with no regard to hygiene.

> With the broken neck of a bottle, the old woman banged hard down, cutting into the upper part of my friend's genitals so as to make a wide a cut as possible since "an incomplete excision does not constitute a sufficient guarantee against profligacy in girls."
>
> The blunt glass of the bottle did not cut deeply enough into my friend's genitals and the exciseuse had to do it several more times.... When the clitoris had been ripped out, the women howled with joy, and forced my friend to get up despite a streaming hemorrhage, to parade her through the town. (p. 151)

The horrors involved in such an account are truly frightening and highlight the physical risks involved in circumcision as practiced in many African countries as a coming-of-age ritual and as discussed in many of the books included in the Novel Guides. But are the physical risks and pain the only issues? After all, removing a tooth is also a painful procedure often imposed on children, which, if performed in nonhygienic conditions, can produce permanent damage. But Westerners are not disgusted by this common practice in their society and consider it as improving body appearance. Consider another common practice in Western society. Are parents who force their children to wear braces mutilating their children's teeth or improving them? While in some instances braces are necessary to promote the longevity of the teeth by improving the bite, in other instances braces are primarily for cosmetic reasons. Therefore, decisions about having braces often depend on one's concept of beauty. Those who see straight, white teeth as beautiful and a sign of good health will spend lots of money permitting their children to experience pain and inconvenience to achieve this goal. They believe these treatments will improve their children's life chances, self-image, and social standing.

Parents who perform female circumcision on their daughters or allow male circumcision at a coming-of-age ceremony invoke precisely the same arguments. For instance, in Somalia "the mother does the excising, slicing, and final infibulations according to time-honored rules. She does this in such a way as to leave the tiniest opening possible. Her 'honor' depends on making this as small as possible, because the smaller the artificial aperture is, the higher the value of the girl" (Daly, 1990, p. 471). Mothers who have their daughters circumcised believe they are doing the right thing because their children would become social outcasts if they did not get circumcised. Nichols (2001) makes this point as follows:

> An uncircumcised woman is labeled unclean, impure, and unfit to marry, bear children, or attain respect in old age. Interviews of the Sabiny people of Uganda state that an uncircumcised woman who marries into the community is always lowest in the pecking order of village women, and she is not allowed to perform the public duties of a wife, such as serving elders. Uncut women are called girls, no matter what their age is, and are forbidden to speak at community gatherings. The social pressures are so intense that uncircumcised wives often become circumcised as adults. (¶ 15)

What about parents in Western culture who indulge their daughters with fad diets that might destroy their teeth, ruin their health, or, in more tragic cases, lead to a potentially life-threatening eating disorder? Do we judge those parents as harshly as we judge parents who insist on circumcision? In both cases, parents sincerely believe they are serving the best interests of their children.

Whether male or female circumcision is practiced in the United States at birth or in African nations at puberty, there are four basic human rights issues that underlie the arguments of social and cultural understandings: children's rights, rites of passage, health issues, and gender relations. The question remains: How might the language of human rights accommodate the diverse people, practices, and circumstances involved?

Children's Rights and the Role of the Parent. The rights of parental decisions and discretion are at stake in questioning either infant circumcision in the United States and other Western countries or male or female circumcision in Africa. While some consider these practices child abuse in that the child is helpless and suffers severe pain, circumcision practices are deeply embedded in the cultures in which they are practiced, and typically the decision-making power comes through the parents. In the United States, a joint publication with the American Academy of Pediatrics and the American College of Obstetricians and Gynecologists (ACOG) concluded in 1997 that "newborn circumcision is an elective procedure to be performed at the request of the parents on baby boys who are physiologically and clinically stable" (AMA, 2005, ¶ 8), and because the procedure is completed in infancy, the boy has no say whatsoever in this decision. In most cases in African nations the woman herself has no choice in the matter and little foreknowledge of what exactly is involved in the process. "It is her family—often the father or elder female relatives—who decide whether she will undergo circumcision. According to one Yacouba [Nigerian] father, '[My daughter] has no choice. I decide. Her viewpoint is not important'" (Althaus, 1997, ¶ 24).

Phillips (1994) contended that circumcisions for personal preference of the parents deny children the basic right to respect and autonomy. People opposing circumcision believe it is the moral duty of educated professionals to protect health and rights of those with little or no social power to protect themselves (Bigelow, 1994). In support of this position, others believe that it is imperative that children have the right to own their reproductive organs and to preserve natural sexual function (Milos & Macris, 1994). Sperlich (1994) asserted that every circumcision is an assault on a child's sexuality and a violation of his or her right to an intact body. Other research has shown that when infants are subjected to intolerable, overwhelming pain, they conceptualize mother as participatory and responsible regardless of mother's intent, and the consequences for impaired bonding between mothers and infants are significant (Laibow, 1991). The fact is that cultural, social, and historical perspectives around infant or adolescent circumcision influence physicians and parents (Stein, 1982). The issue at hand is who determines the rights of children and their parents?

Rites of Passage. Rites of passage are social events that occur in every society that deals with upholding family autonomy, community values, and religious freedom. Within the context of family and friends, individual differentiation and self-determination often take the form of body modification. Body modification can be seen as a sign of self-control, maturity, and personal and social change. For the Kikuyu in Kenya, circumcision was the foundation of "moral self-mastery" for men and women alike (Lonsdale, 1992, p. 390). In the United States or other Western cultures, body piercing and tattooing can be seen as measures of self-control and personal choice, usually occurring during adolescence.

While Westerners do not have formal initiation rites as such, Africans value the initiation ceremony that definitively marks the end of childhood and the beginning of adulthood, and circumcision is often part of the ritual for both boys and girls. While African circumcision is not fundamentally a religious rite, some people do believe this to be the case with Muslims; however, Muslims outside of Africa rarely engage in the practice. For Jews, circumcision is an important aspect of both culture and religion. In any case, finding a marriage partner would be difficult in any society where such beliefs about circumcision are upheld but not adhered to. This, in fact, is the crux on the controversy.

Therefore, because of the sociocultural rationale for the procedure, it is important to acknowledge that many share the view that African women are *not* victims who have no choice, agency, or consciousness and are forced to submit to circumcision practices (Kratz, 1999). Assuming that women are forced into circumcision suggests that these women are unable to act for themselves and that therefore others are justified in intervention strategies meant to save or somehow help these women, often through international action. Critics have called this view a "missionary mentality" (Kratz, 1999, p. 114), in which external values are imposed on these women. In other words, to want to change such deeply ingrained traditional practices through external means is a violation of human rights perhaps as much as the procedure itself. However, these issues do raise fundamental questions. How are such judgments, choices, and even laws to be made in pluralistic societies? And what are appropriate strategies for intervention?

Health Issues. Opponents of genital operations seem to have their strongest argument in the health issues related to circumcision. Any surgical operation holds risks of infection and complications. Complications are often overlooked or unreported. For male and female circumcision, lacerations, skin loss, skin bridges, urinary retention, and hemorrhage are among the common complications (Marshall, 1986). There are intense debates among African activists about whether a medicated, minor form of female modification should be promoted as an interim substitute for more severe operations such as infibulation. Even the circumcision of infant boys in Western countries with anesthetic and under sterile settings can carry risks. And even as "existing scientific evidence demonstrates potential medical benefits of newborn male circumcision," the American Academy of Pediatrics has concluded that "data are not sufficient to recommend routine neonatal circumcision" (AMA, 2005, ¶ 4). The health issues for African girls who undergo far more invasive procedures under unsanitary conditions are even more serious.

The research is not clear as to whether a circumcised woman can experience sexual pleasure. Of course, the answer to that question certainly varies with the kind of operation (Koso-Thomas, 1987; Obiora, 1997; Ogbu, 1997; Parker, 1995). A number of African women also counter the assertion that circumcised women are unable to experience sexual pleasure and go further to question the very definition of sexuality prevalent in the international debates. They see this emphasis on sexual pleasure as primarily reflecting Western concepts of sexuality. In their minds, they enjoy a fulfilling life of motherhood and childbearing that does not diminish their sexuality.

Conclusions and Celebrations

As evidenced by some of the very serious content of this chapter, exploring the life and culture of Africa with Westerners can be a challenging task; however, teachers should remember that along with the weightier issues are the more light-hearted and festive learning opportunities where students take inventory of what they know, identify African nations on the map, consider what they want to learn, and even enjoy African cuisine and mask-making. Opportunities for students to connect ideas and explore themes through Semantic Maps and interviewing African citizens or hearing from a guest speaker from Africa also fit into the foundation of background knowledge that will help students in their literary study and examination of African life and culture. By examining common Western body modifications such as braces and piercings alongside Western and African practices of circumcision—male and female—students will be able to connect what may initially seem like a foreign concept to a much more common pressure: fitting in. Collectively, the information and learning experiences put forth in this chapter will go a long way in facilitating the study of African life and literature.

REFERENCES

Althaus, F.A. (1997). Female circumcision: Rite of passage or violation of rights? *International Family Planning Perspectives, 23*(3). Retrieved from http://www.guttmacher.org/pubs/journals/2313097.html

American Medical Association. (2005). *Neonatal circumcision.* Rep. No. 10 of the Council on Scientific Affairs (I-99). Retrieved January 2, 2007, from http://www.ama-assn.org/ama/pub/category/13585.html

Artyfactory.com. (2005). *African masks—The materials of an African mask*. Retrieved May 8, 2006, from http://www.artyfactory.com/african-masks/context/materials.htm

Bigelow, J. (1994, Summer). Uncircumcising: Undoing effects of an ancient practice in a modern world. *Mothering, 5*, pp. 56–61.

Blachowicz, C.Z., & Ogle, D. (2001). *Reading comprehension: Strategies for independent learners*. New York: Guilford Press.

BrainyQuote.com. (2006). *Maya Angelou quotes*. Retrieved May 9, 2006, from http://www.brainyquote.com/quotes/authors/m/maya_angelou.html

Carrere, R. (n.d.) *Oil palm: The expansion of another destructive monoculture*. Retrieved February 19, 2007, from http://www.wrm.org.uy/plantations/material/oilpalm2.html

Close, C., Farney, S., & Ortman, T. (n.d.) *Female circumcision*. Retrieved January 2, 2007, from http://www2.kenyon.edu/Depts/WMNS/Projects/Wmns36/bloodletting/femframe.htm

Congo Cookbook. (2005). *Yam*. Retrieved June 8, 2006, from http://www.congocookbook.com/c0053.html

Daly, M. (1990). African genital mutilation: The unspeakable atrocities. In E. Ashton-Jones, G.A. Olson, and M.G. Perry (Eds.), *The gender reader* (2nd ed., pp. 462–484). New York: Longman.

Giles-Vernick, T. (1999). On the computer and in the kitchen: Exercises for teaching people-environment relations. In M.L. Bastian & J.L. Parpart (Eds.), *Great ideas for teaching about Africa* (pp. 143–152). Boulder, CO: Lynne Rienner.

Griffin, M. (2006). *Building blocks for children's body image*. Retrieved January 2, 2007, from *Radiance Online* at http://www.radiancemagazine.com/kids_project/body_image.html

Kater, K.J. (2006). *Building healthy body esteem in a body toxic world*. Retrieved January 2, 2007, from http://www.bodyimagehealth.org

Koso-Thomas, O. (1987). *The circumcision of women: A strategy for eradication*. London: Zed Books.

Kouba, L.J., & Muasher, J. (1985). Female circumcision in Africa: An overview. *African Studies Review, 28*, 95–110.

Kratz, C.A. (1999). Contexts, controversies, dilemmas: Teaching circumcision. In M.L. Bastian & J.L. Parpart (Eds.), *Great ideas for teaching about Africa* (pp. 103–118). Boulder, CO: Lynne Rienner.

Laibow, R. (1991, April). *Circumcision: Relationship attachment impairment*. Paper presented at the Second International Symposium on Circumcision, San Francisco, CA.

Lane, S., & Rubinstein, R. (1996, May/June). Judging the other: Responding to traditional female genital surgeries. *Hastings Center Report, 26*(3), pp. 31-40.

Lonsdale, J. (1992). Wealth, poverty, and civic virtue in Kikuyu political thought. In B. Berman & J. Lonsdale (Eds.), *Unhappy valley: Conflict in Kenya and Africa* (pp. 388–397). London: James Currey.

Marshall, F. (1986). Complications: Pediatric circumcision. Urological complications. Medical-Surgical. Year book of medicine (pp. 387–395). New York: Year Book Medical Publications.

Milos, M.F., & Macris, D.R. (1994). Circumcision: Male—Effects on human sexuality. In V.L. Bullough & B. Bullough (Eds.), *Human sexuality: An encyclopedia* (pp. 119–121). New York: Garland.

Murphy, E.J., & Stein, H. (1973). *Teaching Africa today: A handbook for teachers and curriculum planners*. New York: Citation Press.

Natenshon, A. (2006). Childhood fears take new form: Body image concerns in young children. Retrieved January 2, 2007, from http://www.empoweredparents.com/1childhoodonset/childhood_01.htm

Nichols, A. (2001). Female circumcision. Retrieved January 2, 2007, from http://www.siue.edu/~jfarley/nicho490.htm

Obiora, L.A. (1997). Bridges and barricades: Rethinking polemics and intransigence in the campaign against female circumcision. *Case Western Reserve Law Review, 47*(2), 275–378.

Ogbu, M.A. (1997). Comment on Obiora's "Bridges and Barricades." *Case Western Reserve Law Review, 47*(2), 411–422.

O'Hair, S.K. (1995). New crop factsheet: Cassava. Retrieved November 7, 2004, from http://www.hort.purdue.edu/newcrop/CropFactSheets/cassava.html

Parker, M. (1995). Rethinking female circumcision. *Africa, 65*(4), 506–524.

Peel Public Health. (2005). Fostering healthy body image in children and teens. Retrieved January 2, 2007, from http://www.region.peel.on.ca/health/commhlth/fostbi/fostint.htm

Phillips, I. (1994). Advocacy: Rhetoric or practice. *Nursing BC, 26*(4), 38.

Railey, K. (n.d.a). Whole grains: Millet. Retrieved November 7, 2004, from http://chetday.com/millet.html

Railey, K. (n.d.b). Whole grains: Teff. Retrieved November 7, 2004, from http://chetday.com/teff.html

Russell, S. (2005, July 6). Circumcision may offer AIDS hope: Procedure linked to much lower rate of new HIV infections. *San Francisco Chronicle*. Retrieved from http://www.sfgate.com/cgi-bin/article.cgi?file=/c/a/2005/07/06/MNGANDJFVK1.DTL&type=printtableL

Sperlich, B. (1994). Botched circumcisions. *American Journal of Nursing*, [AQ: Please provide vol. number], 16.

Stein, M. (1982). Routine circumcisions: Gap between contemporary policy and practice. *Journal of Family Practice, 15*, 47–53.

Vacca, J.L., Vacca, R.T., Gove, M.K., Burkey, L.C., Lenhart, L.A., & McKeon, C.A. (2005). *Reading and learning to read* (6th ed.). Boston: Allyn & Bacon.

Wikipedia. (2006). Palm oil. Retrieved June 8, 2006, from http://en.wikipedia.org/wiki/Palm_oil

World Health Organization. (2000). Female genital mutilation. Retrieved January 2, 2007, from http://www.who.int/mediacentre/factsheets/fs241/en/index.html

LITERATURE CITED

Kessler, C. (2004). *Our secret: Siri Aang*. New York: Philomel Books.

McCall Smith, A. (1998). *The no. 1 ladies' detective agency*. New York: Anchor Books.

Naidoo, B. (1988). *Journey to Jo'burg: A South African story* (E. Velasquez, Illus.). New York: HarperTrophy.

Rupert, J.E. (1994). *The African mask*. New York: Clarion Books.

wa Thiong'o, N.W. (1965). *The river between*. London: Heinemann.

Williams-Garcia, R. (2004). *No laughter here*. New York: HarperCollins.

PART II

Novel Guides to Explore the Arab World in Northern Africa

CHAPTER 3

Life in Sudan:
From Slavery to Freedom

Jacqueline N. Glasgow

Maps reprinted from *The World Factbook 2007* by the Central Intelligence Agency, http://www.cia.gov/cia/publications/factbook.

Exploring African Life and Literature: Novel Guides to Promote Socially Responsive Learning edited by Jacqueline N. Glasgow and Linda J. Rice. © 2007 by the International Reading Association.

> "No one shall be held in slavery or servitude; slavery and the slave
> trade shall be prohibited in all their forms."
>
> —United Nations, *Universal Declaration of Human Rights*, Article 4, adopted in 1948

E ven though the United Nations (UN) stands strong on its declaration against slavery, Sudan has been embroiled in civil wars in which human rights abuses are widespread. The wars are rooted in northern economic, political, and social domination of Arab Muslims over the non-Muslim, non-Arab southern Sudanese. In 1983, "the second war and famine-related effects resulted in more than 4 million people displaced and, according to rebel estimates, more than 2 million deaths over a period of two decades" (*CIA World Fact Book*, 2007, ¶ 1). While peace talks have succeeded in bringing global awareness to Sudan's engagement in ethnic cleansing, the genocide continues on at least three fronts (in the Nuba Mountains, oil region, and Darfur). The holy wars legitimizing child slave trade and ethnic cleansing are weapons of war that set the stage for the two focal books in this chapter: *Slave: My True Story* (2003) by Mende Nazer and *Escape From Slavery: The True Story of My Ten Years in Captivity—And My Journey to Freedom in America* (2003) by Francis Bok. Supplementary resources for this unit include Niemeyer's *Africa: The Holocausts of Rwanda and Sudan* (2006), which provides students with powerful photography and text that document the genocide and slavery in Sudan. International Rescue Committee's *Making It Home: Real-Life Stories From Children Forced to Flee* (Naidoo, 2004) provides moving stories from refugees. In addition, Mary Williams's *Brothers in Hope: The Story of the Lost Boys of Sudan* (2005) is a picture book that chronicles 30,000 southern Sudanese children who were forced on a trek of nearly 1,000 miles in search of refuge.

The Cross-Curricular Activities for this unit are designed to show the faces of genocide and slavery so that we may see our role in ending these tragedies more clearly. Child slave trade and ethnic cleansing are serious issues that need to be addressed by the global community. To learn more about the political, economic, and religious aspects of life in the Sudan, students capture aspects of the Nuba culture and southern Sudan through Story Impressions, Culture Notebooks, and a Storyboarding Activity. The Making-A-Difference Project for this unit involves students in writing political action letters to influential persons and organizations to stop genocide in Sudan. The overview on page 53 illustrates how the Novel Guides in this chapter and their corresponding activities align with standards for the English language arts (International Reading Association [IRA] & National Council of Teachers of English [NCTE], 1996) and curriculum standards for the social studies (National Council for the Social Studies [NCSS], 1994).

Novels, Activities, and Curricular Standards
for English Language Arts and Social Studies

NOVELS
- *Slave: My True Story* (2003) by Mende Nazer
- *Escape From Slavery: The True Story of My Ten Years in Captivity—And My Journey to Freedom in America* (2003) by Francis Bok

CROSS-CURRICULAR ACTIVITIES
- Story Impressions
- Culture Notebook
- Storyboard Activity

MAKING-A-DIFFERENCE PROJECT
Write a Political Action Letter for Human Rights

STANDARDS FOR THE ENGLISH LANGUAGE ARTS
#1 Students read a wide range of texts to build understanding of the cultures of the world.

#4 Students adjust their use of written language to communicate with different audiences for a variety of purposes.

#7 Students conduct research on issues and interests.

#9 Students develop an understanding and respect for diversity of ethnic groups and social roles.

#11 Students participate as critical members of a variety of literacy communities.

#12 Students use written language to accomplish their own purposes.

Adapted from IRA and NCTE. (1996). *Standards for the English Language Arts*. Newark, DE: International Reading Association; Urbana, IL: National Council of Teachers of English.

CURRICULUM STANDARDS FOR THE SOCIAL STUDIES
#1a Culture: Learners analyze and explain the ways Arab groups address the human needs and concerns of children.

#1f Culture: Learners interpret patterns of behavior such as child slave trade that pose obstacles to cross-cultural understanding.

#3h People, Places, & Environments: Learners examine, interpret, and analyze cultural patterns and their interactions regarding ethnic cleansing.

#4 Individual Development & Identity: Learners analyze the role of perceptions, attitudes, values, and beliefs of Nazer and Bok in the development of their identities.

#9d Global Connections: Learners analyze the causes, consequences, and possible solutions to persistent, emerging global issues such as child slave trade.

Adapted with the permission of the National Council for the Social Studies (NCSS). For the NCSS standards, see the publication *Expectations of Excellence: Curriculum Standards for Social Studies* (Washington, DC: National Council for the Social Studies, 1994). See also www.socialstudies.org.

Social and Historical Context

Sudan, the largest country in Africa, is located in Northern Africa, bordering the Red Sea, between Egypt and Eritrea. When Sudan acquired independence in 1956, the war began between the Sudan Government (GOS) armed by Arab tribes and Sudan People's Liberation Alliance (SPLA), which formed an alliance with the Christian south. In 1988, government forces began systematically killing civilians. "Well over two million southern black Christians, Muslims, and animists in Sudan have died" (Niemeyer, 2006, p. xii). In 1992, the GOS, which had taken Islamic fundamentalism to new extremes, declared a jihad, or holy war, on the Christian south and the people in the Nuba Mountains, which "created a holocaust that rivals the two great genocides in Europe" (Niemeyer, 2006, p. xii). "Eradicating the Nuba," a report by a group of influential Muslim leaders, quickly spread and became the blueprint for killing, the destruction of villages, forced conversions, and forced removals including slavery (Niemeyer, 2004). The government of Khartoum, the capital city of Sudan, sealed off the Nuba Mountains from the outside world for ethnic cleansing purposes that few in the world have heard about.

In addition to this conflagration between the north and the south, a separate conflict broke out in the western region of Darfur. What began in 2003 has resulted in at least 200,000 deaths and nearly 2 million people displaced (*CIA World Factbook*, 2006). In the oil region, Christian flags lead the defensive southern blacks into battle against heavy artillery from Khartoum's governmental forces. "The goal of the north is to create an Arab Muslim state. Their strategy is to displace the southern population from wells and food" (Niemeyer, 2006, p. xii). While peacekeeping troops have been struggling to stabilize the country, many obstacles have obstructed the giving and receiving of humanitarian assistance from around the world.

Slave: My True Story (2003) by Mende Nazer

About the Author

At 12 years old, Mende Nazer was abducted from her village in Sudan, raped, sold into slavery, and kept hostage in Khartoum, the capitol of Sudan, and London, England. In her memoir, *Slave, My True Story* (2003), she describes how she was abused both physically and sexually as a house slave for a wealthy family in Khartoum. After six years, she was sent to London to serve the wife of Sudanese diplomat Abdel Mahmoud al-Koronky. While the family was away vacationing, she managed to escape with the help of a fellow Sudanese in

September 2000. The same year, Nazer applied for asylum for which she was rejected. She then cowrote a book with British journalist Damien Lewis about her ordeal which was published in Germany and became a bestseller. With the support of her readers and human rights activists, the Home Office in Britain reversed its decision and reconsidered her case, granting her asylum. Today she is learning English and speaking for Anti-Slavery International to speak out against children sold into slavery. While her memoir is not in the strictest sense a novel because it is based on real events from her life, this chapter follows the Novel Guide format by providing activities that will meaningfully engage students in considering the main themes of the book, the most important being the issues surrounding child slavery.

Summary

Mende is just drifting off to sleep in her mud hut in the Nuba Mountains in southwest Sudan when she hears a commotion outside. Her father yells, "Fire! Fire in the village!" (p. 2). It only takes a second to realize the Mujahedin, Arab raiders, have arrived to destroy the village. "Run, run to the hills" (p. 2) yells the father. Twelve-year-old Mende grabs her beloved cat, Uran, and hangs on to her father's hand as they run for their lives through the smoke and flames of the grass, thatched roofed huts burning. As they run, they hear crying and screaming in all directions. The raiders are cutting people's throats and grabbing children from their parents' arms. During a cattle stampede, Mende falls to the ground, and a Mujahedin grabs and drags her to the forest's edge. Mende is slung up into the saddle of her captor, and they race through the forest. He molests her along the way and then tries to rape her. Arrival in Khartoum at the home of a wealthy Arab Khartoum marks the beginning of Mende's life as a slave and ends her carefree childhood with the Karko tribe in the Nuba Mountains.

A wealthy Arab couple, Rahab and Mustafa, buy Mende to do domestic work. In this home she sleeps in a shed, eats at a little table apart from the others, and works long hours doing yard work, washing, ironing, cleaning, and supplying childcare. Everything is new to her—from running tap water, to TV/VCRs, and vacuum cleaners—and she works from early morning until late at night. Mende is subjected to appalling physical, sexual, and mental abuse. Her mistress cares nothing for Mende's welfare, even when she is sick with splitting headaches from a beating about her head and, later, with malaria. Mende begins to believe she will never see her family again. While she does contemplate escape, the Arabs seem invincible.

After Mende has been with Rahab for more than six years, she is told she will be going to London to tend to Rahab's sister, Hanan, who just delivered twins. Hanan's husband is the wealthy Abdel al-Koronsky, Sudan's acting charge d'affairs in Willesden, London. In London, her new owners are at first much more humane, but she is still confined to the house, and she works from 6:30 a.m. until late at night. Here Mende is responsible for washing and ironing, cleaning a much larger house, and tending five children. She becomes even more frightened, feels trapped, and considers suicide as the only possible escape. It is only when Hanan takes her family away on vacation and leaves Mende with the Koronskys' family friends that she is treated with respect and her hopes of escape escalate. In this new home, she is free to take the children to the park and to go out alone on short errands. She quickly learns that London is not the crime-ridden, violent place she has been led to believe. Mende seizes her chance and finds a Sudanese person who might help her escape. After several false starts, Mende finds a man who agrees to pick her up in front of the Koronskys' home, makes a dramatic run for her life, and the escape succeeds.

Escape From Slavery: The True Story of My Ten Years in Captivity—And My Journey to Freedom in America (2003) by Francis Bok

About the Author

At the age of 7, Francis Bok was abducted from his village in a Sudanese government slave raid, brought to northern Sudan, and held in bondage by a wealthy Arab landowner. In 1996, he escaped first to Khartoum, then to Egypt, and on to the United States. Today he is is settled in Boston, where he works with the American Anti-Slavery Group. He has testified to the U.S. Senate, met with U.S. Secretary of State Madeleine Albright, carried the Olympic torch, and been honored by the National Council of Teachers of English in Pittsburgh, Pennsylvania, USA, in 2005. In his memoir, *Escape From Slavery: The True Story of My Ten Years in Captivity—and My Journey to Freedom in America* (2003), he describes his experiences of living in a shed near the goats and cattle that were his responsibility. He was fed table scraps, had to learn an unfamiliar language and religion, and had almost no human contact other than his captor's family who abused him. He currently travels and lectures to audiences of all ages and backgrounds about his experiences as a child slave. Like Nazer's book, while this memoir is not in the strictest sense a novel because it is based on real events from Bok's life, this chapter follows the Novel Guide format by providing activities that will meaningfully engage students in considering the main themes of the book, the most important being the issues surrounding child slavery.

Summary

As a young boy, Francis lived on a small farm in the Bahr al-Ghazal region of southwestern Sudan. His early childhood is filled with fond memories of family, friends, and love. His father's farm is full of life—animals, plants, fruit trees, families—and carefree children who play in the sorghum fields. There is no school in Gourion, his village, and like most Dinka boys, Piol (Francis is his Christian name given at his baptism in a Catholic church nearby) spends his day playing with his sisters and friends. He likes to help his father whenever possible, so when his mother asks him to sell hard-cooked eggs and peanuts at the Nyamlell market, he wants to prove his worth as a trader-in-the-making, even though he is very young.

In May 1986, 7-year-old Francis takes his first trip to the market at Nyamlell on his own, when the Murahaliin come and shatter his world forever. These Arab raiders on horseback, armed with rifles and long knives, burst into the quiet marketplace, murdering men and women, and gathering the young children into a group. Strapped to horses and donkeys, Francis and others are taken north, into lives of slavery under wealthy Muslim farmers. Everything he has known for his entire life disappears: his friends, his family, his village. He is now placed in a world different than he could ever have imagined.

At his captor's home, Francis lives alone in a shed near the animals that soon become his sole responsibility. Fed with scraps from the table, slowly learning bits of an unfamiliar language and religion, the child has almost no human contact other than his captor's cruel family. First, Giemma, the father of the family, teaches Francis to graze the goats. Francis is scared of the animals but is more scared of getting beaten, so he complies and learns the routine. During training, Giemma and his son accompany Francis, but soon it is Francis's responsibility to handle and care for the 200 or so sheep and goats. If just one of the animals is missing at the end of the day, he is severely beaten. Francis, however, has no idea how to count them as he can only count to 10. He hates the food and hates the job. Francis decides there is only one answer to the situation—learn the language, learn the religion, learn the territory, and plan the escape. His strategy is to build on Giemma's trust to get as much independence as possible in order to finalize his plan to escape. Francis thinks he will escape when he is a little older, maybe when he is 14.

After two failed attempts to escape—each bringing severe beatings and death threats—Francis finally succeeds at age 17 when he makes a dramatic breakaway on foot. Yet his slavery does not end there, for even as he makes his way toward the capital city of Khartoum, others seek to deprive him of his freedom. In the end, Francis takes a bus and ends up at a refugee camp with other Dinkas. In his desperation to discover what happened to his family on that terrible day in 1986, he shares his story freely. Before long, he is arrested and thrown in jail. There, jailers beat and torture him into making a confession. He denies being a slave and endures the beatings. If he is ever released, he knows he must leave the country, as there will never be any safety in this country as long as the Muslims are at war with the Dinka people.

After seven months of imprisonment, Francis is released on a day of general amnesty. He has heard of people who have gotten a visa to go to Cairo. There are also stories of people who have gone to Cairo and are now living in the United States, England, Canada, and Australia through the help of the United Nations. Francis immediately begins the process to make this happen. His friend, Garang, helps him raise the money and get through the process. Several months later, he is on his way to Cairo, where he wins the attention of United Nations officials. September 15, 1998, he learns the good news that he will be flying to the United States. A year later, August 13, 1999, he makes the journey across the ocean and across the continent to his new home in Fargo, North Dakota. In the United States, Francis becomes a student and an antislavery activist, making it his life mission to combat world slavery. His is one of the first voices to speak for an estimated 27 million people held against their will in nearly every nation, including the United States of America.

Making Connections

Strategic learners have three major strategies they use to generate ideas that serve as a springboard from which to launch new learning (Allan & Miller, 2000). Before reading a new text, strategic readers activate prior experiences and prior knowledge about the topics or themes introduced in the book. Second, strategic readers preview, predict, and reflect on personal purposes for reading the book. They think about what they are likely to learn. Third, they notice unfamiliar words and explore new vocabulary either before they read or as they encounter new words in the text. While strategic readers use these strategies in combination, dependent readers need help in learning these strategies. The Making Connections questions and student responses to these questions will scaffold these strategies (Keene & Zimmermann, 1997). The following list of questions can be used for this unit, and Figure 3.1 shows a sample journal response to a text-to-self question for this Novel Guide created by university student Jessica Radzick.

Making Connections Questions for *Slave: My True Story* (2003) and *Escape From Slavery* (2003)

Text-to-Self	What do I know about child slave trade?
	What do I know about ethnic cleansing?
	What do I know about child abuse?
	What do I know about cultural conflict?
	What do I know about holy wars?

Text-to-Text	What have I read about child slave trade? What have I read about ethnic cleansing? What have I read about child abuse? What have I read about cultural conflict? What have I read about holy wars?
Text-to-World	What countries participate in child slave trade? Where is ethnic cleansing occurring? Where is child abuse legal? Who experiences cultural conflict? What countries experience holy wars?

Figure 3.1. Student Journal Response to a Making Connections Text-to-Self Question

Text–Self: "What do I know about child slave trade?"
I am genuinely disturbed by the human rights that children are denied and the sexual acts that children across the continent are forced to perform. Children are human beings. They have rights that they are entitled to, and they should not be taken advantage of simply because they are children. Their voices are ignored and they have no other choice but to surrender to the traffickers. These victims are not only robbed of their human rights, but they are lied to, beaten, taken advantaged of, raped, and dehumanized.

Critical Exploration of Themes

Through the summaries for these two memoirs, child slavery emerges as one of the primary themes. To discover the prevalent and flagrant abuse of human rights in our modern world through child slave trade, ethnic cleansing, rape, and pillage is both appalling and shocking. In the memoirs of Nazer and Bok, the beauty of the landscape and strong family relationships are sharply contrasted with the violence of the Mujahedin robbing them of their childhood innocence and forcing them into lives of slavery. The following discussion of these themes describes more about the culture in the Nuba Mountains, the slave raiders in Nyamlell, and child slave trade in the world today. It also shows the strength of the human spirit to survive, escape, and lead others to freedom in spite of government oppression.

Culture in the Nuba Mountains: Setting for Nazer's *Slave: My True Story* (2003)

Deep in the heart of the Sudan lie the Nuba Mountains. The Nuba people are the largest of many non-Arab groups in located in the Northern region of Sudan and are the descendants of the people of the Kush kingdom in the 8th century. They are an amalgam of dozens of different tribes with different cultures and languages. But theirs has been a culture of survival against their enemies from early times when Egypt and Assyria were powerful empires. The Kush eventually settled in the Sudan in an area known as the Kordofan Province. But because of the successive attacks by the various Arab tribes who invaded Sudan from the 16th century onward, they retreated to the mountains of South Kordofan. While difficult to evaluate, the best estimate is that over the past 12 years, 200,000 to 300,000 lives, out of approximately 2 million people, have been lost in this small mountainous region (Niemeyer, 2004).

In Part 1 of her book, Mende Nazer shares fond memories of her childhood in the Nuba Mountains. Students should examine the strengths of her culture—the strong family relationships, living conditions, Arab schooling, cultural practices, and Mende's dream for the future. Life in the Nuba Mountains was idyllic for Mende as a child, and making it real through photography serves as a contrast to the Khartoum government's goals of ethnic cleansing.

For more information about the customs and traditions in the Nuba Mountains go to the Nuba Survival Foundation website at www.nubasurvival. com/Nuba%20Culture/Nuba%20Culture%20index.htm (Nuba Survival Foundation, n.d.). This website contains information about Nuba stick fighting, women and marriage in the Nuba tradition, Kambala dance, Fire Sibir (a ceremony after cultivation in November when the stubble is burned), and Nuba songs and poems. It may also be helpful to read about Lucian Niemeyer's visit to the Nuba Mountains and view his photography online at www.lnsart.com/nuba_moun tains.htm (2004) or in his book, *Africa: The Holocausts of Rwanda and Sudan* (2006).

Slave Raiders in Nyamlell, Southern Sudan—Setting for Bok's *Escape From Slavery* (2003)

It has been over 120 years since General Charles Gordon suppressed the slave trade in Sudan. Before he began his campaign, seven out of every eight Sudanese were slaves. Incredible as it may seem, the invasion of slave raiders swooping down on unprotected villages is once again commonplace in Sudan. Tens of thousands of Christian Sudanese men, women, and children, like Francis Bok, have been kidnapped and sold as slaves by government-sponsored soldiers.

In an official report to the UN Commission on Human Rights in Sudan, Gaspar Biro (1996) presented documentation of the systematic pattern of aerial bombardment of civilian targets, arbitrary arrests, detention without due process of law, torture, extra-judicial killings, summary executions, forced removals, forced labor, and slavery by the GOS. According to this report, the slave trade is most prevalent in Bahr-el-Ghazal and the Nuba Mountains. Biro's (1996) report concluded that

> Abduction of southern civilians...has become a way of conducting the war...the abduction of persons, mainly women and children, belonging to racial, ethnic and religious minorities from southern Sudan, the Nuba Mountains and the Ingasemma Hills areas, their subjection to the slave trade, including traffic in and sale of children and woman, slavery, servitude, forced labor and similar practices are taking place with the knowledge of the Government of Sudan...and with the tacit approval of the Government of Sudan. (¶ 11)

Both Mende Nazer and Francis Bok were victims of this religious intolerance condoned by the Sudanese Government.

Child Slave Trade in the World Today

In addition to being victims of religious intolerance, Nazer and Bok were victims of child slave trade that has been one of the consequences of the succession of unstable civilian and military governments in the Sudan. At least 14,000 children have been abducted in the Sudan in the past 20 years of slave raiding. Antislavery activists say that girls working as domestic servants are denied freedom and education and are vulnerable to abuse. Many girls are forced into sex work, while the boys are forced into labor for wealthy Arab militia, often tending their livestock ("Millions 'Forced Into Slavery,'" 2002).

According to reporter Ticky Monekosso (1999), economic pressure and persistent poverty in Africa are also leading to a resurgence of child slave trafficking. These children are for sale in West African countries for domestic and commercial labor as well as for sexual exploitation. Until recently, child slave trade was only practiced in war-ravaged societies such as Angola, Sudan, Somalia, and Chad, where even 10-year-old girls served as servants and concubines at rebel military bases, but now the slave trade is growing in the peaceful areas.

In July 1997, Benin police arrested five West Africans preparing to ship a boat full of 400 children to West African capitals (Monekosso, 1999). Police said the children, some only 8 years old, were bought from families for the equivalent of about US$30. Other children were kidnapped while simply playing outside or after wandering into urban areas. According to investigators, more than 30 kidnapped children cross the Benin–Nigeria border every two months. Of them, almost all are girls under the age of 15, half of whom have never been to school (Monekosso, 1999).

As described in another report, reporter Ian Pannell (2001) traveled to Nigeria and Turin to investigate how traffickers use the United Kingdom as a staging post for child prostitution. He learned that many of the hundreds of girls from Nigeria sold into sexual slavery in Europe each year have been trafficked through England. The report stated that "The children's ordeal begins in Benin City in Nigeria, a dusty, sweaty, frenetic and noisy place. Girls and boys are lured into sexual slavery with tales of riches in far-off lands" (¶ 12).

In addition to those lured into sexual slavery are the cases when parents make the decision to sell their children into slavery. For example, Rafine was just 5 years old when her father hired her out to child traffickers in order to make money on the proceeds of her work ("In the Grip," 2005). When he took a new wife, he did the same with all of Rafine's brothers and sisters. Rafine had to cook, clean, and look after the other children. In return, she slept on the kitchen floor and shared food off the cats' plates before eventually running away. Rafine was just 1 of 50,000 children who are sold each year in Benin when their parents are too poor to resist the trafficker's bribes ("In the Grip," 2005).

Countries in the front line of this trade include Benin, Burkina Faso, Cameroon, Cote d'Ivoire, Gabon, Nigeria, and Togo. Students should research and discuss the causes leading to this child slave market as well as what tasks the children are required to perform at what ages. They should discover what, if anything, is being done to save these children, and research how organizations intervene. Students should discuss human rights for children, especially the right to an education. Who is responsible for educating the children in these countries? How might this right be enforced in the international community as well as in their own? What can our students do to help the situation?

Teacher Talk

Questions have been a part of a teacher's repertoire since Socrates used them as a teaching tool to help students think. Unfortunately, research shows that teachers ask primarily literal, text-based questions (Alexander, Jetton, Kulikowich, & Woehler, 1994). However, by using the following adaptation of Herber's (1978) model, comprised of three levels of comprehension, we can include literal questions and also move to questions that require higher levels of thinking. Literal, text-based questions require students to respond with essential information presented in the text. Interpretive questions require students to recognize implied meanings of the text by integrating information from various sections of the text with their background knowledge. Applied questions require students to synthesize new text information with their background knowledge to extend existing schema knowledge and generalize to new situations or abstract principles. The following questions use Herber's three levels of comprehension to examine the memoirs of Nazer and Bok.

Using Herber's Questioning Levels for Nazer and Bok Memoirs

	Nazer's *Slave: My True Story* (2003)	Bok's *Escape From Slavery* (2003)
Literal Questions	What characterizes Mende Nazer's family life in her early childhood? What does she miss about her childhood home? What were her responsibilities as a slave in Khartoum? How was she treated? Why did her Arab master send her to London? How did she escape from slavery? How did she reconnect with her family in Sudan? What did she think would happen if she was deported back to Sudan? On what basis did the British Home Office deny her asylum? What groups helped her fight the legal battles to live in Britain? What part did her memoir play in securing her freedom? To which ideals is she committed? What is her dream?	What characterizes Francis Bok's childhood experiences? How does his father regard him? How does he learn Arabic? How does he keep track of the goats? What is the punishment for disobedience and escape attempts? How did he manage to escape? Why was he thrown in jail? What groups or people helped him get to Egypt? What part does the UN play in setting him free? How did he make his way to the United States? What were some of the adjustments he had to make in this new country? What are his goals in life? His dream? What are his educational and language development experiences?
Interpretive Questions	What is the basis of the civil conflict between north and south Sudan? What was confusing about living with the Arab family in Khartoum? How did Mende cope with her master's cruelty in Khartoum? How does she find comfort in this harsh environment? What human rights were violated in this situation? What was the most difficult challenge for her to overcome? How would moving to London change her life? Mende's freedom is precious to her, but what made it so terrifying? What were the personal challenges she faced living in England?	What enabled Francis to survive Giemma's cruelty? What are Francis's strengths? What are his weaknesses? How does he find comfort? What drives Francis to pursue freedom at such a great cost? How is learning English critical to his acquiring freedom? How did he get by with a fake passport? What is the purpose for writing the memoir? What is compelling about his memoir? How is Francis establishing his independence as an immigrant to the United States?
Applied Questions	What interest does the United States have in Sudan? What is the basis of the civil war in Sudan? What has been done to stop the genocide in Sudan, including the Darfur crisis?	What is the basis of the civil war in Sudan? What message does Francis want Americans to understand? How have other ethnic and religious groups reacted to persecution?

Applied Questions (continued)	What were the dangers in publishing Mende's book?	Why are so many slave narratives emerging around the globe?

Applied Questions (continued)

What were the dangers in publishing Mende's book?

How differently might this narrative read if written in her Nuba language?

Do we have incidences of government tacit approval of destructive behavior toward the citizenry of the United States? If so, what are they?

What can we do to stop child slave trade?

What can we do to stop human trafficking?

What can we do to support people in Mende's situation?

Do we have a responsibility for social action on Mende's behalf? If so, what should we do?

Why are so many slave narratives emerging around the globe?

What evidence of ethnic interdependence and respect is there in Francis's fugitive narrative?

How differently might this story read in the Dinka language?

How does this story move beyond a slave narrative and become an immigration and Americanization story?

What can we do to fight child slave trade?

Do we have a responsibility for social action on Francis's behalf?

How can we enforce a child's right to an education?

Cross-Curricular Activities

The following classroom assignments are designed to maximize students' understanding and inquiry into major themes, particularly child slave trade, as portrayed in the memoirs of Nazer and Bok. Students will capture aspects of the Nuba culture through a Story Impressions strategy, Culture Notebooks, and a Storyboarding Activity.

Story Impressions

This strategy helps students establish a purpose for reading and form an overall impression of the text through predictions (see All America Reads online at http://www.allamericareads.org/pdf/single/before/storyimpress.pdf for more information on this strategy). The teacher chooses key words, phrases, or concepts from several chapters and lists them in the order in which they appear in the chapters. The list normally consists of 10 to 15 items. Students should be given enough words to form an impression of the chapters but not so many that they would be able to create entire episodes that they will encounter in reading.

First, make a list of words in the order they appear in the story, similar to the following found in chapters 1–3 of Bok's *Escape From Slavery* (2003). Next, display the words in the order that they appear in the text. This strategy will help students when they encounter words or terms that are unfamiliar (see Table 3.1 for a list of words for Story Impressions strategy).

Table 3.1. List of Words for Story Impressions Strategy	
Bok's *Escape From Slavery* (2003)	Nazer's *Slave: My True Story* (2003)
Francis Bok	Beautiful dawn
Peanuts and beans	Fifty cattle
Market at Nyamlell	Father's stories
Catholic Church	Mujahedin
Smoke in the villages	Run, Mende!
Murahaliin	Fire! Fire in the village!
Gun shots	Nuba tribe
Slavery	Mud huts
Small shelter	Curved dagger
Goatherd	Ugly stench
Whip	Blood
Black boys	Terror
Leg cut off	Worst nightmare
Escape	Arab raiders

Have students discuss the keywords so they have the opportunity to figure out words that they do not know before they begin reading. After an initial discussion, ask each student to write a paragraph, using all the words in the given order to predict what she or he thinks the chapters will be about, thus creating a Story Impression. Having students write down all their Story Impressions is important so that they have something to reference once they read the text. Place the students in groups of four or five, and allow the group members time to share their Story Impressions to compare their predictions. After this discussion, give students the opportunity to begin reading the chapters. Decide how much discussion your students need prior to reading.

Culture Notebook for the Nuba

Students acquire and retain knowledge of culture and vocabulary in various ways. An effective method for this unit is through a Culture Notebook. As students read Part 1 of *Slave: My True Story* (2003), "My Childhood With the Nuba," they will encounter unfamiliar words and phrases as Nazer describes her experience. Ask students to enter short passages from the memoir that include the Nuba language, games, relationships, foods, and artifacts in their Culture Notebooks. In most cases, Nuba and Arabic words are explained the first time that they are introduced in the text; however, British English is not. Students should use context clues within a sentence or in surrounding sentences to decode unfamiliar words and then write down their best guesses as to the definition. They should also note the type of context clue they used in order to derive the meaning of the word or phrase. Encourage students to discuss Nazer's reasons for integrating these terms into the story. The Culture Notebook activity provides opportunities to discuss the impact of culture-specific language on the reader's experience. Looking at a short passage illustrates the way the narrator's mixture of Nuba and English enriches the reading experience and offers teachers numerous opportunities for lessons about language and culture. See Figure 3.2 Sample Culture Notebook for *Slave: My True Story*.

Storyboard Activity

The Storyboard Activity involves sketching the most crucial scenes of the story in squares sequentially, as is frequently done by filmmakers (Cox, 2002). After students read the story, ask them to decide on six major scenes that summarize the main events. Crucial lines of text may be inserted into the squares as word balloons or titles. Students should use colors to portray their perceptions of the mood for the scenes and the emotions displayed by the characters.

After students read Part 1 of *Slave: My True Story* (2003), divide them into groups of three or four, depending on the number of students and the size of the

---

Figure 3.2. Sample Culture Notebook for *Slave: My True Story* (Nazer, 2003)

Page Number	Word or Phrase	Meaning	Cultural Impact
2	"Ook tom gua" my father shouted, jumping up.	There's a fire in the village.	Shouting in the Nuba language makes it seem more authentic.
2	"Mujahedin!" my father yelled.	Arab raiders are in the village.	Danger is eminent. It's only natural that he shout in his native language.
4	"Ba! Ba! Ba!" I croaked.	Daddy, Daddy! Daddy!	Of course, Mende would call her father in her Nuba language in such a tragic moment.
5	"Oh Allah, Oh Allah, please save me."	Oh, God, please save me.	As the Arab takes her into the forest Mende is desperate for her and her family to be saved. Her God is "Allah."
9	"My father chose to call me Mende."	Mende means gazelle—the most beautiful and graceful animal in the Nuba Mountains.	We see how special she is to her father. She was her father's fifth and last child. He thought she was the prettiest daughter of all. This close relationship will be a strong resource for her in hard times ahead.

Table 3.2. Minimum Requirements for *Slave: My True Story* (Nazer, 2003) Storyboarding Activity, Scene 1

Scene 1 should include the following:

1. Mende's home with
   a. Shal (p. 9)
   b. Tog (p. 9)
   c. Sheep and goats (p. 9)
   d. Hohua (p. 11)
   e. Durs (p. 13)

2. Hawaja Convoy (p.14)

3. Mende's Family
   a. Ba (pp. 19–20)
   b. Umi (pp. 17–19)
   c. Uran (p. 10)
   d. Shokan (pp. 23–24)
   e. Kunyant (p. 24)
   f. Kwandsharan (p. 24)
   g. Babo (p. 24)

4. Kak or omat huaid (pp. 24–25)

classroom. Assign the first storyboard scene (for the first square) to get them started, and then let them choose the other five scenes for their storyboard. The first square will be based on the setting for the memoir in the Nuba Mountains. This activity will help students not only visualize the setting but also become more familiar with the Nuba language. For scene 1, ask students to create the scene for Mende's home and family. (See Table 3.2 for the minimum requirements for the first scene of the Storyboarding Activity.)

Making-A-Difference Project: Writing a Political Action Letter for Human Rights

Writing strong, informed letters to a real audience that can make a difference is a worthy goal for our English language arts and social studies students. To achieve this goal, the letter must reflect an informed and educated position that is supported with logical and persuasive arguments, research, and examples of good practice, and it must be written in correct business format (see Figure 3.3 for an example of a political action letter written by university student Kaitlin Day to U.S. President George W. Bush, urging him to take steps to stop violence in Sudan).

After reading Nazer's and Bok's memoirs, students can make a difference by supporting the campaigns of human rights organizations like the Human

> **Figure 3.3. Student Political Action Letter to U.S. President George Bush**
>
> 131 South Green Drive
> Apartment 202
> Athens, Ohio 45701
>
> May 8, 2006
>
> Mr. President
> 140 Russell Senate Building
> Washington, DC 20510
>
> Re: Violence in Sudan
>
> Dear Mr. President:
>
> In Sudan's Darfur region, 180,000 Sudanese have been killed. More than two million people have been displaced by violent attacks. These people are near death themselves. They have poor shelter, little nutritious food, dirty water and no guarantee of safety. Everyday more and more people are killed or assaulted.
>
> I recently read Frances Bok's book, *Escape From Slavery*. I understand you have met this brave man. His writing detailed his brutal capture and forced enslavement. I was shocked to read his words and realize that when I was a care-free sixth-grader, Bok, just a few years older than I, was living with the animals and treated as a piece of property.
>
> Please take actions to alleviate the problem. We can make a difference with this situation. Our powerful nation has involved itself in many other world atrocities and made a significant difference. I do not understand why we are not doing more to end these crimes against humanity.
>
> I am saddened and in disbelief that these issues have only lately been acknowledged and brought to our country's attention. I sincerely hope to hear less and less about this issue as time goes on—not because American interest and awareness has tired, but because the problem has been eradicated.
>
> Concerned American,
>
> Kaitlin Daly

Rights Watch, Anti-Slavery International, the National Coalition of Anti-Deportation Campaigns, or Amnesty International (AI). These organizations actively influence legislation and international law to protect human rights around the world. They are all interested in stopping the child abduction and child trafficking in various parts of Africa. The students' projects might be directed at influential persons at the international, national, state, or local levels. For example, students can write a letter to AI in support of its campaigns in Africa. AI is a worldwide movement of people who campaign for internationally recognized human rights:

> AI's vision is of a world in which every person enjoys all of the human rights enshrined in the Universal Declaration of Human Rights and other international hu-

man rights standards. AI is independent of any government, political ideology, economic interest or religion. It does not support or oppose any government or political system, nor does it support or oppose the views of the victims whose rights it seeks to protect. It is concerned solely with the impartial protection of human rights. (Amnesty International, n.d., ¶ 2)

For more information, see the Amnesty International Write for Rights! website at http://web.amnesty.org/pages/writeathon2004-eng. You can also find a letter-writing guide online at www.amnesty.org/campaign/letter-guide.html. The list of political action websites in Table 3.3 on human rights issues of the Sudan may also help inspire students with ideas for their letters.

Table 3.3. List of Political Action Websites on Human Rights Issues in Sudan

1. Stop Africa's Child Trafficking!
   Borzello, A. (2004, April 23). Tracking Africa's child trafficking. *BBC News*. Retrieved from http://news.bbc.co.uk/1/hi/world/africa/3653737.stm

2. Stop Internally Displaced Persons!
   Amnesty International. (2006). *The plight of displaced persons in Sudan*. Retrieved from http://web.amnesty.org/pages/sdn-190406-editorial-eng

3. Stop Genocide in Darfur!
   Darfur crisis is 'as bad as ever.' (2006, April 21). *BBC News*. Retrieved from http://news.bbc.co.uk/2/hi/africa/4926234.stm

4. Stop Sex Slavery!
   Crackdown on sex slavery. (2000, February 23). *BBC News*. Retrieved from http://news.bbc.co.uk/1/hi/world/americas/653648.stm

5. Stop Using African Boys for Human Sacrifice!
   Boys 'used for human sacrifice.' (2005, June 16). *BBC News*. Retrieved from http://news.bbc.co.uk/2/hi/uk_news/4098172.stm

6. Stop Deadly Bird Flu
   Deadly bird flu spreads to Sudan. (2006, April 18). *BBC News*. Retrieved from http://news.bbc.co.uk/1/hi/world/africa/4919852.stm

7. Stop Children as Soldiers!
   Invisible Children Movement. (2006). *Movement*. Retrieved from http://www.invisiblechildren.com/theMovement

8. Stop Abusive Child Labor and Poverty!
   Global Exchange. (2006). *Fair trade chocolate: The sweet solution to abusive child labor and poverty*. Retrieved from http://www.globalexchange.org/campaigns/fairtrade/cocoa

9. Stop Depriving Children of Education!
   Teacher's diary from a Sudan refugee camp. (2006, March 14). *BBC News*. Retrieved from http://news.bbc.co.uk/1/hi/education/features/4794564.stm

10. Stop Western Oil Greed!
   Dixon, N. (2005, February 8). *Sudan: Western oil greed trumps "genocide" concerns*. Retrieved from http://www.worldpress.org/Africa/2025.cfm

For the letter to be effective, it should be 1–2 pages when single-spaced. When readers skim letters, they tend to read the first and last paragraphs and the first sentences of other paragraphs. These are often referred to as "power positions" (Eanes, 2006). Putting the most important information in these power positions is the most effective strategy, because the reader of the letter will take note of the argument placed in these positions. Because the next-to-last paragraph is least important and least likely to be read, counterarguments should be addressed in this position. The last paragraph is most important, so the writer should include important content that leaves the reader with a strong impression of the writer's most important points. This paragraph is not the place to summarize the contents of the letter. In addition, require students to include a separate piece with a bibliography of sources that are current, accurate, and convincing. To facilitate excellence in letter writing, provide students with the Political Action Letter Self-Assessment Checklist adapted from the self-assessment rubric designed by Professor Robin Eanes (see Table 3.4). Emphasize to students that every letter counts.

Table 3.4. Political Action Letter Self-Assessment Checklist

1. The return address and date are complete and positioned correctly.
2. The inside address and salutation are complete and accurate. Subject line is added correctly between the inside address and salutation.
3. The letter immediately applauds the addressee for good practices to establish common ground between the reader and writer and establishes credibility.
4. The introductory paragraph effectively gains and holds attention of audience, and one of the power position paragraphs (first or last) must be used effectively to entice readers into the entire letter.
5. The letter clarifies the writer's personal interests, priorities, and values.
6. The letter reflects an informed and educated position supported with logical and persuasive arguments, research, and good practices.
7. The letter addresses likely concerns of the addressee, including questions for funding.
8. Information is presented in concise and easy-to-read format, including the use of bullets if appropriate.
9. Writing is characterized by appropriate word choice, effective wording and sentence structure, clarity (not vague or ambiguous phrasing) and coherence (good organization, flow, and transitions).
10. The letter is single-spaced and complete in 1–2 pages, using a 12-point font. Grammatical conventions are used correctly. The letter is written in a friendly tone.
11. The letter is accompanied by a separate sheet with a bibliography of sources that are current, accurate, and of appropriate quality.
12. The closing is appropriate, written and typed signatures are present, and enclosure reminder are included if needed.

Conclusion

In the memoirs for this unit, we have seen that Mende Nazer and Francis Bok represent the thousands of other child slaves that have suffered a similar fate. Through the cross-curricular activities, students should come to understand both the beauty of the land and culture Nazer and Bok came from and the appalling abuse they suffered in slavery at such a young age. Students also should understand the power of making a difference in the world through persuasive letter writing to influential people who have the authority to make change.

REFERENCES

Alexander, P.A., Jetton, T.L., Kulikowich, J.M., & Woehler, C.A. (1994). Contrasting instructional and structural importance: The seductive effect of teacher questions. *Journal of Reading Behavior, 26*(1), 19–45.

Allan, K.K., & Miller, M.S. (2000). *Literacy and learning: Strategies for middle and secondary school teachers.* Boston: Houghton Mifflin.

Amnesty International. (n.d.). *About Amnesty International.* Retrieved May 18, 2006, from http://web.amnesty.org/pages/aboutai-index-eng

Amnesty International. (2006). *The plight of displaced persons in Sudan.* Retrieved April 21, 2006, from http://web.amnesty.org/pages/sdn-190406-editorial-eng

Biro, G. (1996, February). *Official report to the UN Commission on Human Rights in the Sudan.* Retrieved December 15, 2004, from http://www.frontline.org.za/printer%20friendly%20version/pf_slaveraiders.htm

Borzello, A. (2004, April 23). Tracking Africa's child trafficking. *BBC News.* Retrieved from http://news.bbc.co.uk/1/hi/world/africa/3653737.stm

Boys 'used for human sacrifice.' (2005, June 16). *BBC News.* Retrieved from http://news.bbc.co.uk/2/hi/uk_news/4098172.stm

Central Intelligence Agency (CIA). *The world factbook: History of Sudan.* Retrieved February 20, 2006, from http://www.cia.gov/cia/publications/factbook/geos/su.html

Cox, C. (2002). *Teaching language arts: A student- and response-centered classroom* (4th ed.). Boston: Allyn & Bacon.

Darfur crisis is 'as bad as ever.' (2006, April 21). *BBC News.* Retrieved from http://news.bbc.co.uk/2/hi/africa/4926234.stm

Deadly bird flu spreads to Sudan. (2006, April 18). *BBC News.* Retrieved from http://news.bbc.co.uk/1/hi/world/africa/4919852.stm

Dixon, N. (2005, February 8). *Sudan: Western oil greed trumps "genocide" concerns.* Retrieved from http://www.worldpress.org/Africa/2025.cfm

Eanes, R. (2006). *Honors 3382 political action letter draft self-assessment rubric.* Retrieved May 10, 2006, from http://www.stedwards.edu/educ/eanes/rubrics/letter_draft_self.htm

Global Exchange. (2006). *Fair trade chocolate: The sweet solution to abusive child labor and poverty.* Retrieved April 21, 2006, from http://www.globalexchange.org/campaigns/fairtrade/cocoa

Herber, H.L. (1984). *Teaching reading in the content areas* (2nd ed.). New York: Prentice Hall.

International Reading Association & National Council of Teachers of English. (1996). *Standards for the English language arts.* Newark, DE; Urbana, IL: Authors.

In the grip of Benin's child traffickers. (2005, May 31). *BBC News.* Retrieved from http://news.bbc.co.uk/1/hi/world/africa/4589731.stm

Keene, E.O., & Zimmermann, S. (1997). *Mosaic of thought: Teaching comprehension in a reader's workshop.* Portsmouth, NH: Heinemann.

Millions 'forced into slavery.' (2002, May 27). *BBC News.* Retrieved from http://news.bbc.co.uk/1/hi/world/2010401.stm

Monekosso, T. (1999, August 6). West Africa's child slave trade. *BBC News.* Retrieved from http://news.bbc.co.uk/1/hi/world/africa/412628.stm

National Council for the Social Studies. (1994). *Expectations of excellence: Curriculum standards for social studies.* Silver Spring, MD: Author.

Niemeyer, L. (2004). *Nuba Mountains—Sudan.* Retrieved December 15, 2004, from http://www.lnsart.com/nuba_mountains.htm

Pannell, I. (2001, January 10). Trafficking nightmare for Nigerian children. *BBC News.* Retrieved from http://news.bbc.co.uk/1/hi/world/africa/841928.stm

Teacher's diary from a Sudan refugee camp. (2006, March 14). *BBC News*. Retrieved from http://news.bbc.co.uk/1/hi/education/features/4794564.stm

United Nations. (1948). *Universal declaration of human rights*. Retrieved December 17, 2004, from http://www.un.org/Overview/rights.html

LITERATURE CITED

Bok, F. (with Tivnan, E.). (2003). *Escape from slavery: The true story of my ten years in captivity—And my journey to freedom in America*. New York: St. Martin's Press.

Naidoo, Beverly. (2004). *Making it home: Real-life stories from children forced to flee*. New York: Puffin Books.

Nazer, M. (with Lewis, D.). (2003). *Slave: My true story*. New York: Public Affairs.

Niemeyer, L. (2006). *Africa: The holocausts of Rwanda and Sudan*. Albuquerque: University of New Mexico Press.

Williams, M. (2005). *Brothers in hope: The story of the lost boys of Sudan*. Ill. Gregory Christie. New York: Lee & Low Books.

CHAPTER 4

The Struggle of Arab Women
to Lead Self-Determining Lives

Jacqueline N. Glasgow

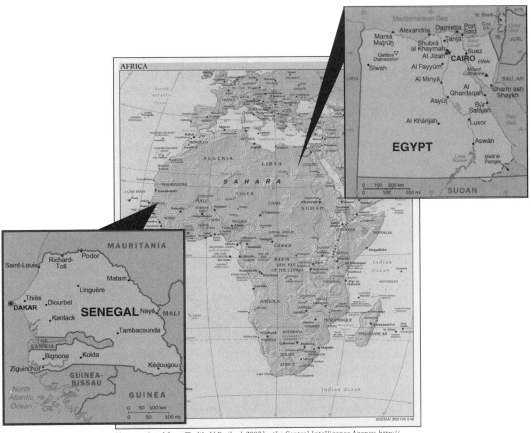

Maps reprinted from *The World Factbook 2007* by the Central Intelligence Agency, http://
www.cia.gov/cia/publications/factbook.

Exploring African Life and Literature: Novel Guides to Promote Socially Responsive Learning edited by Jacqueline N.
Glasgow and Linda J. Rice. © 2007 by the International Reading Association.

"We cannot go forward without culture, without saying what we believe, without communicating with others, without making people think about things. Books are a weapon, a peaceful weapon perhaps, but they *are a weapon*."

—MARIAMA BÂ (CITED IN HARRELL-BOND, 1980, P. 214)

Mariama Bâ said the above words not long before her death. She wanted African women writers to use their writing as a weapon to disrupt the traditional patriarchal hierarchies and take charge of their destiny. African women writers have responded to this challenge by creating spaces for themselves through the act of writing about their experiences. They have also used their writings as weapons to question the oppressive conditions of their post-colonial heritage. These writers speak to women's roles as custodians of oral histories and indigenous forms of knowledge.

This tradition of remembering and retelling is culturally defined as women's work and has been reclaimed in their writings in ways that are empowering and sometimes subversive (Nfah-Abbenyi, 1997, p. 150). By speaking for other African women, these women writers present a platform from which to discuss the changing gender roles. These writers argue for sexual politics that do not view African womanhood as necessarily linked to motherhood. They show how women's bodies and sexualities are not necessarily static areas of oppression but ones that can be contested. As participants in these power struggles, they show that women can effectively reshape gender relations.

While some of the characters in their novels may lead narrow, tragic lives, others "simultaneously juggle the multiple and sometimes contradictory roles that are conferred upon them and are shown to live self-determining lives" (Nfah-Abbenyi, 1997, p. 151). Many female characters confront heavy issues such as class, race, sex, and literacy, but they defy these obstacles and become agents of change. As African women use their writing as weapons, they are no longer left in the shadows of their male counterparts. They have succeeded in offering more dynamic representations of women than the images of subordination often presented by male counterparts. This chapter gives voice to the works of two African women writers: *So Long a Letter* (1989) by Mariama Bâ and *From Sleep Unbound* (1976/1983) by Andrée Chedid.

The Cross-Curricular Activities for this unit are designed to introduce students to Arab women living in Islamic cultures who are struggling to lead self-determining lives. The Prediction Cards Word Sort activity will help students tap into their background knowledge of women's issues such as arranged marriages and polygamy. Students will find exemplary passages that show cultural

Novels, Activities, and Curricular Standards
for English Language Arts and Social Studies

NOVELS
- *From Sleep Unbound* (1976/1983) by Andrée Chedid
- *So Long a Letter* (1989) by Mariama Bâ

CROSS-CURRICULAR ACTIVITIES
- Prediction Card Word Sort
- Sketchbook Journal
- Film Viewing

MAKING-A-DIFFERENCE PROJECT
Reflective Essay That Portrays a Woman's Cultural Conflict

STANDARDS FOR THE ENGLISH LANGUAGE ARTS
#1 Students read texts to build an understanding of themselves and other cultures in the world.

#2 Students read a wide range of literature.

#5 Students employ a wide range of strategies as they write.

#6 Students apply knowledge of language structure, genre, and conventions to create, critique, and discuss texts.

#7 Students conduct research on issues and interests.

#8 Students use a variety of technological and information resources to communicate knowledge.

#11 Students participate as critical members of a variety of literacy communities.

#12 Students use spoken, written, and visual language to accomplish their own purposes.

Adapted from IRA and NCTE. (1996). *Standards for the English Language Arts*. Newark, DE: International Reading Association; Urbana, IL: National Council of Teachers of English.

CURRICULUM STANDARDS FOR THE SOCIAL STUDIES
#1a Culture: Learners analyze and explain ways Islamic cultures address women's needs and concerns.

#1f Culture: Learners interpret patterns of behavior such as polygamy that pose obstacles to cross-cultural understanding.

#3h People, Places, & Environments: Learners examine, interpret, and analyze cultural patterns and their interactions regarding oppression of women.

#4f Individual Development & Identity: Learners analyze the role of perceptions, attitudes, values, and beliefs in the development of the personal identity of the protagonists.

#5f Individuals, Groups, & Institutions: Learners evaluate the role of institutions such as patriarchy in furthering both continuity and change.

#6a Power, Authority, & Governance: Learners examine persistent issues involving the rights, roles, and status of women in relation to the general welfare.

#9h Global Connections: Learners illustrate how individual behaviors and decisions connect with global systems.

Adapted with the permission of the National Council for the Social Studies (NCSS). For the NCSS standards, see the publication *Expectations of Excellence: Curriculum Standards for Social Studies* (Washington, DC: National Council for the Social Studies, 1994). See also www.socialstudies.org.

conflict and have an opportunity to portray them visually in sketchbooks, as drawing and sketching are the graphic equivalents of freewriting. Students create original drawings to illustrate ideas, probe passages, or illustrate quotations. They will view *Osama* (Barmak, 2003), a film about a girl disguised as a boy who tries to support her mother and keep the Taliban from discovering her true identity. Students will then compare and contrast the oppression and resilience of women in the film to the ones in the novels. The Making-A-Difference Project for this unit is a reflective essay on cultural conflicts of women and society. The overview on page 75 illustrates how the Novel Guides in this chapter and their corresponding activities align with standards for the English language arts (International Reading Association [IRA] & National Council of Teachers of English [NCTE], 1996) and curriculum standards for the social studies (National Council for the Social Studies [NCSS], 1994).

Social and Historical Context

The Arab world is diverse economically, socially, historically, and politically, yet the Arab people are linked in a variety of ways. The great majority are linked by common language (Arabic), religion (Islam), and cultural identity and heritage. However, many women are frustrated with Islamic patriarchy. The prevailing gender attitudes continue to exert pressure on all women, regardless of their age, education, or access to the public sphere. While in some countries there have been impressive changes on the legal front, customary treatment of women frustrates formal steps toward full and equal citizenship (United Nations Development Fund for Women [UNIFEM], 2004, p. 2). In a 1991 interview with Lebanese critic Alis Sallum, Chedid spoke of the genesis of her first novel, an account of a young Egyptian woman in an arranged marriage: "*From Sleep Unbound* is the actualization of a human cry that lives within me, and perhaps this cry is there to represent the Arab women's voice.... I lived my childhood in Egypt, and I saw examples of the oppressed woman" (Sallum, 1991, pp. 30–31). At the core of Chedid's writing is the concern not for one race or gender over another but for the spiritual liberation and self-realization of all human beings.

Likewise, Mariama Bâ's *So Long a Letter* (1989) is about women finding hope in a desperate situation. The novel is set in Senegal, where Bâ lived through the tumultuous years leading to independence and through a time of unrest that followed independence. She captures some of these themes in her works, particularly the struggle of women to live self-determining lives within the changing Islamic culture and patriarchy that constrains them. She portrays life realistically and shows that even in "New Africa," it is not easy for women to lead independent lives. The rituals of the Islamic culture that demand obedience to mothers-in-law and their husbands' family members contrast with the autonomy women experience in classrooms. Additionally, she explores the problem of husbands' polygamy. Bâ's characters challenge the civic and religious laws that allow this practice. Seen as a vestige of the past, polygamy undermines the independence many have achieved through their education and careers (Napierkowski, 1998, pp. 8–9).

From Sleep Unbound (1976/1983) by Andrée Chedid

About the Author

Born in Egypt in 1920, Andrée Chedid is a novelist, poet, and playwright of Lebanese descent. She spent her childhood on the banks of the Nile in Cairo, Egypt, frequently visiting Paris. She has made Paris her home since 1946. She completed her secondary education in Paris and then returned to Cairo to study journalism. After receiving her BA from the American University in Cairo and at age 21 marrying Louis Chedid, she moved with her husband to Beirut for three years before returning to Paris, where she has been living since. Most of Chédid's work is in French and has been translated into many languages. Her works include a variety of genres: novels, short stories, plays, essays, and poetry, as well as children's books.

Andreé Chedid's work transcends barriers: geographic, temporal, and linguistic. Her fiction flows easily between France, the Middle East, and Egypt. She is author of 3 volumes of short stories, 2 collections of plays, 3 short prose works, and 11 novels. Her works have been translated into 15 languages. History, both ancient and modern, relationships, and romantic love are recurring themes in both her fiction and drama, and her plays often combine mime, poetry, masque, and music. She is the recipient of many prestigious awards, such as the highest award of the Acadéemie Mallarmé for poetry (1976), the Prix Goncourt for the short story (1979), and the Prix Albert Camus for the novel (1996). She received the French Légion d'Honneur title of commandeur in 2000, and the Académie françasie bestowed on her the Grand Prix Paul Morand in 2001 in recognition of the magnitude and universality of her contribution to French Letters (Cochran & Craver, 2004).

Summary

In the society in which Samya, the protagonist of *From Sleep Unbound* lives, fathers marry off their daughters to acquire more wealth or mend their shabby reputations. Samya is but 15 years old when her father withdraws her from a convent school and forces her into an unwanted arranged marriage with 45-year-old Boutros, whom she has never met.

Without delay, Samya is married and taken to the countryside to live. Her husband oversees a large piece of land, adding title and prestige to his name. Samya is confined to the home. Due to her husband's social position, she is not allowed to enter the city and mingle with the common folks. She is not only isolated from her family and the community but also Boutros is not pleased with her, especially because she appears to be barren. Eight years later, she sees a healer, conceives a child, and gives birth to a baby girl, Mia. With another life to care for, Samya finds a purpose to live, at least for a short time. Mia dies at age six because Boutros refuses to allow proper medical attention, especially since he never wanted a girl anyway.

The story ends approximately 20 years after it begins. Samya is in her late 30s. She is confined to her bed, stricken by an emotional paralysis. Rachida, the sister of Boutros, lives with the couple. She watches over Samya, more with a hateful eye than with compassion. Neither she nor Boutros can understand Samya. No one visits her any longer except for Ammal, a young girl determined to avoid such a loveless and humiliating marriage. Samya's family ignores her situation, and she is forgotten, depressed, and despondent. But Samya does not quit before taking revenge. She has spent too much of her life in passive submission. One day she rises from her sleep of avoidance and shoots Boutros in order to gain emotional freedom.

So Long a Letter (1989) by Mariama Bâ

About the Author

Mariama Bâ was born in 1929 into an influential family in Dakar, Senegal. After the death of her mother, she was brought up by her grandparents in a traditional Muslim environment. She was close to her father, who was the first Minister for Health in the newly independent Senegal. She received a privileged education at a time when many Africans, especially women, had little access to education. Bâ excelled in school and won first prize in the entrance examination for the École Normale de Rufisque, a teacher training school near Dakar. She obtained her teaching diploma in 1947, taught elementary school, and married a member of Parliament, Obèye Diop. They had nine children together, and she later divorced him. After 12 years of teaching, she was forced to resign due to poor health. She asked to take an appointment at the Senegalese Regional Inspectorate of Teaching. In addition to raising the children alone, she was active in women's associations, promoted education, championed women's rights, made speeches, and wrote articles in local newspapers. Bâ died of cancer in 1981, six months after *So Long a Letter* (1989) won the prestigious Noma Award for

Literature. Her second novel, *Scarlet Song* (1995) about the marriage between a European woman and an African man, was published posthumously.

Summary

Set in Senegal and written in epistolary format, the narrative begins as the protagonist, Ramatoulaye Fall, writes a letter to her lifelong friend, Aissatou Bâ, who had moved to the United States after divorcing her husband. Recently widowed, Ramatoulaye not only tells her friend about her husband's death, but she then reminisces about the commonalities of their lives. In her letter, she examines and challenges the issues that face contemporary Africa following de-colonization, particularly the implications of polygamy.

Ramatoulaye's husband, Moudou Fall, died suddenly and unexpectedly of a heart attack. According to her Muslim faith, Ramatoulaye must remain in seclusion for a period of time. She uses this time to construct the long letter to Aissatou. In this letter, Ramatoulaye still ruminates as to why Moudou took a young bride after 25 years of marriage to Ramatoulaye, who bore him 12 children. She is still hurt and baffled by the betrayal and now his death.

Ramatoulaye reflects on Aissatou's decision to leave her husband, Mawdo Bâ. While still in love with Aissatou, Mawdo Bâ succumbed to his mother's pressure to take a wife who shared his same noble blood. Aissatou, who was not accepted by his family in the first place, divorced him and took their four sons to live in the United States. She refused to be bound by the Islamic culture that condones polygamy, which she finds to be humiliating.

In contrast, Ramatoulaye takes a different course after being abandoned by her husband when he marries a young bride. Most of her friends and family expect her to divorce Moudou, especially when they find out that he has abandoned her and quit providing for her and the 12 children. Ramatoulaye decides to remain married and assume the angry, but faithful, position of co-wife. The long letter concludes with a description of other ways her family is being affected by changing traditions. The changes in her children cause her to reflect on their nontraditional behavior: "Does it mean that one can't have modernism, without lowering of moral standards?" (Bâ, 1989, p. 77). Ramatoulaye ends the long letter by looking forward to a visit from her friend, Aissatou, so together they can continue to search for a new way to happiness in spite of the customs of their Islamic culture.

Making Connections

Accessing prior knowledge and experiences is a good starting place when teaching literature because every student has experiences, knowledge, opinions, and emotions that they can draw upon. In this case, students need to think about their concerns for women's issues, such as marriage partners and polygamy, by making text-to-self, text-to-text, and text-to-world connections (Keene & Zimmermann, 1997) between the novels in this unit. The following list of questions can be used for this unit, and Figure 4.1 is a sample journal response written by university student Danielle Moore to the text-to-world question "What choices does a woman have when a man betrays her?"

Making Connections Questions for *From Sleep Unbound* (1976/1983) and *So Long a Letter* (1989)

	Chedid's *From Sleep Unbound* (1976/1983)	Ba's *So Long a Letter* (1989)
Text-to-Self	What dreams do I have for a marriage partner? How do I feel about arranged marriages? Do I expect to have children? What would I do if I could not have children? What are some solutions for abusive relationships? Have I ever felt silenced or oppressed? What freedoms do I cherish the most? Do I think murder is ever justified?	What does it mean to marry for love? Have I ever been betrayed? What does betrayal feel like? How do I deal with bitterness? Hatred? Have I ever sought revenge? What do I think about polygamous relationships? What do I think about divorce? What does a democratic relationship look like? Who do I turn to for strength when I am in trouble? What do I know about Islam?
Text-to-Text	What have I read about arranged marriages? What have I read about childless marriages? What have I read about solutions for abusive relationships? What have I read about women who have been silenced or oppressed? Have I ever read about a murder that was justified?	What have I read about polygamy? What have I read about strong-willed female protagonists? What have I read about characters who are betrayed? What have I read about characters who seek revenge? What have I read about close friendships? What is the most democratic relationship I have read about? What have I read about Islam?
Text-to-World	What are the pros and cons of arranged marriages? What are solutions for abusive relationships? Why is a barren woman rejected? What choices or recourse are available for oppressed women? Is murder ever justified?	What are the pros and cons of polygamy? What choices does a woman have when a man betrays her? What are the consequences of patriarchal use of power? How do Islamic culture and religion impact women's lives?

Critical Exploration of Themes

According to Sehulster's (2004) critique of *So Long a Letter* (1989), Mariama Bâ presents an allegory of the journey from colonization to independence. In her allegory, the predicament of the characters poses as a parallel to that journey. She suggests that while *So Long a Letter* focuses specifically on Senegalese society and on the Islamic patriarchy that controls women's lives, by extension it "also makes a statement about the movement from colonization to independence that all of Africa has faced because of imperialism" (Sehulster, 2004, p. 366). In the allegory, the women represent the colonized and the men the colonizers. Both men and women suffer the pull between tradition and modernity, which is one of the long-range effects of colonization by Westerners. Sehulster posits that just as the colonizers willingly sacrificed the colonized by killing them, enslaving them, or confiscating their lands, in *So Long a Letter*, Moudou Fall and Mawdo Bâ sacrificed their first and second wives for their own, individual gain.

Effects of Islamic Patriarchy

When Moudou Fall deserted Ramatoulaye, he left her destitute. Instead of supporting his large family of a wife and 12 children, he showered his new young bride, Binetou, with lavish gifts such as "the villa, the monthly allowance, and the offer of a future trip to Mecca for her parents" (Bâ, 1989, p. 39). Like the colonizer who sacrificed whole villages' worth of Africans for personal profit, Moudou Fall sacrificed his family to fulfill his desire to acquire a second wife. Just as the colonizer felt pride in conquering a helpless people, Moudou prided himself on winning this young bride, Binetou, who came from a poor and thus easily seduced family (Sehulster, 2004, p. 367). Mawdo Bâ also willingly sacrificed his first wife and four sons in order to obtain his mother's approval. To save his mother from shame, he agreed to wed the girl, Nabou, who she had trained to be a perfect wife for her son. Both men felt justified in abandoning their first wives and taking on wives less educated, less independent, and more likely to exist in a completely servile, sex-slave role than either Ramatoulaye or Aissatou were willing to do. On the other hand, Boutros, not guilty of polygamy, but guilty of emotional abuse of another sort, had enslaved his wife in a loveless marriage.

According to Sehulster (2004), these women became colonized as they performed their sexual and subservient duties. In other words, just as the colonized Africans were expected to accept and to follow their oppressors willingly, the wives of Modou, Mawdo, and Boutros were expected to appreciate and value their roles as wives and mothers. The female characters in these novels were expected to make certain that the household was run smoothly and that their husbands' needs and comforts were met. If they worked outside the home, they still managed all of the traditional duties of the wife and mother, and, in some ways, they defined themselves by those roles. When Aissatou left Mawdo, she lost so much of herself that she had to find a new way to live and define herself as she assumed an appointment to the Senegalese Embassy in the United States. Once Moudo left Ramatoulaye, she was forced to take over Moudo's responsibilities for raising their family in addition to her own. Samya endured an abusive relationship until she could not handle the situation anymore. Rather than adapt and accept their lives in the mold created for them by the colonizers, these women decided not to remain victims of the patriarchy and to pioneer a new way of life.

Women's Determination to Lead Self-Determining Lives

According to Sehulster's (2004) analysis of Bâ's allegory in *So Long a Letter* (1989), each woman represents a successful journey to independence. By the act of writing down her story, Ramatoulaye gives voice to her movement from colonization to independence. She creates her own, new self: someone comfortably still seeking a new way of life. She maintains her traditional belief in motherhood, marriage, and love, though she views marriage without love as an impossibility. She idealizes the marriage of love and equality that her daughter, Daba, and her son-in-law have found. Ramatoulaye offers the traditional Islamic family love to her pregnant, unmarried daughter instead of shunning her as religious traditions would dictate. By writing their stories, Bâ shows that her female characters have "found freedom by remembering, finding, and developing their true selves" (Sehulster, 2004, p. 370). Their writing acts as a changing force as they tell a new history that rejects the Islamic practice of polygamy and foretells a future in which women live independent and self-determining lives, even as they hold on to some of their traditional beliefs.

Resisting the Patriarchy

Just as the friendship between Ramatoulaye and Aissatou sustains them in resisting the Islamic patriarchy, so, too, it is the friendship among women that sustains Samya in *From Sleep Unbound* (1976/1983). Through Samya's story, Chedid shows not only the oppression of women that perpetuates female submission to fathers, brothers, and husbands but also how these women find resources within their community to resist the subjugation. For instance, when Samya arrives home with Boutros, community members secretly form friendships that sustain her. Due to her husband's elevated position in the community, Samya is not permitted to go outside the home or mix with other women. However, Om el Kher, who brings food to the house, defiantly takes Samya into the village to meet her friends while the men are away working in the fields. Om el Kher introduces Samya to her lifetime friend, the old Nefissa, and to Salma, who entertains them all with laughter. Samya meets the openly defiant Ratiba, who calls for the arrest of her brother and father for murdering her sister because they thought she dishonored the family by speaking to a man. These women support each other through subtle exchanges during the day but become dutiful in their homes by evening when the men return. They all silently grieve the loss of a sister with Ratiba and silently grieve the loss of Samya's daughter. These women again demonstrate the solidarity of friendship with Samya after she murders Boutros. They stand silently outside her home, ready to protect her against crowds that might harm her before the police arrive at the scene to take her away.

Another subversive relationship is the friendship that develops as Samya nurtures and protects Ammal. Ammal is a mere 5 years old when she meets Samya. Samya begins sharing stories and dreaming of happiness and freedom. Ammal resists the patriarchy both through the forbidden friendship and through the sculpting of clay figurines. The women of clay represent possibilities of escape from oppressive traditions. Through her artistic forms, Ammal imagines other ways that women can be self-determining and valued for their accomplishments. At the end of the novel when Samya is taken to the police, Ammal, whose name means "hope," runs away, carrying with her the hope of all the women of the village. She is the one who will keep Samya's image alive.

While the women portrayed in Chedid's novel do not lead self-determining lives, they do find strength in each other to deal with their circumstances within the patriarchal structure. The characters, including the women, along with a blind man and an effeminate witch doctor, bond together in forbidden daily exchanges that act as subtle resistance to the patriarchy. Their friendships are based on personal choices to support and protect each other. According to Vitiello (1995), these relationships allow them to overcome their class, religion, age, and, in the case of the men's interactions with the women, gender differences.

Teacher Talk

Questioning Circles (Christenbury, 1994; Christenbury & Kelly, 1983) are useful in helping students combine textual and critical reading with personal connections. In Christenbury's (1994) words, "The questions circle provides a logical, yet flexible, format for questioning" (p. 206). The questioning circles consist of three overlapping areas of knowledge that expert readers bring to bear when reading: knowledge of the matter, personal reality, and external reality. For literature, these three circles represent the text being read (matter), the reader (personal reality), and the world and other literature (external reality). These areas of knowledge also overlap in the center, the area that Christenbury and Kelly (1983) consider the central dense point, where all the different ideas come together, to contain the "central, most important questions...whose answers provide the deepest consideration of the issue" (p. 14). Although these dense questions represent the highest order thinking, students don't necessarily arrive at the answers in a systematic progression. They need to inquire into and reflect upon these complex questions over a period of time. Responding to or posing questions about a text using these multiple perspectives helps to deepen students' understanding. The following questions for *From Sleep Unbound* (1976/1983) were developed by university student Kaitlin Macritchie, and the questions for *So Long a Letter* (1989) were developed by the teacher. Figure 4.2 situates questions for *So Long a Letter* within the Questioning Circle format.

Questions on Chedid's and Bâ's Novels to Use in Questioning Circles

	Chedid's *From Sleep Unbound* (1976/1983)	Bâ's *So Long a Letter* (1989)
Text (the matter)	Why does Samya marry Boutros? How does Boutros deprive her of personal freedom? Who is the blind man and what role does he play in the community? What are the consequences of Mia's death? How did Boutros contribute to Mia's death? Who is Om el Kher and why does she feel uneasy around Samya? What role does Ammal play in the novel? What do her clay statues represent? Why is Rachida so attached to her brother? Who are the villains in the novel, and what makes them so?	Why is Ramatoulaye writing a letter? How would you characterize the relationship between Ramatoulaye and Aissatou? Why did Ramatoulaye marry Modou Fall? How would you describe the first 25 years of the marriage? How did Modou betray her? How does she deal with the pain? Why did she not leave him? What is Modou's relationship to Binetou like? How did he court her? What happened to her when he died? What were the circumstances of Aissatou's marriage to Mawdo?

Text (the matter) (continued)	Why is divorce not a solution? Why does Boutros invite his sister to come live with them? What does "sleep" refer to in this novel? What is it that finally provokes Samya to shoot her husband? Is this murder in self-defense? What do you think will happen to Samya?	How and why did his mother seek revenge for his marriage? Why did Aissatou eventually leave him? What is she doing now? What benevolent act did Aissatou do for her friend, Ramatoulaye? What Islamic practices are portrayed in the novel?
Reader (personal reality)	How do you cope with loneliness or isolation? How do you react when confronted with people who are unhappy or seem strange? How do you protest or resist someone or something that you think is wrong? What do you think about divorce as a possible solution?	Have you ever been betrayed? How do you cope with emotional pain? What characteristics constitute a strong friendship? Relationship? What choices do you have when a relationship does not work? What does your religion say about marriage and divorce? What does your culture say about marriage and divorce?
World (external reality)	In your society, are girls treated differently than boys? What is the most effective means of protest or resistance? What happens to people who are isolated or unhappy? Why do marriages (arranged or not) succeed or fail? How might women resist the patriarchy? What is the punishment for premeditated murder? Is murder for self-defense justifiable?	What does the Quran say about marriage and divorce? What does the Quran say about polygamy? What does a democratic relationship look like? Does your culture have a double standard that privileges males? Under what circumstances does polygamy work well? What are the issues that make it fail? How are women regarded in the Arab world?
Dense Questions	What does it mean to be in a marriage? When being abused—mentally, physically or spiritually—is it acceptable to defend oneself by fighting back? What is the difference between murdering in self-defense and murdering in cold blood? Is it best to obey your parents and elders, even when the orders bring you extreme unhappiness? Why is divorce not an option? How do women find the strength to live day by day?	What constitutes a strong marriage? What are good reasons to marry? What are bad reasons to marry? How does one heal from a betrayal? Under what circumstances is divorce justified? How does religion factor into marriage and divorce? How do men use some aspect of the law to gratify their needs and desires?

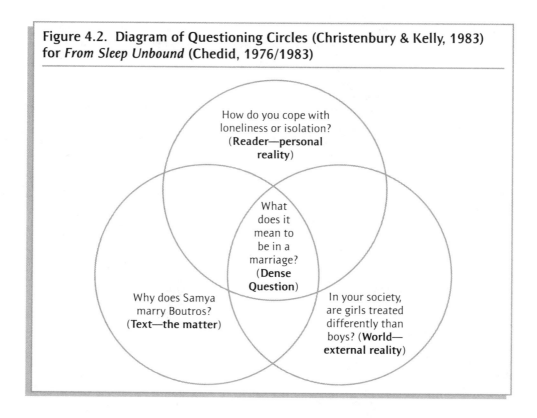

Figure 4.2. Diagram of Questioning Circles (Christenbury & Kelly, 1983) for *From Sleep Unbound* (Chedid, 1976/1983)

How do you cope with loneliness or isolation? (**Reader—personal reality**)

What does it mean to be in a marriage? (**Dense Question**)

Why does Samya marry Boutros? (**Text—the matter**)

In your society, are girls treated differently than boys? (**World—external reality**)

Cross-Curricular Activities

The Cross-Curricular Activities for this unit are designed to introduce students to Arab women's issues as the women struggle to lead self-determining lives. The Prediction Card Word Sort introduces students to the concepts of arranged marriages and polygamy. The film viewing activity portrays the oppression of women due to Taliban restrictions. The Sketchbook Journal activity helps students visualize the cultural conflict that characters experience in the novels.

Prediction Card Word Sort

The Prediction Card Word Sort (adapted from Vacca et al., 2006) allows students to tap into their background knowledge about the topic of a book, share that information with classmates, and make predictions about the content of a piece of literature. At the same time, students can manipulate their vocabulary and share ideas related to word study and comprehension of text.

Before students read a book, select 20–25 words from the book. It is preferable to have words from the front, middle, and ending of the book. Include words students are familiar with, words essential to comprehension of text, and a few unknown words. Print each set of words on index cards and distribute a set of cards to small groups of students. Invite students to assemble the cards into categories of their choosing. Do not tell them a specific number of categories or number of word cards that should be in each grouping. Encourage students to place words in categories according to their own knowledge of those words or their predictions of how those words might be used in forthcoming text. They must have a rationale for each category and also tell why they placed each word into their self-chosen categories.

Invite student groups to share their various categories and groupings and provide their rationale for the placement of word cards within specific groups. Then, invite students to read the text, looking for the words on the index cards. After reading, encourage students to rearrange cards or manipulate words into new categories or groupings based on the information gleaned from the text. Afterward, invite students to discuss reasons for any rearrangements and compare their placements with those of other groups. See Table 4.1 for Prediction Card Labels for *From Sleep Unbound* (1976/1983) and *So Long a Letter* (1989).

Table 4.1. Prediction Card Labels for *From Sleep Unbound* (Chedid, 1976/1983) and *So Long a Letter* (Bâ, 1989)

From Sleep Unbound (1976/1983)	*So Long a Letter* (1989)
Samya	Aissatou
Boutros	Divorce
Jealousy	Heart attack
Rachida	Modou
Bankruptcy	Muslim
Barren	Koran
Arranged marriage	Mourning
Cotton fields	Binetou
Egypt	Ramatoulaye
Boredom	Betrayal
Detachment	Bitterness
Enslaved	Twelve children
Imprisoned	Abandonment
Gun	Co-wife
Typhoid	Torment
Death	Senegal
Suffocated	Emancipation
Artifical flowers	School teacher
Ammal	Modou
Redemption	Mawdou
Liberation	Polygamy
Paralyzed	Friendship
Cripple	
Christian	
Islam	

Film Viewing: *Osama* (Barmak, 2003)

During the Taliban regime (1996–2001), women were not allowed to work or leave their homes without a male relative. This meant that a widow with no brothers or male cousins could not venture out in public even to feed her family. Such was the story in the film *Osama* (Barmak, 2003), filmed in Afghanistan and based on a true story. When a 12-year-old girl and her mother lose their jobs at the hospital due to the Taliban decree for women, they are forced to stay at home. With the mother's husband and son dead, they have no way to survive. Feeling she has no other choice, the mother dresses her daughter as a boy, calls her Osama, and sends her out to find work and barter for food. Osama has many terrifying adventures as she must keep the Taliban from discovering her identity.

If showing a film clip, choose the scene near the end when Osama is in school with boys. In this scene, she is bullied, chased, and eventually discovered to be female. The punishment is cruel, and scenes like this provide a striking and realistic portrayal of the severe treatment of women during hard times under a harsh regime. Use the film to open a discussion on oppression of women and their resilience. As with any film, the visual presentation provided through this medium uses a format that is accessible to students, and the vivid and often graphic representation in this film allows for deeper exploration of the women's issues described in the novels for this unit.

Sketchbook Journal: Portray Cultural Conflicts of Women and Society

Ask students to use sketchbooks to complete at least three visual and written responses that portray the cultural conflicts represented in the novel they read. The written responses and the corresponding visual response will be created on facing pages. In this way, students will be able to read the written response and view the visual response at the same time.

For the visual response, ask students to complete a full-color drawing, painting, or collage that represents an idea or scene from the story that portrays a cultural conflict. The visual may be abstract or representational. It may be completed in any medium, or it may be in mixed media. Tell students to be sure to use all or most of the space. Assessment will be based on completeness and investment of time and effort. Encourage them to be creative.

The written response, single-spaced and mounted on the left page, will include the following: (a) an explanation of the visual (one quarter of a page), (b) two key quotes (include page numbers) from the reading, (c) an explanation as to why the quotes are significant and how they relate to the overall narrative of the novel (one quarter of a page), and (d) a thoughtful personal response and reflection related to the major themes in the reading (one half page). See Figure 4.3

Figure 4.3. Sample Sketchbook Entry

Polygamy

This man's hand with four wedding rings symbolizes the number of co-wives a man might acquire during his lifetime in a polygamous lifestyle. A man in my country might be married four times in his life, but he would marry and divorce one woman at a time.

"Was it madness, weakness, irresistible love? What inner confusion led Modou Fall to marry Binetou?" (p. 11).

"And to think that I loved this man passionately, to think that I gave him thirty years of my life, to think that twelve times over I carried his child. The addition of a rival to my life was not enough for him. In loving someone else, he burned his past, both morally and materially. He dared to commit such an act of disavowal" (p. 12)

These quotes are significant to the narrative in that Ramatoulaye is struggling to understand Modou's betrayal of their relationship throughout her letter to Aissatou, her life-long friend. Aissatou made a decision to leave her husband when he was forced to take a co-wife at his mother's behest. She, too, considered this act to be a betrayal of her relationship to Mawdou.

I personally could never be married to more than one woman at a time. The responsibility and commitment to be fiscally responsible for the home and family of one woman is enough for me. To me, marriage is a life-long commitment. It's enough to handle the jealousy issues between two people, never mind more people. I can't imagine coming home to quarreling, conniving, bitter women, and I can't imagine it wouldn't be otherwise.

for a sample Sketchbook Entry on polygamy created by university students Jeff Schweickert (sketchbook text author) and Amy Spencer (sketchbook artist).

Making-A-Difference Project: Reflective Essay That Portrays a Woman's Cultural Conflict

Writing a reflective essay will give students an opportunity to reflect and comment on what they have read, discussed, written, and learned during this unit. The reading of these books will have raised many issues faced by Arab women living in an Islamic culture. This reflective essay will enable students to focus on a critical issue and explore it more deeply. The reflective essay should be a three- to five-page personal response to the cultural conflict characters experienced in the novels, the film *Osama* (2003), or a current cultural conflict discussed on the Arab Women Connect website found at www.arabwomenconnect.org. Students should exercise critical thinking about the topic and discuss what they have learned in this unit. The essays should be graded, but there should be no "right" or "wrong" answers. Instead, grading of the essay should analyze the following: How well organized is the essay? Does it flow smoothly and logically from one point to the next? Do students back up their points with specific examples? Do they identify their sources? Do they demonstrate an understanding of the culture they are talking about? How thoughtful is the essay? How creative is it? See Table 4.2 for suggested essay topics for reflective essays that por-

---

Table 4.2. Suggested Essay Topics for Reflective Essays That Portray a Woman's Cultural Conflict in the Arab World

Polygamy	Gender and intergenerational relations
Arranged marriages	Violence against women
Bride price/wealth	Resourcefulness for survival
Child brides	Islamic culture
Divorce	Islamic religion
Infertility	Mission schools
Sex slavery	Women's access to education
Ways women resist patriarchy	Solidarity in friendship
Levirate system	Subversive relationships
Class/caste relationships	What do women need to be happy?

Figure 4.4. Excerpt From a Reflective Essay on Polygamy in Bâ's *So Long a Letter* (1989)

Despite their education, both Ramatoulaye and Aissatou learn that even in modern Senegal it is not easy for a woman to determine her own destiny. Both of their marriages were ruined by polygamy. The rituals that demand obedience to the husbands' family members contrast with the autonomy they enjoyed in their classrooms. More importantly, they had to deal with the husbands' polygamy. Aissatou took control of her own life as she divorced her husband and fled to the United states with her children when her husband took a more socially suitable younger bride at the behest of his mother. She let go of her past Islamic customs and began to think for herself about what she believed to be right versus wrong, and respectful versus degrading. I believe this comes from being able to take the time to look outside your own social norms and judge for yourself about the customs, rituals, and beliefs of your society.

In contrast, Ramatoulaye made the decision to remain in her marriage. We felt her pain and sorrow when her now deceased husband took a younger second wife. She quietly sat back and accepted her position of being the first-wife and caring for their twelve children alone. While Ramatoulaye acknowledged the gradual changes of traditions in her life and the affects they had on her family, she seemed stuck between a rock and a hard place. However, even though she did not want to let go of her culture's customs and beliefs, she was able to accept changes in the lives of her children.

Both of these women accepted their roles with grace and beauty as expected by their cultures, but they also objected to the civic and religious laws that allowed polygamy, which victimized them. Both women were both more than capable of meeting their own economic needs. To them, unwanted co-wives undermined the independence they had achieved through their education and careers. While both women became successfully independent, neither of them accepted the position of submissive wife. I respect them both and feel true compassion for them as they struggle with cultural conflicts to find happiness.

tray a woman's cultural conflict and Figure 4.4 for an excerpt from a reflective essay on polygamy written by university student Ann Cugliari.

Conclusion

The Novel Guides in this chapter have examined the struggle of women to live self-determining lives in Islamic cultures in Senegal and Egypt during post-colonial times. Students have been given the opportunity to examine the desires and the obstacles for women to achieve meaningful relationships in Islamic cultures. Students should come to understand the ways women's needs and concerns have been addressed in Islamic cultures. They should reflect on patterns of behavior such as arranged marriages and polygamy that pose obstacles to cross-cultural understanding. Students should also illustrate how individual behaviors and decisions empower women and connect them with global systems. By writing a reflective essay, students can join the literacy community of Mariama Bâ in using words as weapons to imagine, redefine, and represent women's roles in a more dynamic and liberating view of life.

REFERENCES

Christenbury, L. (1994). *Making the journey: Being and becoming a teacher of English language arts.* Portsmouth, NH: Boynton Cook/Heinemann.

Christenbury, L., & Kelly, P.P. (1983). *Questioning: A path to critical thinking.* Urbana: IL: National Council of Teachers of English.

Cochran, J., & Craver, A.D. (2004). Andrée Chedid. In A. della Fazia Amoia & B.L. Knapp (Eds.), *Multicultural writers since 1945: An A-to-Z guide* (pp. 150-154). Westport, CT: Greenwood Press.

Harrell-Bond, B. (1980). Interview: Mariama Bâ, winner of the first Noma Award for publishing in Africa. *The African Book Publishing Record, 6,* 209–214.

International Reading Association & National Council of Teachers of English. (1996). *Standards for the English language arts.* Newark, DE; Urbana, IL: Authors.

Keene, E.O., & Zimmermann, S. (1997). *Mosaic of thought: Teaching comprehension in a reader's workshop.* Portsmouth, NH: Heinemann.

Napierkowski, M.R. (Ed.). (1998). So long a letter: Introduction. In *Literature of developing nations for students* (Vol. 1). Detroit, MI: Gale.

Retrieved April 12, 2006, from http://www.enotes.com/long-letter/14260

National Council for the Social Studies. (1994). *Expectations of excellence: Curriculum standards for social studies.* Silver Spring, MD: Author.

Nfah-Abbenyi, J.M. (1997). *Gender in African women's writing: Identity, sexuality, and difference.* Bloomington: Indiana University Press.

Sallum, A. (1991). Andriyah Sadid: Sarkhah fi Wajh Jidar. *al-Dawliyah, 47,* 30–31.

Sehulster, P. (2004). *So long a letter*: Finding self and independence in Africa. *The Western Journal of Black Studies, 28,* 365–371.

United Nations Development Fund for Women (UNIFEM). (2004). *Progress of Arab women.* Retrieved April 10, 2006, from http://www.arabwomenconnect.org/docs/PAW2004-ch1.pdf

Vacca, J.L., Vacca, R.T., Gove, M.K., Burkey, L.C., Lenhart, L.A., & McKeon, C.A. (2006). *Reading and learning to read* (6th ed.). Boston: Allyn & Bacon.

Vitiello, J. (1995). Friendship in the novels of Andrée Chedid. *Symposium, 49*(1), 65–80.

LITERATURE CITED

Bâ, M. (1989). *So long a letter*. Johannesburg, South Africa: Heinemann.

Bâ, M. (1995). *Scarlet song*. New York: Longman.

Chedid, A. (1983). *From sleep unbound* (S. Spencer, Trans.). Athens: Swallow Press/Ohio University Press. (Original work published 1976)

FILM CITED

Barmak, S. (Director). (2003). *Osama* [Motion picture]. United States: MGM Home Entertainment.

PART III

Novel Guides to Explore the Life and Culture of People in Central Regions of Africa

CHAPTER 5

Voices Resisting Colonial Rule in Nigeria

Jacqueline N. Glasgow

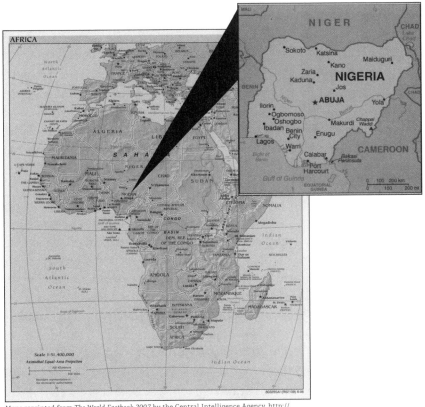

Maps reprinted from *The World Factbook 2007* by the Central Intelligence Agency, http://www.cia.gov/cia/publications/factbook.

Exploring African Life and Literature: Novel Guides to Promote Socially Responsive Learning edited by Jacqueline N. Glasgow and Linda J. Rice. © 2007 by the International Reading Association.

"People go to Africa and confirm what they already have in their heads and so they fail to see what is there in front of them. This is what people have come to expect. It's not viewed as a serious continent. It's a place of strange, bizarre and illogical things, where people don't do what common sense demands."

—Chinua Achebe (BrainyQuote.com, 2006)

Nigeria is a west African country that has suffered through and survived the exploitation of colonialism, gaining independence from Britain in 1960. The country was governed by military rule for 16 years, until a new constitution was adopted in 1999. While institutionalizing democracy, the president faces the task of reforming a petroleum-based economy, whose revenues have been squandered through corruption and mismanagement.

Given the toil in Nigerian history, it is the Nigerian artists who have given voice to the people living through these difficult transitions. The cry of protest has come from Nigerian authors such as Chinua Achebe, Flora Nwapa, Buchi Emecheta, and others who have written novels, plays, and poetry over the last 50 years. They are some of the first African authors to write their works in English to communicate their protest to the rest of the world.

The Cross-Curricular Activities for this unit are designed to introduce students to the Igbo traditions and culture of Nigeria. By creating the Igbo Visual Dictionary, students will learn cultural concepts, foods, and traditions. Because Igbo have a long tradition of storytelling, students will enjoy myths, folk tales, poetry, songs, proverbs, and dances by keeping an Oral Traditions Log. The Making-A-Difference Project invites students to role-play being photojournalists and create a documentary of the lives of Nigerian Igbo women. The overview on page 97 illustrates how the Novel Guides in this chapter and their corresponding activities align with standards for the English language arts (International Reading Association [IRA] & National Council of Teachers of English [NCTE], 1996) and curriculum standards for the social studies (National Council for the Social Studies [NCSS], 1994).

Social and Historical Context

Set in the late 1800s, Chinua Achebe's *Things Fall Apart* (1959/1994) shows how white Christian missionaries invaded Nigerian Igbo communities, bringing not only their religion but also their British government, which stripped the

Novels, Activities, and Curricular Standards
for English Language Arts and Social Studies

NOVELS
- *Things Fall Apart* (1959/1994) by Chinua Achebe
- *Efuru* (1966/1978) by Flora Nwapa
- *The Joys of Motherhood* (1979/2003) by Buchi Emecheta

CROSS-CURRICULAR ACTIVITIES
- Igbo Visual Dictionary
- Igbo Storytelling
- Oral Traditions Log
- African Proverb Project

MAKING-A-DIFFERENCE PROJECT
Photojournalism Documentary of Igbo Women

STANDARDS FOR THE ENGLISH LANGUAGE ARTS
#1 Students read texts to build an understanding of themselves and other cultures in the world.

#2 Students read a wide range of literature.

#5 Students employ a wide range of strategies as they write.

#6 Students apply knowledge of language structure, genre, and conventions to create, critique, and discuss texts.

#7 Students conduct research on issues and interests.

#8 Students use a variety of technological and information resources to communicate knowledge.

#11 Students participate as critical members of a variety of literacy communities.

#12 Students use spoken, written, and visual language to accomplish their own purposes.

Adapted from IRA and NCTE. (1996). *Standards for the English Language Arts*. Newark, DE: International Reading Association; Urbana, IL: National Council of Teachers of English.

CURRICULUM STANDARDS FOR THE SOCIAL STUDIES
#1a Culture: Learners analyze and explain ways in which Igbo cultures address human needs and concerns in a changing society.

#1f Culture: Learners interpret patterns of behavior such as polygamy and female circumcision that pose obstacles to cross-cultural understanding.

#3h People, Places, & Environments: Learners examine, interpret, and analyze cultural patterns and their interactions and cultural transmission of customs and ideas of the Igbo people.

#4f Individual Development & Identity: Learners analyze the role of perceptions, attitudes, values, and beliefs in the development of the personal identity of the protagonists.

Nigerians of their religions, customs, and, in the case of the protagonist Okonkwo, his humanity. With *Efuru* (1966/1978) Flora Nwapa became Africa's first internationally published black female novelist writing in the English language. She is best known for re-creating Igbo life and customs from a woman's viewpoint. She writes about women's issues that are often shrouded in misconceptions and stereotypes, such as female circumcision, bridewealth (payment made by the groom to the bride's family upon marriage), and polygyny (the practice of having more than one wife). Buchi Emecheta's works also deal with the portrayal of the African woman. The main character of her novel *The Joys of Motherhood* (1979/2003), shows what it means to be a woman and a mother in Nigerian urban society. Emecheta looks at how sexuality and the ability to bear children can sometimes be the only way to define femininity and womanhood. The aim of both Flora Nwapa and Buchi Emecheta is not just to present the female point of view but also to subvert patriarchal authority over women in literary history.

Things Fall Apart (1959/1994) by Chinua Achebe

About the Author

The internationally acclaimed West African novelist and essayist and son of a missionary school teacher, Chinua Achebe was born in Ogidi, Nigeria, November 16, 1930. Raised by Christian evangelists in a small village in Eastern Nigeria, Achebe has written eloquently about his childhood alienation from his family's ancestral traditions. He attended Government College in Umuahia, Nigeria, from 1944 to 1947 and University College in Ibadan, Nigeria, from 1948 to 1953, where he studied English, history, and theology and received his Bachelor of Arts. Before joining the Nigerian Broadcasting Company in Lagos in 1954, he traveled in Africa and in the United States and worked for a short time as a teacher. In the 1960s, he was the director of External Services in charge of the Voice of Nigeria, the Federal Radio Corporation of Nigeria. During the Nigerian Civil War (1967–1970), he was in the government service of the Republic of Biafra, a short-lived secessionist state in southeastern Nigeria. It existed from May 30, 1967 to January 15, 1970. He then taught at universities in the United States and Nigeria. Since retiring in 1981, Achebe has been a professor emeritus at the University of Massachusetts, Amherst, USA, and a faculty member at Bard College, New York, USA, a liberal arts school, where he has taught literature to undergraduates (Liukkonen, 2000).

Summary

The bulk of the novel *Things Fall Apart* takes place in Umuofia, a cluster of nine Igbo villages on the lower Niger. Umuofia is a powerful clan, skilled in war and with a large population possessing proud traditions and advanced social institutions. The protagonist of the novel, Okonkwo, has risen from a low reputation he inherited from his father to a high position that he earned. Through hard work, courage, and bravery, he has become a great man among his people. He has taken three wives, and his barn is full of yams, the staple crop. He rules his family with an iron fist.

One day, a neighboring clan commits an offense against Umuofia. To avoid war, the offending clan gives Umuofia a girl and a younger boy. The girl is to become the offended party's new wife. The boy, whose name is Ikemefuna, is to be sacrificed, but not immediately. He lives in Umuofia for three years, and during that time he lives under Okonkwo's roof, becoming like a part of Okonkwo's family. In particular, Nwoye, Okonkwo's oldest son, loves Ikemefuna like a brother. Eventually the Oracle calls for the boy's death, and a group of men take Ikemefuna away to kill him in the forest. Okonkwo, fearful of being perceived as softhearted and weak, participates in the boy's death, against the advice of the clan elders. Okonkwo's son, Nwoye, is spiritually broken by the event.

Later, during a funeral for one of the great men of the clan, Okonkwo's gun accidentally explodes, killing a boy. In accordance to Umuofia's law, Okonkwo and his family must be exiled for seven years. Okonkwo bears the exile bitterly. He flees with his family to Mbanto, his mother's homeland. There his mother's family receives them and treats them generously. His mother's family is headed by Uchendu, Okonkwo's uncle, a generous and wise old man. Okonkwo prospers during those seven years, but regrets every day he spends away from home.

When Okonkwo returns to Umuofia, he finds the clan sadly changed. During Okonkwo's exile, the white man has come to both Umuofia and Mbanto. Along with missionaries, the white man's government has also come to Umuofia. The clan is no longer free to judge their own; a District Commissioner, backed with armed power, judges according to British law. Okonkwo and other tribal leaders attempt to reclaim their hold on their native land, but the District Commissioner takes them prisoner, further humiliates them, and holds them for ransom. When released, embittered and grieving for the destruction of his people's independence, and fearing the humiliation of dying under white law, Okonkwo returns home and hangs himself.

Efuru (1966/1978) by Flora Nwapa

About the Author

Often called the mother of modern African literature, Flora Nwapa, a Nigerian writer, teacher, and administrator, was born in eastern Nigeria in the town of Oguta in 1931 when Oguta was still a British colony. Her parents were teachers who supported her educational pursuits. Nwapa attended University College in Ibadan, Nigeria, graduating with a Bachelor of Arts in English in 1957. She then went on to study at the University of Edinburgh in Scotland, where she gained a Diploma of Teaching in 1958. With *Efuru* (1966/1978), Nwapa became the first Nigerian woman to have a novel published in English and the first African woman to publish in London. She later became the first woman to open a publishing house. She established Tana Press Limited in 1977 for the purpose of publishing her own works.

In addition to authoring novels, short stories, and children's books, Flora Nwapa held a variety of posts in both the teaching and administrative arenas in Nigeria and the United States. From 1959 to 1962, Nwapa was an education officer in Calabar, Nigeria, and an English and geography teacher at Queen's School in Enugu, Nigeria. From 1962 to 1964, she was an assistant registrar at the University of Lagos in Nigeria. When the Nigerian civil war broke out in 1967, she left Lagos and returned to the eastern region. After the war, she served as Minister for Health and Social Welfare for the East Central State in Nigeria from 1970 to 1975, finding homes for 2,000 war orphans. She later worked for the Commissioner for Lands, Survey, and Urban Development in Nigeria. In 1982, the Nigerian government bestowed on her one of the highest honors. The Order of Niger, in her own town, Oguta, awarded her the highest chieftaincy title, *Ogbuefi*, which is usually reserved for men of achievement. Nwapa died in 1993 (Liukkonen, 2002).

Summary

Efuru, the title character in the book, is a beautiful young woman who comes from a distinguished family in eastern Nigeria in the early 20th century. The book opens with Efuru being courted by a man who is looked down upon in her village because of his poverty. Efuru marries this poor man, Adizua, even though he is unable to pay the bride price. This is a disgrace to Efuru's father and family, but she marries him anyway and manages to preserve a special relationship with her father and develop strong relationships with her in-laws.

Efuru is an excellent trader and always does well at market, while Adizua continues to do poorly at farming. Eventually, Efuru becomes pregnant and has a daughter, Ogonim. However, before the girl reaches her second birthday, she dies while having convulsions of some kind. Meanwhile, Adizua has disappeared and does not return for the funeral. However, the entire village takes part in Ogonim's funeral, and because Efuru is so well liked, she has a proper support system for the occasion.

Eventually, another young man, Eneberi (or Gilbert, his Christian name), comes to visit Efuru. Eneberi is handsome and respectable and wants to marry Efuru. Eneberi and some members of his family visit Efuru's father and pay the proper bride price. Efuru and Eneberi are very happy in their first year of marriage. Efuru's excellent trade skills make Eneberi and his family proud. Unfortunately, Efuru is unable to conceive a child, so she agrees to look for another wife for Eneberi, even though he, too, is disappearing for days at a time and fails to attend her father's funeral. Left childless and husbandless, Efuru turns her faith to the worship of the Water Goddess, Uhamiri, who blesses women with beauty and wealth but not with children.

The Joys of Motherhood (1979/2003)
by Buchi Emecheta

About the Author

Buchi Emecheta is one of Africa's most prolific writers, with 20 books—including novels, plays, poetry, essays, and children's books—to her credit. She is an Igbo woman who was born near Lagos, Nigeria, to working class parents. Her father, a railway worker, died when she was very young. In spite of her parents' resistance to education for girls, at the age of 10 she won a scholarship to the Methodist Girls' High School. However, by the time she was 17, she had left school, married, and had a child. She accompanied her husband to London, where he was a student and she a librarian. At age 22, she left him, graduated with a degree in sociology while supporting her five children, and began to write seriously. Buchi Emecheta has made an impressive transition—from a tribal childhood in rural Nigeria to urban life in north London. Writing from a woman's perspective, Emecheta created a portrait of Igbo culture that is very different from Chinua Achebe's. Emecheta was writing 20 years after Achebe, when traditional structures had begun to malfunction under the impact of urbanization. *The Joys of Motherhood* (1979/2003) is a portrait of colonial Nigeria and the fate of a woman trying to stay loyal to traditional Igbo culture in a rapidly changing Lagos (Attree, 2003).

Summary

In *The Joys of Motherhood*, after her first marriage failed, Nnu Ego's father finds her a new husband, one who will love her and take care of her. Nnu Ego travels four days to meet her new husband, Nnaife, in Lagos. He is a washer for a white family and lives in a small hut near the house. He is a heavy man and one who does not live as an Igbo but has converted to Christianity in order to gain his master's approval. Nnu Ego does not like this man; however, this is the man who breaks her bad luck and with whom her *chi* (personal god; see page 105 for more information on Igbo religion) has chosen to give her many children. While she loses her firstborn son, she soon has other children. In 1939, the white family Nnaife works for moves away, leaving him with no job. With no money, Nnu Ego's family moves into a one-room apartment. Nnaife finds another job mowing lawns for the railroad company, but when his brother dies, according to custom he must accept and provide for his brother's two wives and their other children. One of the wives, Adaku, moves in with Nnaife and his family, creating chaos for Nnu Ego, who finds it difficult to adjust to sharing her husband.

As the finances become worse, Nnaife is kidnapped from work, where he and other men are forced by the government to join the army to fight in World War II. Nnaife is only supposed to spend one year in the army but instead spends four years away at war. During this time, Nnu Ego has another baby boy, and the other wife, Adaku, leaves the family with her girls to make a life of her own.

After Nnaife returns, the boys convince their father to send them to a good school. Then, as the oldest son graduates, he goes to college in the United States and marries a white woman, and the second son plans to do the same. Going against tradition, the oldest son rarely sends word to his mother and never sends her the financial support that he is supposed to send as the eldest son. Just as Nnu Ego feared, she dies middle-aged and alone, without her family around her. She is, however, looked upon as a success and held in high regard in her village because she is measured by her children and their success.

Making Connections

To use this strategy effectively, teachers need to spend time modeling how to make meaningful connections. When teachers suspect that students lack the ability to make meaningful connections, classroom instruction is necessary to bridge the gap between students' reading experiences and author assumptions. Throughout instruction, students need to be encouraged to analyze the ways their connections are helping them understand the text. Making connections to the text should lead to better reading comprehension (Keene & Zimmermann, 1997). The following list of questions can be used for this unit, and Figure 5.1 shows a sample journal response to a text-to-world question for *Things Fall Apart* (1959/1994) created by preservice teacher Jessica Radzik.

Figure 5.1. Student Response Journal: Making Connections to *Things Fall Apart* (Achebe, 1959/1994)

Text-to-World: "Where are people oppressed by religion?"

Religion is a sensitive subject around the world. Americans are given the freedom to choose a religion instead of becoming victimized of a forced religion. We do not have the same belief systems, yet we are encouraged to follow the religion that best reflects our opinions and values. Around the world, individuals are not that privileged. It is simple: if you do not believe in the pre-selected religion, you will be killed. Other cultures will not allow for individuals to deviate from the country's religious norms. I am fortunate that I have never been oppressed because of my religion because it does happen on a daily basis.

Making Connections Questions for *Things Fall Apart* (1959/1994), *Efuru* (1966/1978), and *The Joys of Motherhood* (1979/2003)

	Achebe's *Things Fall Apart* (1959/1994)	Nwapa's *Efuru* (1966/1978)	Emecheta's *The Joys of Motherhood* (1979/2003)
Text-to-Self	What do I think are the characteristics of a man of high position?	What do I think happens when people of different classes marry?	What do I believe about motherhood?
	What do I believe about child (human) sacrifice?	What do I think of strong, independent women?	What do I believe is represented in successful children?
	What do I believe about suicide?	What do I know about bride price?	What do I think about polygamy?
	When do I think physical prowess is important in my society?	What do I believe about female circumcision?	What do I think is the best way to plan for a family?
	What do I believe about my religion?	What do I think is the stigma for barren women?	How do I think women's roles are changing?

Text-to-Text	What have I read about men in high positions? What have I read about human sacrifice? What have I read about suicide? What have I read about the importance of physical prowess? What have I read about different religions?	What have I read about marriages between partners of difference classes? What have I read in which women are strong and independent? What have I read about bride price? What have I read about female circumcision? What have I read about barren women?	What have I read about motherhood? What have I read about raising successful children? What have I read about polygamy? What have I read about planning for a family? What have I read about changing roles for women?
Text-to-World	How do the characteristics of men in high positions change from one culture to another? What cultures believe in and practice human sacrifice? What are the causes of suicide in various cultures? What cultures place physical prowess as the most important asset for men? Where are people oppressed by religion?	How do class differences make a difference in marriage partners? How are strong, independent women viewed? Why is bride price important in some cultures? What are the pros and cons of female circumcision? What is the stigma of the barren woman across cultures?	How do different cultures view motherhood? How do various cultures view children? What are the pros and cons of polygamy? How do various cultures plan for families? How are women's roles changing in various cultures?

Critical Exploration of Themes

The central issue in Achebe's *Things Fall Apart* (1959/1994) is the conflict between pre-colonial Igbo traditions and the destruction of Igbo cultural and religious values by the missionary Christians and the colonial powers. The novel depicts a vivid image of the Igbo society at the end of the 19th century. In a society where men wield a great deal of power, as seen in Achebe's *Things Fall Apart*, Nwapa creates female characters fiercely independent, educated, and spiritual. Even though the Igbo society venerated motherhood and placed high stakes on bearing children, Nwapa's characters are empowered by their self-reliance and economic independence. Efuru is a protagonist who lives in a society in which bridewealth, female circumcision, and polygyny are practiced, but one in which Efuru deals with such customs and finds her own place in a spiritual life. A further consideration of patriarchy and polygyny is explored in Emecheta's *The Joys of Motherhood* (1979/2003). This novel tells the story of Nnu Ego, a traditional Igbo woman, who moves away from her Igbo society to make a new life for herself in Lagos. She is caught between two cultures. While she sees that her old customs and beliefs are not conducive to a better life for her, she is unable to come to terms with Lago's different societal rules.

Traditional Igbo Religion and Culture

Before the influence of Europeans and Christian missions, the Igbo traditional religion was organized around four theological concepts: *Chukwu* (Supreme Being, creator of the universe), spirits (deities or oracles), ancestors, and *chi* (personal gods). In *Things Fall Apart* (Achebe, 1959/1994), the people of Umuofia look to the Oracle of the Hills and Caves for major decisions concerning their survival and livelihood. People come from near and far for comfort and counsel.

The Oracle, called Agbala, whose priestess is Chielo, rules with severe consequences to the clan if one defies the Oracle. The Oracle also serves as counselor. Unoka, Okonkwo's father, goes to consult the Oracle's priestess, Chika, to find out why he always has a miserable harvest. It is the Oracle who requires the sacrifice of the boy Ikemefuna, Okonkwo's beloved "adopted" son. Even though the execution runs counter to the clan's regard for Ikemefuna, they go forward with determination to comply with religious duty and faith in the Oracle. Not even the strong paternal feelings of Okonkwo can stand in the way of the Oracle's decree.

Personal gods, *chi*, are also an important part of the spiritual life of the Umuofia. The chi is the guardian spirit granted to every individual at the time of his or her birth and is responsible for the fortunes and misfortunes of each. Unoka is known in his community to have a bad chi who bade him evil fortune that follows him to his death. Even his death is an abomination to the earth goddess because he is afflicted with "swelling in the stomach and the limbs" (Achebe, 1959/1994, p. 18) and is left in the Evil Forest to die. Okonkwo is known in his community to have a good chi. He stores the wooden symbols of this person god and his ancestral spirits in the "medicine house" or shrine (p. 14). There he worships them and prays for his wives and family. Thus, when Okonkwo strives for prosperity, his chi agrees. But when he becomes aggressive, beating his wife and thus breaking the Week of the Peace honoring the earth goddess, his chi disagrees and precipitates his downfall.

Ogbuide, Mammy Water, Uhamiri: Goddess of the River

For all of her strengths (beauty, intelligence, generosity, prosperity), Efuru (Nwapa, 1966/1978) is plagued by infertility, infidelity, and abandonment by two undistinguished husbands. In *The Joys of Motherhood* (1979/2003), Nnu Ego also suffers the disgrace of barren women and abandonment by her husbands. Being unsuccessful with men and childless in a society that values large families is a challenge for both Efuru and Nnu Ego. They lived in a society in which wealth and children are considered identical; in fact, children are valued more than money. It is no wonder that Efuru finally abjures marriage and motherhood and opts for meaningful singlehood as priestess of the goddess of the river, Uhamiri. Uhamiri had been haunting her and calling to her in her dreams throughout much of her life (Drewal, 1988a, 1988b). Uharmiri and Mother of the Lake are names for the female deity, who promises beauty, wealth, and fertility to Efuru as well as Nnu Ego. While Efuru remains infertile, Nnu Ego goes on to another marriage and successfully bears several children, which redeems her from the curse of being barren. In the end, as priestess, Efuru realizes that this devotion brought her fulfillment, in spite of failing the Igbo cultural norms for motherhood. Flora Nwapa may also have been making the social comment that women like Efuru, who are beautiful, intelligent, industrious, and wealthy, may have difficulty finding a suitable partner in the Igbo society of these times.

Bridewealth or Bride Price

The practice of bridewealth is common in most parts of the world in one form or another but is perhaps most prevalent in Africa. Payment is made by the groom and his family to the prospective bride's family in order to begin marriage negotiations. Because this practice is most common in rural areas, bridewealth is often regarded as compensation for the loss of her work on the farm. The payment is commonly in the form of livestock or goods, but it could be paid in cowries (porcelain-like shells used for currency), and in modern days, cash.

While this practice may seem strange to Westerners, students should consider their own practice of the groom buying an expensive diamond ring for his bride. The larger the diamond, the greater the symbol is of wealth and, possibly, commitment. Or is it a sign of how much he loves and cherishes her?

Among the Igbo, the bride price is also made to acquire paternal rights to the children of the marriage and must be returned if the woman is barren or leaves the marriage before producing children. In the opening paragraph of *Efuru* (1966/1978), we find that the protagonist, Efuru, openly disregards the practice of bridewealth with the man she intends to marry. Adizua is a poor farmer and has no money to pay the bride price to Efuru's father. In contrast, Efuru is a remarkable woman who "was distinguished herself and came from a distinguished family" (p. 7). She takes control of the situation, defies traditional customs, and marries Adizua immediately, while deciding to deal with her father's wrath and shame and pay the bride price at a later time.

Efuru's Bath—Female Circumcision

Female circumcision, the partial or total cutting away of the external female genitalia, has been practiced for centuries in parts of Africa, generally as one element of a rite of passage preparing young girls for womanhood and marriage (see chapter 2 for more detailed background information on female circumcision). It is usually performed without anesthetic by lay practitioners using crude instruments. The Igbo culture regards it as an integral part of their cultural and ethnic identity, and some perceive it as a religious obligation. Interestingly enough, the same Efuru who resists the rituals of bridewealth willingly participates in her circumcision. Why does she not choose to resist this ritual as well?

While Western students find this practice blatantly sexist, neither do they examine the practice of infant male circumcision in the United States. While discussing these issues rarely changes students' minds, it does give them pause for thought. See chapter 2 for more discussion of body modifications and the human rights at stake.

Polygyny, Not Polygamy

While polygamy is the practice of having more than one spouse at a time, polygyny is specifically characterized by having more than one wife. In the traditional Igbo arrangement, men attempt to develop large households in order to gain prestige and influence within the community. Consequently, a household head receives the important designation of *ezi*, and the head of a big compound is considered a major leader in village affairs. As a man acquires his wives, he provides each with a personal residence in his compound and a surrounding area where their grown sons and daughters-in-law will eventually set up their own huts. The husband may have a separate hut, which is primarily used as a reception area, but he normally sleeps in one of his wives' rooms according to a scheduled rotation (Schwimmer, 2002).

Whereas Achebe and Nwapa portrayed polygyny in a positive, beneficial way that accomplished the goals of the agricultural Igbo society in the early 1900s, Emecheta gave a glimpse of the degeneration of this practice by mid-century in urban Lagos at the onset of World War II. For example, in *The Joys of Motherhood* (1979/2003) when Nnaife's brother dies, Nnaife inherits two more wives. One of those wives, Adaku and her 4-year-old daughter, come to live with him. From the beginning, Nnu Ego is jealous and fearful of Adaku's beauty and peace. Whereas, Nnu Ego remains the traditional, loyal senior wife, Adaku serves as a co-wife who resists the injustices of their situation. While both women find themselves in a similar circumstance, with an inept husband and excruciating poverty, Adaku is the one who takes the initiative to organize a hunger strike to force Nnaife to leave them more food money. Pregnant Adaku is beaten for it, but in her mind she has made an important statement. Nnu Ego, on the other hand, gives in and cooks Nnaife his favorite food to restore the peace. Nnu Ego does everything she can to make Adaku jealous of her sons, and their friends often have to settle the disputes. The more Adaku parades her wealth, the more jealous Nnu Ego becomes. However, Adaku reaches a breaking point after Nnaife beats her; humiliated and rejected, she leaves this home and strikes out on her own. Polygyny was breaking down in this urban setting, where a woman could make money by trading and become independent as Adaku does, rather than depending on the soil for provisions for her family, as does Nnu Ego.

Changing Roles of Women

The old world was represented by village life in Ibuza, in which women supported their families by farming. Family ties were strong and emotional, and financial support was eminent. On the other hand, the new world, represented by urban life in Lagos, meant quite a departure from traditional family life. Living in cramped conditions, there was no room for extended family support, no land to till, so women had to enter the outside world in order to survive. With the onset of World War II, during which the men were sent away to war, women were forced out of the home and into the trading business.

As in *The Joys of Motherhood* (1979/2003), Nnu Ego struggles to make ends meet—to pay rent, clothe the children, and send the boys to school. She does not leave home to pursue a business enterprise. Although she is resourceful and determined, she mostly does without and lives in poverty. However, we see this is not so for every woman. Unlike Nnu Ego, Adaku, Nnaife's second wife, focuses on her trade and does quite well. With her money, she plans to educate her girls and help them achieve an independent life. She is reluctant to leave their fate to Nnaife, who would undoubtedly marry them early for the best bride price to finance his sons' education. Clearly disgruntled by playing second wife and ridiculed for bearing Nnaife no sons, she leaves the marriage.

This is a courageous move on Adaku's part, given that among the Igbo a free woman like Adaku was considered an *Ajudu* (prostitute) whether or not she solicited men for sexual gratification or economic return. According to Ogunyemi (1996), "this was an unspeakable course of action in the 1940's and one that few women can take at present" in Nigeria (p. 249). In *The Joys of Motherhood* (1979/2003), Emecheta showed that choosing prostitution over marriage may be a desperate means of survival but holding on to an unsuccessful marriage is also harmful for women, as it was for her protagonist, Nnu Ego. Perhaps Emecheta was suggesting that Adaku's actions, while not respectable, were a way of resisting patriarchal power or, at least, creating a space outside of it.

Teacher Talk

Angelo Ciardiello (1998) offered alternative cognitive and metacognitive questioning strategies that are useful in increasing students' reading comprehension. Knowing how to ask good questions enhances comprehension by focusing on main ideas and making connections among ideas. Ciardiello suggested the following four types of questions:

- **Memory**. Memory level questions are those to which answers are found literally within a text.
- **Convergent Thinking**. Convergent thinking questions are those that require the responder to make inferences from the text, but they are close-ended, having a single correct response.
- **Divergent Thinking**. Divergent thinking questions are those that have indirect answers and encourage a number of possible answers that lead to critical thinking, creativity, and problem solving.
- **Evaluative Thinking**. Evaluative thinking questions are those that deal with matters of judgment, value, and choice.

The following questions use Ciardiello's (1998) cognitive and metacognitive questioning strategies to examine the novels of Achebe, Nwapa, and Emecheta.

Using Ciardiello's Questioning Strategies for the Novels of Achebe, Nwapa, and Emecheta

	Achebe's *Things Fall Apart* (1959/1994)	Nwapa's *Efuru* (1966/1978)	Emecheta's *The Joys of Motherhood* (1979/2003)
Memory	What are some of the social customs of the Igbo culture? What are Okonkwo's virtues? What was his tragic flaw? How does one earn titles?	What traditional Igbo practices does Efuru embrace? Which ones does she reject? What are Efuru's virtues? Frailties? What are the gender roles in this Igbo village?	Why does Emecheta tell the story of Ona before the story of Nnu Ego? What is Nnu Ego's family background? How do we know mothers are important in Ibo society?

Memory (continued)	What are the gender roles in the Igbo culture?	What are the relationships among family members?	What is the value of daughters in this culture?
	What is the role of superstition and religion in the Igbo culture?	Why does Efuru go to see the *dibia*?	What is the value of sons?
	Why was Ikemefuna sacrificed?	What are some of Efuru's good deeds?	Why are boys educated but not girls?
	Why did Nwoye convert to Christianity?		Why do you think Nnu Ego refuses to answer the prayers of her children after she dies?
	What is Okonkwo's concept of masculinity?		
Convergent Thinking	What is Okonkwo's relationship to Ezinma and Nwoye?	What were Efuru's motives for marrying Adizua? Eneberi?	What is the rural lifestyle?
	What role do women play Okonkwo's life?	How is Efuru different than other women who live in other polygamous villages depicted by Achebe and Emecheta?	What is the urban lifestyle?
	What Igbo customs have changed over time?		What are the expectations of each lifestyle in terms of marriage, children, housing, supporting parents, occupation?
	Why do some of the villagers welcome the British?	How does Efuru compare with Nnu Ego as a business woman?	What are Nnu Ego's experiences?
	What about their culture allowed the British to take over?	What part do spirits play in the lives of the Igbo in this village?	How are her two husbands, Amatokwu and Nnaife, alike and different?
	Compare Okonkwo to Obierika.	What form of communication do local and regional news take?	How does Nnaife prove his manhood?
	Compare marriage customs of the Igbo to those in your own country.	What is the impact of a woman having or not having children?	What is the purpose of having children in this culture?
	Compare the differences and attitudes between Mr. Brown and Mr. Smith.		How does the colonial influence create the dilemma Nnu Ego faces?
Divergent Thinking	What are the advantages and disadvantages of this polygamous social structure?	How do Efuru's husbands each represent colonial power?	What are the coping mechanisms Nnu Ego uses to make the transition from rural to urban living?
	Why does this novel end with the District Commissioner musing about the book he is writing on Africa?	Why does Efuru turn to Uhamiri, Goddess of the Lake?	What Igbo customs and beliefs does she move away from?
		What are the ways in which Ajanupu mothers Efuru?	What new ideas does she embrace or reject?
		What is the role of the proverb in this culture?	

Divergent Thinking (continued)	How do things fall apart in the destruction of the tribal ways and customs? What does the *egwugwu* tribunal say about the nature of justice in this culture? What are the ways in which the Igbo perceive animals that differ from your own, and how do these different beliefs shape behavior?	How is storytelling the same or different than what you know? What are the ways that Efuru finds satisfaction and contentment in her life? What does a successful marriage depend upon in Nwapa's novel?	In what ways does Nnu Ego become enslaved or imprisoned by the life in Lagos? What sacrifices did Nnu Ego make on her children's behalf? Why doesn't Nnu Ego realize she had the ability to change her circumstances? How is she to blame for her circumstances?
Evaluative Thinking	Was it moral of the Christian missionaries to impose their beliefs and education upon the Africans? Which system, colonial or Igbo, is more primitive? How does Achebe see the role of the writer/storyteller? In what ways does he use fiction as a means of expressing and commenting on history? To what extent is *Things Fall Apart* successful in communicating an alternative narrative to the dominant Western history of missionaries in Africa and other colonized societies?	Does it take a village to raise a child? Explain. What power do women have in this novel? In what ways does your religion compare to Efuru's goddess worship? What did you learn about the life of rural African women and African culture by reading this novel? Does Efuru appear as a feminist?	How successful is Nnu Ego while living in the city or urban area rather than a rural one? How successful is she according to colonial culture? How do the transitions in Nnu Ego's life and the interplay of cultures determine her fate? What kind of support do adult children owe their aging parents whether in poor health or not? From what should a mother's joy be derived? What would empower women like Nnu Ego? Was she ever fulfilled on her own?

Cross-Curricular Activities

The classroom assignments for these novels focus on helping students develop a deeper understanding of the Igbo culture. By researching the terms for the Igbo Visual Dictionary, students will learn important concepts and traditions of the Igbo people mentioned in the novels. By attending to the African oral tradition, students will extend their understanding of the novel and think critically about this important literary form. As photojournalists, students will create a visual documentary of the family, work, and play of the Igbo woman.

Igbo Visual Dictionary

To assist students in learning about the Igbo culture and language, assign each student one of the words in Table 5.1 to research. Make an Igbo Dictionary by asking each student to compose a page for the word they choose or are assigned from the list. These terms, cultural concepts, and traditions come from the text of either Achebe's *Things Fall Apart* (1959/1994) or Nwapa's *Efuru* (1966/1978). Students should define the term, describe its importance to the culture, and find and create a visual aid to support the meaning. When the assignment is submitted, ask students to present their dictionary page to the rest of the class. The Igbo Dictionary can be displayed around the room for easy reference or compiled in book format and copied for each student to have for their own review and artifact of the culture. Encourage students to add other terms they find in their reading. (See Figure 5.2 for an Igbo Visual Dictionary entry for *kola nuts* created by university student Jeffrey Fisher.)

Table 5.1. Igbo Terms, Cultural Concepts, and Traditions for Visual Dictionary

Afo day	Great River	Onwasato festival
Agbala	Harmattan	Osu
alligator pepper	Ibo	Ozo
Asa fish	Igbo engagement ceremony	palm wine
bride price	Igbo funeral ritual	plantain
bridewealth	Ilo	polygyny
Camwood	Iroko tree	rainy season
Chi	Jigida	Schnapps
Chielo	Kola-nuts	Singlet
Cowry shells	Machet	ten pounds
Crayfish	New Yam Festival	ten shillings
Dibia	Ngwo	titles
dowry	Nkwo day	Udu
Egwugwu ceremony	Obi	Uhamiri
Eke day	Ogbanje	Uli
Ekwe	Ogbono	Uziza
Evil Forest	Oguna fish	Week of Peace
female circumcision	Oguta Imo	wrappa
Fufu	okra	yams
Funeral ceremony	Oracle	yaws
Gari	Orie day	

Oral Traditions Log

Traditionally, the art forms of many African cultures are rooted in their oral tradition. African stories are created to be verbally and communally performed as an integral part of dance and music as they draw on the collective wisdom of oral peoples. In writing *Things Fall Apart* (1959/1994), Achebe incorporated Igbo oral traditions as a way of preserving the stories and introducing readers to the Igbo culture. Achebe also used African oral traditions as a way to subvert the colonialist language and culture. As students read the novel, ask them to create an Oral Traditions Log by recording as many oral forms as possible, identifying the type of element (e.g., myth, folk tale, poetry, proverb, song), and describing its relation to the novel's story and message. Students may also want to add rituals and festivals to this chart. (See Figure 5.3 for a sample of a completed Oral Traditions Log.)

After completing the Oral Traditions Log, ask students to write an essay on one of the following:

1. Discuss narrative customs in relation to the Igbo people's rituals, ceremonies, literature, and informal education.

Figure 5.3. Sample Oral Traditions Log

Page Numbers	Oral Form (Myths, Folk Tales, Proverbs, Poetry, Songs)	Title/Example	Summary, Interpretation, or Message	Connection to the Novel
96–98	Folk tale	"Tortoise and the Birds" (Found in chapter 11 of *Things Fall Apart*)	Explains why the tortoise shell is "not smooth." Greedy Tortoise manages to trick the birds out of the food at the feast. He is punished for his selfishness. He falls from the sky and breaks his shell into pieces. He is restored back to society after he is patched up.	Selfishness will be punished. It foreshadows Okonkwo's fate.

2. Discuss the importance of folk stories in traditional Igbo informal education.

3. Discuss the types of folk stories Nwoye liked in *Things Fall Apart* (Achebe, 1959/1994).

African Proverb Project

After students have completed the Oral Traditions Log, ask them to take a closer look at African proverbs. Proverbs are the distilled genius of oral cultures, perhaps even an encapsulation of the whole. They identify and dignify a culture, bringing life into wisdom and wisdom into life. Achebe (1959/1994) said, "Proverbs are the palm oil with which words are eaten" (p. 7). Unfortunately, their potential value for modern thought and life is often overlooked, so this project is designed to help students learn the wisdom of the African proverb. Ask students to choose a proverb from *Things Fall Apart* (Achebe, 1959/1994) or from the following website that features an African Proverb of the Month: www.afriprov.org. After students select a proverb that is meaningful to them, have them complete one of the projects that will inspire creative thinking and writing found in Table 5.2, which provides different options for the African Proverb Project. Ask students to choose one of the activities to do independently or with a partner.

> ### Table 5.2. African Proverb Project Options
>
> 1. Choose a proverb and write a story that leads to the lesson to be learned. Select images or African symbols that strengthen the story line. Put the story parts with pictures in a Microsoft PowerPoint slide presentation to share with the class.
> 2. Choose a proverb and translate it into a visual metaphor by creating a symbol, braiding and weaving (http://www.imonk.com/angela/lessons/weaving.html), dance, work of art, work of architecture, currency, a song, or a poem. Write a narrative explanation.
> 3. Write Readers Theatre script that leads to the lesson to be learned. Perform the Readers Theatre adding music (such as drumming), costumes, and props to complement the story.
> 4. Create a mask that illustrates or interprets the proverb.
> 5. Dance to your own interpretation of a proverb.
> 6. Make a quilt square that explains a proverb using symbols and combine it with others to create a wall hanging.
> 7. Write an essay discussing the cultural roles proverbs play in Igbo society.

Making-A-Difference Project: Photojournalists Document the Lives of Nigerian Igbo Women

For this Making-A-Difference Project, students will play the role of a photojournalist and be assigned to "travel" to Nigeria to produce a documentary of the lives of traditional Nigerian Igbo women. Because this traditional culture is changing rapidly, it will be up to them to capture and preserve the Igbo traditions. The documentary will be based on the life of Nnu Ego in Emecheta's *The Joys of Motherhood* (1979/2003) or Efuru in Nwapa's *Efuru* (1966/1978). References to women in Achebe's *Things Fall Apart* (1959/1994) are also appropriate. This documentary should highlight the many aspects of a woman's life in the Igbo society, such as marriage, bridewealth, gender roles, family ethics, polygyny, hospitality, feeding the family, education, religion, child rearing, trading, and effects of colonialism and urbanization.

Divide students into teams and "send" them to Nigeria to document the lives of Nigerian Igbo women. Each team of photojournalists will be responsible to do the following:

- Have each group member assume one of the following roles: Lead Historian (organizes the information found by group members), Literary Luminary (collects quotes from the novels to use as captions for the slides or parts of the narration), Media Specialist (acquires multimedia materials for the documentary), or Slide Show Engineer (constructs the Microsoft PowerPoint presentation).

- Each team researches the various aspects of the lives of traditional Igbo women as discussed above. (See Table 5.3 for a list of suggested library or media center resources and Table 5.4 for a list of suggested Internet resources.)
- Each team prepares the script to use for the narration in the documentary.
- The team collaboratively creates and edits a documentary using either Windows Movie Maker or Microsoft PowerPoint, including appropriate cultural images, captions, and script or voice-over narration for at least 15 slides.
- The team presents the documentary to the class.
- Each member of the team writes a self-reflection paper describing her or his participation in the project.

Conclusion

The authors in this unit gave voice to men and women who resisted colonial rule in Nigeria. Chinua Achebe wrote about the white Christian missionaries who invaded Igbo communities and succeeded in stripping the Igbo of their religions, customs, and traditions. Flora Nwapa and Buchi Emecheta gave voice to the cries of woman struggling against colonialism and patriarchy to lead self-determining lives in a time when women's roles were changing. In the Cross-Curricular Activities, students will explore the strengths and weaknesses of the Igbo culture, folklore, and literature. As photojournalists, students will produce a documentary of Nigerian women that highlights many aspects of a woman's life in the Igbo society—and in doing so, they will have participated in the struggle for human rights that challenges women worldwide.

Table 5.3. List of Suggested Library or Media Center Resources for Making-A-Difference Project

Amadiume, I. (1987). *Male daughters, female husbands: Gender and sex in an African society.* London: Zed Books.
Arinze, F. (1970). *Sacrifice in Ibo religion.* Ibadan, Nigeria: Ibadan University Press.
Bleeker, S. (1969). *The Ibo of Biafra.* Illustrated by Edith Singer. New York: Morrow.
Hodder, B.W. (1969). *Markets in West Africa: Studies of markets and trade among the Yoruba and Ibo.* Ibadan, Nigeria: Ibadan University Press.
Leith-Ross, S. (1965). *African women: A study of the Ibo of Nigeria.* New York: F.A. Praeger.
Lieber, J.W. (1971). *Ibo village communities.* Ibadan, Nigeria: Ibadan University Press.
Umeasiegbu, R.N. (1969). *The way we lived: Ibo customs and stories.* Ibadan, Nigeria: Ibadan University Press.

Table 5.4. List of Suggested Internet Resources for Making-A-Difference Project

AllAfrica.com
http://allafrica.com
This website is continually updated with stories from over 80 African news agencies. You can search the site by region, country, or subject matter. There is a section of the site dedicated to African books and a section of the site for women and gender issues. The site also includes a photo essay of many cultural experiences.

African Studies Center, University of Pennsylvania: Nigeria Page
www.sas.upenn.edu/African_Studies/Country_Specific/Nigeria.html
This website covers many topics related to Nigerian customs, language, religions, folk stories, photographic archive, and literature.

Other Nigerian, Igbo, and African Resources
www.geocities.com/Athens/Acropolis/3629/links.html
This website covers Nigerian, Igbo, and African Resources on language, people, art, widowhood, and other cultural information.

Colonial and Postcolonial Literary Dialogues: *The Joys of Motherhood*
www.wmich.edu/dialogues/texts/joysofmotherhood.html
This webpage focuses on Emecheta and *The Joys of Motherhood* and covers gender discrimination, videos, discussion questions, and links to more information.

Art and Life in Africa: Yoruba Information
www.uiowa.edu/%7Eafricart/toc/people/Yoruba.html
The Yoruba Information webpage provides information about Yoruba art, history, religions, economics, and so forth.

Art and Life in Africa: Igbo Information
www.uiowa.edu/%7Eafricart/toc/people/Igbo.html
The Igbo Information webpage includes information on Igbo art, history, economy, politics, and religion.

G.I. Jones Photographic Archive of Southeastern Nigerian Art and Culture
http://mccoy.lib.siu.edu/jmccall/jones/
This archive is a great website for viewing artifacts from Nigeria circa 1930.

Smithsonian Natural History: African Voices
www.mnh.si.edu/africanvoices
This website provides rich resources of African people, art, history, and culture.

Motherland Nigeria
www.motherlandnigeria.com
This website contains almost everything you would want to know about Nigeria, past and present. This is the best site out there about Nigeria. It also includes links to Igbo recipes, samples of Nigerian music, current affairs, travel information, games, stories, and much more.

REFERENCES

Amadiume, I. (1987). *Male daughters, female husbands: Gender and sex in an African society*. London: Zed Books.

Arinze, F.A. (1970). *Sacrifice in Ibo religion*. Ibadan, Nigeria: Ibadan University Press.

Attree, L. (2003, March 28). *Buchi Emecheta: Profiles*. Retrieved February 20, 2005, from http://people.africadatabase.org/en/profile/2442.html

Liukkonen, P. (2000). *Chinua Achebe (1930–)—In full Albert Chinualumogu Achebe*. Retrieved February 17, 2005, from http://www.kirjasto.sci.fi/achebe.htm

Liukkonen, P. (2002). *Flora Nwapa: 1931–1993*. Retrieved February. 17, 2005, from http://www.kirjasto.sci.fi/nwapa.htm

Bleeker, S. (1969). *The Ibo of Biafra*. New York: Morrow.

BrainyQuote.com. (2006). *Chinua Achebe quotes*. Retrieved June 7, 2006, from http://www.brainyquote.com/quotes/authors/c/chinua_achebe.html

Central Intelligence Agency (CIA). *The world factbook: History of Nigeria*. Retrieved February 20, 2006, from http://www.cia.gov/cia/publications/factbook/geos/ni.html

Ciardiello, A.V. (1998). Did you ask a good question today? Alternative cognitive and metacognitive strategies. *Journal of Adolescent & Adult Literacy, 42*, 210–219.

Drewal, H.J. (1988a). Mermaids, mirrors, and snake charmers: Igbo Mami Wata shrines. *African Arts, 21*(2), 38–45, 96.

Drewal, H.J. (1988b). Performing the other: Mami Wata worship in Africa. *The Drama Review, 32*, 160–185.

Hodder, B.W. (1969). *Markets in West Africa: Studies of markets and trade among the Yoruba and Ibo*. Ibadan, Nigeria: Ibadan University Press.

International Reading Association & National Council of Teachers of English. (1996). *Standards for the English language arts*. Newark, DE; Urbana, IL: Authors.

Keene, E.O., & Zimmermann, S. (1997). *Mosaic of thought: Teaching comprehension in a reader's workshop*. Portsmouth, NH: Heinemann.

Leith-Ross, S. (1965). *African women: A study of the Ibo of Nigeria*. New York: F.A. Praeger.

Lieber, J.W. (1971). *Ibo village communities*. Ibadan, Nigeria: Ibadan University Press.

National Council for the Social Studies. (1994). *Expectations of excellence: Curriculum standards for social studies*. Silver Spring, MD: Author.

Ogunyemi, O.C. (1996). *Africa wolman palava: The Nigerian novel by women*. Chicago: University of Chicago Press.

Schwimmer, B. (2002). *Igbo residence*. Retrieved February 17, 2005, from http://www.umanitoba.ca/faculties/arts/anthropology/tutor/case_studies/igbo/residence.html

Umeasiegbu, R.N. (1969). *The way we lived: Ibo customs and stories*. Ibadan, Nigeria: Ibadan University Press.

LITERATURE CITED

Achebe, C. (1994). *Things fall apart*. New York: Anchor Books. (Original work published 1959)

Emecheta, B. (2003). *The joys of motherhood*. New York: George Braziller. (Original work published 1979)

Nwapa, F. (1978). *Efuru*. Oxford: Heinemann. (Original work published 1966)

CHAPTER 6

Conflicts in Rituals and Politics in Kenya

Linda J. Rice

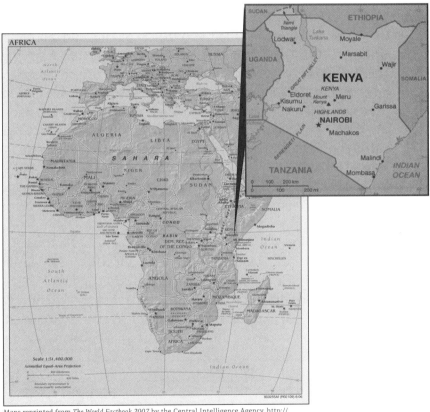

Maps reprinted from *The World Factbook 2007* by the Central Intelligence Agency, http://www.cia.gov/cia/publications/factbook.

Exploring African Life and Literature: Novel Guides to Promote Socially Responsive Learning edited by Jacqueline N. Glasgow and Linda J. Rice. © 2007 by the International Reading Association.

"Following the tribal custom, I had to pass through several stages of initiation along with my age-group.... Although men do not witness the physical operation on the girls, they are not ignorant of its details, as the young initiates of both sexes talk freely to each other about it afterwards."

—JOMO KENYATTA, FORMER PRIME MINISTER AND PRESIDENT OF KENYA (DELF, 1961, P. 42)

This chapter focuses on two novels, *The River Between* (1965) and *Weep Not, Child* (1964), by native Kenyan writer Ngugi wa Thiong'o. The novels explore the ritual of female circumcision as a rite of passage, the clash between indigenous tribal customs and teachings by Christian missionaries, and the conflicts of land and labor that resulted from British colonialism. Through its presentation of themes, connections, discussion questions, and Cross-Curricular Activities, this chapter is designed to deepen students' understanding of the two featured novels and Kenya's past and present. The Cross-Curricular Activities for this unit involve students in analyzing literary passages then turning them into poetry and then exploring the culture and rituals of Kenya through research and creative means of expression to include slide shows, artifacts, music selections, video clips, and authentic Kenyan foods. The Making-A-Difference Project engages students in investigative reporting to examine the World Free Press Institute, an agency geared to improve and support free press and the USAID Program which, besides giving money, also seeks volunteers to help in the areas of health care, natural resources management, and basic education. The overview on page 121 illustrates how the Novel Guides in this chapter and their corresponding activities align with standards for the English language arts (International Reading Association [IRA] and National Council of Teachers of English [NCTE], 1996) and curriculum standards for the social studies (National Council for the Social Studies [NCSS], 1994).

Social and Historical Context

The Kenyan ritual of female circumcision, sometimes known as female genital mutilation (FGM), provides the focal point for a clash in cultures in *The River Between* (wa Thiong'o, 1965) the first of two novels discussed in this chapter. Ngugi addresses the issue by presenting two perspectives, one viewing the ritual as a life-giving tradition of the tribe and another viewing the practice as a matter of miseducation that the Christian missionaries and converts are trying

Novels, Activities, and Curricular Standards for English Language Arts and Social Studies

NOVELS
- *The River Between* (1965) by Ngugi wa Thiong'o
- *Weep Not, Child* (1964) by Ngugi wa Thiong'o

CROSS-CURRICULAR ACTIVITIES
- Passage Analysis and Poetry
- Exploring the Culture and Rituals of Kenya

MAKING-A-DIFFERENCE PROJECT
Investigative Report of the World Free Press Institute and USAID Program

STANDARDS FOR THE ENGLISH LANGUAGE ARTS
#5 Students employ a wide range of strategies as they write and use different writing process elements appropriately to communicate for a variety of purposes.

#7 Students conduct research on issues and interests by generating ideas and questions, and by posing problems.

#8 Students use a variety of technological and informational resources to gather and synthesize information and to create and communicate knowledge.

Adapted from IRA and NCTE. (1996). *Standards for the English Language Arts*. Newark, DE: International Reading Association; Urbana, IL: National Council of Teachers of English.

CURRICULUM STANDARDS FOR THE SOCIAL STUDIES
#2c Time, Continuity, & Change: Learners identify and describe the influence of colonialism on farmers and the Mau Mau resistance.

#4c Individual Development & Identity: Learners describe ways family, religion, gender, education, and other cultural influences influence how people view various rituals of the Kikuyu.

#9b Global Connections: Learners explain conditions and motivations related to Kikuyu custom and Christianity that contribute to conflict, cooperation, and interdependence.

Adapted with the permission of the National Council for the Social Studies (NCSS). For the NCSS standards, see the publication *Expectations of Excellence: Curriculum Standards for Social Studies* (Washington, DC: National Council for the Social Studies, 1994). See also www.socialstudies.org.

to eradicate. *The River Between* effectively shows the delicate balance involved in bridging, or eliminating, traditional practices with new ways of thinking; it also highlights the consequences of forcing change rather than letting it take root in people's thinking and evolve through time and education. Ngugi's novel neither promotes nor demonizes the ritual of female circumcision; rather, it shows its devastating consequence—death—for one character, Muthoni, who chooses the rite even though her father, a Christian convert, condemns the practice. Chapter 2 of this book includes an extensive section exploring body modification that can be used to build a context to teach about female circumcision. Chapters 5 and 7 also explore the controversy surrounding FGM, so teachers who want to address the issue may want to pair Ngugi wa Thiong'o's *The River Between* with the novels featured in those chapters: Flora Nwapa's *Efuru* (1966/1978), Buchi Emecheta's *The Joys of Motherhood* (1979/2003), Cristina Kessler's *Our Secret, Siri Aang* (2004), and Rita Williams-Garcia's *No Laughter Here* (2004).

Because Kenyans connect the rite of circumcision with reducing promiscuity, girls who have not been circumcised are regarded as "impure" (p. 11) and considered to be "outcasts" (p. 8) (Jaldesa, Askew, Njue, & Wanjiru, 2005). According to the *Kenya Demographic and Health Survey, 1998* (Nyong'a, 1999), nearly 40% of Kenyan women have undergone some form of genital circumcision. In Kisii, a rural area southwest of Nairobi, that figure rises to 97% (Nyong'a, 1999). *National Geographic Today* reporter Kristin Whiting (2002) gives a detailed account of one such circumcision performed in Kisii in 2001. The story is available online and worth reading to see what actually happens during the ceremony and its aftermath, to include the reporter's standing outside "the hut where the cutting took place" and hearing the cries of pain that were "beyond disturbing" (¶ 18).

In December 2001, 36 years after the publication of *The River Between* (1965), President Daniel Arap Moi of Kenya outlawed female genital mutilation. The ban, however, is difficult to enforce, especially as "parents are circumcising their girls at a younger age to avoid government intervention and potential defiance from the girls themselves" (Whiting, 2002, ¶ 23). A number of grassroots African organizations and the Program for Appropriate Technology in Health (PATH), a nonprofit organization based in Seattle, Washington, USA, have collaborated with Kenyan mothers seeking to find new ways to help usher their daughters into womanhood. They have formed a new group called "Ntanira na Mugambo," which loosely translates as "circumcision through words" (Mohamud, Ringheim, Bloodworth, & Gryboski, 2002, p. 74). This group supports the ban on circumcision and replaces it with "a new approach to initiation into womanhood that includes song, education, celebration, and a week of seclusion" ("Alternative Rituals," 2005, ¶ 3). The group performed its first ceremony in 1996 and has been growing ever since.

The Mau Mau Revolt provides the backdrop of the second novel, *Weep Not, Child* (1964), discussed in this chapter. Still in its mode of colonial rule after World War I, Britain rewarded its war veterans by giving them plots of land in Kenya. The Mau Mau were a group of native Kenyans who banded together in

1947 with the intent of reclaiming the land that was taken from them (Anderson, 2005). Members of the Kikuyu tribe, believing they were destined to live in and rule their ancestral lands and determined to make this happen, formed the core of the resistance of the Mau Mau. Before the official beginning of the revolt, the Mau Mau made strikes against the "loyalists," Kenyans loyal to colonialism (Martin, 2006, p. 5). After a five-year period of covert planning and organizing, the Mau Mau launched their insurgency in 1952 (Martin, 2006). The Kenyan government declared a state of emergency in 1953 when the Mau Mau made strikes against both loyalists and colonists through strategies of guerilla warfare (Anderson, 2005). Eventually, the revolt of the Mau Mau was subdued by the combined forces of the British army and the imperial Kenyan army. Only 15,000 of the initial 120,000 Mau Mau were left to continue the cause (Martin, 2006). The Mau Mau did not disintegrate completely for another 10 years when, in 1961, Jomo Kenyatta was released from prison. Kenyatta, along with other prominent leaders, had been arrested for allegedly organizing the Mau Mau (Maxon, 1997). Two years after Kenyatta's release from prison with hard labor, he was elected Prime Minister of Kenya and supported reconciliation between native Kenyans and white settlers. Then, when Kenya became an independent republic in 1964, Kenyatta became president, serving from 1964 to 1978 (Maxon, 1997).

The River Between (1965) and *Weep Not, Child* (1964) by Ngugi wa Thiong'o

About the Author

Ngugi wa Thiong'o, named James Thiong'o Ngugi by his parents, was born in 1938 in Limuru, Kenya, as the fifth child of the third of his father's four wives (Liukkonen, 2000). His father had been a peasant farmer who was reduced to a squatter after the British Imperial Act of 1915 (Liukkonen, 2000). Raised in British-ruled Kenya, Ngugi saw firsthand the collisions of European and traditional African cultures. As a child, Ngugi attended a mission school and then moved to an independent Gikuyu school during the Mau Mau Revolt (Sicherman, 1990). Some of Ngugi's family members were involved in the revolt against colonial rule, and during that time his stepbrother was killed and his mother was tortured (Liukkonen, 2000). For safety and increased opportunity during the insurgency, Ngugi attended high school (1955–1959) and college (1959–1964) in Uganda ("Biography," 2006).

At the time Kenya gained its independence from Britain in 1963, Ngugi was still a devoted Christian and deeply committed to the notion that education changes things. Following his first publication in 1962, a play entitled *The Black Hermit*, Ngugi wa Thiong'o published his first two novels, *Weep Not, Child* (1964) and *The River Between* (1965). After earning his Bachelor of Arts in English and working as a journalist for Nairobi's *Daily Nation*, Ngugi went to Leeds, England, to pursue a degree in literature (Liukkonen, 2000). He then returned to Kenya from 1967 to 1969 to teach at the University College in Nairobi (Liukkonen, 2000). In the 1970s, Ngugi rejected Christianity, changed his original name (James) due to its colonial ties, and began to write in his native Gikuyu (Liukkonen, 2000). The political nature of his writings led to his arrest and imprisonment by the Kenyan government in 1977–1978 (Reboussin, 2003). Upon his release, he left the country in self-imposed exile, living in London for a while and then teaching at Yale University in New Haven, Connecticut, USA, for several years before becoming a professor at New York University in New York City, New York, USA, in 1993 (Reboussin, 2003).

Summary (*The River Between*)

The River Between (1965) tells the story of two communities, Kameno and Makuya, that are separated by the Honia River and represent different beliefs and cultures. Key characters who live in Kameno are Chege, who is said to have magical powers and is a highly respected elder, and his son, Waiyaki. Although Chege sees the presence of Christian missionaries as a threat to the native culture, he sends his son to Siriana for a white man's education so that he will be able to learn their ways and ultimately protect his tribe from them. In contrast to Chege, two other elders, Joshua and Kaboyni, abandon the tribe, convert to Christianity, and settle in Makuya. Joshua has two daughters, Muthoni and Nyambura, whom he forbids to partake in female circumcision as a rite of passage. Muthoni desperately wants to be circumcised, although she is a Christian. Nyambura is fearful for her sister because of her father's strictness, and Muthoni sneaks away to her aunt's house so that she can be part of the rites with the other girls and boys her age.

The night before the circumcision, the adolescents gather near the Honia River and dance. Chege's son, Waiyaki, sees Muthoni and asks why she chose to rebel against her father. She answers that she wants to become a woman of the tribe, and Waiyaki is completely taken by her. The two are circumcised the following day, and while Waiyaki heals, Muthoni becomes ill and dies a few days later. From this point, tensions mount as the groups living on each ridge community blame one another for Muthoni's death.

Loyalties are divided and jealousies surge as Nyambura feels guilt over her sister's death but finds herself in love with Waiyaki and thus torn between being a part of the tribe and honoring her father. Kabonyi leaves Joshua in preference of the ways of the tribe, and both Waiyaki and Kabonyi's son, Kamau, fall in love with Nyambura. Waiyaki desires for the two ridges to accept each other's views and stop their fighting. In the end, Wiayaki comes to the river where people from both ridges are waiting for him. The elders, the Kiama, bring out Nyambura who is deemed impure because she is uncircumcised and instruct Waiyaki to refuse her in order to keep the tribe pure. He embraces his love for her instead, and the novel ends with the Kiama agreeing on a trial to decide their fate, the implication being that they will be put to death.

Summary (*Weep Not, Child*)

Weep Not, Child (1964) tells the story of a young boy named Njorge and his family during the Mau Mau revolt. While Njorge himself focuses on earning a good education and is not involved in the insurgency against colonial rule, his family becomes irreversibly intertwined in the dispute. Njorge is in love with Mwihaki, the daughter of a rich African farmer, Jacobo. Mr. Howlands, a British settler, serves as the district officer and appoints Jacobo to the position of chief over the workers. Njorge's father, Ngotho, and Mwihaki's father, Jacobo, clash throughout the novel, as Jacobo finds opportunities for advancement under colonial rule and Ngotho stands up for his sons, who are part of the Mau Mau. One of Ngotho's sons kills Jacobo, and this breaks Njorge's heart as he knows it may push Mwihaki away from him forever. Another of Ngotho's sons kills Mr. Howlands. The book ends as Njorge, in despair of how peace will ever return, decides to hang himself from a tree one night. As he is adjusting the rope in the darkness, he hears a voice and realizes his mother is frantically searching for him. Torn between relief and defeat, Njorge comes down from the tree and walks home with his mother as a voice inside his head tells him he is a coward.

Making Connections

Because it is so important to connect literature with students' lives, the following questions are included to prompt students to take inventory on what they know in conjunction with the themes of Ngugi's writing and the culture and history of Kenya. Making these connections between text-to-self, text-to-text, and text-to-world (Keene & Zimmermann, 1997) causes students to bridge their personal existence with the world around them, a key aim of this book. Figure 6.1 shows a sample journal response to a text-to-self question for this Novel Guide created by university student Ann Cugliari.

Figure 6.1. Student Journal Response to a Making Connections Text-to-Self Question

Text-to-Self: "What do I think about colonialism?"
I do not agree whole-heartedly about colonialism, even though that is how the United States of America was created and established. The reason for this being that in order for colonization to occur is that the indigenous people are to be conquered and killed, or conquered and converted, or conquered and pushed out of their homes. This then creates the colony to be of the superior race, religion, and belief which is called to be cultural arrogance. The entire country of the United States of America is founded on stolen land (with stolen labor when you pull into the accounts of the chattel slavery) and cultural arrogance. The entire continent of Africa was divided up like a pie by seven European countries for colonization during the "Scramble for Africa" with no consideration for the indigenous people of the entire continent. So while I don't particularly agree with colonialism because of the injustices that go with it, I do realize that it was influential in creating this place I live, the republic of the United States where I have the freedom to believe what I want and voice my opinions.

Making Connections Questions for *The River Between* (1965) and *Weep Not, Child* (1964)

	Ngugi wa Thiong'o's *Weep Not, Child* (1964)	Ngugi wa Thiong'o's *The River Between* (1965)
Text-to-Self	What do I believe about the connection between education and a better life? Do I think that cultures can blend peacefully, even if they have different beliefs? If so, how would this work? If not, what are the barriers? What do I know about the Mau Mau war? What do I think about colonialism?	Where have I seen clashes between people with different belief systems or faiths? When have I clashed with my family over our views on some issue or tradition? What do I know about the history and culture of Kenya?
Text-to-Text	What books have I read or films have I viewed that have to do with white minorities ruling over black majorities? What books have I read or films have I viewed that showed someone ruling unjustly over someone of the same race?	What books have I read or films have I viewed that have to do with Kenya, its people, conflicts, and culture? In literature and film, where have I seen clashes between people with different belief systems or faiths?
Text-to-World	Where are Peace Corps volunteers, the United Nations, missionaries, or other social servants working to better peoples' lives in the world through education today, and how are they doing this? What remnants of colonialism exist in modern Kenya?	Where and to what degree is "female circumcision," or "female genital mutilation," practiced in the world today, and is any progress being made to stop this? What is it like to be or work with a missionary today, and what are examples of missionaries peacefully coexisting with native people?

Critical Exploration of Themes

This section includes a discussion of four themes that are applicable to both *The River Between* (1965) and *Weep Not, Child* (1964). The themes examine the power of religion and education to transform individuals and divide communities; the interplay of freedom, choice, happiness, and fulfillment; the connection between wisdom and open-mindedness, and the responsibility of those in power to govern justly. Each theme is supported by specific examples from Ngugi's novels.

Religious Conversion and Education Can Be Both Transformative and Divisive

While *The River Between* (1965) and *Weep Not, Child* (1964) demonstrate the transformative power of religious conversion and education, both also show how these can cause great divisions among tribes and even within families. In *The River Between* the river serves as a symbolic divider between the people living on the two ridges, one ridge representing the traditions of the tribe, the other ridge representing the influence of "the white man" and Christianity. Chege sends his son to the white man's school, Siriana, to learn all that the white man has to teach, but his purposes are to use this knowledge to conquer the white man and preserve the traditions of the tribe. Once friends of Chege, Joshua, and Kabonyi convert to Christianity, they support its traditions over those of the tribe, including the elimination of female circumcision as a rite of passage.

While Joshua's religious conversion is connected with a better education and free choice of marriage partners for his daughters, Muthoni and Nyambura, Joshua rules his home with a heavy, often violent hand that is inconsistent with a Christ-like love or servanthood. While Nyambura highly reveres her father and his stand against female circumcision, Muthoni rebels against him and chooses to escape to the other side of the river and take part in the ritual, believing that it would make her a real woman and true member of the tribe. Upon finding out that Muthoni has escaped to be circumcised, Joshua disowns his daughter. Several days after the ritual, however, Muthoni dies, causing an even greater division between the two ridges. Ngugi wa Thiong'o effectively complicates and connects the issue of female circumcision, tribal practices, and education, as evidenced in the following quote from *The River Between* (1965):

> Circumcision of women was not important as a physical operation. It was what it did inside a person. It could not be stopped overnight. Patience, and above all, education, were needed. If the white man's religion made you abandon a custom and then did not give you something else of equal value, you became lost. An attempt at resolution of the conflict would only kill you, as it did Muthoni. (p. 142)

Weep Not, Child (1964) also shows the duality of education's ability to transform and divide. In this story, young Njorge yearns for an education more than anything. No one in Njorge's family has ever attended school, and when he is presented with the opportunity from his mother, Nyokabi, he feels very honored. Njorge understands that he is to attend school in order to learn and educate the rest of his family. While attending school, Njorge learns to read and write and interacts with Mwihaki, the daughter of the town's most wealthy black farmer. Njorge enjoys both his education and the opportunity to interact with a higher class of people, something that becomes a conflict because Njorge's father and Mwihaki's father are at odds over a workers strike. Although Njorge keeps his focus on his schooling, his brothers, Boro and Kamau, become deeply involved in the jungle movement, the Mau Mau revolt. Njorge sees education as the key he needs to help him save his country, but his attendance at Siriana Secondary School also removes him from the death and destruction that await him in his war-torn village. Njorge is beaten in an interrogation about his family, and he later learns that his father admitted to killing Mwihaki's father. This news severs the bond between Mwihaki and Njorge, as Mwihaki is no longer interested in making a life with Njorge and decides it is her duty to stand up for the people of Kenya and not lose hope while Njorge has lost all hope and wishes to give up his fight and leave the country.

Freedom and Choice Do Not Guarantee Happiness and Fulfillment

While freedom and choice are certainly integral to personal growth and a democratic society, they are not guarantees of happiness or fulfillment, as evidenced in Ngugi wa Thiong'o's *The River Between* (1965) and *Weep Not, Child* (1964). Daughters of a Christian convert who denounces the practice of female circumcision, Muthoni and Nyambura could both see themselves as free of that oppressive, life-endangering rite into womanhood. However, while Nyambura respects her father's views, Muthoni chooses to go behind his back, escape to the other side of the river, and be part of the ritual with the other girls and boys in Kameno. Her sister, Nyambura, knowing how her father will disapprove of Muthoni's actions, chooses to keep Nyambura's whereabouts a secret. Reflective of the severe health risks that accompany female circumcision, Muthoni experiences complications and infection and writhes in pain and delirium for several days before finally dying. Muthoni's intent was to become a real woman and true part of the tribe while still being a Christian; however, her choices collide with unsanitary conditions and result in tragedy. Nyambura, too, suffers the consequences of guilt for not intervening and telling her father the truth of Muthoni's whereabouts in time for him to remove his daughter from the ritual.

Waiyaki is circumcised the same day Muthoni is, though his comparatively simple circumcision heals without complications (chapter 2 of this book provides background information on Western and African practices of circumcision, which teachers may want to share with their students before studying this aspect of Ngugi's novel). The night before the ritual, Waiyaki and Muthoni dance together and clearly develop a passion for one another. Waiyaki grieves Muthoni's death and forges a bond with her sister, Nyambura. Waiyaki professes his love for Nyambura and proposes, but she refuses, even though she has feelings for him, to honor her father. The controlling father that he is, Joshua, upon hearing rumors of Waiyaki and his obedient daughter, forbids Nyambura from seeing Waiyaki again, threatening to disown her if she does. Waiyaki tries to protect Joshua's family by warning Joshua of rumors that a group of young men is headed over the slopes to attack them, but Joshua, caught up with different rumors, stubbornness, and his own authority, fails to see the good in Waiyaki's actions. Eventually Nyambura chooses to flee with Waiyaki, understanding this could be of great cost. The deaths of Waiyaki and Nyambura are implied in the end of the book, which Ngugi used to showed that freedom and choice are not guarantees of happiness and fulfillment, though he also conveyed the importance of striving for unity and standing up for love.

In *Weep Not, Child* (1964), Njorge has freedoms that others do not by nature of being chosen by his family to attend school. Njorge is passionate about the opportunity to become educated and sees it as a way to better the lives of his family and even the nation. School also provides him with a forum to interact with Mwihaki, the daughter of the town's most wealthy farmer, Jacobo, who is eager to please "the white man" because doing so enables him to grow in wealth, power, and status. Despite the freedom and safety that school provides Njorge, his life ultimately turns toward hopelessness and a sense of despair so deep that the book closes with his thwarted suicide. Though Njorge himself is free and makes choices not to be a part of the violence surrounding the Mau Mau Revolt, the actions of others, particularly his family members, derail his pursuit of happiness and fulfillment.

Wisdom Is Less About Age Than Understanding

In both *The River Between* (1965) and *Weep Not, Child* (1964), Ngugi wa Thiong'o invests young characters with wisdom while at the same time some of the older members of each related society appear foolish and preoccupied with selfish ambitions and power. In *The River Between*, it is Waiyaki who decides that the people on both ridges need to accept each other's ways and work toward a peaceful existence. Even though he is regarded by the people of Kameno as having a more powerful presence than his father, Chege, Waiyaki does not seek power as much as he seeks to understand the Christians and their reasons for standing against female circumcision. Waiyaki pursues an education and is respected as "the Teacher" among the most prominent in his village. While Waiyaki seeks to please everyone in his tribe, he shows compassion for Nyambura when her sister dies and does not judge Nyambura for not being circumcised. All of Waiyaki's energies after the death of Muthoni are directed toward unifying the people, even though in the end the efforts appear fruitless because others insist on seeing themselves as right instead of accepting one another's ways and growing together through education.

In *Weep Not, Child* (1964), education and the young mind also unite to show wisdom. While Jacobo has his mind set on obtaining more property and authority over the peasant farmers, and Mr. Howlands easily agrees to allow Jacobo to imprison Ngotho—an action more about personal resentment than actual wrong—young Njorge pursues education as a way to gain the kind of understanding that he hopes will build a better Kenya. Likewise, Njorge's schoolmate and love, Mwihaki, also sees education as the foundation for a more free and egalitarian society. Unlike her father, Mwihaki does not use her family's wealth as license to look down on or exert control over other people. Even when her father is murdered, she stays the course of understanding and focuses on her duty to continue her education and serve her country. In an unfortunate contrast, Njorge lets despair overtake him, thus losing the maturity of wisdom and a vision for a better tomorrow.

Those Invested With Power and Authority Have a Responsibility to Govern Justly or Face Fierce Consequences

Joshua in *The River Between* (1965) and Jacobo and Mr. Howlands in *Weep Not, Child* (1964) all demonstrate rigidity; harsh, judgmental attitudes or indiscriminate decision making; and abuses of power that ultimately result in their personal or familial demise. Joshua's abusive and controlling tendencies with his wife and daughter create a sense of fear and intimidation rather than inspiring the kind of honor that stems naturally from love. Rather than Joshua demonstrating an open mind that is willing to listen and converse with his daughter Muthoni, his dogmatic ways cause Muthoni to seek the rite of circumcision in secret. A more approachable father might have been able to reason his daughter into making a better decision, but Joshua's inflexible manner closes conversation and makes Muthoni's desire all the more fervent, even though it proves to be fatal. Despite the fact that Joshua disowns Muthoni upon learning that she has escaped to participate in the rite of circumcision, which she believes makes her a real woman and true part of the tribe, he must feel some sense of grief over the loss of his daughter. If he had been more moderate and approachable, the tragedy might not have occurred.

The trajectory of events that unfold after Muthoni's death draw in additional characters who choose to abuse their power and influence rather than strive toward unity. In the end, this leads to the implied death sentence of Waiyaki and Nyambura. Even as they are convicted of their wrongs, pride and stubbornness keep the people from changing their course of action for the good. This is reinforced with Ngugi wa Thiong'o's (1965) last line: "For [the elders and villagers] did not want to look at the Teacher [Waiyaki] and they did not want to read their guilt in one another's faces" (p. 152).

In *Weep Not, Child* (1964), Jacobo is the wealthiest farmer among the people. Instead of using his influence to provide a greater realm of opportunities for his fellow citizens, he becomes consumed with protecting his position and not allowing others to attain his status. He stands against the striking workers and harbors a personal resentment toward Ngotho, whom he convinces the district officer, Mr. Howlands, to arrest. Mr. Howlands removes Ngotho, whom he once very much admired as one of his best workers, for his alleged involvement in the workers strike. Mr. Howlands then appoints Jacobo to the position of chief to oversee his affairs. Jacobo is opportunistic and wields his power openly, though in fact he is more of a puppet enacting the violent will of the European colonists as represented in the character of Mr. Howlands. While Mr. Howlands sends his wife and son to England for safety, Njorge, son of Ngotho, cannot afford such a luxury. As it is rumored that Ngotho's brother, Boro, is involved with the jungle movement, Njorge is taken by police, questioned, and beaten to near-death. His other family members are tortured and interrogated in a similar fashion. In his own quest for justice, Boro kills Jacobo and Mr. Howlands.

Teacher Talk

As can be derived from the exploration of themes present in Ngugi wa Thiong'o's novels, there are many points of discussion that emerge from *The River Between* (1965) and *Weep Not, Child* (1964). The following discussion questions use major literary theories to inspire different approaches to the novels. The questions are broad in nature to provide maximal room for analysis and interpretation. The theories may be viewed as critical lenses through which readers see the texts; different lenses bring about different focal points and subsequently influence interpretation, understanding, and, in essence, what readers read into, experience, or carry away from the text. Steven Lynn's *Texts and Contexts: Writing About Literature With Critical Theory* (2005) offers a primer on the major critical theories for which specific questions related to Ngugi's novels have been drawn.

	wa Thiong'o's *Weep Not, Child* (1964) and *The River Between* (1965)
Formalism/New Criticism	What literary devices and techniques work together to provide unity in *Weep Not, Child* and *The River Between*? What are the major themes and how do they emerge in Ngugi's writing?
Feminism/Gender Criticism	How are women represented in Ngugi's novels? How are gender and power related in Ngugi's novels? In what issues in *Weep Not, Child* and *The River Between* does gender play a particularly vital role?
Marxist/Economic Criticism	What political and economic structures are at work in *Weep Not, Child* and *The River Between*? Who, why, and how are the various characters and groups empowered and disenfranchised in Ngugi's novels?
Reader Response Criticism	What is your personal response to Ngugi's writing? What life experiences, beliefs, and preconceived notions entered into your reading and interpretation of *Weep Not, Child* and *The River Between*?
Deconstructive Criticism	In what places does the text seem to fall apart or work against itself (i.e., do the opposite of what the words seem to say)? How is language used in contradictory ways in *Weep Not, Child* and *The River Between*?
Historical/Biographical Criticism	How might Ngugi's life have influenced his writing? What was going on in Kenya and the world when Ngugi wrote *Weep Not, Child* and *The River Between*?
Freudian/Psychological Criticism	What motivates Waiyaki's actions in *The River Between*? What motivates Njorge's actions in *Weep Not, Child*? Where do you see evidence of repression, projection, displacement, denial, or other coping mechanisms in Ngugi's writing?

Cross-Curricular Activities

The Cross-Curricular Activities for this unit engage students in creative writing, literary analysis, and research. In particular, students will identify the most important passage from an assigned chapter of *The River Between* (1965) or *Weep Not, Child* (1964) and turn an aspect of the passage into a poem. Students will also conduct research exploring the culture and rituals of Kenya as a way to broaden their contextual understanding of that nation's uniqueness and the backdrop of Ngugi's writing.

Passage Analysis and Poetry

For this first activity, the teacher will assign each student (or each pair of students, if the teacher would like the activity to involve discussion and collaboration) a chapter from either book, *The River Between* (1965) or *Weep Not, Child* (1964), and ask students to identify the most important passage in that chapter. Students will have to make a case for why the passage they chose is the most significant, which requires discernment and critical thinking. Students should limit the passage to 100 words, use a word-processing program for presenting the passage, and attach the passage to the related essay. When students are allowed time to share their choices of the "most important passage" in class, this activity serves as an effective way to review the text while also hearing Ngugi's writing style.

After students have selected and analyzed their choice of a most important passage, they are to write a poem as a way to think more deeply about and creatively interpret the passage. The poem should be extensive enough to show the development of the novel up to the point where the passage occurs, thus providing some history and context for the passage. Figure 6.2 features an excerpt from an essay written by university students Leah Francescani and Heather Warnecke about a passage from the last chapter of *Weep Not, Child* in which the students identified with the hopelessness and sadness of Njorge as he pondered suicide by hanging. While Leah and Heather's reflections on the

---

Figure 6.2. Student Passage Analysis for *Weep Not, Child* (wa Thiong'o, 1964)

The silver lining of this passage is simply that Njorge did not kill himself. While this seems like a small thing, it is really quite significant. The book may end, but Njorge's story does not. Once someone hits rock bottom, the only way to go is up....

After reading this passage and finishing the book, I had many questions for Ngugi. One, why does Njorge consider himself a coward? Is it because he did not go through with the suicide or that he was considering it at all? Is he a coward for letting down his family and country or for letting down himself? "The voice" asks him why he "didn't do it," but I wonder, what is "it"? Is "it" the suicide? Or is "it" saving his people? In order to be at peace with the ending, I decided that "it" could be either of these things or even both.

Another question that plagued me was, did he not go through with the suicide because he did not really want to die or because his mother came and basically stopped him? ...the fact that he felt so guilty when his mothers came for him shows that he was not mentally prepared to end his life....

To me, the most important part of this passage is the very last line. After paragraphs of depression and despair, the last line makes me think that Njorge is going to begin climbing back up to his usual, positive self.... I was uplifted with hope when, at the end, Njorge ran ahead to hold the door of his mothers, because I felt like the country of Kenya had its savior back.

final chapter of *Weep Not, Child* show a great deal of reader optimism, they also reveal a sincere connection with the text as well as serious consideration of the possibilities that lie beyond it. This is further reflected in the students' poem that appears in Figure 6.3.

Exploring the Culture and Rituals of Kenya

As a way to involve students in research and help increase their knowledge of the culture and rituals of Kenya, the teacher should have students investigate assigned topics and report their findings to the class. Table 6.1 offers a list of possible topics for students' exploration. Students' investigation may be reported in the form of one-minute vocabulary reports during which they offer a simple definition and explanation of their assigned term, supported by a picture or symbol and posted on the class bulletin board, or more extensively in research papers of 3–5 pages. Results could also be shared in a Microsoft PowerPoint presenta-

---

Figure 6.3. Students' Poem to Accompany Passage Analysis of *Weep Not, Child* (wa Thiong'o, 1964)

The Path of the Young One

"Education is for you" is what his mother said,
My family depends on me, he knew in his head.
Meeting Mwihaki and chatting each day,
Becoming friends, enduring come what may.
A strike of the workers and war in the lands,
Fathers against fathers; friendship disbands.
Tomorrow will be better is what the young boy said.
Past hate, evil feelings, and unfounded fear must be shed.
Brother in the forest fighting and killing for a cause,
Do you know where he is, his oath, he broke the laws.
The questions and beatings to pay for the dead,
A father stood firm till his last breath.
What to do now? Is he still the savior? Can he help them at all?
Mwihaki and he should escape and leave, avoid his call.
Tomorrow will be better the young girl now said.
I will not leave with you. Let's have hope instead.
Exasperated the young boy now sulks,
This was not the same, not like the other talks.
Going home disheartened he knows what he must do,
In the darkness he goes to the tree to complete what must ensue.
Njorge hears his mother call.
He's a coward. Again his plans fall.
Will tomorrow be better? Should hope remain?
Will the young boy his calling regain?

Table 6.1. Research Topics for Exploring Kenyan Culture and Ritual

Bridewealth or bride price	Language (Swahili in particular)
Music and dance	Health epidemics (AIDS in particular)
Celebrations	Food (including recipes)
Dress (Kanga in particular)	Tribes (Kikuyu in particular)
Face paint	Rites of passage
Dreadlocks (symbol of transition)	• Birth
Oaths (Mau Mau in particular)	• Naming
Medicine men	• Circumcision
Diviners	• Marriage
Rainmakers	• Elderhood
Priests	• Death
Religion in Kenya today	

tion or through other forms that integrate visuals such as pictures and arti-facts. Musical selections, video clips, and authentic Kenyan food dishes should also be encouraged to broaden students' exposure to Kenyan culture.

Making-A-Difference Project: An Investigative Report of the World Free Press Institute and USAID Program

In closing out this unit of study, students should work in groups of four or five to research the World Free Press Institute (WFPI) and the United States Agency for International Development (USAID) programs. To avoid overlap in report content, the teacher should require students to specify their particular focus of research after having an opportunity to conduct a preliminary investigation of the various facets of work conducted by the WFPI and USAID. Students may share their findings in an essay, speech, or Microsoft PowerPoint presentation, so long as the emphasis is on reporting how these agencies make a difference for the nation and citizens of Kenya. Information about WFPI is based on the be-lief that "Democracy cannot function without a free and informed media" (WFPI, 2004c, ¶ 1).

From this conviction the WFPI has established its mission "to improve, sup-port, and strengthen a free press in its role as an opponent of tyranny around the world" (WFPI, 2004a, ¶ 1). With headquarters in Nairobi, Kenya, the East Africa Media Support Program is a joint initiative between the Network for the Defense of Independent Media in Africa (NDIMA) and WFPI (WFPI, 2004a, ¶ 2). The collaborative efforts of NDIMA and WFPI are aimed at assisting "the region's independent media" in combating a range of problems from "govern-ment repression, lack of professional training, and a lack of solidarity among journalists" (WFPI, 2004a, ¶ 2). Specifically, these efforts include the following (WFPI, 2004a):

- Assistance in empowering and networking East African journalists
- Creation of training materials specific to East African media managers' needs
- Providing temporary food and shelter to journalists expelled by their countries
- Providing computers to local journalism organizations
- Providing communication to outside organizations on media repression
- Hosting the annual East Africa Free Press Assembly, that brings together leading journalists from countries throughout the region. (¶ 3)

Major providers of funding for the World Free Press Institute and its Nairobi-based support program include the United Nations Educational, Scientific, and Cultural Organization (UNESCO) as well as the American-based Ford Foundation and Upjohn Foundation (WFPI, 2004d). Private individuals who share a commitment to the free exchange of ideas and information may also contribute financially to help WFPI counter "repressive governments around the world [that are] continuing their attacks on free and independent media" (WFPI, 2004b, ¶ 1). As a class project, students should learn about and educate others on the ways in which WFPI works for democracy, with a culminating ac-tivity being collecting donations to send to the WFPI. Such a collection could take place in a school cafeteria where students set up a table with a slideshow on a laptop computer or a tri-fold display about WFPI and ask peers and teach-ers to leave their change in support of the organization. Providing handouts or bookmarks with information about WFPI would also be nice touches. Alternately, students could present such information at a school open house.

Students around the globe will also benefit from knowing what kinds of foreign aid support Kenya, in particular USAID, which is the world's leading donor to Kenya. According to USAID (2005), "Overall development assistance to Kenya totals about $700 million per year. The United States and the United Kingdom are Kenya's first and second largest bilateral donors, respectively" (¶ 9), and other supportive countries include The Netherlands, Denmark, Sweden, Germany, and Canada. Beyond the numerical data, students should especially look at the aims associated with the financial aid. USAID's primary website, www.usaid.gov, offers specific details of U.S. foreign assistance for countries around the globe, including links to the Department of State's Fiscal Year Congressional Budget Justification for each. This site offers an education on aid from the U.S. people, including USAID's history, which dates back to the Marshall Plan for the reconstruction of Europe after World War II (USAID,

2006a). Following the Truman Administration's Point Four Program, President John F. Kennedy in 1961 "signed the Foreign Assistance Act into law and created by executive order USAID. Since that time, USAID has been the primary U.S. agency to extend assistance to countries recovering from disaster, trying to escape poverty, and engaging in democratic reforms" (USAID, 2006a, ¶ 2–3).

In fiscal year 2006, USAID gave Kenya over $36 million in aid directed toward health issues, natural resources management, democracy and governance, increasing rural household incomes, and basic education (USAID, 2005). This aid package funded five specific objectives outlined in the USAID Program Elements for Kenya in 2006:

1. Improving the balance of power among institutions of governance;
2. Promoting sustainable use of natural resources;
3. Improving rural incomes by increasing agricultural and rural enterprise opportunities;
4. Improving health conditions;
5. Providing education support for children of marginalized populations. (USAID, 2005, ¶ 6)

Students should also investigate two particular programs that are a part of USAID—the Colours of Life campaign, which is helping to market goods made by women living in the poorest suburbs of Nairobi (USAID, 2006b), and Volunteers for Prosperity, a program launched by President and Laura Bush in 2003 that enlists the aid of doctors, nurses, teachers, engineers, economists, computer specialists, and others to work on development initiatives (USAID, 2003). By exposing students to special programs such as Colours of Life and Volunteers for Prosperity, teachers can plant seeds within their students of future service with a global vision.

Conclusion

Through his writing, Ngugi effectively presents readers with complex themes that help them recognize problems associated with religious conversion, particularly as they can affect tribes and families. He also leads the reader to question issues of freedom and choice by showing that these are not guarantees of happiness and fulfillment. Additionally, Ngugi creates complex characters who prompt readers to consider what it means to have wisdom and to govern justly or face fierce consequences. While Ngugi wa Thiong'o's *The River Between* (1965) and *Weep Not, Child* (1964) depict conflicts in rituals and politics that were prevalent in Kenya when the novels were written in the 1960s, those who study

Kenya today realize that although the Mau Mau Rebellion is history, female circumcision continues to be widely practiced and thus remains a serious concern. Kenya's 2006 profile from USAID highlights other current problems facing the nation to include crumbling infrastructure, delivery of social services, environmental exploitation, poverty, prevalence of HIV/AIDS, child mortality, and school drop-out rates. That information combined with the study of Ngugi's novels and the range of activities presented in this chapter help students gain a better understanding of Kenya past and present.

REFERENCES

Alternative rituals raise hope for eradication of female genital mutilation. (2005). McLean, VA: Christian Connections for International Health. Retrieved June 15, 2006, from http://www.ccih.org/forum/9810-06.htm

Anderson, D. (2005). *Histories of the hanged: The dirty war in Kenya and the end of empire.* New York: W.W. Norton.

Biography of Ngugi wa Thiong'o. (2006). Retrieved June 20, 2006, from http://www.youressay.com/biographies/Ngugi_wa_Thiongo-32662.html

Delf, G. (1961). *Jomo Kenyatta: Towards truth about "The light of Kenya".* Garden City, NY: Doubleday.

International Reading Association & National Council of Teachers of English. (1996). *Standards for the English language arts.* Newark, DE; Urbana, IL: Authors.

Jaldesa, G.W., Askew, I., Njue, C., & Wanjiru, M. (2005). *Female genital cutting among the Somali of Kenya and management of its complications.* Washington, DC: USAID. Retrieved February 21, 2007, from http://www.intact-http://www.popcouncil.org/pdfs/frontiers/FR_FinalReports/Kenya_Somali.pdf

Keene, E.O., & Zimmermann, S. (1997). *Mosaic of thought: Teaching comprehension in a reader's workshop.* Portsmouth, NH: Heinemann.

Liukkonen, P. (2000). *Ngugi wa Thiong'o—Formerly known as James Ngugi.* Retrieved June 20, 2006, from http://www.kirjasto.sci.fi/ngugiw.htm

Lynn, S. (2005). *Texts and contexts: Writing about literature with critical theory* (3rd ed.). New York: Pearson.

Martin, F. (2006). *Clash of cultures; Mau Mau and the problematic interaction between Christianity and native Kikuyu beliefs in British colonial Kenya.* University Honors Capstone manuscript, American University, Washington, DC. Retrieved June 20, 2006, from http://www.american.edu/honors/Honors%20Activities/2004%20capstones/Martin.pdf

Maxon, R.M. (1997). Jomo Kenyatta. In *Microsoft Encarta online encyclopedia 2006.* Retrieved June 20, 2006, from http://encarta.msn.com/encyclopedia_761552618/Jomo_Kenyatta.html

Mohamud, A., Ringheim, K., Bloodworth, S., & Gryboski, K. (2002). Girls at risk: Community approaches to end female genital mutilation and treating women injured by the practice. In *Reproductive health and rights—Reaching the hardly reached* (pp. 69–85). Washington, DC: PATH. Retrieved June 15, 2006, from http://www.path.org/files/RHR-Article-8.pdf

National Council for the Social Studies. (1994). *Expectations of excellence: Curriculum standards for social studies.* Silver Spring, MD: Author.

Nyong'a, V. (1999). Female circumcision. In *Kenya demographic and health survey, 1998* (pp. 167–174). Calverton, MD: Macro International. Retrieved June 20, 2006, from http://www.measuredhs.com/topics/gender/FGC-CD/pdfs/Kenya1998chapter.pdf

Reboussin, D. (2003, December 18). *Thiongo.* Retrieved June 20, 2006, from African Collection, George A. Smathers Libraries, University of Florida: http://web.uflib.ufl.edu/cm/africana/thiongo.htm

Sicherman, C. (1990). *Ngugi wa Thiong'o: The making of a rebel: A sourcebook in Kenyan literature and resistance.* New York: H. Zell.

U.S. Agency for International Development (USAID). (2003, May 23). *President Bush launches "volunteers for prosperity": USAID and USA Freedom Corps will mobilize volunteers.* Retrieved June 20, 2006, from http://www.usaid.gov/press/releases/2003/pr030523_1.html

U.S. Agency for International Development (USAID). (2005). *Budget.* Retrieved June 15, 2006, from http://www.usaid.gov/policy/budget/cbj2006/afr/ke.html

U.S. Agency for International Development (US-AID). (2006a). *About USAID.*. Retrieved June 15, 2006, from http://www.usaid.gov/about_usaid

U.S. Agency for International Development (US-AID). (2006b). *Colours of life program empowers co-op in Kenya* . Retrieved June 20, 2006, from http://www.usaid.gov/stories/kenya/ss_kenya_coop.html

Whiting, K. (2002, February 19). Reporter's notebook: Female circumcision in Africa. *National Geographic Today*. Retrieved June 15, 2006, from http://news.nationalgeographic.com/news/2002/02/0220_020219_TVcircumcision.html

The World Free Press Institute (WFPI). (2004a). *East Africa media support program.* Retrieved June 20, 2006, from http://www.worldfreepress.org/content/nairobi2002.asp

The World Free Press Institute (WFPI). (2004b). *A free press needs your help.* Retrieved June 20, 2006, from http://www.worldfreepress.org/supportus.asp

The World Free Press Institute (WFPI). (2004c). *Home.* Retrieved June 20, 2006, from http://www.worldfreepress.org/wfpi.asp

The World Free Press Institute (WFPI). (2004d). *Our mission.* Retrieved June 20, 2006, from http://www.worldfreepress.org/ourmission.asp

LITERATURE CITED

Kessler, C. (2004). *Our secret, Siri Aang.* New York: Philomel Books.

wa Thiong'o, N. (1962). *The black hermit.* Portsmouth, NH: Heinemann.

wa Thiong'o, N. (1964). *Weep not, child.* Portsmouth, NH: Heinemann.

wa Thiong'o, N. (1965). *The river between.* Portsmouth, NH: Heinemann.

Williams-Garcia. R. (2004). *No laughter here.* New York: HarperCollins.

CHAPTER 7

Rites of Passage for Young Girls in the Central Regions of Africa

Jacqueline N. Glasgow

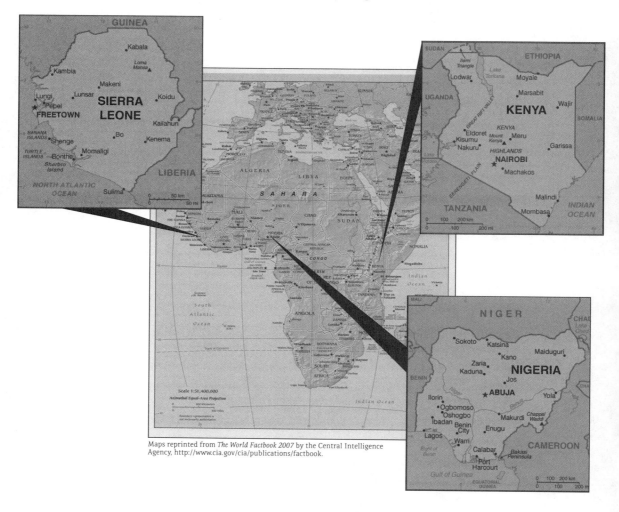

Maps reprinted from *The World Factbook 2007* by the Central Intelligence
Agency, http://www.cia.gov/cia/publications/factbook.

Exploring African Life and Literature: Novel Guides to Promote Socially Responsive Learning edited by Jacqueline N.
Glasgow and Linda J. Rice. © 2007 by the International Reading Association.

> "Of all passages, coming of age, or reaching adolescence, is the purest, in that it is the loneliest. In birth one is not truly conscious; in marriage one has a partner; even death is faced with a life's experience by one's side."
>
> —David Van Biema (1991, p. 31)

The initiation process is a basic one in human development, for it takes us from the protected and ideal world of childhood into the real and sometimes discouraging world of adulthood, where disillusionment and disappointment are commonplace. Through a healthy initiation process, we gain a realistic recognition of those goals that we can achieve as adults and, conversely, those values and modes of behavior that we should discard. In every case, there is a loss of innocence and a consequent gain in experience.

Adolescence is a separation from childhood and a preparation for adulthood, and often the teenager has to go outside mainstream society in order to achieve some individual identity before returning to that society as an adult. The rite of passage varies from one culture to another. While the 18th birthday is a formal legal marker in the United States (and other Western countries have similar formal legal markers), there is no national or cultural ritual that marks for the child, or for his or her society, that passage into adulthood. However, in other cultures, the rite of passage is ceremonial, sacred, and essential to enter the adult community. In the novels selected for this chapter, the rite of passage for adolescent girls is female circumcision, an issue that has recently attracted global attention. While many consider the practice barbaric, other cultures consider an uncircumcised female as "unclean" and therefore unmarriageable (see chapter 2 for more detailed background information on this practice). Many people in these communities are often unwilling to change these customs because they have always done them this way.

In the novels selected for this chapter, the protagonists grapple with and challenge female circumcision as their rite of passage. In doing so, they make costly sacrifices in resisting the traditions of their cultures. For example, in Kessler's *Our Secret, Siri Aang* (2004), the protagonist's choice between whether to preserve or resist cultural traditions affects not only human rights but also animal rights. The protagonist in this novel publicly embarrasses her mother by refusing her ceremony in order to protect an endangered rhinoceros, which she would be forbidden by the elders to do afterward. In Kessler's *No Condition Is Permanent* (2000), the protagonist interferes with her friend's ceremony when she finds out about what is happening. In Collins's *The Fattening Hut* (2005),

Novels, Activities, and Curricular Standards
for English Language Arts and Social Studies

NOVELS
- *Our Secret, Siri Aang* (2004) by Cristina Kessler
- *No Condition Is Permanent* (2000) by Cristina Kessler
- *The Fattening Hut* (2005) by Pat Lowery Collins
- *No Laughter Here* (2004) by Rita Williams-Garcia

CROSS-CURRICULAR ACTIVITIES
- Mind's Eye Predictions
- Q-Sort for Animal Rights
- Anticipation Guide for Female Circumcision

MAKING-A-DIFFERENCE PROJECT
Multigenre Research Paper Advocating for Change in Cultural Rites of Passage or Exposing Environmental Issues

STANDARDS FOR THE ENGLISH LANGUAGE ARTS
#2 Students read a wide range of literature.

#5 Students employ a wide range of strategies as they write.

#7 Students conduct research on issues and interests.

#11 Students participate as critical members of a variety of literacy communities.

#12 Students use spoken, written, and visual language to accomplish their own purposes.

Adapted from IRA and NCTE. (1996). *Standards for the English Language Arts.* Newark, DE: International Reading Association; Urbana, IL: National Council of Teachers of English.

CURRICULUM STANDARDS FOR THE SOCIAL STUDIES
#1a Culture: Learners compare similarities and differences in the coming-of-age rites for girls in Kenya and Nigeria.

#3h People, Places, & Environments: Learners examine, interpret, and analyze physical and cultural patterns and their interactions to show the Maasai migration patterns and ecosystem changes for Black Rhino survival.

#4e Individual Development & Identity: Learners identify and describe ways ethnic cultures influence individuals' coming-of-age ceremonies.

#9b Global Connections: Learners analyze examples of conflict, cooperation, and interdependence concerning Maasai survival and rhino extinction.

Adapted with the permission of the National Council for the Social Studies (NCSS). For the NCSS standards, see the publication *Expectations of Excellence: Curriculum Standards for Social Studies* (Washington, DC: National Council for the Social Studies, 1994). See also www.socialstudies.org.

the protagonist escapes her circumcision and embarks on a terrifying journey through the wild forests in hopes of surviving with her life. In Williams-Garcia's *No Laughter Here* (2004), the protagonist is not able to spare her friend the circumcision, but the girls initiate a public awareness campaign as human rights activists. Any of these novels could be read by the whole group, or they could be options for literature circles, as each novel brings a unique perspective on resistance to this age-old ritual. Also appropriate as a literature circle option is Farmer's *A Girl Named Disaster* (1996; see the Novel Guide for *A Girl Named Disaster* in chapter 13 of this book). As the issue of female circumcision becomes a controversial global issue, the authors of these novels connect young people across the continents in challenging the tradition.

The Cross-Curricular Activities for these novels are designed to help students to learn more about the consequences of resisting the rites of passage for young women and to understand the consequences of this resistance from various perspectives. The activities include Mind's Eye Predictions, a Q-Sort, and an Anticipation Guide discussing female circumcision. The Making-A-Difference Project invites students to create Multigenre Research Papers advocating for change in coming-of-age rituals or exposing environmental issues such as poaching, rhinoceros extinction, and the invasion of oil companies in the Niger Delta. The overview on page 142 illustrates how the Novel Guides in this chapter and their corresponding activities align with standards for the English language arts (International Reading Association [IRA] & National Council of Teachers of English [NCTE], 1996) and curriculum standards for the social studies (National Council for the Social Studies [NCSS], 1994).

Social and Historical Context

Kessler's inspiration for writing *Our Secret, Siri Aang* (2004), set in Kenya, came from observing the changes imposed on the Maasai people by the African government as well as wanting to capture their traditions before they became lost. All of the semi-nomadic tribes of Africa are being forced into sedentary lifestyles by outside forces, and often when they lose the right or ability to wander to graze their animals, they also lose their traditional ways. The Maasai, located in Kenya and Tanzania, are known for their love of nature and the freedom to relocate based on availability of water and grasslands for grazing their animals. The traditional Maasai lifestyle centers around their cattle, which constitutes the primary source of food. The Tanzanian and Kenyan governments have instituted programs to encourage the Maasai to abandon their traditional nomadic lifestyle and adopt an agrarian lifestyle instead. Kessler's desire is "to celebrate the Maasai as they have lived for uncountable years"

(AuthorsTalk.com, 2006, ¶10). Through her novel, she hopes readers will empathize with people who must yield their traditional ways of living to the modern world.

Just as the Maasai struggle to maintain many of their cultural traditions while engaging in contemporary conflicts of economic, social, and political forces, the pressure on the dwindling rhino species is another issue that is explored in *Our Secret, Siri Aang*. The rhino horn has been in demand for more than 1,000 years by various peoples around the world. Even though all rhino species face the threat of extinction, people still covet their horns as status symbols, powerful medicines, and aphrodisiacs. Conservation groups are faced with the challenge that to stop poaching, they must discourage the demand for the rhino horn that drives the price up to astronomical heights.

In *No Condition Is Permanent* (2000) Kessler explores another tradition that is challenged by those moving forward into the modern world: female circumcision as a rite of passage. Pat Lowery Collins and Rita Williams-Garcia also challenge the controversial issue of rites of passage for young women that require female circumcision, whether in Africa or in other places around the world. Many consider the practice to be barbaric, yet those who adhere to the practice of female circumcision have many justifications for continuing in the traditional ways (see chapter 2, pages 42–46). Fortunately, as women learn about the health risks that circumcision represents, they are more likely to seek out more sanitary conditions in hospitals, and some have even established initiation without cutting programs so that the girls still go through some initiation rites, but without any blood (see page 122 in chapter 6 for more information on this topic and for more information on what grassroots organizations and the Program for Appropriate Technology in Health are doing to address the dangers of the ritual of circumcision).

Our Secret, Siri Aang (2004) and *No Condition Is Permanent* (2000) by Cristina Kessler

About the Author

Cristina Kessler is the award-winning author of children's picture books and young adult fiction. Kessler grew up in Los Altos, California, USA, but has not lived there since joining the Peace Corps in 1973, where she met and married her husband while volunteering in Honduras. Since that time, she has followed her husband's job with CARE, an organization dedicated to fighting poverty, and has spent 28 years working and traveling to all seven continents, from Africa to Antarctica. Kessler said in an interview, "Any trip, anywhere, any time is my philosophy in life. This gives me plenty to write about, and hopefully after 19 years in Africa, credibility. I try to take my readers, from 4 years and up, on a trip to Africa" (AuthorsDen, 2007, ¶ 1). Drawing on her experience, journals, and photographs, Kessler's stories capture the beauty and harmony of African culture, wildlife, and landscape, which spark the imaginations of young readers and take them on trips to the African continent whether or not they have passports.

In addition to writing books for children, Kessler has written for magazines and worked for various international organizations as a writer, photographer, and layout designer. She has used these skills to help women in Ethiopia and Mali publish their own magazines such as *Women to Women* in Ethiopia and *La Parole aux Femmes* (Women Speak Out) in Mali. The magazines support women's issues and provide information to their readers ("Bring Cristina Kessler," 2006).

Summary (*Our Secret, Siri Aang*)

One day 12-year-old Namelokis is gathering firewood in the bush and stumbles upon a pregnant rhino giving birth. She names the baby Siri Aang (our secret) and vows to protect the animals according to her Maasai tradition. As a semi-nomadic people living mostly in Kenya, the Maasai frequently move their families and animals to better grazing grounds. In this case, Namelok's father moves his family to an area close to a Kenyan national park, where they are introduced to tourists, commerce, and radio communication from the outside world. As the Maasai become more desperate to provide for their families, they are tempted to make money from the tourists. Furthermore, as Namelok is pressured toward her initiation ceremony, which requires female circumcision as a rite of passage, she realizes she will no longer be allowed to wander in the wild to visit the animals, and her dream of attending school will be lost. But when Namelok discovers that poachers have killed the mother rhino, she is determined to protest her rite of passage into womanhood and both find the poachers and make sure the baby rhino is safe. Namelok tracks the baby through the bush for days, surviving on berries and tree bark, and even encounters a lion. In the end, she discovers that her desperate father had enabled the poachers to find the rhino in order to ensure survival of his family. The novel ends with a moving scene of forgiveness and restitution between father and daughter. So far, Namelok succeeded in her activism for animal rights, but readers are left wondering how far she will go in protesting female circumcision.

Summary (*No Condition Is Permanent*)

Fourteen-year-old Jodie Nichols accompanies her mother on a trip from California to a village in Sierra Leone to do fieldwork for a research project.

Jodie suddenly finds herself immersed in a new culture with no electricity and no indoor plumbing. Furthermore, she must learn the Krio language if she is to make friends. Despite the culture shock and language barrier, she befriends Khadi, a village girl her age, and they enjoy doing their chores together—carrying water, collecting firewood, and working in the rice fields together. But when Khadi is inducted into the women's Secret Society for her coming-of-age ceremony, which includes female circumcision, Jodie must decide whether or not to interfere. Hoping to spare her friend this practice, Jodie persists in getting involved, even though the consequence might be to alienate her from her friend and banish her and her mother from the country.

The Fattening Hut (2003) by Pat Lowery Collins

About the Author
The award-winning poet and author Pat Lowery Collins lives in Gloucester, Massachusetts, USA, where she writes, paints and illustrates full time. She was born and raised in Hollywood and received her bachelor's degree in English from the University of Southern California, USA. Most of her adult life has been spent in New England where she and her husband, Wallace, have raised five children. During some of that time she also studied art at the DeCordova Museum School in Lincoln, Massachusetts, USA. She has been writing children's books and poetry for publication for the last 25 years (Collins, 2007) She enjoys teaching workshops in creative, writing, and life drawing, and she also gives readings and visits schools as a guest author. In addition to *The Fattening Hut* (2003), other works include *Just Imagine* (2001), and *Signs and Wonders* (1999), as well as the picture book *Tomorrow, Up and Away* (1990).

Summary
In *The Fattening Hut* (2005), a story told in narrative poetry, 14-year-old Helen is placed in the "fattening hut," accompanied by her older sister who is married and nursing her first child. She is placed there by her mother, who according to tribal custom has sent her there to fatten her up, making her more beautiful and more marriageable. She is to eat all the food until she is given in marriage to the man chosen by her parents. She realizes she can't do what her mother is asking and begins her rebellion by either refusing to eat or by vomiting and burying it. Meanwhile, her Aunt Margaret secretly visits her in the night and leaves her reading material that Helen hides under her mattress. Through her reading she discovers the initiation ceremony includes "cutting" or

female circumcision. She now understands why Aunt Margaret is shunned for refusing the cutting ritual and that she, too, may have other choices. Even though she is warned of a dismal future with no husband, no children, no future without the ceremony, she manages to escape the fattening hut and embarks on a terrifying journey through the wild forest in hopes of surviving.

No Laughter Here (2004) by Rita Williams-Garcia

About the Author

Rita Williams-Garcia, renowned African American author, was born in Queens, New York, USA. Because her father was in the U.S. Army, the family traveled and lived throughout the United States. After living in Seaside, California, where Williams-Garcia enjoyed a carefree, happy childhood, the family moved back to Jamaica, New York, where she weathered adolescence and resides today. By age 14, she sold her first story to *Highlights Magazine*. After a false start majoring in economics at Hofstra University, she switched to arts and sciences. Thanks to a fiction workshop, she was inspired to begin writing again. While participating in a sorority community outreach literacy program in which she tutored four high school girls who read below fourth-grade level, she realized the lack of relevant young adult novels available that could speak to those girls. She began recording their dialogue, stealing bits and pieces of their conversations. These pieces were worked out in her writing workshop and became the first draft for *Blue Tights* (1988). From there, she wrote *Fast Talk on a Slow Track* (1991), *Like Sisters on the Homefront* (1995), *Every Time a Rainbow Dies* (2002), and *No Laughter Here* (2004). Living in a multicultural setting, Williams-Garcia is known for her complex character development and insight into adolescent emotions, conflicts, and cross-cultural issues. While avoiding racial issues per se, she does provide strong role models for black adolescents (Pais, Brown, & Gartner, 2006).

Williams-Garcia writes to give a voice to young African American and African girls. She always knew she would write a book about female circumcision because, she says, girls who must undergo this procedure have no voice or say in what happens to them. According to Williams-Garcia, many Westerners have little or no knowledge about this subject as it is usually happens within Africa and only happens to black girls. If something like this happens, Williams-Garcia feels she should write about it (Rowe, 2003, ¶ 15). "If I can raise awareness about the plight of girls, I will. If I can help a reader value herself even more, I will" (Rowe, 2003, ¶ 15). She believes her readers should know about these issues and arm themselves with knowledge so that they will be ready to face the tough reality that Akilah and Victoria encounter in *No Laughter Here* (2004).

Summary

Set in the United States, the novel begins with a typical fifth grader, 10-year-old Akilah Hunter, waiting to receive a letter from her best friend, Victoria Ojike, who is spending the summer with her grandmother in Nigeria, her birthplace. Akilah is worried because the letters have stopped coming regularly. She suspects things are changing and rightly so. When Victoria returns to the United States, she is silent and withdrawn—not the outspoken, studious e-mail partner Akilah used to enjoy. However, after a sexual education video in class, Victoria shares her secret with Akilah. While in Nigeria, she was circumcised against her will by her mother, her aunts, and her grandmother. While she was put to sleep for the operation, she suffered a lot of rage and pain. She says, "I don't look like that. I no longer have what other girls have" (Williams-Garcia, 2004, p. 70). Horrified, Akilah promises to keep the secret while searching the Internet for more information. However, it is not long until her mother discovers what Akilah is researching. After an awkward confrontation between the two mothers, Akilah is no longer welcome at Victoria's house. Akilah tells Victoria that she got her period, and Victoria tells Akilah that she is bleeding, too, but not from her period. The two girls decide to speak out against the atrocities of female circumcision by putting Victoria's story on the Internet. Victoria realizes that her secret needs to be shared with girls around the world to prevent future acts of female circumcision. These two young activists want to stop this practice because no girl deserves to lose what they call her laughter.

Making Connections

In preparation for reading the novels in this unit, students need to connect their personal lives with the major ideas presented in the text. "When readers make connections with the text, they understand how characters feel and the motivation behind their actions" (Tovani, 2000, p. 73). In this case, the students will be asked to think about themes such as rites of passage, including female circumcision; relationships with family and friends; rhino extinction; and Maasai survival. The following Making Connections questions for the novels in this unit will help students explore text-to-self, text-to-text, and text-to-world connections (Keene & Zimmermann, 1997). Figure 7.1 shows a sample journal response to a text-to-world question for this Novel Guide created by university student Lauren Berg.

Making Connections Questions for *Our Secret, Siri Aang* (2004), *No Condition Is Permanent* (2000), *No Laughter Here* (2004), and *The Fattening Hut* (2005)

	Kessler's *Our Secret, Siri Aang* (2004)	Williams-Garcia's *No Laughter Here* (2004)	Kessler's *No Condition Is Permanent* (2000)	Collins's *The Fattening Hut* (2005)
Text-to-Self	Do I have any secrets? Why do people keep secrets? How does one come of age in my culture? What age should I be to get married? What do I know about female circumcision? What animals do I know of that are endangered? How do I feel about my education?	What characteristics must I have in a friend? What characteristics of a friend can I not stand? How supportive are my parents when I have a problem? How does one come of age in my culture? What do I know about female circumcision? What would I like to learn about female circumcision?	Have I ever experienced culture shock? Have I ever been in a situation where I couldn't understand the language people were speaking around me? Have I ever studied a foreign language? What experiences have I had when I had to use outdoor latrines and no electricity? What does it mean to be best friends?	What do I know about how beauty is determined in other cultures? How would I define beauty? How would I react to being stuck in a fattening hut for the purposes of making me more marriageable? What *does* make me marriageable in my society? How would I survive if I ran away from home? What do I know about female circumcision?

Text-to-Text	What else have I read about how adolescents come of age? What have I read about female circumcision? What else have I read about endangered species?	What else have I read in which there are strong friends and strong families? What have I read about female circumcision? What coming-of-age stories have I read?	What else have I read about people living abroad? What have I read about female circumcision? What coming-of-age stories have I read?	What else have I read about marriage customs in other cultures? What have I read about ways to make one more marriageable? What coming-of-age customs have I read about?
Text-to-World	How do other cultures celebrate rites of passage? What are the problems connected to female circumcision? Should female circumcision be stopped? What threatens a culture's survival? Who is marginalized by our education system? What animals are endangered around the world? How can poaching be stopped?	How do other cultures celebrate rites of passage? What are the problems connected with female circumcision? Should female circumcision be stopped? Why or why not?	How do other cultures celebrate rites of passage? What are the problems connected with female circumcision? Should circumcision be stopped? Why or why not?	How do other cultures celebrate the right of passage? What are the dangers of female circumcision? What are the consequences of resisting female circumcision in a society that believes so strongly in it? How would one survive without family, friends, and culture?

Critical Exploration of Themes

Resistance to oppressive cultural practices takes many forms, and in the novels selected for this Novel Guide unit, the protagonists make significant sacrifices by making the choice to oppose the age-old customs and traditions of their communities. The risks taken by these young activists often mean making sacrifices for themselves, their families, and their cultures, and these young women must deal with the consequences that result from these choices.

One consequence resulting from their resistance to female circumcision is to bear the shame associated with remaining uncircumcised and become alienated from the home community. In *The Fattening Hut* (2005), Helen escapes the ceremony by running away, but if captured, will face the shame of disappointing her parents and community as well as being shunned in the same way as her Aunt Margaret has been. She would have to live alone and bear her shame in solitude as a spinster, as no man in her society would marry an uncircumcised woman. She would bear no children and have no family to support her. However, thanks to her childhood friend, Ashanti, and Western supporters, she survives and is rescued, but, of course, can never rejoin her culture.

Like *The Fattening Hut*, *Our Secret: Siri Aang* (2004) focuses on a female protagonist who chooses to claim freedoms and rights that challenge cultural practices. Also present in this story are themes of the Maasai protection of animals, and the struggle to preserve their tribal culture, life, and lands. The Maasai are pastoralists who live close to the earth and believe it is their duty to protect not only the cattle, but all wild animals. In this story, Namelok is conflicted between preserving her commitment to protecting a mother rhino and its newborn baby and her own initiation into womanhood.

Once the initiation is complete, she would be prohibited from visiting the rhinos and freely roaming the land. Therefore, she chooses to accept her activist role in the tribe by pursuing the poachers who killed the mother rhino and to challenge the initiation tradition. She succeeds in hiding her menstruation from her mother for at least three months and finds creative ways to visit the rhinos. Once discovered, she is forced to submit to the circumcision ceremony that would make her a woman and require her to enter an arranged marriage. However, inspired by a voice on the radio telling young girls not to be initiated, Namelok begins her resistance. One day as the women and children are gathered together making jewelry, Namelok asks the group, "Why can't I go to school and marry later?" (Kessler, 2004, p. 101). Challenging the traditions of her mother, grandmothers, and great-grandmothers is strictly forbidden and brings shame on herself and on her family. However, because Namelok observes that Maasai ways are changing, she has high hopes those changes will include other ways for her to become a woman.

In the other two novels in this unit, the protagonists explore cross-cultural connections that challenge the practice of female circumcision from an outsider's point of view. In *No Condition Is Permanent* (2000), Jodie, the American protagonist living in Sierra Leone, can't understand why Khadi never questions the Secret Society that practices female circumcision as part of the initiation of young girls. For Khadi, however, this practice is part of the cultural norm, something that she has learned from her grandmother and will pass on to her daughters and granddaughters. When Jodie advises her to ask some questions and get some answers as is done in America, Khadi cuts right in with, "Dis no be America" (Kessler, 2000, p. 103). Jodie is warned by her mother and by Khadi to stay away from the Secret Society activities that no white woman can attend. But after Jodie finds out what is going on, she ignores the warnings and searches for a way to save her friend from circumcision. Because she takes an activist stance in attempting to thwart Khadi's initiation, Jodie and her mother are consequently banished from the country.

In *No Laughter Here* (2004), Victoria makes the trip from the United States back to her native Nigeria with her mother and grandmother, not knowing that the purpose is her circumcision. She is quite angry when she discovers what has happened to her after waking up from the surgery. Returning back to the United States, Victoria is estranged from her best friend, Akilah. She remains quiet, withdrawn, and sad until Akilah persists in finding out what happened. Akilah is outraged, but keeps her friend's secret until her mother discovers that Akilah is reading about female circumcision on a website and guesses the reason why. Akilah's mother, also angered, confronts Victoria's mother with the issue, which causes a rift between the two families. Eventually the relationship between the girls is restored. Together as activists, the girls plan to post a public awareness letter about the dangers of FGM on the Web for girls around the world to see.

Teacher Talk

The goal of the Great Books Foundation (2006a) Great Books programs is to instill the habits of mind that characterize a self-reliant thinker, reader, and learner. The Great Books Foundation recommends the shared inquiry method of leading a discussion in which participants search for answers to fundamental questions raised by the text. The foundation believes that the kind of question a leader asks determines the kind of discussion and the kind of thinking that will happen. The three types of questions for leading a shared inquiry discussion are factual, interpretive, and evaluative questions (Great Books Foundation, 2006b). The following questions can be used when leading a shared inquiry discussion. Preservice teacher Adam Brenner developed the questions for *Our Secret, Siri Aang* (2004), preservice teacher Lauren Berg developed the questions for *No Laughter Here* (2004), and the instructor (Glasgow) developed the questions for *No Condition Is Permanent* (2000) and Collins's *The Fattening Hut* (2005).

Using Questions for a Shared Inquiry Discussion

	Factual	Intepretive	Evaluative
Kessler's *Our Secret, Siri Aang* (2004)	What does Namelok's name mean? What does Siri Aang mean and who is it given to as a name? What does Namelok do to insult the elders in her enkang? Who does Namelok discover took part in the poaching? What does Namelok think about education? Why does Reteti dislike living in this particular enkang? Why did Loitipitip not move with his family when they left their last enkang? What motivates Reteti to help the poachers?	Why does Namelok have such a love for Yieyio Emuny Narok and Siri Aang? Why are Namelok's parents so upset by her request to want an education? Do you think that Namelok was inspired by reasons other than finding the poachers when she went out in the copse? Does Namelok really forgive her father or does she feel like she has to because he is her father? What motivates Namelok more: to find Siri Aang or find the people responsible for killing Yieyio Emuny Narok?	If you were in Reteti's position, would you have helped the poachers in order to better your family's way of life even if it meant going against your beliefs? If you were Namelok, would you be able to forgive Reteti for helping the poachers? Imagine yourself living in the same enkang as Namelok and her family. What would be the best and worst part of life? Imagine being told you were not allowed to go to school and that as soon as you come of age, you had to be married. How would you react?
Williams-Garcia's *No Laughter Here* (2004)	What is the setting? What does Akilah struggle with regarding Victoria? Why did Akilah act up in class? What happened with Akilah and Juwan? What is the matter with Victoria? What vow did Akilah make to Victoria	Why is the setting important? Tell about one event in the story. What is the theme of the book? Why? Who is Girl Warrior and why is she called that? Why is female genital mutilation (FGM) done? Why did Rita Williams-Garcia write this book? For whom?	Why do you think female circumcision is still practiced today even though it is illegal? If you were Akilah's mother, would you have dealt with the situation differently? Why or why not? Should Victoria have told Akilah what happened? Should Akilah accept this fact or try to persuade Victoria to do something about it?

| Kessler's *No Condition Is Permanent* (2000) | Where is the setting?
How does Jodie deal with the culture shock?
What was Jodie's new environment like?
What changes did she have to make to adjust to the African village?
How does Khadi help her adjust?
What languages do people speak in Sierray Leone? | What does it mean when Jodie's mother says, "no condition is permanent"?
Why does Jodie feel so connected to Khadi?
How does Jodie overstep the boundaries of the village culture?
When does Jodie understand that she really does fit into the culture?
What does Jodie have to offer Khadi? | How did Jodie spoil the happiest months of her life in the village?
Why doesn't Khadi question the activities of the Secret Society?
What are the consequences of resisting circumcision?
Is there any good coming out of the Secret Society?
What drives Jodie's motivation in breaking the taboo to learn more about the activities of the Secret Society? |
| Collins's *The Fattening Hut* (2005) | Why did Helen hate the fattening hut?
What are the ways she defied her mother's intentions to fatten her up in preparation for the initiation ceremony?
How is beauty defined in Helen's culture?
What's in the package that her Aunt Margaret sneaks in to her?
How does Helen resist her mother's intentions to fatten her up for marriage? | What has Helen learned from reading the books Aunt Margaret gave her?
How does her sister explain the initiation ceremony?
How is Aunt Margaret regarded in the community? Why?
What is the relationship between Helen and Ashani?
How does Helen bring shame upon her mother? | How does Helen come to question the initiation ceremony?
Why does Helen decide to escape the fattening hut?
How does she manage to survive in the wilderness?
What price does she pay for her resistance to the traditional customs?
How is she rescued from her flight?
What cost does she pay for her freedom? |

Cross-Curricular Activities

The Cross-Curricular Activities for this unit are designed as prereading strategies to prepare students to deal with the controversial issues raised in the novels. The Mind's Eye activity invites students to visualize and make predictions after seeing and hearing a list of terms from the novel. The Q-Sort activity requires students to evaluate various aspects of animal rights. To access students' prior knowledge and opinions concerning female circumcision, use the Anticipation Guide to stimulate discussion before reading any of the novels dealing with female circumcision. The Making-A-Difference Project for this unit is a Multigenre Research Paper in which students advocate for change in cultural rites of passage or expose environmental issues. This project allows students to report their research in creative formats in lieu of the traditional research paper.

Mind's Eye Predictions

To create the Mind's Eye Predictions activity, construct a list of 20 to 25 important words that appear in the first three chapters of the book and arrange them sequentially on an overhead transparency. Then read the words slowly and thoughtfully to the class and ask students to formulate mental images of what might be happening in the novel *Our Secret, Siri Aang* (2004) by Cristina Kessler. After hearing and reading the words and creating visualizations in their heads, students should do one of the following activities:

- Draw a picture based on your visualization as the basis for prediction.
- Formulate questions you hope the text will answer.
- Use the words to write a paragraph predicting the events in the novel.
- Describe the feelings, words, and mental images called forth in your visualization and predict what will happen in the story (adapted from Brownlie & Silver, 1995).

See Figure 7.2 for the Words for Mind's Eye Prediction Activity with responses and predictions created by preservice teacher Adam Brenner.

Q-Sort for Animal Rights

The purpose of a Q-Sort is to get students thinking about a topic or concept that you want them to evaluate. In this case, the topic is animal rights, and students will consider the moral judgments connected with this topic. The Q-Sort technique (Stephenson, 1953) helps facilitate the task of ranking or prioritizing valuable, complex, and partially overlapping items. It can be used as a before-reading strategy to access and activate prior knowledge, an important part of active reading. For this activity, students are given nine statements with various perspectives on the animal rights controversy. Each statement should be placed individually either on sentence strips or index cards so that each person in the class has a copy of each of the statements. For examples, see the Q-Sort Statements for Animal Rights in Table 7.1. Students do the Q-Sort activity for five minutes individually by placing each of the statements on the

Figure 7.2. Words for Mind's Eye Prediction Activity and Student Response With Predictions

Namelok	Marriage
Maasi	Coming of age
Community	Sacrifice
Enkang	School
Black Rhinos	Shame
Protector	Poachers
Wild animals	Tourists
Secret	Money
Government warriors	Kenya
Emuratare	Bush

Student's Response and Predictions

The first thing I noticed when I looked at the words, were the many different foreign words that I did not know how to pronounce. Upon further examination, I would guess that they would be the names of the main characters in the novel. I realize that this is a unit on African Literature so I am guessing that those are African names, most likely from Kenya. It appears that the family and community and the wild animals are important to the people of the novel. The sacrifice, shame and poachers all present images in my mind that make me think that someone may have done something that they regret and could have something to do with the wild animals mentioned earlier. The money and tourists seem to have a connection in that maybe tourists visit their town and their money helps support the inhabitants financially and allows them to survive and protect their families, community and the wild animals. The book appears to be set in a jungle or desert type area because it is in Kenya, a country in Africa and the presence of wild animals appear to make it in the wilderness or bush of some type.

Table 7.1. Q-Sort Statements for Animal Rights

1. Hunting animals is never justified.
2. Animal testing is necessary to advance medical research.
3. Animal farming (chickens, fish, cattle) should be illegal.
4. Using animals for entertainment (circuses, aquariums, zoos) should be banned.
5. Animals should not be made to suffer unnecessarily.
6. Vegetarianism should be mandated.
7. Hunting animals for food and medicinal purposes is justified.
8. Humans should continue to exploit other animals for their own welfare and survival.
9. Leather products should be banned.

Q-Sort Continuum based on their opinions that range from one with which they "Most Agree" to one for which they "Least Agree." These responses form a ranking similar to the bell-curve in that the greatest number of responses are the neutral ones in the middle while the tails of the bell-curve reflect the more discrete opinions (see Figure 7.3 for the Q-Sort Continuum). Then, arrange stu-

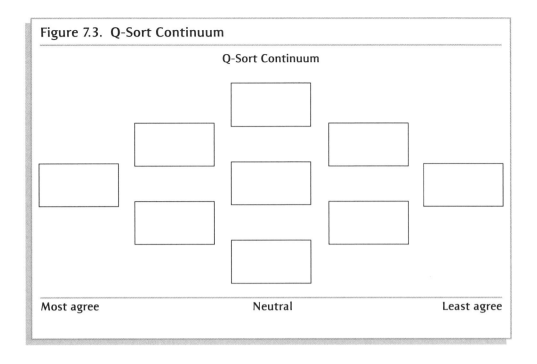

Figure 7.3. Q-Sort Continuum

Q-Sort Continuum

Most agree   Neutral   Least agree

dents in groups of three or four and ask them to negotiate their opinions and come to consensus by creating one continuum that reflects the group members' beliefs. Each group then shares with the class the choices they made and the conflicts they had during the negotiations. If desirable, the class members can work toward consensus for a whole-group continuum that gives a portrait of the beliefs held by the entire class.

Anticipation Guide for Female Circumcision

The Anticipation Guide is used as a means to access a class's prior knowledge by anticipating some of the themes and issues before they begin reading a novel. According to Tierney, Readence, and Dishner (1995), Anticipation Guides that present students with a set of generalizations related to the theme of the novel help dependent readers in particular to construct meaning of the text before they begin reading it. Statements in the Anticipation Guide should be ambiguous and controversial in order for students to examine their beliefs and make predictions about key issues in the novel. Students should respond first in writing and then discuss the responses as a whole group. See Table 7.2 for an Anticipation Guide for female circumcision. Students should revisit the Anticipation Guide after reading the novel and note ideas and connections they have made that might have changed.

Table 7.2. Anticipation Guide for Female Circumcision

Directions: Read each statement and put a check mark in the Yes column if you believe the statement and could support it, or put a check mark in the No column if you do not believe the statement and could not support it.

Yes   No   Statement

1. Because female circumcision is a social custom, not a religious practice, it is an acceptable practice.

2. The Qu' ran, Hebrew scriptures (Old Testament), and Christian scriptures are all silent on the subject of female circumcision.

3. The United Nations should support the right of member states to grant refugee status to women who fear being mutilated through female circumcision if returned to their country of origin.

4. Educated women do not adhere to this traditional rite of passage.

5. Female circumcision is justified as part of an initiation ritual.

6. The act of circumcising girls favors the girl because they will find sexual intercourse more pleasurable.

7. Female circumcision promotes female hygiene.

8. Female circumcision is a violation of individual human rights.

9. Female circumcision exists solely as a means of control by men.

10. The fact that this procedure is carried out without anesthesia and under unsanitary conditions in practicing countries is acceptable because of their culture.

Making-A-Difference Project: Multigenre Research Papers Advocating for Change in Cultural Rites of Passage or Environmental Issues

The Making-A-Difference project for this unit is a Multigenre Research Paper to advocate for change by having students choose a controversial topic—such as female circumcision, poaching, animal rights, rhino survival, or the invasion of oil companies in the Niger Delta—take a stand on the issue, and advocate for change. The multigenre research paper is a creative alternative to the traditional research paper. Students select a topic, gather information from reliable sources, and conduct interviews just as they would for a traditional research paper. The difference is that students report their findings in creative formats such as letters, diary entries, poetry, stories, editorials, and various other creative formats. These creative pieces are connected together with pieces that Tom Romano (2000) called "repetends" (graphics, quotes, memos, and so forth, that students have written themselves or documented from other sources) in order to tell a story and make a powerful statement. In this way students develop strong, personal voices to express the multiple perspectives they are representing. At the end of the multigenre research paper, students provide a notes page describing the inspiration for their creative pieces and a works cited page to document their resources. Students also prepare a presentation to the class to share their research findings by reading some of their pieces, maybe providing a musical background, using a visual aid, or putting pieces into a Microsoft PowerPoint presentation. For more information and student examples about this type of research paper, see Romano's *Blending Genre, Altering Style: Writing Multigenre Papers* (2000) or Glasgow's *Strategies for Engaging Young Adult Readers: A Social Themes Approach* (2005). Table 7.3 provides a suggested list of requirements for the Multigenre Research Project and instructions for students are as follows.

First, provide a choice of appropriate topics for students to research. The topics could range from male and female circumcision, coming-of-age rituals, or African marriage rituals to animal rights, rhino survival, oil companies in the Niger Delta, and so forth. Then ask students to prepare a prospectus that states their topic, interest, purpose, audience, and resources they will use for information. As students find information on their topic, ask them to keep a journal entry for each resource to record their findings and their reactions to what they are reading. Require them to find information using at least three different types of sources (e.g., Internet, magazines, newspapers, interviews). These journal entries will be helpful in drafting the creative writing pieces.

Table 7.3. Suggested Multigenre Research Paper Requirements

Minimum Requirements for the Multigenre Paper	Due Date
Prospectus (topic, interest, purpose, audience, and resources)	
Table of contents	
Prologue (provides a context for the reader; tells the reader how to read the paper)	
At least five original pieces (representing four different genres)	
Repetends (to connect the creative pieces)	
Notes page (reflective in nature; describes the inspiration for each of the pieces and repetends in the project)	
Works cited page	
Plan for a five-minute presentation to the class (must include a visual)	

In class, have students practice reading informational text and reporting it in poems, letters, diary entries, and other creative formats. Students should always ask themselves the question, what did I learn about the topic in the creative piece? In other words, the creative pieces must be informative and show evidence of the research. For instance, see Figure 7.4 for an original found poem created by preservice teacher Julianne Oliver based on passages from *No Laughter Here* (2004) and the author's notes at the end of the book, or see Figure 7.5 for a poem in two voices on rhino poaching by preservice teacher Will Hanek.

As students begin drafting creative pieces for the final paper, make sure they experiment with various voices, perspectives, and genres. A genre is a form of

---

Figure 7.4. Student Found Poem Based on *No Laughter Here* (Kessler, 2004)

For marriage, a woman must be clean. Proper.
Why are you here?
AKILAH!
I couldn't move,
I was running out of hiding places,
I do not have joy,
She made a sound. Not a scream, but like a cry,
That sick feeling came over me,
I do not laugh,
Over two million girls mutilated each year.

Figure 7.5. Student Poem in Two Voices on Rhino Poaching

Black Rhino	Hunter
	I hunt for a living
I roam for a living	
I sleep	I sleep
I graze	
	I shoot
to take care of my young	to take care of my young.
I die	
at the crack of the gun	at the crack of the gun
	I claim my booty,
my horn	the horn
is removed	
	and sold for a price
a price too great to pay	
to save the earth	
	to save mankind.

Figure 7.6. Repetends Using Statistics to Help Save the Black Rhino

- Rhino Horns have no medicinal value
- Between 1970 and 1992, the Black Rhino population declined by 96%.
- It is thought that 90% of rhinos are killed by poachers for their horns.
- Black Rhinos have no predators in the wild; human beings, mainly poachers, pose the biggest threat to rhinos.

To help save Black Rhinos visit www.rhino-irf.org

writing such as short stories, diary entries, news articles, letters, memos, and so forth. The final paper should include at least four different genres. The best papers are cohesive, meaning that some structure holds the creative pieces together. Look for images, quotes, photographs, statistics, or other devices that would be appropriate as "repetends," or connecting pieces of the creative pieces, which move along the story, argument, or main point. See Figure 7.6 for an example of repetends using statistics to help save the Black Rhino by preservice teacher Adam Brenner.

When projects are complete, choose a day for presentations to be shared. Provide a sign-up sheet so that students can prepare for the event. Invite parents, caretakers, administrators, and other classes to join in the celebration. These papers are often the students' best work of the year. Students take great pride in their accomplishments. They are sure to make a difference, not only in their own thinking but also in the minds of those who hear their ideas for change.

Conclusions

Through reading, research, and discussion, students have had the opportunity to explore coming-of-age rituals at home and abroad. They have examined characters who chose to comply with their culture and submit to circumcision in order to preserve their places in their indigenous cultures. They have also examined books in which protagonists have resisted ceremonies that include female circumcision and made the sacrifices necessary to secure their freedom. In addition, students have made cross-cultural connections that come with travel into the international community and immigration to other countries where they bring native traditions with them. If students have read *Our Secret, Siri Aang* (2004), they have also discussed issues of animal rights, poaching, and possible extinction of the Black Rhino, as well as the encroachment of the modern world on the Maasai way of life. Through this examination of other cultural traditions through reading literature, students will come to appreciate the difficulty of finding the dividing line between a need for tolerance of other cultural practices and the need for basic human rights.

REFERENCES

AuthorsDen.com (2006). *Interviews: Christina Kessler*. Retrieved February 17, 2007, from http://www.authorsden.com/cristinakessler

AuthorsDen.com (2007). *No condition is permanent: Author review*. Retrieved February 17, 2007, from http://www.authorsden.com/visit/viewwork.asp?AuthorID=880&id=12925

Bring Cristina Kessler to Your School! (2006). Retrieved February 2, 2006, from http://www.authorsinschools.com/author_details.aspx?AuthorID=48

Brownlie, F., & Silver, H.G. (1995, January). *Mind's eye*. Paper presented at the seminar "Responding Thoughtfully to the Challenge of Diversity," Delta School District Conference Center, Delta, British Columbia, Canada.

Collins, P.L. (2007). *My Life*. Retrieved February 16, 2007, from http://www.patlowerycollins.com/bio.htm

Glasgow, J. (2005). *Strategies for engaging young adult readers: A social themes approach*. Norwood, MA: Christopher-Gordon.

Great Books Foundation. (2006a). *Great Books*. Retrieved February 3, 2006, from http://www.greatbooks.org/about.html

Great Books Foundation. (2006b). *Philosophy: Great Books discussions and shared inquiry*. Retrieved February 3, 2006, from http://www.greatbooks.org/programs-for-all-ages/gb/gbphilosophy.html

International Reading Association & National Council of Teachers of English. (1996). *Standards for the English language arts*. Newark, DE; Urbana, IL: Authors.

Keene, E.O., & Zimmermann, S. (1997). *Mosaic of thought: Teaching comprehension in a reader's workshop*. Portsmouth, NH: Heinemann.

National Council for the Social Studies. (1994). *Expectations of excellence: Curriculum standards for social studies*. Silver Spring, MD: Author.

Pais, S., Brown, P., & Gartner, A. (with Vandergrift, K.E.). (2006). *Learning about Rita Williams-Garcia*. Retrieved February 6, 2006, from http://www.scils.rutgers.edu/~kvander/williamsgarcia.html

Romano, T. (2000). *Blending genre, altering style: Writing multigenre papers*. Portsmouth, NH: Boynton/Cook.

Rowe, B. (2003, February). *Rita Williams-Garcia [Interview]*. Retrieved February 6, 2006, from http://www.myshelf.com/haveyouheard/03/garcia.htm

Stephenson, W. (1953). *The study of behavior: Q-technique and its methodology*. Chicago: University of Chicago Press.

Tierney, R.J., Readence, J.E., & Dishner, E.K. (1995). *Reading strategies and practices: A compendium* (4th ed.). Boston: Allyn & Bacon.

Tovani, C. (2000). *I read it, but I don't get it: Comprehension strategies for adolescent readers*. Portland, ME: Stenhouse.

Van Biema, D. (1991, October). The journey of our lives. *Life, 14*(12), 31.

LITERATURE CITED

Collins, P.L. (2003). *The fattening hut*. New York: Houghton Mifflin.

Farmer, N. (1996). *A girl named disaster*. New York: Puffin Books.

Kessler, C. (2000). *No condition is permanent*. New York: Philomel Books.

Kessler, C. (2004). *Our secret, Siri Aang*. New York: Philomel Books.

Williams-Garcia, R. (1988). *Blue tights*. New York: Dutton.

Williams-Garcia, R. (1991). *Fast talk on a slow track*. New York: Lodestar Books.

Williams-Garcia, R. (1995). *Sisters on the home-front*. New York: Lodestar Books.

Williams-Garcia, R. (2001). *Every time a rainbow dies*. New York: HarperCollins.

Williams-Garcia. R. (2004). *No laughter here*. New York: Amistad.

CHAPTER 8

Connections and Communication Across the Continents: From Ethiopia to the United States

Alexa L. Sandmann

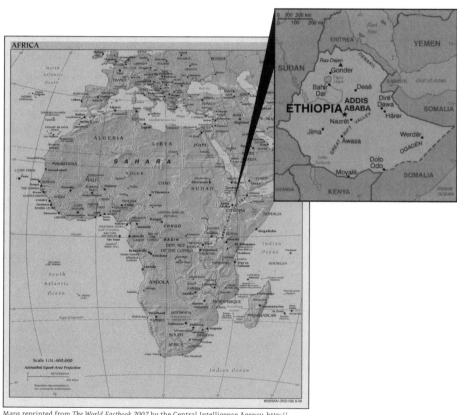

Maps reprinted from *The World Factbook 2007* by the Central Intelligence Agency, http://
www.cia.gov/cia/publications/factbook.

Exploring African Life and Literature: Novel Guides to Promote Socially Responsive Learning edited by Jacqueline N.
Glasgow and Linda J. Rice. © 2007 by the International Reading Association.

Jane Kurtz was born in Portland, Oregon, but moved to Ethiopia when she was two years old and lived there for most of her childhood. She visited Boise, Idaho, for one year when she was seven, and she spent one year in Pasadena, California, when she was thirteen. She says she "grew up as someone who is sometimes labeled a 'third-culture kid,' a person who doesn't fully belong in her parents' culture but doesn't fully belong in the culture around her, either."

—Jane Kurtz, in *Memories of Sun* (2004, Book Jacket)

O ver the years, author and editor Jane Kurtz has discovered a way to share connections from Ethiopia to the United States by writing books for children and young adults. As she reveals on her website, "It's been a healing and inspiring experience to reconnect with my childhood and also be able to help people know just a little bit of [Ethiopia] the beautiful country where I grew up" (Kurtz, 2003, ¶ 3). Creating literature that has honored her transcontinental experience, Kurtz has produced 11 books to date that connect to her Ethiopian years. Kurtz has written 14 other books as well, including 3 professional texts (see Table 8.1 for a bibliography of books by Jane Kurtz). This chapter focuses on two of Kurtz's works. *Jakarta Missing* (2001) is a novel that traces the concept of "home" while *Memories of Sun: Stories of Africa and America* (2004) is Kurtz's edited collection of poems and stories, which explore the same theme. Cross-Curricular Activities for this chapter include a Student-Directed Inquiry Into Ethiopia and a chart Comparing Life in Africa to America. The Making-A-Difference project for this chapter is Supporting Literacy in Ethiopia. Teachers and students are invited to visit www.ethiopiareads.org online to find out about literacy in Ethiopia and how they can make a difference in the literacy lives of children. Various projects that both adults and children can complete are suggested. Any of the projects would help to improve literacy and nurture a culture of reading in Ethiopia, which would bring hope, vision, and educational skills to the current generation of children. The overview on page 166 illustrates how the Novel Guides in this chapter and their corresponding activities align with standards for the English language arts (International Reading Association [IRA] & National Council of Teachers of English [NCTE], 1996) and curriculum standards for the social studies (National Council for the Social Studies [NCSS], 1994).

Social and Historical Context

A country of over 65 million people, Ethiopia is the only African nation that was not colonized by Europeans, although it was briefly occupied by the Italians

Novels, Activities, and Curricular Standards for English Language Arts and Social Studies

NOVELS
- *Jakarta Missing* (2001) by Jane Kurtz
- *Memories of Sun: Stories of Africa and America* (2004) edited by Jane Kurtz

CROSS-CURRICULAR ACTIVITIES
- Student-Directed Inquiry Into Ethiopia
- Comparing Life in Africa to Life in America

MAKING-A-DIFFERENCE PROJECT
Supporting Literacy in Ethiopia

STANDARDS FOR THE ENGLISH LANGUAGE ARTS
#3 Students draw on their prior experience and their knowledge of word meaning and of other texts, their word identification strategies, and their understanding of textual features.

#8 Students use a variety of technological and information resources to gather and synthesize information and to create and communicate knowledge.

#9 Students develop an understanding of and respect for diversity in language use, patterns, and dialects across cultures and geographic regions.

Adapted from IRA and NCTE. (1996). *Standards for the English Language Arts.* Newark, DE: International Reading Association; Urbana, IL: National Council of Teachers of English.

CURRICULUM STANDARDS FOR THE SOCIAL STUDIES
#1c Culture: Learners explain and give examples of how language and stories of Africa and the United States contribute to the development and transmission of culture.

#3b People, Places, & Environments: Learners use research sources and maps to investigate features of various countries and plot them in relation to one another.

#4a Individual Development & Identity: Learners describe personal connections between stories from the United States and various countries in Africa.

Adapted with the permission of the National Council for the Social Studies (NCSS). For the NCSS standards, see the publication *Expectations of Excellence: Curriculum Standards for Social Studies* (Washington, DC: National Council for the Social Studies, 1994). See also www.socialstudies.org.

between 1936 and 1941 (Embassy of Ethiopia, 2001a, 2001b). According to the Embassy of Ethiopia, Washington, DC, website, "Ethiopia is a mosaic of diverse people who live peacefully, side-by-side speaking a multitude of different tongues, practicing different religions and customs, and celebrating a rich and eclectic history" (2001b, ¶ 4). Victorious over Italy at the Battle of Adwa, Ethiopia established itself as the first African nation to defeat a European colo-

Table 8.1. Bibliography of Books by Jane Kurtz

Children's Picture Books
Kurtz, J. (1994). *Fire on the mountain* (E.B. Lewis, Ill.). New York: Simon & Schuster.
Kurtz, J. (1995). *Pulling the lion's tail* (F. Cooper, Ill.). New York: Simon & Schuster.
Kurtz, J. (1997). *Only a pigeon* (E.B. Lewis, Ill.). New York: Simon & Schuster.
Kurtz, J. (1997). *Trouble* (D. Bernhard, Ill.). San Diego, CA: Gulliver.
Kurtz, J. (2000). *Faraway home* (E.B. Lewis, Ill.). New York: Gulliver.
Kurtz, J. (2002). *Water hole waiting* (L. Christiansen, Ill.). New York: Greenwillow Books.

Nonfiction
Kurtz, J. (1991). *Ethiopia: The roof of Africa*. New York: Dillon Press.

Novels
Kurtz, J. (1998). *The storyteller's beads*. San Diego, CA: Gulliver.
Kurtz, J. (1999). *I'm sorry, Almira Ann* (S. Havice, Ill.). New York: Henry Holt.
Kurtz, J. (2001). *Jakarta missing*. New York: Greenwillow.
Kurtz, J. (2003). *Bicycle madness* (B. Peck, Ill.). New York: Henry Holt.
Kurtz, J. (2003). *Saba: Under the hyena's foot* (J.P. Tibbles, Ill.). Middleton, WI: Pleasant.
Kurtz, J. (2004). *The feverbird's claw*. New York: Greenwillow.

Anthology of Short Stories and Poems
Kurtz, J. (Ed.). (2004). *Memories of sun: Stories of Africa and America*. New York: Greenwillow.

Professional Books
Buzzeo, T., & Kurtz, J. (1999). *Terrific connections with authors, illustrators, and storytellers: Real space and virtual links*. Englewood, CO: Libraries Unlimited.
Buzzeo, T., & Kurtz, J. (2002). *35 best books for teaching U.S. regions*. New York: Scholastic.
Kurtz, J. (1999). *The American Southwest resource book, Vol. 1: The people and culture*. New York: Eakin Press.

nial power. In 1974, after a period of extended conflict with neighboring nation Eritrea and severe famine, a coup d'état led by Lieutenant Colonel Mengistu Haile Mariam overtook Ethiopia's Emperor Haile Selaise I (who had reigned since 1930) and reoriented the government and national economy from capitalism to Marxism. "During the 17 years of the military controlled government, the economy deeply worsened, while civil unrest grew beyond the control of the military" (Embassy of Ethiopia, 2001b, ¶ 8). This led to an uprising of the Ethiopian citizenry to form the Ethiopian Peoples' Revolutionary Democratic Front (EPRDF). The EPRDF toppled the communist dictators, and between 1991 and 1995 formed a transitional government leading to a new constitution, bicameral legislature, judicial system, and guarantee of "equal rights and freedom of expression to all Ethiopian citizens" (¶ 9). In May 1995, Ethiopia's first free and democratic elections resulted in the election of a Prime Minister, Meles Zenawi, and a President, Negasso Gidada. It is within this modern democratic context that the stories of Jane Kurtz are told.

Jakarta Missing (2001) by Jane Kurtz and *Memories of Sun: Stories of Africa and America* (2004) edited by Jane Kurtz

About the Author/Editor

Imagine a childhood without television, radios, or movies but instead a childhood of climbing mountains, wading in rivers, and making up and dramatizing stories for days at a time. This is the childhood of Jane Kurtz, who moved to Ethiopia as a 2-year-old because her parents worked for the Presbyterian church in that country (DownHomeBooks, 2003). When she was 4, she moved to a rural area near the small village of Maji, located in the southwest corner of Ethiopia. She and her sisters were the only white children as well as the only children who spoke English in that whole region (DownHomeBooks, 2003, ¶ 13). Because classes in the school their parents helped with were taught only in Amharic, then the official language of Ethiopia, Jane and her siblings were homeschooled by their mother.

Jane thought when she returned to the United States for a visit at age 7 that she would have only comfortable feelings of belonging. To her surprise, she felt even more like an outsider in the United States than she had in Ethiopia (DownHomeBooks, 2003). Her family returned to Ethiopia, and in fourth grade, Jane went to a boarding school in Addis Ababa, where instruction was in English. With the exception of one other visit to the United States, Jane remained in Ethiopia until she returned to attend college in Illinois, USA. There, she used her grandmother's Des Moines, Iowa, address in the student directory so she would not have to answer questions about Ethiopia. She was determined to learn what it meant to be an American (DownHomeBooks, 2003).

Since college, Jane has lived in southern Illinois, Colorado, North Dakota, and Kansas in the United States. Beginning with her college years, and until she was in her late 30s, Jane was convinced that there was no way for her to share her childhood with people in the United States, no way to talk about it, to help Americans understand what it was like because her experiences growing up in various African countries were so distinctly different. Jane says perhaps it was the extremely cold winters of North Dakota that prompted reveries of her younger years, of the flowers, sun, fog, and mountains of her youth. She missed the feeling that overtakes her now each time she visits Ethiopia. As she states in an interview with DownHomeBooks, "Now when I visit Ethiopia, I have the instant sensation of warmth and comfort. All the sights, sounds, smells, tastes and textures shout, 'You are here; you are home'" (DownHomeBooks, 2003, ¶ 5).

Summary (*Jakarta Missing*)

Jakarta Missing (2001) is a novel of 12-year-old Dakar, her 16-year-old sister Jakarta, and their parents, who vowed "not to say no to any adventure" (Kurtz, pp. 50–51). As the novel begins, Dakar is living in North Dakota, USA, with her parents, after having lived in various countries in Africa since she was born. Her mother had yearned to return to the United States, the country she knew as a child, and her father acquiesced although it was difficult for him, being an activist for social justice and in continual need to live out his beliefs. Dakar's sister had been allowed to stay in Kenya until there is a bombing in the town of her school, and then she is immediately sent to the States, much to her displeasure. Ironically it is Jakarta who seems to adjust more quickly to life in Cottonwood, North Dakota, perhaps because she makes the basketball team. Her teammates quickly become her friends when they realize what talent she has, and that she uses her talent to make them all perform better—Jakarta is the ultimate team player. Dakar has only one friend, Melanie, and being brave enough to do things even with her is a stretch for Dakar, who misses the land of her childhood. When their mom goes to visit her Aunt Lily and their father goes on a relief trip to Guatemala without telling his wife, the girls are on their own. When their mom finds out, she returns home, with Aunt Lily accompanying her. Together once again, the family realizes it needs some resolution to the Africa–America dilemma. Who wants to stay in the United States? Who wants to return to Africa?

Summary (*Memories of Sun: Stories of Africa and America*)

Memories of Sun: Stories of Africa and America (2004) is a collection of short stories and several poems, edited by Kurtz, that explores the feeling of displacement and the search for where to call "home." The stories and poems are placed into one of three sections: Africa, Americans in Africa, or Africans in America. Table 8.2 offers a brief summary of each of the 15 works in *Memories of the Sun: Stories of Africa and America* along with their title, author, and section.

Making Connections

The Making Connections questions for this chapter are, by far, the most extensive in the book because they are designed to address each of the 15 stories and poems that make up Kurtz's edited collection *Memories of Sun: Stories of Africa and America* (2004) as well as her novel *Jakarta Missing* (2001). As a unique feature of this chapter, the text-to-self, text-to-text, and text-to-world connections (Keene & Zimmermann, 1997) in this section each correlate with a quote

Table 8.2. Summary of Kurtz's Edited Anthology of Short Stories and Poetry

Africa

"Bagamoya" by Nikki Grimes describes what is special about the Tanzanian town of that name in a poem that captures the actual, as well as the spiritual, connections to place.

"Ella's Dunes" by Elana Bregin relates 14-year-old Annette's two-week sojourn with her father so that her mother can go on a trip with her boyfriend. Annette, who has not seen her father since she was 6, is unhappy at the prospect, and arriving in Magliesberg at the Bushman Farm in South Africa does not make her any happier because she believes the Bushmen are being exploited by her father. His explanation helps a bit, but it is through becoming friends with Ella that Annette understands the truth of the Bushmen's survival in a modern world. Even more importantly, with Ella and her people, Annette understands what it feels like to belong.

"Scenes in a Roman Theater" by Elsa Marston features Hedi, a young boy who sells hats to tourists in a Roman theater in Tunisia to help support his family. There, he meets an artist who paints so that her husband can sell her paintings, her artistic expression trapped in his financial expectations about her art. Deciding to protect the artist from tourists' questions and pushy vendors, Hedi gets to know her and realizes that being an artist is something he would like to explore.

"October Sunrise" by Monica Arac de Nyeko is the story of a 14-year-old girl, Auma Adoch, who does not understand why she lives with her grandmother instead of her parents. When the mother unexpectedly brings Auma home, her husband is furious and takes out his fury on Auma. Still confused, Auma finally hears from her sister that the reason is that Auma is not his child. Grandma Esteri arrives soon after to take "her child" home in the Agora Hills at the border of Sudan and Uganda.

"Kamau's Finish" by Muthoni Muchemi features 11-year-old Kamau, who yearns for his father's approval, especially when he runs the 800-meter race on Sports Day at school in Nairobi. As he nears the finish line, he is tied for first, and then he trips. Planning to pretend his leg is broken to defer the shame in not winning, he hears the crowd chanting his name and his father's voice in particular, "Run, son! Get up and run!" Kamau finishes the race, knowing his father is pleased because "effort is what matters" and "problems help us grow" (p. 78).

Americans in Africa

"Into the Maghreb," a poem by Lindsey Clark, opens the second section. The narrative poem recounts a daughter's visit to her mother's homeland of Morocco. When she returns, she realizes that she now knows a country that is "no longer far away / but part of me" (p. 93).

"Our Song" by Angela Johnson reveals how the song 9-year-old Josie's great-great grandmother Ole Ma has sung to Josie all her life brings her comfort and connects her to her grandparents' homeland of Senegal. When Josie's family accompanies Ole Ma on a visit to her village, Josie hears the song sung in English for the first time and finds a kinship between this life and her own.

"The Homecoming" by Maretha Maartens is about the return of Lincoln's father to his native South Africa after he has lived in America for 15 years. Lincoln, who is now attending Afrikaan's Senior Primary school, is finding the adjustment quite a challenge, but his friend Manfred eases it, inviting him to his home. There, Lincoln meets Manfred's

(continued)

Table 8.2. Summary of Kurtz's Edited Anthology of Short Stories and Poetry (continued)

grandfather, who eventually asks him the pivotal question: "Are you glad [your father brought you home to his country]?" Lincoln answers, "Yes, I'm glad we came."

"What I Did on My Summer Safari" by Stephanie Stuve-Bodeen is a humorous story of one family's adventures. As the daughter of an American diplomat, Sarah receives a safari through Ruaha in central Tanzania as her sixth-grade graduation present. Immersed in the text are Sarah's "Safari Tips" such as "Number One: There are no rest areas in Tanzania" (p. 139), but through appreciation of the nighttime calls of the lions to one another, Sarah finds the beauty of Africa.

"Her Mother's Monkey" by Amy Bronwen Zemser is about a mother's attachment to the monkey her English-teacher-turned-amateur-veterinarian husband decides to nurse back to health in Liberia. Despite her initial and ongoing protests, she comes to love the little creature and can hardly bear to leave it when the school term ends.

Africans in America

"an african american" is a poem by Meri Nana-Ama Danquah that proudly states the lineage and blessings of the narrator of the poem. Her conclusion? "i am / in the truest sense of the word / an african American" (p. 174).

"My Brother's Heart" by Mawi Asgedom recounts a father's story of how small lies or instances of thievery can grow to become habits of life. After escaping Ethiopia to the Sudan and finally America, Tewolde and his younger brother steal a parking meter—and remember both their father's story and his admonition to treat all strangers as angels sent from heaven to "test the goodness inside us" (p. 186). Years later, Tewolde cares for a stranger, his little brother a witness to both of their developing hearts.

"Flimflam" by Jane Kurtz highlights the ongoing turmoil between Eritrea and Ethiopia through the story of a young girl, Loly, who lives with her grandmother in the United States because her parents were killed in the war. Loly accuses her best friend, the narrator, of being "an ugly American.... You Americans treat my people like bugs." The narrator, never named, is unwilling to accept that Loly, so caught up in understanding her people's troubles, will not attend an important concert with her, one that will positively affect their social standing at school. The narrator responds with "Go back to Africa, if that's all you can think about" and then, in the last sentence, understands why Loly can not enjoy herself at a concert when people in her country are dying.

"Soldiers of the Stone" by Uko Bendi Udo is an intense story of territorialism. At 15, Kulaja was a soldier in Sierra Leone's civil war. Now he is in Los Angeles, California, USA, with Abu, six years his senior. When a Mexican youth makes his tag by spray painting Abu's house, Kulaja wants the Mexican to be held accountable and so Kulaja, who has killed before during his time as a soldier, almost kills again—but killing over something so minor as spraypainting would make him a soldier of the stone, someone who fights and kills for vain or senseless causes. A conversation with the "Angel of Death," a pseudonym for the Mexican youth Marco, enables Kulaja to turn away from his previous life, determined never to be a soldier of the stone again.

"Lying Down With the Lion" by Sonia Levitin is teenager Ajang's story of learning what America is like after a childhood in the Sudan. His neighbor Terry invites him to dinner, but Ajang does not understand why since they do not have a daughter of marriageable age, nor does Terry seem like he needs help. At dinner, he tells a story that, through metaphor, enables Terry's father to give Terry permission, finally, to crew on his uncle's fishing boat for the summer. Like the father in Ajang's tale, Terry's father is able to "lie down with the lion" and allow his son to pursue his dream.

or allusion from one of the literary texts followed by a prompt. Figure 8.1 shows a sample journal response to a text-to-self question for this Novel Guide, created by university student Holly Willis.

Figure 8.1. Student Journal Response to a Making Connections Text-to-Self Question

Text-to-Self: "Tell a story, as Ajang does, of a time your parents allowed or did not allow you to do something that you felt was important to whom you were becoming."

When two friends and I were asked to perform at the halftime show of the Citrus Bowl, I was worried my parents weren't going to let me go. Even though we would have a strict schedule of practice and meetings, we wouldn't have a full-time chaperone. Luckily, my parents let me go! I had a great time hanging out with my friends and being on my own. One of my friends, Nicole, turned out to be the leader of the three of us. I was the jokester making everyone laugh when practice was delayed because of rain. My other friend, Kylee, stepped into the role of the mediator. We did some pretty amazing things, like going to Sea World and Disney World, and the best part was that we were on our own. We never split up and never strayed far from our group, but we all gained a sense of independence that we had never had before. That trip not only solidified our friendships but also gave us a new perspective on ourselves, our capabilities, and our limitations.

Making Connections Questions for *Jakarta Missing* (2001) and *Memories of Sun* (2004)

	Literature	Quote/Allusion	Prompt
Text-to-Self	"Bagamoya" by Nikki Grimes	"...and calling my name" (p. 11).	The town of Bagamoya is forever captured in Nikki Grimes's memory. What place is forever captured in your memory and why?
	"Ella's Dunes" by Elana Bregin	"I'd noticed before the way she always said we, seldom I. As if the group all shared the same thoughts, as if one heart drove them" (p. 31).	Belonging is critically important to Annette. Tell of a time when you felt like the outsider and when the feeling changed.
	"October Sunrise" by Monica Arac de Nyeko	"'I have come to take my child'" (p. 73).	"October Sunrise" captures a pivotal day in Auma Adoch's life. Discuss a pivotal day from your life and name it according to a month and sunset or sunrise.

Text-to-Self	"Our Song" by Angela Johnson	"I like my whole family more, and I don't even know why. Daddy says it's because I've made room for more family and I've got heart space now" (p. 104).	If your family had a song, what would it be and why?
	"Her Mother's Monkey" by Amy Bronwen Zemser	"She couldn't have come with us to say good-bye for all the diamonds in the Ivory Coast" (p. 164).	Tell about a pet that is special to you. What adventure would you like to have with your pet?
	"an african american" by Meri Nana-Ama Danquah	"open your ears / my children / and listen to this griot / talk of history / being made / i wanna tell you this story / of my life" (p. 172).	If you were to write a poem about yourself and your desires, what would you make sure to include?
	"Lying Down With the Lion" by Sonia Levitin	"a story is a story and a good listener is always a friend" (p. 238).	Tell a story, as Ajang does, of a time your parents allowed or did not allow you to do something that you felt was important to whom you were becoming.
	Jakarta Missing by Jane Kurtz	"True stories of mysterious and unexplained things I know about personally," which begins on page 54.	Create a list of "mysterious and unexplained things" and come up with action plans to see if any are solvable or if research could at least shed some light on the subjects.
	Jakarta Missing by Jane Kurtz	Dakar says she has an "invisible cloak" (p. 22).	Did you ever feel like you had or wish you had an "invisible cloak"? Do you think that would be desirable or not? Explain.
Text-to-Text	"Scenes in a Roman Theater" by Elsa Marston	"'I suppose a person can feel locked up in almost any place,' she said quietly, 'even one of sheer beauty'" (p. 52).	If you were going to create a variation of this story using the "Scenes in a ____" structure, where would your story take place and why?

Text-to-Text (continued)	"Kamau's Finish" by Muthoni Muchemi	"'Run, son! Get up and run!'" (p. 84)	Kamau's father was proud of his son, even if he wasn't first in the race. What other stories have you read in which winning was not the primary goal, even though competition was involved?
	"Into the Maghreb" by Lindsey Clark	"And I know a country no longer far away but part of me" (p. 93).	If you were to visit the country of your ancestors, where would it be? Visit it or research it, find connections and then write about it, just as the author of this poem does.
	Jakarta Missing by Jane Kurtz	Share Charles Kingsley's *The Water-Babies* (1997) first published in England in 1863. It is the story of a boy who discovers a world under the waves, the land of the Water Babies.	Do you think Dakar and Jakarta might have heard or read this story as children? Do you think it might have influenced Dakar and Jakarta's play with "water babies"? Why or why not?
	Jakarta Missing by Jane Kurtz	Read aloud Geraldine McCaughrean's 2004 retelling (written for those in grades 5 through 9) of Homer's *Odysseus*.	Why does Kurtz use Odysseus as a point of comparison for Dakar? Discuss what Kurtz's purpose for this might be.
	Jakarta Missing by Jane Kurtz	Numerous allusions are made to Cleopatra in the novel.	Why does Cleopatra make numerous "appearances" in *Jakarta Missing*? What might Kurtz's purpose for this be?
Text-to-World	"The Homecoming" by Maretha Martens	"He had to laugh at himself. *Flippit* seemed to be one of the most frequently used words on South African school grounds. He was picking up words without even realizing it" (p. 108).	What helpful information would you give to a newcomer to South Africa? Create a pamphlet detailing this information.

Text-to-World (continued)	"What I Did on My Summer Safari" by Stephen Stuve-Boden	"My dad insisted it would be a crash course in the culture and landscape of the country we'd called home for almost a year" (p. 138).	What tips would you give a traveler about to go on a safari? Make a "top ten" list.
	"My Brother's Heart" by Mawi Asgedom	"For we knew that the exchange of gifts blesses the giver even more than the receiver" (p. 184).	What are varying views of gifts and blessings in the world? Interview as many people as you can find from around the world and record their answers.
	"Flimflam" by Jane Kurtz	"I'm sorry, but you can just donate your suffering.... You Americans treat my people like bugs. But we kneel to no one" (p. 200).	How might you go about relieving suffering for people in various countries? Design an action plan and then implement it.
	"Soldiers of the Stone" by Uko Bendi Udo	"He was not a soldier of the stone...those that die fighting for vain causes" (pp. 224–225).	What are some things people across the globe believe are worth dying for? Survey texts of various kinds and talk with as many people as possible to create a record of their opinions.

Critical Exploration of Themes

This section addresses two vitally important themes in Kurtz's writing that focus on the similarities and differences between life in various African countries and the United States. Careful consideration of any of Kurtz's writings will reveal that concepts of home vary greatly, while sharing underlying factors of friends, familiarity, and family. Kurtz's work further highlights that as vast as the distance is between Africa and the United States, people share values, feelings, and experiences that make the human experience somewhat universal. These are the key ideas discussed in more detail in the section that follows.

Concepts of Home Vary Greatly

Throughout her writing, Jane Kurtz deals with the concept of home. As evidenced by sisters Jakarta and Dakar in *Jakarta Missing* (2001), even children raised by the same parents can have quite different feelings about where they want to live, what they value, and where they feel most comfortable. Kurtz also shows the conflict that can result when individual family members disagree about where home is. For instance, while Jakarta wants to be American and stay in North Dakota, Dakar misses Ethiopia and Kenya, the land of her childhood, even though a bombing of a school in the town makes it unsafe. Throughout *Jakarta Missing*, the reader is able to identify with the differing characters' perspectives, including those of the parents. Their mother wants to return to the United States, the country she knew as a child, and to be close to her relatives. Their father agrees to the move, but with hesitation because he finds his conviction of working toward social justice more needed in Ethiopia and Kenya than in the United States.

As readers analyze what Jakarta, Dakar, and their parents value, the concept of home becomes linked with friends, familiarity, and family. For example, part of Dakar's unhappiness stems from the fact that she has only one friend, Melanie. But Dakar also misses the landscape of Kenya that she knew and loved. Jakarta herself, while initially not wanting to leave Kenya, is the most adaptable, seeing home as where one is at any given moment. When she makes the basketball team in North Dakota, she settles in and enjoys the camaraderie of her teammates, who praise her skill on the court.

Kurtz's edited collection of short stories and poems *Memories of Sun: Stories of Africa and America* (2004) also explores the feeling of displacement and the search for where to call home. What is particularly unique about this collection is that it covers not only Ethiopia, Kenya, and North Dakota, but also other parts of the African continent and the United States. The collection, organized in three parts (Africa, Americans in Africa, and Africans in America) highlights concepts of home in Tanzania, South Africa, Tunisia, Sudan, Uganda, Kenya, Morocco, Liberia, Ethiopia, and Eritrea, as well as Los Angeles, California, USA. The summary of the 15 short stories and poems (see Table 8.2) will give additional insight into how the concept of home emerges in Kurtz's edited work.

By Nature of Shared Values, Feelings, and Experiences, People Connect and Communicate Across Continents

The heart of Kurtz's writing makes the world seem smaller, friendlier, and more connected. While some students might think of moving to Ethiopia or Kenya as undesirable, Kurtz's own experiences, embedded richly into *Jakarta Missing* (2001), paint a different picture: one of a beautiful country that sisters Jakarta and Dakar miss while in the United States. The love of the land and the friends in other countries shines through *Jakarta Missing* and the same appears throughout *Memories of Sun: Stories of Africa and America* (2004). Additionally, Kurtz's edited collection of short stories and poems lets readers know that whether they live in Africa or the United States, they share values, feelings, and experiences with people across continents. For instance, favorite memories come through "Bagamoya" by Nikki Grimes, a sense of belonging is captured in "Ella's Dunes" by Elana Bregin, a pivotal life moment is the subject of "October Sunrise" by Monica Arac de Nyeko, family stories are prized in "Our Song" by Angela Johnson, and the value of pets and individual identity come through "Her Mother's Monkey" by Amy Bronwen Zemser and "an african american" by Meri Nana-Ama Danquah. The idea of children becoming independent of their parents is at the center of "Lying Down With the Lion" by Sonia Levitin, and a child's desire to make his father proud is the universal idea present in "Kamua's Finish" by Muthoni Muchemi. Family celebrations, the ability to adapt, the desire to seek adventure, a value of serving others, and what it means to cope with pain and suffering are other common experiences captured throughout the three sections of Kurtz's edited collection of stories and poems, *Memories of Sun*. Due to the universal nature of the values, feelings, and experiences reflected in these works, the vast distance between Africa and the United States suddenly seems smaller, and the idea of global connectedness becomes so much larger.

Teacher Talk

To assist students in becoming more proficient readers who gain a deeper understanding of the text, the teacher must "draw on instructional activities prior to reading, during reading, and following reading" (Ryder & Graves, 2003, p. 108). As such, the questioning strategy for this unit organizes questions for use before, during, and after reading for Kurtz's novel *Jakarta Missing* (2001) and her edited collection of stories and poems representing various aspects of life and travel in Africa and America, *Memories of Sun* (2004). Teachers and students can readily adapt the questions to form the basis for much more extensive creative writing, research, and visual projects.

Using Before-, During-, and After-Reading Questions for Kurtz's Novels

	Kurtz's *Memories of Sun: Stories of Africa and America* (2004)	Kurtz's *Jakarta Missing* (2001)
Before Reading	What do you know about Africa? What do you want to know about Africa? Why do you think this collection of poems and stories is called *Memories of Sun*?	What is your concept of "home"? What feelings do you associate with home? The book jacket for *Jakarta Missing* reads, "My whole life has been shaped by that feeling of never

Before Reading (continued)	In the Introduction, Kurtz quotes Dr. Spencer Wells as saying, "We are all African under the skin" (p. 1). What do you think that means? Preview the three sections of the book: Africa, Americans in Africa, and Africans in America. What section do you think will be the most challenging to read and why?	being able to go home again." What do you think that means, and can you relate to that? The book jacket also states, "Luckily for me, my writing can transport me anyplace in the world." Does writing work that way for you? Does reading work that way for you? Why do you think that statement is included on the book jacket? What do you know about Egypt, Ethiopia, Kenya, and Senegal, and which can you locate on a map?
During Reading	What words were new to you while reading? What do you think they mean? What did you learn about the words when you looked them up? Where does each story take place, what characteristics of each place stand out to you, and why? What animals are mentioned in the stories? If you had to put them into categories of pets, possible pets, and impossible pets, which animals would go in which category and why? What have you learned about the various countries and peoples of Africa in your reading?	What words did Dakar find to be interesting? (e.g., "chiding," p. 31). What words did you find interesting while reading? Dakar's dad shares various "Words for Living" (see examples below). What makes these fitting for him, based on what you learned about him in your reading? • "It's a poor life in which there is no fear" (p. 3). • "Don't mope, do something. Big problems require big solutions" (p. 13). • "Meet people where they are. Just be quiet and listen to what people have to tell you about their lives" (p. 71). • "You are the hero of your own life" (p. 169). • "I'd rather encourage mending and building in my children than crushing and winning" (p. 240).
After Reading	What questions remain for you after reading Kurtz's collection of poems and stories? What selection was your favorite and why? If you could write a letter to one of the authors represented in Kurtz's book, which one would you choose and what would you say?	What "Words for Living" do you think the cook and Lily would offer if speaking to your class? In what ways do you think Mr. Johnson was right in telling his students, "You are the engineers of the world's future" (p. 65)? Do you feel that applies to you and your classmates? Would you be more like Jakarta or Dakar in terms of your response to the culture shock both experienced upon their return from Kenya? If Dakar were to travel to a new country, where do you think she might go and why?

Cross-Curricular Activities

The Cross-Curricular Activities for this chapter engage students in research to learn more about Ethiopia and compare life there with life in the United States. The research activity begins with a look at some of Kurtz's children's picture books and then expands on students' own questions about Ethiopia. The comparison activity involves charting specific aspects of life in Africa and the United States as depicted in Kurtz's *Jakarta Missing* (2001) and *Memories of Sun: Stories of Africa and America* (2004).

Student-Directed Inquiry Into Ethiopia

To open this activity, have students read aloud one or more of Jane Kurtz's picture books of Ethiopia (see the picture book section in Table 8.1). This makes for a wonderful introduction to the country, which many students may not even be able to locate on a map of the continent of Africa.

Once students have been engaged in at least one of these richly authentic stories, ask them what they want to know about the country. Write these questions on chart paper and then ask students to sort themselves into research groups, each group tackling a different question. Provide needed time to research and then ask each group to present their information. One particularly helpful resource is Kurtz's own nonfiction text about Ethiopia, part of the Discovering Our Heritage Series, *Ethiopia: The Roof of Africa* (1991). The book provides extensive information about the country, written with an insider's perspective and heart. Students will also find the websites in Table 8.3 to be particularly helpful.

Comparing Life in Ethiopia to Life in the United States

Kurtz's novel, *Jakarta Missing* (2001), and her edited collection of poems and short stories, *Memories of Sun* (2004), richly characterize various aspects of life in both Ethiopia and the United States. This cross-curricular activity is designed to help students focus on the ways in which life in Africa and life in the United States are alike and different. As students read the two books featured in this chapter, they should complete the comparison chart in Table 8.4. To promote active readership, the teacher should also ask students to note chapters in *Jakarta Missing* or titles of poems and stories from *Memories of Sun* in which specific examples appear. While the comparison chart depicted in Table 8.4 is quite simple, teachers can easily expand this activity to include quotes from the text and supporting pictures or illustrations. Such visual depictions effectively signify the layering, texture, and richness of Kurtz's cross-continental stories.

Table 8.3. List of Websites for Researching Ethiopia

The CIA World Factbook: Ethiopia
www.cia.gov/cia/publications/factbook/geos/et.html
Sponsored by the Central Intelligence Agency of the United States, this site provides an introduction to Ethiopia, plus geography, people, government, economy, communication, transportation, military, and transnational issues.

Embassy of Ethiopia
www.ethiopianembassy.org/index.shtml
This site gives up-to-date information about life in Ethiopia as well as information through "Country Profile," "Business/Economy," "Government/Politics," and "Travel and Culture" tabs. Information about "Consular/Visa" issues is also provided. "Links" at the top of the page provides even more detailed information about specific agencies and companies in Ethiopia.

African Studies Center, University of Pennsylvania: Ethiopia Page
www.sas.upenn.edu/African_Studies/Country_Specific/Ethiopia.html
This website provides extensive information and links on a myriad of topics about Ethiopia.

The Library of Congress
www.loc.gov/index.html
This site, a research center for the Library of Congress, offers extensive information about Ethiopia. After accessing the main webpage, type "Ethiopia" in the Search box to see a summary of related articles.

Table 8.4. Comparison Chart of Life in Ethiopia and Life in the United States

	Africa	America
Safety of small town versus big city		
Favorite sport		
Kind of school		
Chickens		
Fruit		
Pets		
Telephone		
Music		
Adventures		
Trees		
Fences		
Rain		
Cleaning		
Shopping		

Making-A-Difference Project: Supporting Literacy in Ethiopia

Children's librarian and native of Ethiopia Yohannes Gebregeoris organized a nonprofit organization, the Ethiopian Books for Children and Educational Foundation (EBCEF) in 1998 (Goering, 2006a). As he worked on the project, he contacted Jane Kurtz, knowing she had grown up in Ethiopia and written books for children set in that country (Goering, 2006a). As Gebregeoris and Kurtz collaborated, their idea was not just to collect books but to open a free public library for the children in Addis Ababa, a city of more than 3 million people. Through a grant from the EBCEF and a significant amount of money raised by members of Kurtz's church in Grand Forks, North Dakota, USA, the library opened in Addis Ababa on April 7, 2003, housing approximately 15,000 books with seating for 126 children. In its first year, the library staff, trained by Yohannes, recorded 40,000 visits from children who had never before had access to books (Goering, 2006a).

The EBCEF also published *Silly Mammo* (2002), a traditional Ethiopian folk tale retold by Yohannes Gebregeoris. The story is written in both English and Amharic, and the profits from the book help support the center. In 2005, EBCEF received a grant from the Canadian Council and Room to Read to produce a new printing of *Silly Mammo* that will be given away or sold at cost to schools and children in Ethiopia (Goering, 2006b). A second local language book was scheduled for production in 2006, and more will follow in Ethiopia's various languages. EBCEF has also established the Golden Kuraz award for excellence in children's books published in Ethiopia as one way to encourage authentic Ethiopian literacy materials (Goering, 2006b).

In the "How You Can Help" section (Goering, 2005) of the EBCEF website (www.ethiopiareads.org), Kurtz suggests ways that children, adults, and community organizations, such as Boy or Girl Scout troops, might complete projects to support the center. She hopes that those who read about Ethiopia Reads will be motivated to do something to support the literacy lives of children in Africa by taking on one of these projects, most of which will generate books or money for the emerging libraries. For those people who cannot donate money or complete fundraising projects, she hopes they will at least include information about this effort through articles in their organizations' newspapers or newsletters. For a news article indicating support of the center through book collection, see the teacher-created model by Linda Rice in Figure 8.2.

Through its vibrant transnational connection, the EBCEF provides a way for people of multiple cultures to share their stories—the essence of who they are—and supporting the center makes a difference to both the giver and the re-

Figure 8.2. Teacher-Created Sample News Article to Support Literacy in Ethiopia

CENTRAL MIDDLE SCHOOL

SUPPORTING LITERACY

VOLUME 1, ISSUE 1   SPRING 2007, MISS RICE'S CLASS

KIDS IN ETHIOPIA NEED OUR HELP

Our eighth grade class has been reading books by Jane Kurtz this nine weeks, and we have learned a great deal about Ethiopia, Kenya, and Eritrea. We have also learned that kids in Ethiopia don't have access to books and libraries like we do, and we want to help change that. In 1998 native Ethiopian and children's librarian Johannes Gebregeoris teamed up with Jane Kurtz to start the Ethiopian Books for Children and Educational Foundation (EBCEF). They collected over $30,000, and that enabled them to open a library that had 40,000 visits during its first year, 2003. The center needs our help to keep its doors open and serve the children of Addis Ababa, a city with more than three million people. We hope you enjoy this issue of *Supporting Literacy*. There is a lot of good information that will teach you about authors, countries, and EBCEF. You can even test your own knowledge.

IMPORTANT NOTES:

- *Book collection will take place in Miss Rice's room*
- *New and gently used books for school age kids*
- *Cash donations will help with shipping*
- *Deadline May 1st*

INSIDE THIS ISSUE:

JANE KURTZ: AUTHOR PROFILE	2
WHO IS YOHANNES GEBREGEORIS?	2
HISTORY OF EBCEF	2
SUMMARY OF CLASS PROJECTS	3
TEST YOUR KNOWLEDGE OF ETHIOPIA	4
CONNECTING AFRICA AND AMERICA	5
MAPS AND BIBLIOGRAPHY	6

PLEASE SUPPORT OUR PROJECT

There are two ways that you can help us to support the Ethiopian Books for Children and Educational Foundation. First, we will be collecting books for school age kids. We accept picture books, young adult novels, and even classics. These may be brand new or gently used. While we want to send the kids of Ethiopia lots of books, we also need money because books are heavy, and it will cost a lot to mail the boxes of books across the world. So you can also donate cash for postage. All donations are tax-deductible.

Created by Linda J. Rice

---

ceiver. As Jakarta's father says, "I've ended up with the same compulsion [as my parents]—to make a difference. To leave the world a better place than I found it" (Kurtz, 2001, p. 50), and by supporting the Ethiopian Reads effort through fundraising, students, too, can help make the world a better place.

Conclusion

When I asked Jane Kurtz to autograph my copy of *Jakarta Missing* (2001), she wrote the following inscription: "May your heart always find its home." This sentiment is a perfect reflection of Kurtz's books discussed in this chapter. At the end of *Jakarta Missing*, sisters Jakarta and Dakar each come to their own decision about where home is. It is a contemporary story and one with which increasing numbers of children can relate as more and more children come from other countries to make the United States their new place of residence and, in time, a true home. Whether reading *Jakarta Missing* or the poems and stories from *Memories of Sun* (2004), researching Ethiopia to learn more about the nation's history and culture, comparing life in Africa to life in the United States, or donating funds to support literacy in Ethiopia, students will leave Kurtz's books with greater understanding and connectedness.

REFERENCES

DownHomeBooks. (2003, September). *Author interviews: Jane Kurtz.* Retrieved June 21, 2006, from http://www.downhomebooks.com/kurtz.htm

Embassy of Ethiopia, Washington, D.C. (2001a). *History.* Retrieved June 15, 2006, from http://www.ethiopianembassy.org/history.shtml

Embassy of Ethiopia, Washington, D.C. (2001b). *Population.* Retrieved June 15, 2006, from http://www.ethiopianembassy.org/population.shtml

Goering, R. (2005). *How you can help!* Ethiopian Books for Children and Educational Foundation. Retrieved June 16, 2006, from http://www.ethiopiareads.org/help.htm

Goering, R. (2006a). *History.* Ethiopian Books for Children and Educational Foundation. Retrieved June 16, 2006, from http://www.ethiopiareads.org/history.htm

Goering, R. (2006b). *Ethiopia Reads.* Ethiopian Books for Children and Education Foundation. Retrived February 14, 2007, from http://www.ethiopiareads.org

International Reading Association & National Council of Teachers of English. (1996). *Standards for the English language arts.* Newark, DE; Urbana, IL: Authors.

Keene, E.O., & Zimmermann, S. (1997). *Mosaic of thought: Teaching comprehension in a reader's workshop.* Portsmouth, NH: Heinemann.

Kurtz, J. (2003). *Biographical information: Jane Kurtz.* Retrieved June 16, 2006, from http://www.janekurtz.com/biography.html

National Council for the Social Studies. (1994). *Expectations of excellence: Curriculum standards for social studies.* Silver Spring, MD: Author.

Ryder, R.J., & Graves, M.F. (2003). *Reading and learning in content areas* (3rd ed.) New York: John Wiley & Sons.

LITERATURE CITED

Gebregeoris, Y. (2002). *Silly Mammo = Kilu Mammo: An Ethiopian tale* (B. Belachew, Ill.). Oakland, CA: African Sun Press.

Kingsley, C. (1997). *The water-babies* (J.W. Smith, Ill.). New York: Morrow.

Kurtz, J. (2001). *Jakarta missing.* New York: Greenwillow.

Kurtz, J. (Ed.). (2004). *Memories of the sun: Stories of Africa and America.* New York: Greenwillow.

McCaughrean, G. (2004). *Odysseus.* Chicago: Cricket Books.

PART IV

Novel Guides to Explore the Life and Culture of People in Sub-Saharan Africa

Exploitation Through Child Labor and Animal Poaching in 19th-Century South Africa

Linda J. Rice

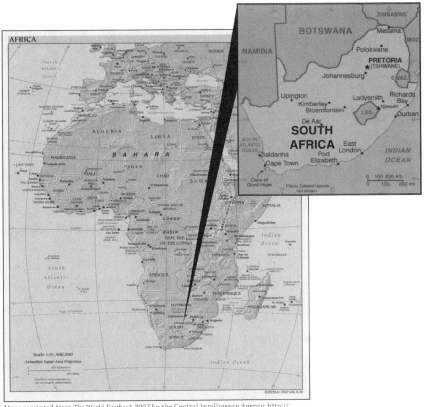

Maps reprinted from *The World Factbook 2007* by the Central Intelligence Agency, http://www.cia.gov/cia/publications/factbook.

Exploring African Life and Literature: Novel Guides to Promote Socially Responsive Learning edited by Jacqueline N. Glasgow and Linda J. Rice. © 2007 by the International Reading Association.

"He had not gone far, when a branch suddenly snapped close by him
in the Forest. He stopped dead, felt the direction of the wind and
waited. There was something in the thickets but he could not make
out if it was a buck or an elephant. He tried to breathe more quietly
but found it difficult.... When the second branch snapped, there was
no doubt left in him—there was an elephant somewhere in the
moonlit thickets east of the road, and he could not make out
whether it was coming nearer him or going away."

—DALENE MATTHEE (1986, P. 304)

S outh African novelist Dalene Matthee is best known for her "forest novels," *Circles in a Forest* (1984) and *Fiela's Child* (1986), popular literature
that highlights the Knysna Forest region and the 19th-century lives of
woodcutters and elephant poachers. *Circles in a Forest* develops man in
the dual roles of predator and kin, as one character is in pursuit of Old Foot for its
ivory tusks while another character seeks to protect Old Foot, the oldest elephant of the forest, and subsequently develops a kind of spiritual relationship
with the animal. Matthee's *Fiela's Child* also involves the reader with racial issues as a colored family raises a white boy, who showed up at their doorstep at the
age of 3, only to have the child taken away when the woman who claims to be
his mother wants him back. While many events of the two novels take place in the
forest, other events span a village, the seacoast, and the Long Kloof farming region, thus showing the diversity of the Knysna region and elements that define
its place in the history and culture of the South African people.

The Cross-Curricular Activities for the novels featured in this chapter involve students in music, creative writing, storyboarding, and research. The
Making-A-Difference Project bridges historical aspects of Matthee's novels with
their contemporary relevance as students research adoption, child labor, or animal poaching and report their findings in the form of a Slideshow
Documentary. The overview on page 189 illustrates how the Novel Guides in this
chapter and their corresponding activities align with standards for the English
language arts (International Reading Association [IRA] & National Council of
Teachers of English [NCTE], 1996) and curriculum standards for the social studies (National Council for the Social Studies [NCSS], 1994).

Social and Historical Context

Today the Knysna Forest is known as a beautiful destination for tourists from
around the world. Part of South Africa's Garden Route that spans the south-

Novels, Activities, and Curricular Standards
for English Language Arts and Social Studies

NOVELS
- *Fiela's Child* (1986) by Dalene Matthee
- *Circles in a Forest* (1984) by Dalene Matthee

CROSS-CURRICULAR ACTIVITIES
- Song Adaptations and Poetry
- Readers Theatre
- Narrative Storyboard

MAKING-A-DIFFERENCE PROJECT
Slideshow Documentary on Adoption, Child Labor, or Animal Poaching

STANDARDS FOR THE ENGLISH LANGUAGE ARTS
#5 Students employ a wide range of strategies as they write and use different writing process elements appropriately to communicate with different audiences for a variety of purposes.

#6 Students apply knowledge of language and media techniques to create, critique, and discuss print and nonprint texts.

#7 Students conduct research on issues and interests by generating ideas and questions, and by posing problems. They gather, evaluate, and synthesize data from a variety of sources (e.g., print and nonprint texts, artifacts, people) to communicate their discoveries in ways that suit their purpose and audience.

Adapted from IRA and NCTE. (1996). *Standards for the English Language Arts*. Newark, DE: International Reading Association; Urbana, IL: National Council of Teachers of English.

CURRICULUM STANDARDS FOR THE SOCIAL STUDIES
#1g Culture: Learners construct reasoned judgments about interracial adoption and animal poaching.

#7h Production, Distribution, & Consumption: Learners apply economic concepts and reasoning when examining the forest industry, elephant poaching, and ostrich farming in Knysna and the Long Kloof.

#10b Civic Ideals & Practices: Learners identify, analyze, interpret, and evaluate sources and examples of citizens' rights and responsibilities in relation to adoption and child labor.

Adapted with the permission of the National Council for the Social Studies (NCSS). For the NCSS standards, see the publication *Expectations of Excellence: Curriculum Standards for Social Studies* (Washington, DC: National Council for the Social Studies, 1994). See also www.socialstudies.org.

western Cape region, the Knysna Forest is known for its natural beauty, old trees, and miles of hiking trails. The area, now extinct of elephants that roamed in the hundreds at the turn of the 19th century, is still home to blue duiker, bushpig, lynx, genet, and bushbuck (iAfrica.com, 2006). Knysna was founded in the early 1800s and within the following hundred years became a financial haven for timber merchants who sold the wood throughout the country (Choice Garden Route Property Group, 2004). The merchants lived apart from the wood-cutters, who were known to be rugged and "fiercely independent" people (Matthee, 1984, back cover). In South Africa, most homes are made of brick covered with stucco, as compared to timber frame homes. Wood is considered to be a valuable commodity in South Africa and in modern times is showcased in fine furniture and collectibles. In the 19th century, the wood was used for furniture, boats, and homes. Trees indigenous to the Knysna Forest include yellowwood, ironwood, white pear, and stinkwood, all of which are considered to be quite valuable (iAfrica.com, 2006).

In addition to the timber, ivory became a treasured commodity, and hunters were known to kill elephants only for the tusks. The Sans were the original inhabitants of the southern Cape, and they considered the elephants to be a "power animal" from which they drew spiritual and religious connections (Patterson, n.d., ¶ 3). In 1908, elephants were declared "royal game," subsequently decimating the elephant population (du Toit, 1998, ¶ 1). It was not until 1978, when the elephant was threatened with extinction and listed as such by the Convention for International Trade of Endangered Species, that a ban was made on the trade of ivory products (Bennett, 1997). Of the estimated 500 elephants that inhabited the Knysna Forest region in 1870, the time setting for Matthee's novels, just 10 remained 100 years later. By 1990, that number was 4, and at the turn of the millennium, there was only 1 survivor (Lovell, 1999; Seymour, 2001).

Although slavery ended in South Africa in 1834, severe limitations were imposed on black and colored families. For instance, as black farmers began to succeed in the marketplace near the end of the 19th century, the white government "intensified legislative suppression" by enacting a law in 1890 that limited "individual black land ownership to ten acres" (Spiro, 1987, ¶ 17). Child labor was also a problem in 19th-century South Africa because in the villages "at least some freed families appeared to have depended on children's immediate economic contribution to the household" (Scully, 1997, p. 98). There were also accounts of settlers on the lookout for child labor. Farmers traveling with their wagons were known to

> pick up children—and always boys—on the pretence of finding them hungry and naked and in a state of destitution and upon producing such children to the Magistrate teach them, perhaps, how to tell their story, or a story, and all this because it has been the practice to indenture such children to the finder unless on advertisement a relative may claim them. (Scully, 1997, p. 130)

The rugged lifestyle of the woodcutters, the presence of child labor, the opportunism of the timber merchants, and the exploitation of the land and the elephants are all apparent in *Fiela's Child* (1986) and *Circles in a Forest* (1984). Matthee's novels convey a passionate concern for racial and economic fairness and environmental protection. Her writing also provides many entry points for those who wish to understand more about the Knysna Forest and the woodcutters, elephants, farmers, ostriches, villagers, and seamen that inhabit it and its surrounding coastal region.

Fiela's Child (1986) and *Circles in a Forest* (1984) by Dalene Matthee

About the Author

A descendent of Scottish novelist Sir Walter Scott, Dalene Matthee (1938–2005) was born Dalene Scott in Riversdale, South Africa. Matthee's novels focus on the forests and foresters of the Knysna region in the southeastern Cape Province. Written in Afrikaans, Matthee's novels have been translated into 14 other languages, and *Circles in a Forest* (1984) and *Fiela's Child* (1986) have also been made into films. Best known for her "forest novels," which are the focus of this chapter, Matthee has been regarded by fellow authors as "one who successfully bridged the gap between quality and popular literature" (Pople, 2005, ¶ 7). The Afrikaanse Taal En Kultuurvereniging (ATKV) is a cultural organization through which Afrikaans culture is "experienced, promoted, enhanced and expanded, so as to make an indispensable contribution in Southern Africa" (ATKV, 2005, ¶ 1). In her lifetime, Matthee won the ATKV Prose Award four times and the South African Institute of Forestry Award twice (Contemporary Africa Database, 2006). She also won the Stab Award, a Swiss literature prize for her "energetic literary work and her passionate interest in nature conservation" (Pople, 2005, ¶ 24). Known as a feminist, an ecologist, an advocate of nonracialism, and a prize-winning author, Matthee invested seven years of research to write her forest novels (Newmarch, 2005). A wife and mother to three daughters, Matthee, who died during the writing of this book (February 2005), has been regarded by the South African people as "one of the most well-loved popular novelists in Afrikaans" noted for getting "the general Afrikaans public [to] read again" (Pople, 2005, ¶ 7).

Summary (*Fiela's Child*)

Fiela's Child (1986), set in the Knysna Forest region of South Africa in the late 19th century, tells the story of Benjamin Komoetie. The novel begins with a scene in which a small boy, the child of Elias and Barta Van Rooyen, disappears from a forest village. Months after the boy's disappearance, bones are found along the banks of a river, and it is assumed that they are the boy's bones, although some believe the bones may be those of a baboon. Next, the reader is introduced to the Komoetie family, which consists of parents Fiela and Selling and their children Kittie, Dawid, Tollie, Emma, and Benjamin. Fiela refers to Benjamin as her "handchild," for he was a child who appeared at their home one day and whom she and Selling had taken in and raised as their own. The family lives in Long Kloof, an open area north of where the story begins. The Komoeties are a loving, hard-working family who are presently trying to breed ostriches. One day census takers arrive and ask Fiela to provide names and birth dates of her children. Fiela prays silently during the census takers' visit that God keep Benjamin away from the house. As she provides the census takers with the birth dates of Kittie, Dawid, Tollie, and Emma, "she glanced at Selling and pretended to read [Benjamin's birth date] straight from the Bible" (Matthee, 1986, p. 27). Then Benjamin walks into the room, and the census takers cannot believe that the Komoeties' youngest child, Benjamin, is a white boy in a colored family. The census takers immediately think of the small boy who went missing on the other side of the mountain nine years earlier. Although Fiela does not believe Benjamin could possibly be that child, for he would have had to cross over the mountain at the age of 3, the men say that it will be a matter for the magistrate to decide.

From this point on, the story alternates chapters that show the lives of the Van Rooyens in the forest, with a particular focus on the father's abusive nature, and the Komoetie family. Benjamin stands before the magistrate and Barta Van Rooyen, who decides that Benjamin is her lost son Lukas. Benjamin is ordered to leave the Komoeties and live with the Van Rooyens. Elias Van Rooyen forces Benjamin to accept the name Lukas by beating him when he fails to respond. Elias is hard on all of his children, making them work long hours cutting beams and hauling wood from the forest and beating them for any disobedience. He is particularly abusive to his daughter, Nina, whom Benjamin/Lukas has developed feelings for, something that confuses him as he is her brother. One subplot involves Nina's travels to the village by the ocean to escape her father and look for work to support herself. Another involves Elias's intensive greed that causes him to seek devious ways to trap and kill elephants for their tusks. Nina and Lukas are heartbroken when an elephant calf dies in a pit Elias forced them to dig to trap a large elephant. In a kind of natural vengeance, elephants later attack Elias for killing their young. Lukas continues to question his identity and at one point forcefully confronts Barta as to whether he is really her son. Initially she lies and says yes, but later, in poor health, she admits that he is not Lukas. Upon realizing this, Benjamin becomes free to have feelings for Nina, and the ending implies that the two will go back to Long Kloof.

Summary (*Circles in a Forest*)

Like *Fiela's Child* (1986), *Circles in a Forest* (1984) is set in the Knysna Forest region of South Africa in the latter half of the 19th century. The novel's central character is Saul Barnard, who has a special kinship with the elephants, in particular one known as Old Foot. Old Foot is currently being pursued by Fred Terblans, a hunter who was called in to shoot the elephant by Saul's brother Jozef. Although Jozef wants Old Foot dead, thinking it was the elephant that killed his son, Fred's primary motive for killing the elephant is to take its ivory tusks. Saul would rather kill Old Foot himself than have the animal face the humiliation of having its ivory tusks removed in death. Saul also desires to protect the forest from opportunistic timber merchants who care little about preserving the forest or being fair to the woodcutters. The title refers to both the instinct of the elephant and the story's structure, which makes frequent shifts from past to present, interweaving rather tragic elements associated with Saul's childhood to include the death of his sister and mother and an incident when Saul saw his father belittled while selling wood. Saul is torn up inside as he is made to chop down trees in the forest and sees his family members involved in hunting elephants. At various points in the novel, Old Foot makes appearances when Saul has faced suffering. For this reason, Saul recognizes that Old Foot has chosen him as his "man-brother," and Saul likewise chooses Old Foot as his "animal-brother" (p. 354). The book comes full circle in the end as Saul spends five days searching for Old Foot but learns that some gold diggers from the village who had gone hunting for ivory one day killed the elephant. Saul cries in agony and feels as though part of the forest died with Old Foot.

Making Connections

Matthee's novels easily engage readers with sympathy for those who face hardship due to poverty, physical abuse, and racial discrimination. The books also help readers to identify with the beauties and hardships of relying on the natural world—forest and animals—for their livelihood. And while both books evoke sorrow for the hunted elephant, both also evoke a kinship with animals for prosperity and friendship, as evidenced by the Komoeties' faith in the ostriches in *Fiela's Child* (1986) and Saul's relationship with Old Foot in *Circles in a Forest* (1984). The questions that follow are designed to help students make connections text-to-self, text-to-text, and text-to-world (Keene & Zimmermann, 1997) between significant aspects of Matthee's novels and their own lives, other texts, and the world around them. Figure 9.1 shows a sample journal response to a text-to-text question for this Novel Guide created by university student Amy Watt.

Figure 9.1. Student Response Journal to a Making Connections Text-to-Text Question

Text-to-Text: "What books have I read or films have I viewed that dealt with interracial relationships?"

Within the past year, I read the novel *The God of Small Things* by Arundhati Roy. This fascinating book dealt with the caste system in India and the hypocrisy behind it. In the novel, the children's mother engages in a relationship with someone who does not have the same status as her. As a result, the two lovers can never be together as they wished they could. This shows how when cultures place restrictions on interracial relationships, hurt and despair are all that follow. A film that also showed interracial dating was *Save the Last Dance*. In this, a white girl from the suburbs moves into the inner city to live with her father. She dates a fellow black student, and instantly there is trouble. Many of their friends shun them, and her black girl friends say that white women are taking away all the good black men. In the end, they win the battle against injustice, but this film does a good job of showing how hard it can be to date interracially in a world that may not be ready for it yet.

Making Connections Questions for *Fiela's Child* (1986) and *Circles in a Forest* (1984)

	Matthee's *Fiela's Child* (1986)	Matthee's *Circles in a Forest* (1984)
Text-to-Self	What do I think of parents raising children of different races? Have I ever seen abuses in child labor? What do I know about ostriches? What do I envision as the benefits and hardships of life as a woodcutter, sailor, and farmer?	When have I seen cruelty to animals? Tell of a time when I or someone I know had a special bond with an animal. Tell of a time an animal protected me. What do I know about elephants? How do I see elephants (friendly, fierce, other)?
Text-to-Text	What books have I read or films have I viewed that dealt with adoption? What books have I read or films have I viewed that dealt with interracial relationships? What books have I read or films have I viewed that conveyed a connection between the judicial system and racism?	What other books have I read or films have I viewed where there was a significant connection between a person and an animal? What other books have I read or films have I viewed that showed tension between siblings followed by reconciliation?
Text-to-World	How serious is the issue of child labor in the world today? How does the timber industry work in South Africa today?	To what extent is animal poaching an issue in the world today? What is being done to protect endangered species?

Critical Exploration of Themes

Both set in the Knysna Forest and its surrounding regions, *Circles in a Forest* (1984) and *Fiela's Child* (1986) depict humans in relation to the environment. For example, the relationship between Saul and Old Foot depicted in *Circles in a Forest* shows man's reliance on animals for protection, but other characters in the book who hunt Old Foot for his ivory tusks show man's exploitation of animals. As depicted in *Fiela's Child*, the resources of the forest make the owners and merchants of the timber industry quite wealthy, while their greed causes them to dole out only modest incomes for the woodcutters. Injustices rooted in abuses of power and racial and economic exploitation are also embedded in Matthee's novels. These ideas are discussed in detail in this section, supported by specific examples from the texts.

Humankind Has a Spiritual Connection With and Reliance on Animals

As evidenced in the character of Saul in *Circles in a Forest* (1984), some people have a special connection with animals. Not only does Saul regard the elephant Old Foot as a living creature whose life is a symbol of the vitality of the forest, but he seeks to protect the animal, even after it kills his nephew. When a hunter, Fred Terblans, is called in to kill Old Foot, Saul decides he would rather shoot the animal himself than have it suffer the indignity of having its tusks removed while its body is left to rot. As it turns out, several gold miners poach Old Foot before Saul can find him, but when Saul finds out, he runs to the dying elephant and chases off any who dare come near it. Saul's presence with Old Foot does come to an end, however, as his friend Maska pulls him away before the other elephants come to mourn. Although Old Foot was the most feared elephant in the forest, he seemed to have a special protective connection with Saul. In some ways it seemed as though Old Foot was more of a father to Saul than his actual father. Old Foot protected Saul when he was sick, showed up and comforted Saul when bad things happened, and respected Saul more than any other person or animal in the novel. Because of the ways in which Old Foot had appeared at various times in Saul's life, Saul believed the elephant had chosen him as his "man-brother," and in kind, Saul chose Old Foot as his "animal-brother."

While the relationship between Saul and Old Foot models a protective relationship and positive connection in *Circles in a Forest* (1984), the connection between man and animal in *Fiela's Child* (1986) is a grim one. Although he could make ends meet by selling beams from the forest, woodcutter Elias Van Rooyen wants more and sees the ivory-tusked elephant as the solution to his financial woe. Elias is intent on hunting and killing an elephant and making a small fortune by selling its ivory tusks to traders in the village. Hunting the elephants becomes a personal mission, almost to the point of obsession for Elias. He even forces Lukas and Nina to dig a hole, where he hopes an elephant will fall. An elephant does fall into the pit; however, it is just a calf with no tusks. The calf is unable to get out of the pit and dies, and from that point on Elias lives in fear, believing the elephants will not forget his scent and have marked him for death. *Circles in a Forest* and *Fiela's Child* reveal much about the nature of elephants, and *Fiela's Child* implies that elephants can even distinguish those, like Lukas and Nina, who were merely forced to dig the pit, from "the hunter," Elias, who made the demand. Although Elias buys a gun for protection, the elephants ultimately do catch up with him and attack him in an apparent act of vengeance, and he nearly dies.

Fiela's Child (1986) also shows how animals can offer a source of hope and prosperity. Woven throughout the Komoeties' story are the ostriches Kicker and Pollie. It is understood that if and when the two finally breed, the Komoetie family will have increased wealth and opportunity. Great care is invested in these animals, and by the end of the book their prosperity parallels that of Benjamin, who has found fulfillment realizing he is free to love Nina, since she is not, after all, his sister, and to return to the Kloof now that Barta Van Rooyen has revealed that he is not, in fact, her son.

Exploitation Comes in Various Forms, Each Involving an Abuse of Power

Land, animals, and people each face exploitation in Matthee's novels. While the government marks some trees for preservation, the greed of the timber merchants causes them to demand larger beams from the woodcutters. As a result, the land is exploited as the forest is robbed of some of its oldest trees. This particularly grieves Saul, the protagonist of *Circles in a Forest* (1984), who views the trees as living creatures. At one point Saul's unwillingness to cut down the trees causes so much arguing between him and his father that his father sends him out of the forest to work for MacDonald, the wood buyer known for taking advantage of the woodcutters. Elephants are equally exploited as greedy poachers, eager only for ivory, relentlessly hunt the animals, cut off their tusks, and leave the rest for dead. Perhaps most tragic of all are the exploitations of people.

In addition to the economic exploitation the timber merchants impose on the woodcutters by not paying them fairly for their work, others abuse based on race. Specifically, the key conflict in *Fiela's Child* exists because the white census takers cannot accept that Benjamin, a white boy, is being raised in a colored family. When the case is referred to the magistrate, he gives the child to the supposed mother, Barta Van Rooyen, who claims he is her Lukas, thought to have been lost nine years earlier when he wandered away from the forest at age 3. It is unclear what Barta's motives were that day before the magistrate, but in chapter 29, she states clearly "I took somebody else's child that day. I only found out when it was too late, after we came home with him. I thought it was my imagination and I pushed it away but it would never stay away for long and now it never goes away.... Our Lukas's bones were picked up along the Gouna River; he got lost and the angels took him" (Matthee, 1986, p. 345). Also in this chapter, Barta reveals that she had been tipped off by one of the court employees as to which child was Benjamin when he was placed in a lineup of children. Barta's choice not to make the truth known years earlier, the court employee's willingness to assist, and the magistrate's low standards for investigating the case all resulted in hurt to the Komoetie family, including Fiela's handchild Benjamin.

Readers conclude that Benjamin's presence in the Komoetie family would never have been questioned if he were colored or if the situation were reversed; that is, there is little doubt that the census takers would have been so deliberate to pursue the case had a colored child been taken in by a white family. The attribution of power to the whites is reiterated throughout *Fiela's Child*. But even though the Van Rooyens are white, they are not exempt from hardship because another abuse highlighted in Matthee's writing is that which stems from the greed of the wealthy. For example, the Van Rooyen family is unable to get ahead financially, despite putting in long days in their forest village and having all of the children work.

Teacher Talk

Like class discussions, Socratic Seminars create a "spirit of joint adventure where students' questions are encouraged and their viewpoints are valued" (Guthrie & Wigfield, 1997, p. 164). The Socratic Seminar is based on Socrates' idea of the dialectic, where he, the scholar, would pose thought-provoking questions to his students. The questions are broad in nature, allowing much room for discussion and debate. Socrates was not there to deliver the answer, but to prompt deeper, reflective thinking and a careful analysis of one's ideas and logic. A key characteristic of the seminar is that once a question has been posed by the teacher/facilitator, he or she backs out and becomes an intentional listener, putting the bulk of the dialogue on the students, though periodically intervening to ask clarifying questions. Desks should be arranged in a circle, symbolic of equal voice, for a Socratic Seminar.

Socratic Seminars consist of three types of questions, and all three types are applied to Matthee's novels. The Opening Questions are designed to connect aspects of the text with the readers' personal experiences. The Opening Question of the Socratic Seminar is the only one all participants are required to answer—because everyone must share something, the teacher/facilitator should offer all three questions upfront and have students choose the one to which they will respond. The Core Questions make up the bulk of the seminar and are linked directly to the text while still allowing much room for differing ideas and interpretations. A good Core Question can easily prompt 10 to 15 minutes of student-owned discussion. The Closing Questions are designed to bridge aspects of the literary text with the students' lives and world. For a more extensive explanation of Socratic Seminars and how to create them consult Rice's *What Was It Like? Teaching History and Culture Through Young Adult Literature* (2006).

Using Socratic Seminar to Explore *Fiela's Child* (1986) and *Circles in a Forest* (1984)

Socratic Seminar

Matthee's *Fiela's Child* (1986)

Opening Questions

1. When was there a time that you have been lost or scared?
2. What incidents of racism have you witnessed?
3. Was there ever a time when your identity (or that of someone you knew) was mistaken? Explain.

Core Questions

1. Why do you believe Fiela is so drawn to protect Benjamin? Is this draw disproportionate to her relationship with her other children? Explain.
2. What do you think of the relationship between Elias and Barta Van Rooyen versus Fiela and Selling Komoetie? (Consider coffee how coffee is used as a symbol.)
3. What role do faith and superstition play in the story?
4. What evidence is there of racial and social class conflict in the book? (Consider the use of the word *master*, ownership of property, and how Fiela prepares Benjamin to meet the magistrate.)
5. What is the role of Nina in the story?
6. What is the view of law represented by the book? (See chapter 13 of the novel.)
7. In what ways is this story one of determination and resignation?

Matthee's *Circles in a Forest* (1984)

Opening Questions

1. When have you seen circles (i.e. cycles, cyclical patterns) in your own life experience?
2. What animals are special to you?
3. Was there ever a time when an animal protected you or someone you knew? Explain?

Core Questions

1. How is social class an issue in this novel?
2. What political aspects play into the novel?
3. To what extent are the circles physical, spiritual, and relational?
4. How does greed drive action in the novel?
5. What life truths appear in the novel?
6. Who and what does Saul seem to value most and why?
7. Did your view of Old Foot change throughout the novel? If so, how?
8. To what extent is this novel a critique of government and materialism?
9. Do you see Kate and Saul's relationship as one based more on similarity or difference and why?

Closing Questions

1. If you could give this novel a different title, what would it be and why?
2. Who would you recommend this book to and why?

Matthee's *Fiela's Child* (1986) (continued)

8. How might the situation with the ostriches (Kicker and Pollie) parallel human aspects of the book? (See chapters 15 and17 of the novel.)

9. What is the role of Petrus Zondagh in the book? Does he emphasize the Komoeties dependence? Is he exercising power or truly other oriented? How do you know?

10. Why, given an opportunity, did Benjamin decide not to go back to Fiela?

11. Elias was mauled by elephants—was this poetic justice? Sweet vengeance? How did you read this scene? What did it make you think or feel?

12. Why do you think Barta waited so long to tell the truth?

Closing Questions

1. What would you like to have happen at the end of the book?

2. Which family—the Van Rooyens or Komoeties—would you rather be a part of and why?

3. In the end, whom do you admire most and why—Fiela, Nina, or Benjamin?

4. If Nina and Benjamin were to marry, would they make good parents? Explain.

Matthee's *Circles in a Forest* (1984) (continued)

3. What questions did you leave this book with?

4. How has the book influenced your view of the relationship between humans and animals or nature?

Cross-Curricular Activities

The Cross-Curricular Activities for this chapter encourage creative connections and responses to Matthee's novels while deepening students' understanding of how conflict, character, theme, and plot are developed in literature. In the first activity, students will rewrite a song or poem of their choosing and relate this to *Circles in a Forest* (1984) or *Fiela's Child* (1986). The second activity also involves creative writing stemming from the text as students compose a Readers Theatre script. The third activity combines visual and written artistry as students create a Narrative Storyboard.

Song Adaptations and Poetry

Most song lyrics, written in line rather than sentence form, offer teachers a way to engage their students with poetry in a nonthreatening way. For this activity, students can either compose an original poem to highlight a theme or retell some aspect of one of Matthee's novels or adapt lyrics of a song they like for the same purpose.

While there is no prescribed length for the poem, students' writing should be sufficiently well developed to capture an experience or convey an emotion in conjunction with the text. Students opting to do the song adaptation should change at least one third of the lyrics and be aware of rhythm and syllable count in order to maintain the feel of the original song. Students should accompany their poem or song adaptation with a written explanation of what they set out to accomplish. Students who adapt a song should include a copy of the original lyrics and, in their adaptation, put their adapted lyrics in bold print.

Excerpts from a song adaptation by university student Gabriel Durham appear in Figure 9.2, accompanied by an excerpt from his essay explaining what song he chose and what parallels he made between the song and *Fiela's Child*.

Figure 9.2. Student's Song Adaptation and Essay for *Fiela's Child* (Matthee, 1986)

Excerpts for Adapted Song Lyrics

Set to "Fear of a Black Planet" by Public
    Enemy

Magistrate, you ain't gotta
Worry 'bout a thing
'Bout **da Komoeties**
Nah she ain't my **color**
(But supposin' **she really is my mother**)

Magistrate, calm **highness self** down, don't
    get mad
I'm not Woodcutter's son
(But supposin' **Fiela** said she loved me)
Would you **believe her**

Thru **the forest and the mountains**
Then **they would ask how I could have
    made it**

But did you know **I'm not Lukas**
Man c'mon now, I don't want **your family**
Stop **cryin'. I'm not the child you lost.**

I'm just a **Ostrich talker**
Sendin' boats into the water
Breakdown **19th century**
Might be best to be **loved**
Or just **safe from an Elias beatdown**

Explanation for Choice of Song

I chose the song "Fear of a Black Planet" by Public Enemy because I wanted to find a song that would exemplify the tensions between whites and blacks. *Fiela's Child* is about a white child that is taken from a black family and placed into a white family and I wanted to select a song that would highlight some sort of tension between people of two different races. I came across the Public Enemy song because I know this rap group to be one of the more controversial rap groups because of their inflammatory lyrics that highlight racial differences. Most of the songs that I found by this group would have worked because they dealt with the racial divide but they contained some rather explicit language and I did not feel that they would be appropriate selections to use in a classroom. The original song highlights aggression toward those who have problems with interracial relationships and seemed like a near perfect fit for describing the situation that Benjamin/Lukas is placed in when the magistrate takes him away from his black family.

Figure 9.3 provides an example of an original poem by university student Byron Keith Greene. The poem highlights Nina's discovery of the dead elephant calf along with the intense resentment she held toward her father, who made her dig the pit. Accompanying Byron's poem is his explanatory paragraph.

Readers Theatre

Readers Theatre does not involve memorizing, props, costumes, or sets, but it does involve students in writing a script for oral performance. The script of the Readers Theatre emerges from the novel itself as students select lines from throughout the text as a way of creating a dialogue (see *A Comprehensive Guide to Readers Theatre* by Alison Black and Anna Stave [2007] for more detailed information on Readers Theatre and using literature to create scripts). Students' scripts should be 1 to 3 pages long and developed to sustain a theme or trace some incident of conflict from the novel. Students should use short lines in order to move the story forward quickly and thus engage the audience when the Readers Theatre is performed. A sample Readers Theatre appears in Figure 9.4,

---

Figure 9.3. Student's Poem for *Fiela's Child* (Matthee, 1986) and Explanation

Cruel Discovery!	Explanation
That is what she found.	The idea I wanted to convey through my
A pit.	poem was what discoveries Nina really
She knew it well,	made once she found the calf in the pit. The
For it was formed with her hands,	poem symbolizes how cruel certain
Though not for its purpose.	discoveries can be. Nina discovers many
No, that was concealed.	things when she finds the elephant calf in
This pit hid many things.	the pit. She discovers the cruelty her pa has
Purpose!	inside himself. She discovers how her
Greed!	innocence could be used against her and
Deceit!	taken away. She discovers the nature of
Innocence!	greed. She discovers how intent and
A lifeless calf lay there.	responsibility are two different things. Nina
Hiding what?	feels betrayed by her father and also feels
Cruel Discovery!	her father has taken away the beauty the
Manner of man is weak.	forest has always held for her. Nina spent
Pa's flesh holds such weakness.	her life discovering the forest; that's what
Can't forgive!	made her happy. The discovery of the calf
Nor will the calf's mother.	seems much crueler because the pit hid far
Hiding its purpose,	more than just a dead animal; Nina is
Both pit and father.	devastated by this discovery. It opens her
Can't forgive!	eyes to a world that is far crueler than a
Won't forget!	whipping with an ox rein.
Cruel Discovery!	

Figure 9.4. Readers Theatre Script for *Fiela's Child* (Matthee, 1986)

Barta:	Elias, don't you have Lukas? (p. 4)
Elias:	What's wrong with you, Barta? Can't you keep an eye on your son? (p. 6)
Malie:	God alone knows where that child is right now, lost in the woods. (p. 9)
Constable:	You must accept that the child could no longer possibly be alive. (p. 9)
Fiela:	A child was crying outside and woke me from my sleep. (p. 22)
Tall One:	Whose child is this? (p. 21)
Fiela:	The boy is mine. (p. 21)
Tall One:	But the child is white. (p. 21)
Fiela:	He is my "hand child." (p. 21)
Short One:	A number of years ago, a child was lost in the forest. (p. 23)
Fiela:	Are you suggesting that a child of three could have made it through the forest, over the mountain, and to my doorstep in the Kloof? This is crazy talk. (p. 24)
Tall One:	We must take the matter to the magistrate. He will decide. (p. 25)
Barta:	Will I recognize my son? It's been so many years. (p. 81)
Elias:	I'm sure the magistrate will give you sufficient time. (p. 81)
Barta:	But Elias, do you think I'll really recognize him after all these years? (p. 83)
Magistrate:	Initially, Lukas, you will find it difficult to be back with your own family, but soon you will feel right at home. (p. 93)
Feila:	I am heartbroken. Here I have waited for hours, and for what? Just to find out that they are not bringing my Benjamin back to the Kloof. (p. 100)
Barta:	Elias, why won't the child talk? (p. 102)
Benjamin/Lukas:	You will see. My mother will come to get me. (p. 121)
Nina:	You're my brother Lukas. (p. 121)
Benjamin/Lukas:	No, I am not your brother. I am Benjamin Komoetie. (p. 121)
Nina:	Well, brown people can't have white children. You are Lukas Van Rooyen, the boy who disappeared. (p. 123)
Fiela:	Here I am still waiting, though they said they would bring Benjamin home on Saturday. (p. 151)
Magistrate:	Lukas is with his rightful parents, Ms. Komoetie. You must accept that this case is closed. (p. 170)
Fiela:	I beg you, please tell me where the child is and who he is with. (p. 172)
Magistrate:	You may not go near the child any more. (p. 172)
Elias:	"I'm your pa! That's who I am! And who are you?" (p. 159)
Benjamin/Lukas:	"Benja—Lukas." (p. 159)
Elias:	"Lukas who?" If you don't get it right, I will beat you again. (p. 159)
Benjamin/Lukas:	"Lukas van Rooyen." (p. 159)
Nina	Lukas, are you ok? (p. 251)
Benjamin/Lukas:	Nina, go home and tell pa I am done with the forest. I won't be coming back. (p. 251)

(continued)

Nina:	You'd better hope he doesn't find out you've run off. (p. 283)
Benjamin/Lukas:	I don't care if he finds out. No matter what, I am not going back. (p. 283)
Nina:	The boy was from Long Kloof, and said he was sent to tell Benjamin that his brother Dawid had died. (p. 287)
Benjamin/Lukas:	Ma, I am here. Please stop crying. (p. 302)
Fiela:	"What difference can it make now?" (p. 305)
Benjamin/ Lukas:	"I feel I don't know who I am." (p. 305)
Fiela:	Your skin is white and ours is brown, but your soul will tell you who you are. (p. 306)
Benjamin/Lukas:	As soon as I came back and stood looking down the road, I knew I was home again. (p. 306)
Barta:	Elias, I swore falsely and took the wrong child. "He is not Lukas." (p. 337)
Benjamin/Lukas:	"From now on I will be known as Benjamin Komoetie. It's not a new name, it's my old name." (p. 349)

Note. All of the lines in this script are paraphrased based on information found on their corresponding page number from *Fiela's Child* (Matthee, 1986) except where lines appear in quotation marks, in which case they are direct quotes from Matthee's novel.

adapted from a script written by university student Stacey Tucker. With the script's lines paraphrased from *Fiela's Child* (1986), the reader will note the script's focus on issues of race, power, and identity.

Narrative Storyboard

Moviemakers use storyboards to plot out the action, voice, and visuals that transform print text into film (Hart, 1999). Creating a storyboard involves students in critical thinking as they consider what matters about the text and how they can convey it. Students can use storyboards as a vehicle for exploring themes, characters, settings, and conflicts. For Matthee's novels, students could choose to create a storyboard based on the scene in the book that moved them most, such as the separation of Benjamin from the Komoeties in *Fiela's Child* (1986) or Old Foot's death in *Circles in a Forest* (1984).

While storyboards can be elaborated to include such elements as timing for each frame, camera angle, music, sound effects, and dialogue (Rice, 2002), the Narrative Storyboard presented here is comparatively simple, including only a visual and corresponding narration. In assigning the storyboard, teachers could ask students to represent a theme from the book or, for more detailed coverage, divide the book by chapters and ask each student to create a storyboard to show the incident from that chapter they believe to be the most important. Students' storyboards should have at least 10 frames, each with a narrative voice-over to accompany the picture. Figure 9.5 shows several frames from a Narrative Storyboard created by university student Christen Kegler in response to *Fiela's Child* (1986).

Figure 9.5. Excerpts From Student's Narrative Storyboard for *Fiela's Child* (Matthee, 1986)

Sketch 1 of 10

It was early one morning with the night mist still lingering on in the rise of the new sun. When Fiela opened her door she saw a small child standing there. Fiela took him in calling him her "hand child," Benjamin. Fiela loved him from the moment she saw him and decided to raise him as one of her own.

Sketch 2 of 10

The magistrate wanted to see Benjamin and to give Barta a chance to see if it was her son. Little did Benjamin or Fiela know that it would be the last time they saw each other for seven years.

Sketch 4 of 10

Benjamin tried to runaway and return back to Fiela. However, he was unfamiliar with the forest and was eventually found by Elias.

Sketch 9 of 10

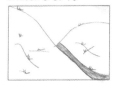

When a boy came to tell Benjamin about the death of his brother, Dawid, he knew in an instant that Fiela still loved him, and he knew that he really did belong with them. They were his family. So, Benjamin began his journey back.

Sketch 10 of 10

Finally, Benjamin returned home for good. His family cried at the sight and were so happy to have a member of the family back. Fiela knew that God had returned her hand child. Meanwhile, during his journey home, Benjamin put the pieces together from the day he left and what society had tried to do to him. Benjamin and Fiela knew all along that time, distance, and man could not keep them apart forever. Furthermore, a mother is not determined by her skin color, the house, her bank account, or social status, but by the love and compassion she shows a child. Fiela was Benjamin's mother, and no one could tell him any differently.

Making-A-Difference Project:
Slideshow Documentary on Adoption, Child Labor, or Animal Poaching

The Making-A-Difference Project for this chapter involves students in researching adoption, child labor, or animal poaching; relating these issues to Matthee's novels set in 19th century South Africa; and reporting their findings in the form of a Slideshow Documentary using software such as Microsoft PowerPoint. The slideshow should be informative in nature and blend historical aspects and contemporary relevance. While the slideshow itself may consist mostly of pictures, students should accompany the collection of slides with a script that becomes the informative basis of the documentary. The show should consist of at least 20 slides, including at least 5 with quotes from *Circles in a Forest* (1984) or *Fiela's Child* (1986), thus establishing the literary roots of the project. As part of their research, students should identify relevant organizations that protect children and animals from the injustices and cruelties conveyed in Matthee's novels.

Conclusion

Although the novels by Dalene Matthee featured in this chapter are set in the 1870s, the struggles they depict have enduring relevance. As students examine various aspects of exploitation through *Circles in a Forest* (1984) and *Fiela's Child* (1986), they realize that greed and selfishness perpetuate serious problems such as child labor, animal poaching, discrimination, and unnecessary abuses of the environment. The Knysna Forest is now extinct of elephants that numbered over 500 less than 150 years ago. And while the ban on ivory and elephant parts came too late to rescue the elephants of the Knysna Forest, fortunately a system of forestry management was introduced in time to "put an end to the unthinking and rapid devastation" of the forest itself (du Toit, 1998, ¶ 1).

Environmental preservation and human justice were clearly issues dear to Dalene Matthee's heart and mind. Her portrayal of the interconnectedness of people, animals, and natural resources reminds readers to care for all of these aspects of life. And while relatively few readers of Matthee's novels may actually have the opportunity to travel to South Africa's Knysna Forest, those who do will see this magnificent region, which today is one of the country's most sought after natural tourist destinations, against the backdrop of a history of woodcutters, timber merchants, ostrich farmers, and families whom Dalene Matthee brought to life after seven years of research (Pople, 2005, ¶ 22).

REFERENCES

ATKV. (2005). *The ATKV: Your One-Stop Cultural Home*. Retrieved February 23, 2007, from http://www.atkv.org.za/content.cfm?ipk CategoryID=480

Bennett, A. (1997). Ivory trade and elephant preservation. *Sustainable development case studies*. Colby College. Retrieved June 15, 2006, from http://www.colby.edu/personal/t/thti eten/end-bots.html

Black, A. & Stave, A.M. (2007). *A comprehensive guide to Readers Theatre: Enhancing fluency and comprehension in middle school and beyond*. Newark, DE: International Reading Association.

Choice Garden Route Property Group. (2004). *Knysna*. Retrieved June 20, 2006, from http://www.choicenet.co.za/index.php?page=knysna

Contemporary Africa Database. (2006). *People: Dalene Matthee: South African Novelist*. Retrieved February 23, 2007, from http://people.africadatabase.org/en/person/18367.html

du Toit, T. (1998, September 9). *Knysna forests*. Retrieved June 15, 2006, from http://www.knet.co.za/knysna/

Guthrie, J.T., & Wigfield, A. (Eds.). (1997). *Reading engagement: Motivating readers through integrated instruction*. Newark, DE: International Reading Association.

Hart, J. (1999). *The art of the storyboard: Storyboarding for film, tv, and animation*. Woburn, MA: Focal Press.

iAfrica.com. (2006, November 27). *Explore the Knysna forest*. Retrieved January 31, 2007, from http://travel.iafrica.com/searchsa/garden route/hotspots/278110.htm

International Reading Association & National Council of Teachers of English. (1996). *Standards for the English language arts*. Newark, DE; Urbana, IL: Authors.

Keene, E.O., & Zimmermann, S. (1997). *Mosaic of thought: Teaching comprehension in a reader's workshop*. Portsmouth, NH: Heinemann.

Lovell, J. (1999, July 18). Elephants back in South Africa's Knysna forest. *Reuters Limited*. Retrieved June 15, 2006, from http://forests.org/archive/africa/elebacsa.htm

National Council for the Social Studies. (1994). *Expectations of excellence: Curriculum standards for social studies*. Silver Spring, MD: Author.

Newmarch, J. (2005, March 9). *Goodbye, Dalene Matthee*. Retrieved June 15, 2006, from http://www.iafrica.com/pls/procs/SEARCH.AR CHIVE?p_content_id=421574&p_site_id=2

Patterson, G. (n.d.). *Knysna elephants*. Retrieved June 15, 2006, from http://www.garethpatterson.com/Elephants/elephants.htm

Pople, L. (2005, February 23). SA writers mourn Dalene Matthee. *The Namibian*. Retrieved June 15, 2006, from http://www.namibian.com.na/2005/February/national/0598CC15E5.html

Rice, L.J. (2002). Conformity and individuality in Cormier's the chocolate war. In J. Glasgow (Ed.), *Using young adult literature: Thematic activities based on Gardner's multiple intelligences*. (pp. 200–201). Norwood, MA: Christopher-Gordon.

Rice, L.J. (2006). *What was it like? Teaching history and culture through young adult literature*. New York: Teachers College Press.

Scully, P. (1997). *Liberating the family: Gender and British slave emancipation in the rural Western Cape, South Africa, 1823–1853*. Portsmouth, NH: Heinemann.

Seymour, C. (2001). *Knysna–Amatole Montane Forests*. Retrieved June 15, 2006, from http://www.worldwildlife.org/wildworld/profiles/terrestrial/at/at0115_full.html

Spiro, P.J. (1987, January 27). *Better now than never: Economic and social reforms in South Africa* (Cato Policy Analysis No. 81), Retrieved June 15, 2006, from http://www.cato.org/pubs/pas/pa081.html

LITERATURE CITED

Matthee, D. (1984). *Circles in a forest*. London: Penguin.

Matthee, D. (1986). *Fiela's child*. London: Penguin.

CHAPTER 10

Racial Tensions, Injustice, and Harmony in South African Literature

Linda J. Rice

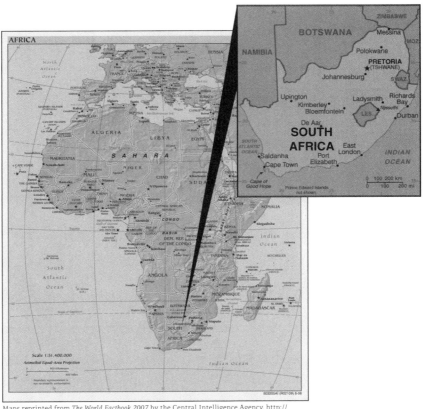

Maps reprinted from *The World Factbook 2007* by the Central Intelligence Agency, http://www.cia.gov/cia/publications/factbook.

Exploring African Life and Literature: Novel Guides to Promote Socially Responsive Learning edited by Jacqueline N. Glasgow and Linda J. Rice. © 2007 by the International Reading Association.

"My vision is of a South Africa that is totally non-racial...a new South Africa, a free South Africa, where all of us, black and white together, will walk tall; where all of us, black and white together, will hold hands as we stride forth on the Freedom March to usher in the new South Africa where people will matter because they are human beings made in the image of God."

—Bishop Desmond Tutu (cited in Landis, 2006, ¶ 1)

South Africa, the setting for the novels in this chapter, is the southern-most country of the African continent. A traveler to South Africa's Cape Town may stand at the point where the Atlantic and Indian Oceans meet. To many citizens and tourists, South Africa is a country known for its immense game reserve, Kruger National Park, which is as large as England; for its wine region in the Western Cape; for its prestigious college town, Stellenbosh; for its beautiful coastal towns like Plettenburg Bay and Port Elizabeth; for its keen competition in rugby and soccer; for its beautiful parliament buildings; for its magnificent modern cities such as Johannesburg, Pretoria, and Cape Town that boast the arts, entertainment, luxurious shopping, accommodations, and skyscrapers; and for its abundance of natural resources including gold and diamonds. But South Africa is also known for its juxtapositions of wealth and poverty, for its shantytowns and unemployment, and for its turbulent history of racial injustice. While apartheid officially ended in 1994, studying South African history and culture while omitting the literature of the apartheid era would be like studying contemporary American race relations while ignoring the influence of slavery, Jim Crow laws, and the Civil Rights Movement. Therefore, this chapter will help readers understand crucial aspects of South Africa's history.

The Cross-Curricular Activities for the two novels featured in this chapter, *Cry, the Beloved Country* (1948/1987) by Alan Paton and *July's People* (1981) by Nadine Gordimer, are designed to help students understand why the writings of Abraham Lincoln were influential to those who sought to end apartheid and to envision connections between the writings of Paton and Gordimer and the non-fiction film portrayal of the negotiations between Nelson Mandela and F.W. de Klerk that brought apartheid to an end. The Making-A-Difference Project requires students to go beyond the perspectives of two white South African writers, Paton and Gordimer, whose work is featured in this chapter, and deliberately consider the black South African perspective by reading additional novels in literature circles where they can freely discuss their novels. In their literature circles, students will examine the similarities and differences be-

Novels, Activities, and Curricular Standards
for English Language Arts and Social Studies

NOVELS
- *Cry, the Beloved Country* (1948/1987) by Alan Paton
- *July's People* (1981) by Nadine Gordimer

CROSS-CURRICULAR ACTIVITIES
- Examining and Comparing the Writings of Abraham Lincoln With Those of Arthur Jarvis From *Cry, the Beloved Country* (1948/1987)
- Viewing, Comparing, and Contrasting *Mandela and de Klerk* (1997) with *Cry, the Beloved Country* (1948/1987) or *July's People* (1981)

MAKING-A-DIFFERENCE PROJECT
Reading Feast Day

STANDARDS FOR THE ENGLISH LANGUAGE ARTS
#1 Students read print and nonprint texts to build an understanding of texts and of the cultures of the world.

#7 Students gather, evaluate, and synthesize data from a variety of sources to communicate their discoveries in ways that suit their purpose and audience.

#8 Students use a variety of technological and informational resources to gather and synthesize information and to create and communicate knowledge.

Adapted from IRA and NCTE. (1996). *Standards for the English Language Arts.* Newark, DE: International Reading Association; Urbana, IL: National Council of Teachers of English.

CURRICULUM STANDARDS FOR THE SOCIAL STUDIES
#1d Culture: Learners compare and analyze societal patterns for preserving culture while adapting to change resulting from moves from village to city and city to village.

#4g Individual Development & Identity: Learners compare and evaluate the impact of stereotyping and acts of altruism between blacks and whites in South Africa.

#6a Power, Authority, & Governance: Learners examine apartheid as it affected the rights, roles, and status of the individual.

#6e Power, Authority, & Governance: Learners compare race conflicts in 1948 South Africa with those of Civil War–era United States and identify representative political leaders (Lincoln, Mandela, & de Klerk) from historical and contemporary settings.

Adapted with the permission of the National Council for the Social Studies (NCSS). For the NCSS standards, see the publication *Expectations of Excellence: Curriculum Standards for Social Studies* (Washington, DC: National Council for the Social Studies, 1994). See also www.socialstudies.org.

tween books written by black South Africans and the books by Paton and Gordimer. The culminating event for students' study of South African literature will be a Reading Feast Day in which they will promote the novel and novelist studied in their literature circles and enjoy authentic South African cuisine.

The overview on page 209 illustrates how the Novel Guides in this chapter and their corresponding activities align with standards for the English language arts (International Reading Association [IRA] & National Council of Teachers of English [NCTE], 1996) and curriculum standards for the social studies (National Council for the Social Studies [NCSS], 1994).

Social and Historical Context

South Africa was colonized predominantly by Dutch and English settlers in the 17th century (Chokshi, Carter, Gupta, Martin, & Allen, 1995). The Dutch descendents, known as Boers or Afrikaners, established their own settlements, called the Orange Free State and Transvaal (Chokshi et al., 1995). When diamonds were discovered in that region in 1899, the English invaded, and the Boer War began (Chokshi et al., 1995). The war, known as the Second Boer War, between the English and the Dutch, lasted from 1899 to 1902 and resulted in a victory for the English (Crystal, 1993). After the Second Boer War, the Dutch and the English shared political power in South Africa through their respective parties, the Afrikaner National Party and the National Party. The power sharing was tense and uneasy at times, but both parties supported the enactment of apartheid laws in 1948 that had the effect of institutionalizing racism (Chokshi et al., 1995).

Apartheid laws placed many restrictions on the nonwhite population including the prohibition of marriage between whites and nonwhites and the sanctioning of "white-only" jobs (Chokshi et al., 1995, ¶ 3). The Population Registration Act of 1950 required all South Africans to be "racially classified into one of three categories: white, black (African), or colored (of mixed decent)" (Chokshi et al., 1995, ¶ 2). The colored category "included major subgroups of Indians and Asians" (Chokshi et al., 1995, ¶ 2). Blacks were required to carry "pass books" with identifying fingerprints and photograph when traveling to nonblack areas (Chokshi et al., 1995, ¶ 2).

In 1951, the Bantu Authorities Act created "homelands," independent states to which each African was assigned by the government (Chokshi et al., 1995, ¶ 3). All political rights, including voting, held by Africans were restricted to the designated homeland, thus denying black citizens the right to vote or be involved with the South African Parliament (Chokshi et al., 1995). In 1953, the passage of the Public Safety and Criminal Law Amendment Acts increased penalties for those who protested or supported the repeal of apartheid laws (Chokshi et al., 1995). Penalties included fines, whippings, and imprisonment (Chokshi et al., 1995). Apartheid policies and the Bantu Authorities Act effectively secured preferential treatment for whites. For example, while composing only 18% of South Africa's population, whites were allocated 87% of the land, 75% of the national income, and a per pupil expenditure for education that was 12 times greater than the per pupil expenditure for blacks (Leonard, 1983). Infant mortality rates were 10 times greater in the black population, largely due to inadequate medical facilities and an insufficient number of doctors. While there was one doctor for every 400 members of the white South African population, there was one doctor for every 44,000 members of the black South African population (Leonard, 1983). Teacher–pupil ratios were also disproportionate, with one teacher for every 22 white students and one teacher for every 60 black students (Leonard, 1993).

In 1990, under the leadership of South African President F.W. de Klerk, apartheid laws were dismantled, the ban on the African National Congress (ANC) was lifted, and Nelson Mandela, who spent 27 years in prison for treason due to his resistance to apartheid, was released (Crystal, 1993). In 1993, South Africa adopted a new constitution, including the governance of a 400-seat national assembly and 90-seat senate (Crystal, 1993). The 1994 election resulted in a victory for the ANC and the nation's first black president, Nelson Mandela.

Cry, the Beloved Country (1948/1987) by Alan Paton

About the Author

Alan Paton was born in 1903 in Pietermaritzburg, in the province of Natal, South Africa (Marais, 2003a). He attended Pietermaritzburg College and Natal University, where he was particularly active in the Student Christian Association, an organization near to the heart of Paton's mentor, the South African political leader Jan Hofmeyr. Paton began his professional life teaching in an all-white school in the rural village of Ixopo. At age 30, Paton was stricken with a severe case of typhoid fever for which he was hospitalized for more than two months. During his illness, Paton engaged in serious personal reflection and decided he did not want to spend his life teaching the children of rich South Africans (Marais, 2003a). In 1935, Paton accepted the position of principal at Diepkloof Reformatory, a prison for delinquent black boys near Johannesburg. In his tenure at Diepkloof, Paton implemented numerous reforms and had the bars and barbed wire removed. Upon his retirement from the reformatory, Paton wrote many articles on South African affairs and helped to form the Liberal Association of South Africa, which later emerged as a political party devoted to eradicating apartheid (Brennan, 2006).

Summary

Cry, the Beloved Country (1948/1987) tells the story of a black South African, Stephen Kumalo, and his son, Absalom. Stephen, a reverend from the small rural town of Ndotsheni, travels to Johannesburg upon hearing that his sister Gertrude has fallen into trouble. Stephen finds his sister and learns that she has turned to prostitution and an immoral life. While trying to help Gertrude and her infant child, Stephen learns that his son Absalom has encountered an even more serious problem. Absalom, along with his cousin Matthew Kumalo and a friend Johannes Parfuri, break into the house of a white South African, Arthur Jarvis, and murder him. The three accomplices intended to commit a robbery for clothes and money; they did not intend to commit murder. When Arthur's servant saw the intruders, he shouted "master, master" (p. 160). Johannes struck the servant over the head with an iron bar, and when Arthur appeared in the passageway, Absalom fired the gun in fear. The irony of the murder is that Arthur was a strong advocate for equality, despite his upbringing by parents who justified separation and inequality between the blacks and whites. Before the murder, Arthur's father, James Jarvis, was unaware of his son's passionate commitment toward racial equality. While going through his son's office, James discovers Arthur's essays discussing the causes of native crime and the problem of the inauthentic Christians justifying the oppression of black South Africans. James is hurt and angry at first but eventually comes to terms with the truth of his son's arguments.

Leading up to Absalom and his accomplices' day in court, Stephen urges his son to tell the truth on the stand. Absalom explains that he pulled the trigger out of fear, not malice or intent to kill. While Absalom's cousin and friend deny even being in the house or taking part in the robbery and are set free, Absalom is sentenced to death by hanging. Two fathers, one black and one white, grieve their sons' deaths. Stephen Kumalo goes to the home of James Jarvis to tell Jarvis that it was Absalom who killed Arthur. As a sign of forgiveness and reconciliation, James gives money for Stephen to build a new church and dam in Ndotsheni, and he provides milk for the people who live there.

Beyond the pivotal relationship between the Kumalo and Jarvis families, *Cry, the Beloved Country* (1948/1987) also depicts the "brokenness" of the tribes and land of South Africa, the dangers of city life, and the lack of available housing for blacks. The story also weaves in arguments for labor unions, with Stephen's brother John acting as a major proponent, and the difficulty blacks have handling money and power without becoming corrupted due to lack of educational opportunity and practice using resources responsibly. The story is ultimately one of accountability, reconciliation, healing, love, and brotherhood. Paton's writing has as its core that unity and equality are essential for social progress and justice. Particular evidence of this is found in those who assist Stephen on his journey to find his sister and son, including Msimangu, Mrs. Litebe, Father Vincent, and Mr. Carmichael, the young white man who took Absalom's case *pro deo* (for God; i.e., without pay).

July's People (1981) by Nadine Gordimer

About the Author

Nadine Gordimer was born in 1923 in Springs, a small gold-mining town in the province of Transvaal, South Africa (Liukkonen, 2003). Her father was a Jewish jeweler, originally from Latvia, and her mother was of British decent. Gordimer attended college for one year at Witwaterstrand University in Johannesburg. She wrote from the time she was a child and had her first published work at age 14 in a South African magazine called *Forum*. Gordimer's first book was published in 1953, and since then she has written a total of 14 novels and 11 short story collections (Liukkonen, 2003). Recognized as a political activist and champion of the disenfranchised, Gordimer is one of the world's most decorated writers, the recipient of literary awards from many nations and 15 honorary degrees from universities in the United States, England, Belgium, and South Africa (United, 2006). Gordimer was awarded the Nobel Prize for Literature in 1991 (Marais, 2003b).

Summary

While Alan Paton wrote *Cry, the Beloved Country* (first published in 1948) in 1946, two years before the official establishment of apartheid laws, Nadine Gordimer wrote *July's People* in 1981, over 30 years since apartheid had been in place. Gordimer's novel was written in the aftermath of the uprisings that took place in South Africa during the 1970s, a decade in which neighboring nations Angola, Mozambique, and Zimbabwe declared independence from colonial rule. Gordimer's novel presents the fictional account of a violent revolution in South Africa, told from the perspective of a liberal white family who, due to fears of being robbed or murdered, flee their wealth and home and find refuge living with their servant's family. Bam and Maureen Smales, along with their three children, Royce, Victor, and Gina, leave their affluence behind and live in a mud hut with a thatch roof belonging to the mother of their servant, July.

July worked for the Smales for 15 years, and although the Smales viewed themselves as superior liberals who were kind to their servant and granted him many rights, including the right to have an affair with his lover, Ellen, on their property, the role reversal in the story highlights the Smales's many inconsistencies. For all of their internal talk about how they treated July as an equal, they still want the upper hand, even when living on July's property. They resent the fact that July keeps the keys to their *bakkie* (car), that July must accompany them to see the chief, and that they must rely on him for mealies and pap (staple foods).

Beyond the novel's focus on role reversal, *July's People* (1981) also invites the lenses of psychological and gender criticism. While the Smales's children readily adapt to life in the bush, trading in their electric race track and Superman comics for the joys of hopping like frogs over the stones in the river and befriending the other children regardless of race, their mother, Maureen, is unable to adapt. Maureen grows disgusted with her husband, lashes out at July, and gradually unravels. The book's climax occurs at the end when Maureen hears the beating of helicopter propellers and runs. It is unclear whether the helicopter offers safety or combat, but Maureen's resolve is clear that a better life awaits, so she runs—away from her husband, away from her children, away from July's people, trusting only in herself. Compared to Maureen, July's wife, Martha, is a much more passive and subservient character. When July stayed in town with the Smales, he carried on an affair with a woman who cleans offices and only returned to his wife every two years, each time leaving her pregnant. Though at one point in the story, July tells Martha that the next time he goes back to work he will take her with him, she is incapable of imagining a life away from her village of mud huts.

The careful reader will note the many historical allusions embedded in Gordimer's novel, such as the pass burnings of the 1950s, the Soweto Riots of 1976, and the imprisonment of Nelson Mandela. The text also highlights many cultural shifts, human cravings, lost privileges, and basic necessities. For example, there is no toilet paper, and the Smales worry about contracting bilharzias (a disease caused by parasitic worms that live in the small veins that carry blood from the intestine to the liver) from the water. Sexual relations between Bam and Maureen are thwarted. Maureen bathes naked in the rain and on a separate occasion drowns a cat so as not to have one more mouth to feed. In contrast to these fears and choices, which signify the Smales's new life focus on health and survival, *Fah-Fee* (gambling) and the *gumba-gumba* (traveling entertainment) serve as symbols for how simple moments provide happiness for the people who live in the bush. The gumba-gumba is described as "the red box... someone had brought back from the mines [with] a battery-operated amplifier [that would be set up in the village and] attached to a record player" (p. 140). Collectively, these aspects of the text depict the range of human emotion, shifting priorities, and adaptation which the reader donning the lens of psychological criticism will find to be most interesting.

Making Connections

While exploring the writings of Alan Paton and Nadine Gordimer, teachers and students will also want to make connections between the texts, *Cry, the Beloved*

Country (1948/1987) and *July's People* (1981), and aspects of their own lives and the world around them. As students make such connections from text-to-self, text-to-text, and text-to-world, they draw on prior knowledge and experience in meaningful ways that increase comprehension (Keene & Zimmermann, 1997). The Making Connections questions for this chapter can aid teachers and students in making connections while exploring racial tensions, injustice, and harmony in South African literature. Figure 10.1 shows a sample journal response to a text-to-self question for this Novel Guide created by university student Cherish Odom.

Figure 10.1. Student Journal Response to a Making Connections Text-to-Self Question

---

Text-to-Self: "What do I believe is really important in life?"

One thing that I consider really important in life is family. I rely on my family for so many things. They are the ones that I go to when I am in trouble; likewise, they are the ones that come to me when they are in trouble. I do not limit family to blood relations but also to close friends and people I can truly count on. It takes a lot to trust someone, especially with your life or secrets that truly matter to you, which is why I think it is important to have someone like that you can rely on. Take for example my sister. My sister and I do not get along by any stretch of the imagination. However, I know that my sister is someone I can rely on if I get into a jam or if I need her help. We may not have the friendship that I want but we will always have that sisterly bond that no one else has.

Making Connections Questions for *Cry, the Beloved Country* (1948/1987) and *July's People* (1981)

	Paton's *Cry, the Beloved Country* (1948/1987)	Gordimer's *July's People* (1981)
Text-to-Self	When and where have I seen racial tensions?	When and how have I felt taken advantage of, and when and how have I taken advantage of others?
	When and where have I seen injustice?	
	When and where have I seen divided factions come together in harmony through arduous negotiation?	When did I want to leave my home and why?
		When was I away from my home and wanted to return and why?
	What does equality mean to me?	When did I grow apart from someone I cared about, and why did that happen?
	When and why have I had to rely on someone else?	
	What are my strengths and weaknesses in working with others?	When did my priorities change and why?
		How adaptable am I to changing circumstances?
	How willing am I to forgive? How willing am I to be forgiven?	What do I believe is really important in life?

Text-to-Text	How does Lincoln's *The Gettysburg Address* (1863) relate to the novel?	What texts will show me Kruger National Park and what the mud huts that the main characters lived in might have looked like?
	How does what Lincoln said in his Second Inaugural Address (1865) relate to the opposing sides of apartheid?	What books have I read in which people were living in fear or had to change their lifestyle radically?
	How does *The Long Walk Home* (1991) parallel the bus boycott Stephen encountered on his journey to find his son?	What texts will help me to learn more about the Ndbele?
	How does Chief Joseph's "I Have Heard Talk and Talk" parallel the state of the tribes depicted in the novel?	What other stories have I read or viewed in which the ending is unclear?
	How might Stephen Kumalo's journeys to the mountain be compared to stories of Moses in the Old Testament?	What texts can help me understand more about the riots that happened in South Africa during the 1970s?
Text-to-World	What do I know about racial inequality in different parts of the world?	What minority populations are living in fear in the world today, and where are they?
	What is South Africa really like? In particular, how does Johannesburg differ from the rural areas, and what are some of the nation's natural resources?	To what extent does South Africa have a class system today, and what kind of jobs do people who live there have?
	How might apartheid practices in South Africa be compared to Jim Crow laws in the United States?	What are the different housing styles and standards of living in South Africa today?
	How do unions function?	What are some examples of political and social uprising in the world, past and present?
	What are some examples of where negotiation is being used to change governments and policies in the world?	What are some examples of role reversal in the United States and the world?
	What do the Army Corps of Engineers and the Peace Corps do, and how could they have helped the people of Ndotsheni?	What system of government does South Africa have today?

Critical Exploration of Themes

This section includes a discussion of three themes that are applicable to both *Cry, the Beloved Country* (1948/1987) and *July's People* (1981). Although other themes could be added, the three presented here provide rich opportunities to synthesize the different texts, examine similarities and differences, and show the trajectory of apartheid practices and how, ultimately, as Gordimer's novel suggests, the policies, had they not been overturned, eventually would have backfired, causing further violence and role reversal. The themes explored here emphasize the importance of relying on others, being adaptable to changing circumstances, reconciling differences, keeping an open mind, and living one's faith through action and mercy.

The Willingness to Depend on Others and Adapt to Changing Circumstances Is Integral to Progress and Personal Development

Paton's *Cry, the Beloved Country* (1948/1987) and Gordimer's *July's People* (1981) both demonstrate how people must depend on one another in order to deal effectively with the problems they face. In *Cry, the Beloved Country*, Stephen Kumalo depends on the support and kindness of others at many stages of his journey. From the moment Stephen receives a letter telling him his sister Gertrude is in trouble, his wife comes to his aid, offering all of the money that has been saved in a tin for her new stove. While she is fearful of what Stephen's journey will hold, she is supportive, even in her silence. Later, when Stephen travels from Ndotsheni to Johannesburg and is robbed, his friend Theopholis Msimangu helps Stephen—a simple country minister who is not equipped to face the city and its dangers alone—navigate through the city to find his sister Gertrude and later his son, Absalom. This journey includes many stops, each redirecting Stephen in his search. Because he is determined to support the bus boycott, Stephen continues to walk—he walks to Doornfontein, to Sophiatown, past shantytowns, to Mrs. Mkize's house, to Orlando, to the reformatory where Absalom had been sent, to Pimville where Absalom and his girlfriend were living for a time, to Springs and Absalom's workplace, and finally to prison, where Absalom awaits trial for murder. Yet at each step of the way, Msimangu is with Stephen, and each step of the way others, too, offer kindness, even when they are fearful of getting involved. For example, Stephen has to depend on the Mission House and the kindness of strangers to give him places to eat and sleep.

Stephen's willingness to depend on others and the willingness of others to extend their support greatly influence many outcomes. Stephen's dependence on others does not save Absalom's life, but it does allow him to see and embrace his son before the trial. It also allows him the opportunity to perform a marriage ceremony for Absalom and his girlfriend and to bring home the young girl and her child to Ndotsheni, where both would have a better life and be part of Kumalo's family. Stephen's dependence on others does not save Gertrude from city life, as she chooses to stay rather than return to Ndotsheni, but it does allow him to adopt her child and raise him as his own, perhaps filling part of the void Absalom's death will leave. Stephen's journey also helps him to see that even in the city that he viewed to be so evil and destructive, there are good and caring people—

people such as the young man from the reformatory who showed compassion and a willingness to give Absalom a second chance and Mr. Carmichael, said to be one of the greatest lawyers in South Africa, who takes Absalom's case for free.

In *July's People* (1981), Bam and Maureen Smales have little choice but to depend on their servant, July. The long-brewing violent revolution against apartheid results in murders of white South Africans and arson of their houses. July offers his former employers the refuge of moving to the bush and living in one of his family's mud huts. While Bam is relatively open to this new way of life and willing to learn from July's people, Maureen initially makes requests of July, as though he is still her servant. She resists dependence and as a result becomes increasingly self-absorbed, to the point of taking the largest portions of food, depriving her own children from vaccines so that she can have them, and ultimately leaving everyone, including her own family, behind. In the book's final scene, Maureen's running is described as that of "a solitary animal at the season when animals neither seek a mate nor take care of young, existing only for their lone survival, the enemy of all that would make claims of responsibility" (Gordimer, 1981, p. 160).

While Maureen's actions may be progressive in terms of fighting for survival, they are simultaneously extreme and show an inability to adapt or rely on others. Through their willingness to depend on others, Bam and the children are able to find simple moments of happiness with their new life and contribute to the common good of the village whether by gathering water or hunting. But Maureen's arrival in the bush starts a serial decline in which she turns inward, can scarcely nurture her own children, no longer holds her husband in high regard—now that his material wealth is useless—and harbors nothing but resentment toward July, whom she does not trust to care for the bakkie and who has been caught with stolen items from her home. This brings out the point that a willingness to be dependent on others requires a degree of trust, and trust comes naturally when people prove themselves to be trustworthy and reliable. Maureen's knowledge of July's thievery and affair with Ellen may undermine her willingness to depend on July, but it seems Maureen's most significant limitations are her pride and inability to adapt to the role reversal.

Reconciliation and an Open Mind Are Crucial to Growth

Paton's *Cry, the Beloved Country* (1948/1987) takes readers on a heart-wrenching journey of two fathers who ultimately lose their sons and then binds the fathers and sons together with renewed understanding and reconciliation. Stephen Kumalo goes to the home of James Jarvis to tell him personally that it was his son, Absalom, who killed James's son, Arthur. Kumalo says, "this thing that is the heaviest thing of all my years, is the heaviest thing of all your years also" to which Jarvis replies, after a long silence, "I have heard you. I understand what I did not understand. There is no anger in me" (Paton, 1987, pp. 180–181). The magnitude of Jarvis's heartfelt reconciliation with Stephen comes through additional acts of kindness and generosity, for Jarvis sends milk to the people of Ndotsheni and provides money to build a dam and a new church. James's words to Stephen signify another point of reconciliation, that between James and his own son, Arthur.

While the book holds no indication that the father and son had a particularly poor relationship, it does reveal that Arthur felt he had been misled by his parents about issues of race. He wrote in an essay called "Private Essay on the Evolution of South Africa" about his parents: "They were upright and kind and law-abiding; they taught me my prayers and took me regularly to church; they had no trouble with servants and my father was never short of labour. From them I learned all that a child should learn of honour and charity and generosity. But of South Africa I learned nothing at all" (Paton, 1987, p. 174). Upon reading this and others of his son's essays, James is very hurt: "For a moment he felt something almost like anger, but he wiped his eyes with his fingers and shook it from him" (Paton, 1987, p. 174). James's openness to his son's essays gives him the opportunity to know his son more fully, even in death, and to gain the capacity to change his views for the good and potentially carry on his son's legacy of justice. As James sits in his son's study with pictures of Christ crucified and Abraham Lincoln, "there was increasing knowledge of a stranger. He began to understand why the picture of this man was in the house of his son, and the multitude of books" (Paton, 1987, p. 155). James's ready offering of forgiveness to Stephen is no doubt influenced by his reading and careful consideration of his son's essays, such as the one his son was supposed to have delivered the night of his death, titled the "The Real Causes of Native Crime."

In *July's People* (1981), Maureen and her daughter Gina become foil characters in regard to open-mindedness and reconciliation. While Maureen seems unable to look upon her new circumstances with anything but contempt and longing for the many material possessions she left behind, Gina readily makes friends with Nyiko, one of the black children from their new home in the bush. Maureen appears bound by her racial vision, making her emotions fluctuate from fearful to superior, but Gina is colorblind and remains on the lookout for opportunities to reach out to her new neighbors. For instance, when the Smales open a tin of sausages and Gina decides Nyiko should have one, Maureen puts the sausage on the tip of a penknife and holds it out to the child, who receives it with an attitude of "receiving grace" (Gordimer, 1981, p. 43). Maureen's response is to give the knife back to Bam without wiping it off, as if she wants no physical contact with the child. She then says to her husband in a sarcastic tone:

"If only ours'd pickup the good manners along with the habits of blowing their noses in their fingers and relieving themselves where they feel like it" (Gordimer, 1981, p. 43).

Maureen's frustration with her situation causes her to push away, even from her husband. Her words are often hostile as she is steeped in resentment and inflexibility that keep her from respecting July and the ways of his people. She cannot release the notion that July should still be subservient to her needs. While Maureen's bitterness and inability to seek reconciliation with July intensify throughout the novel, Gina's openness brings her closer to July's people. Gina grows to care so much for her young playmate Nyiko that a rivalry develops. At one point, Gina wanted to bring Nyiko on a trip to see the chief and "yelled in his language, which she was learning in the form of 'private talk' between Nyiko and herself, He's *my* friend, mine!" (Gordimer, 1981, p. 106). Similarly, while Gina is open to enjoying the gumba-gumba and revels in its entertainment as something "new to the world," Maureen shows no interest in it whatsoever, choosing instead to relive past memories of her childhood servant, Lydia (Gordimer, 1981, p. 140).

Piety Should Be Accompanied by Godly Action, Justice, and Mercy

The protagonist of *Cry, the Beloved Country* (1948/1987), Stephen Kumalo, relies heavily on his Christian faith. While he desires for his sister Gertrude and son, Absalom, to admit their wrongs and repent, he openly admits his own imperfections and models the importance of humility and prayer. Stephen exemplifies authentic faith in the way he is convicted and moved to apologize to those he has hurt, as was the case with his harsh treatment of Absalom's girlfriend. Stephen also made trips to the mountaintop to get close to God, ask forgiveness, seek help in avoiding temptation, and pray for his son on the day of the hanging. Stephen's helpers in Johannesburg call him *unfundisi* (parson) to acknowledge his position as a parson and as a sign of respect. Msimangu, who identifies himself as Kumalo's "brother in Christ," models virtuous action as he assists Stephen on his journey to find Absalom, traveling many miles on foot and opening doors so that he might find safety. Msimangu also shows mercy and understanding, offering a shoulder to lean on and never judging Stephen's family, despite their obvious shortcomings. Father Vincent also intervenes positively by introducing Stephen to Mr. Carmichael. Each of these characters demonstrates that religious devotion ought to be accompanied by action, justice, and mercy. They also connect justice with truth. While Stephen's brother John intends to lie and connive to keep his son out of jail, although his son was an accomplice to the murder of Arthur Jarvis, Stephen insists that Absalom and his lawyer tell the truth. The tragic loss of Arthur sparks a spiritual journey for James Jarvis as he reexamines his beliefs about racial separation and offers mercy to the father of his son's murderer. And perhaps most poignant, the writings of Arthur Jarvis shine the light of truth as they carefully examine the irony of a Christian civilization that seeks to justify apartheid. He concludes, in the essay he was writing at the time of his death, "The truth is that our civilization is not Christian; it is a tragic compound of great ideal and fearful practice, of high assurance and desperate anxiety, of loving charity and fearful clutching of possessions" (Paton, 1987, p. 155). What *Cry, the Beloved Country* emphasizes is that a true Christian faith must be bolstered by right and moral actions that uphold both justice and mercy.

Compared to *Cry, the Beloved Country* (1948/1987), *July's People* (1981) is far less spiritual and not overtly Christian in terms of its imagery. The book is written from a more secular point of view, making occasional reference to prayer, but not developed around characters who rely on faith in times of need. In this light, therefore, piety is not equated directly with religious devotion but rather with personal, self-righteous attitudes. Bam and Maureen both exhibit a sense of superiority, especially when they first flee their home to live with July. While Bam adapts somewhat readily, Maureen harbors her sense of self-righteous superiority and routinely uses it to remind July that she *was* a kind, permissive, and generous employer. The very fact that Maureen is so intent on repeating to July how good she was to him draws into question whether her actions reflected that she really viewed July as equal or whether she simply wanted to profess a politically correct position. At one point, Maureen seems to become so agitated that she "put a fist, hard claim, upon his arm" saying, "I've never made you do anything you didn't think it was your job to do. Have I? *Have I?*... Tell me. When did we treat you inconsiderately—badly? I'd like to know, I really want to know" (Gordimer, 1981, pp. 70–71). July suggests that Maureen's questions were never really about asking at all, but making commands. Then he refers to Bam as "the master," to which Maureen replies, "*The master*. Bam's not your master. Why do you pretend? Nobody's ever thought of you as anything but a grown man" (Gordimer, 1981, pp. 70–71). While these arguments may initially sound logical on Maureen's behalf, her merciless outburst against July in the second to last chapter of the book reveals that she did view July with disdain and contempt.

Teacher Talk

This Teacher Talk section offers a list of questions designed to engage students in high-order critical thinking as they consider the significance of various events and character behaviors, recognize literary conventions, examine reading as a transaction whereby the author leads the reader through a story, and analyze the author's agenda and their own. These four question categories are what Wilhelm (1997) calls the Reflective Dimension, which encourages students "to be spectating on the reading experience and reflecting on it" (p. 74). The open-ended nature of the questions allows plenty of room for students to offer interpretations and negotiate meaning while still ensuring that they draw on their knowledge of the text to render responses that demonstrate careful analysis (Wiggins & McTighe, 2005). Besides class discussion, teachers will find these questions useful for creating a range of writing assignments from informal journals to in-depth literary essays.

Using Reflective Dimension Questions for *Cry, the Beloved Country* (1948/1987) and *July's People* (1981)

	Paton's *Cry, the Beloved Country* (1948/1987)	Gordimer's *July's People* (1981)
Considering Significance	How do the speeches and actions of John Kumalo contribute to the meaning of the story (particularly of unionization and the mining industry in South Africa)? What is significant or symbolic about each work of art in Arthur Jarvis's study? What is significant about the reformatory? How are women represented in the book?	Who is running and where at the end of the book? Why do you think the outcome is unclear? Why is Lydia in the story? What was the significance of the gumba-gumba? What role do the children play in the book?
Recognizing Literary Conventions	How did the author create parallels between the brokenness of the people and the brokenness of the land? What are the various meanings of the book's title? How did the author develop a sense of racial solidarity in the story? What ironies do you see in the story?	How does the author develop changing values through the way the children progress in the novel? How does the author create for the reader a kind of love–hate relationship for Maureen? What are the symbols of ownership in the novel? How are these gradually transferred from white to black?
Recognizing Reading as a Transaction	How do Arthur and James Jarvis view one another while living? How does James's view of his son change after the murder and why? How did Paton make this a story of personal and communal faith? How did Paton make this a story of forgiveness, redemption, and hope?	How does the author make you aware of gender when reading the novel? How do psychological aspects (stability, instability, denial, repression, transference) stand out in the novel? The Smales clearly believe they have been good to July. How does the author challenge this notion?

Evaluating an Author, and the Self as Reader

How do the white fears and perspectives portrayed in chapter 12 influence your view of Stephen Kumalo and the court scene that follows?

What messages do you think Paton wanted to send about race, power, and corruption in chapter 7?

To what extent is the legal system presented as just in the novel? What other people and institutions does Paton seem to critique through this novel? Do you agree with his critique?

How do you think the author wants you to view the Smales family throughout the novel? How do you view the Smales? In particular, how do you view Maureen?

How do you think the author wants you to view July throughout the novel? How do you view July?

How does July change during the course of the novel? Are his changes believable? Why or why not?

Cross-Curricular Activities

The first Cross-Curricular Activity to be used to deepen students' understanding examines and compares two influential speeches of Abraham Lincoln with the writings of Paton's character, Arthur Jarvis. The second engages students with a film, *Mandela and de Klerk* (Sofronski & Sargent, 1997) to show the problems of apartheid and how it finally came to an end in 1994. Critical–analytical questions link the film with the writings of Paton and Gordimer.

Examining and Comparing the Writings of Abraham Lincoln With Those of Arthur Jarvis From *Cry, the Beloved Country* (1948/1987)

The connection Arthur Jarvis felt with Abraham Lincoln in *Cry, the Beloved Country* was considerable. Students should read Lincoln's *Gettysburg Address* (1863) and his Second Inaugural Address (1865) in order to better understand the connection between the fight to end slavery in America and the fight to end apartheid in South Africa. Both are short and should be read aloud in class and then compared with the excerpted essays by Arthur Jarvis that appear in chapters 20, 21, and 24 of *Cry, the Beloved Country*. See Table 10.1 for questions to help guide the discussion.

Viewing, Comparing, and Contrasting *Mandela and de Klerk* (1997) with *Cry, the Beloved Country* (1948/1987) or *July's People* (1981)

Both Sidney Poitier and Michael Caine received Emmy nominations for their performances in the 1997 film *Mandela and de Klerk* (Sofronski & Sargent). The

> **Table 10.1. Discussion Questions for Exploration of Writings by Abraham Lincoln and Arthur Jarvis**
>
> 1. Why did James Jarvis admire Abraham Lincoln?
> 2. In what ways are Jarvis's writings similar to Lincoln's in both content and form?
> 3. How do Jarvis and Lincoln envision the roles of man and God in fighting great moral battles?
> 4. What do Jarvis's and Lincoln's writings reveal about their beliefs of government and its role?
> 5. How would you describe the tone of Jarvis's writing as compared to Lincoln's? Which would be more apt to offend an audience and why?

film portrays the effects of institutionalized racism, the imprisonment of Nelson Mandela, and the hard fight to freedom that began when South African President F.W. de Klerk replaced President Botha and began the process of dismantling apartheid. The film includes actual footage of South Africa in the wake of violence and riots, some of which were orchestrated by the government, and also depicts the relationship between Nelson and Winnie Mandela, including Nelson's criticism of her love affairs while he was in prison and alleged violent activism. One of the most graphic scenes depicts the "necklace of shame" in which black South Africans put tires over those who are believed to be traitors in their communities, douse them with gasoline, and burn them to death.

While the film is realistic in its portrayal of violence and the hard processes of negotiation, it is also inspiring as it shows what people working together can do for the common good. This film will help students complete the picture that began with the institution of apartheid policies in 1948, the same year *Cry, the Beloved Country* was published. It also shows the effects of the policies and backlash on the white community, as depicted in *July's People*, and ends with the revocation of apartheid laws and election of Nelson Mandela in 1994, which provides a historical context for both novels. To encourage students to critically view the film and connect it with the writings of Paton and Gordimer, teachers should ask them to respond to one or more of the questions in Table 10.2. Per their discretion and in consideration of class time available, teachers may elect to have students respond to these questions in a class discussion or individually in writing.

Making-A-Difference Project: Reading Feast Day

As veteran English teachers in U.S. high schools know, *Cry, the Beloved Country* (1948/1987) is well rooted in the nation's public schools. *July's People* (1981),

Table 10.2. Questions Linking South African Literature and Film

1. What did you learn from watching the film *Mandela and de Klerk* (Sofronski & Sargent, 1997). What moved you? What actions disturbed you? How does this relate to *Cry, the Beloved Country* or *July's People*?

2. Explore the complexity of Apartheid—if the whites knew it was morally wrong, then why did they continue it for so long? Look to the human heart, the head, the spirit—what tensions exist? What was there to gain with and without apartheid? What was there to lose? Incorporate your related understanding of *Cry, the Beloved Country* or *July's People* into your response.

3. Compare any one aspect of the film with Paton's *Cry, the Beloved Country* (e.g., the trial, shantytowns, housing situation, white fears, aspects of violence, inequity). Use specifics from both the film and the book in responding to this—you might begin by quoting an excerpt from the book and then follow it with a discussion of the same aspect represented by the movie.

4. Discuss the process of F.W. de Klerk and Nelson Mandela's hammering out a new policy of peace, justice, and equality for all. What did you see as the integral challenges, risks, and barriers? What made it finally work? What if Maureen Smales and July had been the negotiators? What would have been the challenges? Would they have been able to achieve resolution? Explain.

5. Do you admire Winnie Mandela or not? (Or are you somewhere in the middle?) Explain. Discuss the ways in which she supported and interfered with her husband's plan. What character from *Cry, the Beloved Country* or *July's People* do you think is most like Winnie Mandela and why? Which character would be Winnie's best foil character and why?

6. Choose one person from the movie and one character from *Cry, the Beloved Country* or *July's People* that you find most comparable. Discuss the two in relation to one another, with an emphasis on similarities in thought and action.

while not as commonly taught in U.S. high schools, remains a popular text in college classrooms both within and outside of the United States. However, while both of these literary works are exceptional in their depiction of racial conflict in South Africa, it is important to note that they are also written from a white perspective. As a prominent South African novelist and colleague who currently teaches at Ohio University, Zakes Mda pointed out in personal communication (May 22, 2006), "However liberal [the voices of Paton and Gordimer] may be, there are others who have told the South African story from a totally different perspective." It is Mda's insight that provides the impetus for the Making-A-Difference Project that follows.

In order to expand their understanding of the racial issues in South Africa and deliberately consider the black South African perspective, students should read one of the novels in Table 10.3. Some of these can be difficult to find in large quantities, so teachers should plan ahead when obtaining copies. All of the books on the list are available through Amazon.com and have accompanying editorial reviews.

> ### Table 10.3. Selected Novels by Black South African Writers
>
> **Peter Abrahams**
> *Mine Boy.* (1970). London: Faber and Faber.
> *Tell Freedom: Memories of Africa.* (1982). London: Faber and Faber.
>
> **Alex La Guma**
> *In the Fog of the Season's End.* (1992). London: Heinemann.
> *Time of the Butcherbird.* (1987). London: Heinemann.
> *A Walk in the Night and Other Stories.* (1968). Evanston, IL: Northwestern University Press.
>
> **Sindiwe Magona**
> *Push-Push & Other Stories.* (1996). Johannesburg, South Africa: David Philip.
> *Mother to Mother.* (1998). Boston: Beacon Press.
> *Living, Loving, and Lying Awake at Night.* (1991/2003). Johannesburg, South Africa: David Philip.
> *To My Children's Children.* (1990/2005). Johannesburg, South Africa: David Philip.
>
> **Zakes Mda**
> *The Heart of Redness.* (2003). London: Picador.
> *The Madonna Excelsior.* (2005). London: Picador.
> *She Plays With the Darkness.* (2004). London: Picador.
> *Ways of Dying.* (2002). London: Picador.
> *The Whale Caller.* (2005). New York: Farrar, Straus and Giroux.
>
> **Es'kia Mphahlele**
> *Down Second Avenue.* (1985). London: Faber and Faber.
> *Renewal Time.* (1988). London: Readers International.
>
> **Sol Plaatje**
> *Mhudi.* (2006). London: Penguin Global.
>
> **Miriam Tlali**
> *Between Two Worlds.* (2004). Calgary, AB: Broadview Press.

Students should work in literature circles in which they can freely discuss their chosen or assigned novel, making a point to examine what similarities and differences exist between these books and those of Paton and Gordimer. For more information on structuring literature circles, consult Harvey Daniels's *Literature Circles: Voice and Choice in the Student-Centered Classroom* (1994).

In order to transform their reading into a Making-A-Difference Project, each group of students will research the author, find a creative way to share the literature they read, and make a promotional brochure enticing others to read the book. A teacher model promotional brochure appears in Figure 10.2. The teacher should give each group several South African recipes to choose from; these can be found easily by doing a general Internet search. Then, on "Reading Feast Day," each group will bring their dish, and students will enjoy authentic South African cuisine while sharing stories by some of South Africa's best

A Great Novel by South African "Renaissance Man"

Personal Context:

- Imagine having to move because your property is taken from you and people are at war in your own back yard...
- Imagine being on the run with the one you love...

Promotional Summary:

- **Mhudi** is the story of an African man and woman living in South Africa during the Boer expansion.

Author & Book:

- The contributions of **Sol Plaatje**, one of South Africa's true renaissance men, have gone underreported. But now, thanks to Penguin Global, **Mhudi** is in print again (2006).

Additional Importance:

In 1914, Mhudi became the first novel by a Black South African to be published in English.

known writers: Peter Abrahams, Alex La Guma, Sindiwe Magona, Zakes Mda, Es'kia Mphahlele, Sol Plaatje, and Miriam Tlali.

Conclusion

As students explore *Cry, the Beloved Country* (1948/1987) and *July's People* (1981) and additional novels by black South African writers (see Table 10.3) through discussion, connections with other texts, current events, and related self-reflection questions, they will have a twofold opportunity: studying great literature and understanding the history of a great and diverse nation, South Africa. Through the serious exploration of race, injustice, negotiation, and harmony that emerges in this Novel Guide, students move beyond stereotypical views of Africa as a country or South Africa as a region in a vast continent and begin to define the uniqueness of the nation of South Africa, its struggle, its people, and their commitment to change. By making connections between apartheid and the writings of Abraham Lincoln, by linking themes of Paton and Gordimer's works with current events, and by looking at issues of race from the perspectives of white and black authors alike, students start to see how much different times and different places have in common and how globally connected they are.

REFERENCES

Brennan, S. (2006). "Alan Paton: Biography." Retrieved May 10, 2007 from http://www.answers.com/topic/alan-paton

Chokshi, M., Carter, C., Gupta, D., Martin, T., & Allen, R. (1995, Spring). The history of apartheid in South Africa. In *Computers and the apartheid regime in South Africa.* Retrieved June 19, 2006, from http://www-cs-students.stanford.edu/~cale/cs201/apartheid.hist.html

Crystal, D. (Ed.). (1993). *The Cambridge factfinder.* New York: Cambridge University Press.

Daniels, H. (1994). *Literature circles: Voice and choice in the student-centered classroom.* York, ME: Stenhouse.

Hayes, S. (2005). *The liberal party of South Africa.* Retrieved February 21, 2007, from http://www.geocities.com/athens/7734/liberal1.htm

International Reading Association & National Council of Teachers of English. (1996). *Standards for the English language arts.* Newark, DE; Urbana, IL: Authors.

Keene, E.O., & Zimmermann, S. (1997). *Mosaic of thought: Teaching comprehension in a reader's workshop.* Portsmouth, NH: Heinemann.

Landis, M. (2006). *Desmond Tutu.* Retrieved June 15, 2006, from http://www.wagingpeace.org/menu/programs/youth-outreach/peace-heroes/tutu-desmond.htm

Leonard, R. (1983). *South Africa at war: White power and the crisis in southern Africa.* Westport, CT: L. Hill.

Lincoln, A. (1863). The Gettysburg address. In *Abraham Lincoln online: Speeches and writings.* Retrieved February 21, 2007, from http://showcase.netins.net/web/creative/lincoln/speeches/gettysburg.htm

Lincoln, A. (1865). The second inaugural address. In *Abraham Lincoln online: Speeches and writings.* Retrieved June 15, 2006, from http://showcase.netins.net/web/creative/lincoln/speeches/inaug2.htm

Liukkonen, P. (2003). *Nadine Gordimer.* Retrieved June 20, 2006, from http://www.kirjasto.sci.fi/gordimer.htm

Marais, E. (2003a). *Biographies: Alan Paton.* Retrieved June 20, 2006, from http://zar.co.za/

Marais, E. (2003b). *Biographies: Nadine Gordimer.* Retrieved June 20, 2006, from http://zar.co.za/

National Council for the Social Studies. (1994). *Expectations of excellence: Curriculum standards for social studies.* Silver Spring, MD: Author.

United Nations Development Programme—South Africa (2006). Retrieved May 10, 2007 from http://www.undp.org.za/docs/misc/gordimerbio.html

Wiggins, G., & McTighe, J. (2005). *Understanding by design* (2nd ed.). Alexandria, VA: Association for Supervision and Curriculum Development.

Wilhelm, J.D. (1997). *"You gotta BE the book": Teaching engaged and reflective reading with adolescents.* New York: Teachers College Press/National Council of Teachers of English.

LITERATURE CITED

Gordimer, N. (1981). *July's people.* London: Penguin.

Paton, A. (1948/1987). *Cry, the beloved country.* New York: Macmillan.

Plaatje, S. (1914/2006). *Mhundi.* London: Penguin.

FILMS CITED

Pearce, R. (Producer) & Atkins, E. (Director). (1991). *The long walk home* [Motion picture]. United States: Artisan.

Sofronski, B. (Producer) & Sargent, J. (Director). (1997). *Mandela and de Klerk* [Motion picture]. United States: Showtime Original Pictures.

CHAPTER 11

The Struggles for Human Rights in the Young Adult Literature of South Africa

Jacqueline N. Glasgow

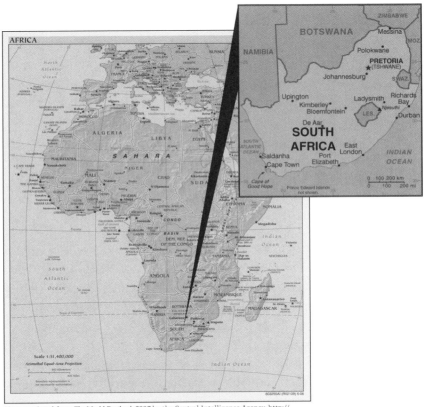

Maps reprinted from *The World Factbook 2007* by the Central Intelligence Agency, http://www.cia.gov/cia/publications/factbook.

Exploring African Life and Literature: Novel Guides to Promote Socially Responsive Learning edited by Jacqueline N. Glasgow and Linda J. Rice. © 2007 by the International Reading Association.

"Approximately 95% of AIDS orphans live in Sub-Saharan Africa."

—AVERT (2006)

South Africa, located in the southern region of sub-Saharan Africa, is known for its pristine beaches, majestic mountains, and abundant wildlife. However, despite its attractive climate and vast natural beauty, South Africa has been a place of civil unrest in recent history. Until 1994, the South African government enforced apartheid, a form of institutionalized racism that gave preferential treatment to people classified as white. The Population Registration Act of 1950 required all South Africans to be "racially classified into one of three categories: white, black (African), or colored (of mixed decent)" (Chokshi, Carter, Gupta, Martin, & Allen, 1995, ¶ 2), and apartheid laws placed many restrictions on the nonwhite population, including the prohibition of marriage between whites and nonwhites and sanctioning of "white-only" jobs (Chokshi et al., 1995, ¶ 3; see chapter 10 for more in-depth discussion of apartheid). After the fall of the apartheid structure, black South Africans gained the majority rule in a new democratic government in 1994, and the people of South Africa have struggled to ease racial tension and develop equality and peace in the post-apartheid years. In addition to difficult racial issues, the post-apartheid era has brought other struggles for human rights. South Africa must find solutions for the crisis created by HIV/AIDS, the struggle against poverty, and the need for better access to education.

The Novel Guides for this chapter illustrate some of the struggles for human rights that South Africans have encountered in the apartheid and post-apartheid years and reveal some of the issues this country must face as it makes the transition from a rigid apartheid structure toward new possibilities for peace, harmony, and a democratic government. In Beverley Naidoo's *Journey to Jo'Burg: A South African Story* (1988) and the sequel, *Chain of Fire* (1989), the protagonists struggle for freedom and human rights during the apartheid era. In Sheila Gordon's *Waiting for the Rain: A Novel of South Africa* (1987), the protagonist fights for racial equality and access to education. In Allan Stratton's Printz Honor Book, *Chanda's Secrets* (2004), set in a fictional country in sub-Saharan Africa, the protagonist struggles with the survival of her family against HIV/AIDS, an issue that is of major concern in South Africa, as illustrated in this chapter's opening quote. To expand students' understanding of these novels and the struggle for human rights existing during this progression from apartheid into the post-apartheid era, students can also read an additional novel from the list in Table 11.1 and then work in literature circles to discuss the books they read, as described in chapter 10.

Novels, Activities, and Curricular Standards
for English Language Arts and Social Studies

NOVELS
- *Journey to Jo'Burg* (1988) and the sequel, *Chain of Fire* (1989), by Beverley Naidoo
- *Waiting for the Rain* (1987) by Sheila Gordon
- *Chanda's Secrets* (2004) by Allan Stratton

CROSS-CURRICULAR ACTIVITIES
- Completing a Photo Essay
- Conducting Fictional Interviews With People Living With HIV/AIDS
- Public Awareness Posters

MAKING-A-DIFFERENCE PROJECT
Process Drama on HIV/AIDS in South Africa: "What Needs to Happen?"

STANDARDS FOR THE ENGLISH LANGUAGE ARTS
#2 Students read a wide range of literature to understand human experience.

#7 Students conduct research on issues and interests.

#8 Students use a variety of technological and informational resources to gather and synthesize information and to create and communicate knowledge.

Adapted from IRA and NCTE. (1996). *Standards for the English Language Arts.* Newark, DE: International Reading Association; Urbana, IL: National Council of Teachers of English.

CURRICULUM STANDARDS FOR THE SOCIAL STUDIES
#1a Culture: Learners analyze the ways the cultures deal with apartheid issues and the HIV/AIDS epidemic.

#4b Individual Development & Identity: Learners describe personal connections associated with the global concerns and interconnectivity of the HIV/AIDS pandemic.

#9f Global Connections: Learners demonstrate understanding of post-apartheid and HIV/AIDS issues related to universal human rights.

#10j Civic Ideals & Practices: Learners participate in cross-cultural activities designed to strengthen the "common good."

Adapted with the permission of the National Council for the Social Studies (NCSS). For the NCSS standards, see the publication *Expectations of Excellence: Curriculum Standards for Social Studies* (Washington, DC: National Council for the Social Studies, 1994). See also www.socialstudies.org.

The Cross-Curricular Activities for these novels are designed to introduce students to life and human rights struggles in South Africa and serve as preparation for the Making-A-Difference Project. Students will create a photo essay, conduct a "mock interview" with a person living with HIV/AIDS, and create a public awareness poster. The Making-A-Difference Project for this unit is a process drama about HIV/AIDS titled "What Needs to Happen?" By participating

> **Table 11.1. Selected Novels With Post-Apartheid Themes**
>
> - Ellis, D. (2004). *The heaven shop*. Markham, ON: Fitzhenry & Whiteside.
> - Ferreira, A. (2002). *Zulu dog*. New York: Farrar, Straus and Giroux.
> - Gordon, S. (1988). *Unfinished business*. New York: Random House.
> - Gordon, S. (1991). *The middle of somewhere*. Danbury, CT: Orchard Books.
> - Naidoo, B. (1995). *No turning back: A novel of South Africa*. London: Penguin.
> - Naidoo, B. (2001). *The other side of truth*. New York: HarperCollins.
> - Naidoo, B. (2003). *Out of bounds: Seven stories of conflict and hope*. New York: HarperCollins.

in the process drama, students become personally engaged in the struggle for human rights in sub-Saharan African countries, especially the struggle to obtain medical treatments. The overview on page 231 illustrates how the Novel Guides in this chapter and their corresponding activities align with standards for the English language arts (International Reading Association [IRA] & National Council of Teachers of English [NCTE], 1996) and curriculum standards for the social studies (National Council for the Social Studies [NCSS], 1994).

Social and Historical Context

After the British seized the Cape of Good Hope area in 1806, many of the Dutch settlers (the Boers) migrated north to establish their own republics. The discovery of diamonds (1867) and gold (1886) spurred wealth and immigration and intensified the subjugation of the native inhabitants. The Boers resisted British encroachments but were defeated in the Boer War (1899–1902). Following independence from England, an uneasy power sharing between the two groups, the Boers and the British, held sway until the 1940s, when the Afrikaner National Party was able to gain a strong majority. Strategists in the National Party invented apartheid as a means to cement their control over the economic and social system. With the enactment of apartheid laws in 1948, racial discrimination was institutionalized in South Africa. In white-ruled South Africa, black people were denied basic human and political rights. Their labor was exploited and their lives segregated (see chapter 9 for more background information on apartheid). It was not until the 1990s that an end to apartheid politically ushered in black majority rule (Central Intelligence Agency [CIA], 2006).

The apartheid system created educational inequalities through overt racist policies. The Bantu Education Act of 1952 ensured that blacks received an education that limited their educational potential and kept them in the working class. This policy directly affected the funding and the content of learning to further racial inequalities by preventing access to further education. The Bantu Education Act created separate Departments of Education by race, and it gave less money to black schools while giving most to whites. In addition to content and funding inequities, apartheid legislation affected the educational potential of students. The number of schools for blacks increased during the 1960s, but their curriculum was designed to prepare children for menial jobs. Verwoerd, minister of native affairs in 1953, said black Africans "should be educated for their opportunities in life," and that there was no place for them "above the level of certain forms of labour" (Byrnes, 1996, ¶ 15).

It is not surprising, then, that many young people during the 1980s were committed to destroying the school system because of its identification with apartheid. Student strikes, vandalism, and violence seriously undermined the schools' ability to function. By the early 1990s, shortages of teachers, classrooms, and equipment had taken a further toll on education. In August 1993, de Klerk gathered together leading experts on education in the National Education and Training Forum to formulate a policy framework for restructuring education. He earmarked 23.5% of the national budget in fiscal year 1993 to 1994 for education. He reorganized the Department of Education and when the new school year began in January 1995, all government-run primary and secondary schools were officially integrated (Byrnes, 1996, ¶ 25). Since then, other inequities have been addressed, such as funding, compulsory education, and curriculum revision.

In addition to the struggle for racial equality and quality education for all citizens, South Africa is currently struggling with one of the most severe HIV epidemics in the world. By the end of 2005, there were five and a half million people living with HIV in South Africa, including 250,000 children younger than 15 years old (UNAIDS & World Health Organization, 2006, p. 17). In addition to the many children being infected with HIV in South Africa, many more are suffering from the loss of their parents and family members from AIDS. UNAIDS estimated that there were 1.2 million South African children living as orphans due to AIDS in 2005, compared to 780,000 in 2003 (UNAIDS & World Health Organization, p. 17). Once orphaned, these children are then likely to face poverty, poor health and a lack of access to education.

According to the UNAIDS and the World Health Organization's 2006 report, the epidemic in South Africa disproportionately affects women. Young women (15–24 years) are four times more likely to be HIV-infected than are young men (p. 17). Prevalence of HIV among women attending public antenatal clinics was more than one third (35%) higher in 2005 than it had been in 1999. While HIV infection levels among young pregnant women appear to be stabilizing, they continue to increase among older women. The epidemic is having a significant impact. Death rates from natural causes for women aged 25–34 years increased fivefold between 1997 and 2004, and for males aged 30–44 they more than doubled. A large part of those increases is due to the AIDS epidemic, and the increasing death toll has driven average life expectancy below 50 years in at least three provinces (p. 12). However, the sheer scale of need in this region means that a little less than one quarter (23%) of the estimated 4.6 million people in need of antiretroviral therapy in the region are receiving it (p. 16).

Journey to Jo'Burg (1988) and *Chain of Fire* (1989) by Beverley Naidoo

About the Author

Beverley Naidoo was born in Johannesburg, South Africa, in 1943, where she grew up under strict apartheid laws that gave privilege to white children. She attended a white-only school and never questioned the way blacks were treated. She graduated from the University of Witwatersrand in 1963 and at this time began to question the racism that surrounded her, eventually becoming a civil rights activist. At one point, Naidoo was arrested for taking part in the resistance movement; she commented, "Eight weeks of solitary confinement in jail, when I was twenty one, gave me a sense of how the country was a giant jail for most of its people" (Naidoo, 2006, ¶ 2). In 1965, Beverley was exiled to England and married a black South African exile. Apartheid laws forbade marriage between white and black people and barred them from living together with their children in South Africa, but they were, of course, free to do so in London. She left for England in 1965 and studied at the University of York, training to become a teacher. After graduating, Beverley Naidoo taught primary and secondary school in London for 18 years. She obtained a doctoral degree from the University of Southampton in 1991 and worked as Adviser for Cultural Diversity and English in Dorset. For her doctorate, she explored issues of racism with young people through literature and in fact continues to work tirelessly to promote children's entitlement to grow up free from racism and injustice. It was during the time of exile in England as her own children were growing up that Naidoo began to write her novels (Naidoo, 2006). She wasn't allowed to return to South Africa until after Nelson Mandela was released from prison in 1991.

Summary (*Journey to Jo'Burg*)

Mma lives and works in Johannesburg, far from the village where her children, 13-year-old Naledi; her younger brother, Tiro; and their baby sister, Dineo, call home. When Dineo suddenly becomes very sick, Naledi and Tiro know that their mother is the only one person who can save her. With a bag of sweet potatoes and a bottle of water, they set off on foot for a 300-kilometer (188-mile) journey to find Mma and bring her home. They conquer their fear of walking through towns without a "pass" that would permit them to be on the streets. They receive help from many people, both young and old, on their journey to the city of gold, Jo'Burg. Mma gets permission to leave the following day and return home to tend to her sick child. It is during this trip that Naledi and Tiro come to understand the dangers of being black in the city of Johannesburg. The children quickly learn that the struggle for freedom and dignity comes at the price of police brutality and death. They also realize the consequences of poverty, which deprives children of proper nutrition.

Summary (*Chain of Fire*)

This book, the sequel to *Journey to Jo'Burg*, begins with the sudden announcement from a white man from the government that the people of Naledi's village are to be relocated to "the homeland" in Bophurhatswana, an outlying area of Jo'Burg, now considered to be the townships. Chief Sekete, the landowner, too weak to stand up for his people, has betrayed them and the whites are now in control. With every reason to believe few would survive the removal, the villagers begin to resist. Relying on the strength of her friend, Taolo, who has witnessed resistance of blacks in Soweto (a suburb of Johannesburg), Naledi, now 15 years old, joins his resistance and consequently suffers a caning from the headmaster for discussing politics on the schoolyard. Taolo is expelled and events accelerate. Due to government forces and control, churches and homes are bulldozed, families are separated, and Taolo's father is murdered. The removal is accomplished, and, for the moment, it seems the white government has won. But Naledi and her neighbors are no longer the same villagers who once clung passively to subsistence. Lengthening their chain of fire from the new "homeland" in Bophurhatswana to friends in Soweto, they are becoming a unified people, determined to withstand the oppression and establish freedom.

Waiting for the Rain (1987) by Sheila Gordon

About the Author

Sheila Gordon was born January 22, 1927, in Johannesburg, South Africa. She received her bachelor's degree in 1946 from the University of Witwatersrand in Johannesburg, South Africa and later moved to New York City. Many of her books focus on the issues of South Africa, including *Unfinished Business* (1988), *The Middle of Somewhere* (1991), and *Waiting for the Rain* (1987). The latter two books were both awarded the Jane Addams Children's Book Award by the Jane

Addams Peace Association and the Women's International League for Peace and Freedom. Gordon has also written an autobiography entitled *A Modest Harmony: Seven Summers in a Scottish Glen* (1982) in which she describes simple living during her family's vacations in Scotland (Lechtman & Watta, 1996).

In an interview with *The Atlantic Monthly's* Tony Lechtman and David Watta (1996), Sheila Gordon described her inspiration for writing *Waiting for the Rain* (1987). She said the idea for the novel came from watching a television show in which a group of white soldiers rode into a township to quell an uprising of black schoolchildren.

> I saw how scared the white soldiers looked; the same fear was on the faces of the black children—who were the same age as the soldiers. I was moved to pity by the situation; these children were pitted against one another by the conditions adults had laid down for them. (Lechtman & Watta, 1996)

Out of this brief image a whole novel developed in which the characters Tengo and Frikkie lose the innocence of their childhood relationship when both are forced into the apartheid conflict.

Summary

Waiting for the Rain (1987) highlights and brings to life the tragedy and inhumanity of racial discrimination through the story of two boyhood friends, Tengo (black) and Frikkie (white), and their experiences with apartheid in South Africa. Tengo works on a farm owned by Oom Koos, Frikkie's uncle. Frikkie, who loves farm life over city life, spends much of his time on the farm, and they become fast friends. Tengo desperately wants to learn and go to school, but there are no schools for him, a black boy, to attend. After an altercation between the boys during a birthday party at the master's house, Tengo's parents realize they must send him to Johannesburg to get his education. With time, Tengo adjusts to city life and is a top student in his school. Everything goes well until the massacres begin, and there are riots close to the black school. Tengo's dreams of becoming a college student are shattered when he joins in a black mob pressing for freedom that is met by the open fire of the white army and police. Stunned by the violence, Tengo flees, hotly pursued by Frikkie, who had joined the army and thought that the running Tengo was the black man who had killed his friends. When threatened, Tengo strikes Frikkie with a crowbar and renders him helpless. Through this ordeal, Frikkie's truly realizes the suffering that his race has inflicted upon the blacks. Despite all of the anger and desire for vengeance that have built up inside of Tengo, he releases Frikkie and realizes that Frikkie is not responsible for the disastrous times that are occurring in Africa. It is the misunderstandings on both sides that have caused the boys to be so polarized and forced to fight each other.

Chanda's Secrets (2004) by Allan Stratton

About the Author

Allan Stratton is an award-winning, internationally published and produced playwright and novelist. His two young adult novels have won numerous awards, but of special interest is *Chanda's Secrets* (2004), a novel that won the prestigious 2005 Michael L. Printz Honor Book Award for literary excellence in young adult literature as well as the 2005 Children's Africana Best Book Award. *Leslie's Journal* (Stratton, 2000), a novel about sexual abuse in adolescent dating relationships, was one of the American Library Association's "Best Books for Young Adults" in 2002. Stratton began his professional arts career while still in high school when his first play was published. He performed with the Stratford Festival and the Huron Country Playhouse while attending the University of Toronto in Canada. Throughout this period he continued to write and eventually became successful enough to write full time.

While the idea of writing *Chanda's Secrets* started with a conversation with his editor, the book itself grew out of Stratton's experiences in Africa, as well as the times he spent as caregiver for friends in the final stages of AIDS. In preparation to write *Chanda's Secrets*, Stratton traveled to South Africa, Zimbabwe, and Botswana, where various agencies introduced him to those who live with and those who are working to fight HIV/AIDS. He met with dozens of families living with HIV/AIDS in Monarch Township in Botswana and with many herbal doctors, spirit doctors, and clinic workers in the villages and cattle posts outside Francistown. From his travels, Stratton crafted Chanda's world by placing her in a small, fictional city in sub-Saharan Africa (Stratton, n.d.). In his forthcoming book, *Chanda's War* (in press), Chanda travels with her younger brother and sister to their ancestral village of Tiro to heal a family rift. A civil war breaks out in the neighboring country of Ngara and spills over the border, and Chanda's young siblings are stolen to become child soldiers. Chanda must find them or lose them forever (Stratton, n.d.).

Summary

Chanda's home was not always a shantytown in the fictional city of Bonang. Through a series of devastating deaths and moves, Chanda and her family end up living with a drunken philanderer in a small house inherited by Mama from a prior marriage. While illness and death are commonplace in Chanda's world, lies and secrets cover the unmentionable epidemic of AIDS. Instead, the deaths are attributed to cancer, tuberculosis, and hunting accidents. Families, including Chanda's, suffer in silence from this tragic disease to avoid the shame and social death that come with admitting the disease. While Chanda slowly realizes the truth about AIDS in her life, her stepfather, Jonah, turns to alcohol, the poor man's antidepressant, to cope with his disease. When her mother, who also has HIV/AIDS but doesn't disclose it to her children, pretends to leave to visit family back at the cattle post, Chanda is left to care for her younger siblings and her best friend, Esther, who becomes infected after turning to prostitution to support herself. Eventually, Chanda finds a way to bring her ill mother home so she can die in dignity, surrounded by her family who love her. The book ends with Chanda facing her fear of knowing the truth as she arranges AIDS testing for herself, her friend, and her siblings.

Making Connections

Schema theory explains how previous experiences, knowledge, emotions, and understandings affect what and how people learn (Harvey & Goudvis, 2000). Schema is the background knowledge and experience readers bring to the text, and when students are taught how to connect to text, they are able to better understand what they are reading. According to Keene and Zimmermann (1997), reading comprehension improves when students make text-to-self, text-to-text, and text-to-world connections. The following list of questions can be used for this unit, and Figure 11.1 shows a sample journal response to a text-to-text question for this Novel Guide created by preservice teacher Brett Sutton.

Figure 11.1. Student Journal Response to a Making Connections Text-to-Text Question

---

Text-to-Text: "What else have I read about HIV/AIDS?"

I have read some startling statistics on HIV/AIDS. From various handouts and class notes I have received in past Health and Geography classes I have taken, over an estimated 25 million people have died from AIDS in the last 25 years. While America may have its run-ins with AIDS, other countries suffer far more from the sickness. In Africa there are an estimated 11 million orphaned due to AIDS. I have also seen a film about the spread of AIDS through the pop-culture of America's youth. This film is *Kids* (1995) directed by Larry Clark. This film is about an unknowingly HIV positive teenager who sets out to deflower as many virgins as possible. The film takes a sharp turn toward reality when a girl he slept with in the past was told she had contracted the virus. This girl was later date raped on a couch at a party by the main character's best friend. The cycle continues in Middle America.

Making Connections Questions for *Journey to Jo'Burg* (1988), *Chain of Fire* (1989), *Waiting for the Rain* (1987), **and** *Chanda's Secrets* (2004)

	Naidoo's *Journey to Jo'Burg* (1988) and *Chain of Fire* (1989)	Gordon's *Waiting for the Rain* (1987)	Stratton's *Chanda's Secrets* (2004)
Text-to-Self	What do I know about living in poverty? What do I know about people who do not have medical insurance? How do I feel about my freedom to attend school? What do I know about segregation? What do I know about proper nutrition?	How do I feel about my rights to an education? What do I know about segregation in this country and apartheid in South Africa? Is my education worth fighting for? If my freedom worth fighting for? What would I fight for?	What do I know about HIV/AIDS? What experiences have I had with sickness and death? What do I know about burial ceremonies? What would I do if I lost both of my parents?
Text-to-Text	What else have I read about people living in poverty? What have I read about people that cannot afford medical treatment? What have I read about children who are denied access to education? What have I read about racial discrimination? What have I read about malnutrition?	What have I read about children who are denied an education? What have I read about racial discrimination and apartheid? What have I read in which children march for a cause they believed in? What have I read about children fighting for freedom and their rights as children?	What have I read about HIV/AIDS? What have I read about sickness, death, and burial ceremonies? What have I read about children surviving without their parents?
Text-to-World	What are the consequences of living in poverty? What happens to people who cannot afford medical treatment? What conditions prevent children from attending school? Why does racial inequality still exist? Why does hunger still exist in the world today?	What are children's rights to attend school? What conditions prevent children from attending school? Where does racial discrimination still exist? What issues are worth fighting for? How can we support equal rights issues?	What has created the pandemic of HIV/AIDS? Why is it spreading so rapidly? What can be done to help people with HIV/AIDS? What is the HIV/AIDS situation in my country?

Critical Exploration of Themes

The authors of the novels discussed in this chapter all have firsthand experience with the struggles for human rights existing in South Africa. Both Beverley Naidoo and Sheila Gordon grew up in Johannesburg, South Africa, during the era of apartheid (1948–1994). As Gordon said, "While growing up in South Africa, I found myself observing an officially sanctioned, unjust society, and I could see how everyday lives were shaped by the politics of apartheid" (Lechtman & Watta, 1996, ¶ 5). Both authors wrote compelling novels in which their young characters experience devastating consequences for their involvement in the politics of apartheid, whether they are black or white. The setting for their novels takes place in or about Johannesburg, South Africa. On the other hand, Allan Stratton was influenced by the dramatic spread of HIV/AIDS in southern Africa and the consequences to families affected by it. The following describes some of the key components of apartheid and HIV/AIDS that can be used as background knowledge and discussion of the novels.

Apartheid and the Struggle for Equality

In the novels by Naidoo and Gordon, the protagonists become involved in the politics of apartheid. The apartheid government devised complex, discriminatory criteria to determine the four racial groups: black, white, Indian, and colored. Inequities created by this law that are experienced by young characters in the novels include substandard housing (rare plumbing or electricity), poor medical treatment, inadequate salaries to pay for basic needs, and inadequate education for nonwhites (International Marketing Council for South Africa, 2006). In Naidoo's *Journey to Jo'Burg* (1988), the children become desperate when their baby sister is suffering and possibly dying, not from an incurable disease, but from starvation. Their mother, who works as a maid for a wealthy doctor's family, does not make enough to buy substantive food for her children, never mind afford medical treatment. In Gordon's *Waiting for the Rain* (1987), the black protagonist, Tengo, lives in poverty on a wealthy Afrikaaner's farm where his parents serve the master. Although he does learn to read and write, he desires a formal education. Tengo eventually receives an inferior Bantu education designated for blacks only in Johannesburg that is in sharp contrast to the school opportunities of his white friend from the farm, who receives an excellent, free education. Influenced by the Soweto Massacre, Gordon's and Naidoo's characters go on to show the strength of the black student activists in Johannesburg who boycott the Bantu schools and fight for equal educational opportunities.

HIV/AIDS in Sub-Saharan Africa

One of the most serious challenges that face African countries and their partners in the global community is the stigma and discrimination that prevent people from getting the medical support they need. Stratton's *Chanda's Secrets* (2004) shows the consequences of one family that is challenged by HIV/AIDS. The story begins with Chanda's youngest sister dying of AIDS, and soon her stepfather becomes quite ill, as does her mother and her best friend. While Chanda's mother leaves her family to die alone, Chanda's love for her enables her to bring her mother back home. The solidarity of the family gives them the courage to face the stigma and acquire some medical aid. However, in reality, most are not so fortunate. People with or suspected of having HIV may be turned away from overburdened health care services, lose employment, or be evicted from their homes by their own families. Women and girls are particularly vulnerable and are commonly discriminated against in terms of access to education, employment, credit, health care, land, and inheritance. Infected members of the family frequently find themselves stigmatized and discriminated against within the home. While Chanda's immediate family support one another, her ill mother was discriminated against by family members when she returned to her ancestral village, Tiro. The stigma can extend into the next generation, placing an emotional burden on those left behind, especially if communities fail to acknowledge the problem and provide for the children ("HIV & AIDS," 2006).

Teacher Talk

In 1956, Benjamin Bloom headed a group of educational psychologists who developed a classification of levels of intellectual behavior important in learning. Bloom found that over 95% of the test questions students encountered required them to think only at the lowest possible level, the recall of information. As a result, he identified six levels of thinking or learning that range from the simple recall or recognition of facts, at the lowest level, through increasingly more complex and abstract mental levels, to the highest order, which is classified as evaluation. The taxonomy provides a useful structure in which to categorize discussion questions that evoke higher levels of thinking from the students (Learning Skills, 2003). The following questions apply each of Bloom's levels of thinking to further explore the novels discussed in this chapter.

Using Bloom's Taxonomy to Structure Discussion Questions for *Journey to Jo'Burg* (1988), *Chain of Fire* (1989), *Waiting for the Rain* (1987), and *Chanda's Secrets* (2004)

	Naidoo's *Journey to Jo'Burg* (1988) and *Chain of Fire* (1989)	Gordon's *Waiting for the Rain* (1987)	Stratton's *Chanda's Secrets* (2004)
Knowledge	What did Naledi and Tiro sacrifice to try and help their baby sister? What are some examples of racism given in the novel? What are some examples of poverty represented in the novel? What were some of the reasons that the community did not want to move?	What does Frikkie love about the farm? What do Frikkie and Tengo enjoy doing together? What were they not allowed to do together? What does Tengo want to do more than anything else? What are some of the inequities Tengo begins to notice at the farm?	What are some terms that convey death and mourning? What are Chanda's secrets? What are some of the contrasts that depict underdevelopment versus development or modernization.
Comprehension	What were the reasons that Mma lived in Jo'Burg? What made Naledi and Tiro's journey to Jo'Burg complicated? Why was Grace's brother, Dumi, arrested? What were the major events of the journey that changed Naledi's outlook in life?	What does Tengo learn about life in the city and apartheid from his cousin Joseph? How does Tengo feel about Frikkie's offer to make him boss-boy? What does Tengo take away from the history lesson from Oom Koos? What happened to Tengo at Oom Koos's birthday party?	What characterizes rural life compared to urban life? What personal and social factors motivate Mama to marry the men she does? What is the difference between a rural education and an urban one?
Application	What are slogans for potential banners that reflect the feelings of the characters? What freedoms would you consider marching for? What rights should children have? Do you agree with the students' decision to march against being moved to a "homeland"? Why or why not?	How does Tengo change and adjust to school and to city life? How does Frikkie change as he matures and joins the Army? What is the purpose of a school boycott?	What part do unions and mining play in South Africa and in this novel? How does Mrs. Tafa use power in this novel? What are the causes and effects of global sex trade?

Analysis	What are the effects of apartheid represented in the novel?	Why does Tengo begin to avoid Frikkie?	What are some of the reasons why Jonas drinks?
	Do you see Bophelong as a place that is giving its people life? Why or why not?	What makes Tengo feel helpless and powerless?	How are HIV/AIDS victims treated in this novel?
	How did Mr. Molaba's treatment of Naledi make you feel? Do you think he was justified in punishing Naledi? Why or why not?	What fuels Tengo's thirst for knowledge?	What are the symptoms of AIDS, especially in Sara's case?
		How did the events at Soweto change Joseph?	From what might Sara have died? Why do you think that?
		What are the problems with Bantu education?	
		What characterizes white liberals? Why is Joseph opposed to them?	
Synthesis	How did Naledi mature in this novel? What did she learn from her journey?	How has apartheid shaped Frikkie's attitudes toward blacks?	What impact does poverty have on the characters in this novel?
	What are some of the ways in which the people of Bophelong were being pushed around?	How has apartheid shaped Tengo's attitudes toward whites?	How do social and economic conditions affect moral choices in the novel?
	How is the enemy like a machine?	What factors contribute to Tengo's joining the resistance group to fight apartheid?	What characterizes Chanda's bravery and courage in the novel?
	Do you think that the resistance movement has a strong voice? What have they accomplished with their actions?	How does Tengo deal with his rage?	
		Claire wants to design ideal community projects. What would that look like?	
Evaluation	What would you have done in Naledi and Tiro's situation?	What good is education to a kaffir (black African)?	At what age should a child be told about a family member's death?
	What could you do to help the health care crisis in South Africa?	Why might violence be necessary to bring about change?	What should they be told? Why?
	Naledi feels guilty about fibbing to her grandmother, yet she also believes that the work she is doing is very important. Do you think Naledi is making the right decision? Why or why not?	Could there be a peaceful solution to racial inequities?	What should be the role of health care in a stable society?
		How should Tengo deal with the violence of his comrades who turned activist?	How do silence, shame, and secretiveness operate as forms of social control in the novel?
		Did Tengo make the right decision in joining the African National Congress freedom fighters? What choices did he have?	

Cross-Curricular Activities

The Cross-Curricular Activities for this unit serve as preparation for students to participate in the process drama that constitutes the Making-A-Difference Project. Students will create a class photo essay, conduct a fictional "mock" interview of a person living with HIV/AIDS, and create a public awareness poster. They will use these projects during the process drama that follows in the Making-A-Difference Project.

Completing a Photo Essay

In order to create a class photo essay, ask each student in the class to download and print a photo documenting HIV/AIDS in Africa. The PBS Photoscope of Africa website at www.pbs.org/wnet/africa/photoscope/index.html and photos by Gideon Mendal found online at www.ayudaenaccion.org/contenidos/documentos/previo/Speaking-out%20ingl.pdf are excellent sources for photos by outstanding photographers from around the world.

After students acquire the photographs, ask them to frame them on construction paper. Create a visual display by posting the photographs on a classroom wall. As they take ownership of their photos, students should write a one-page rationale for their choice. They should also discuss obstacles, both concrete and abstract, that prevent the persons in their photographs from receiving the medical and emotional support they need.

Conducting Fictional Interviews With People Living With HIV/AIDS

For this activity, students need to conduct a fictional interview with a man, woman, or child living with HIV/AIDS. An excellent resource for this activity is an Internet site on HIV/AIDS in Africa found at http://allafrica.com/photoessay/womenaids/photo1.html. This website features photos and stories of real African women who are living with AIDS, and students can use these real people and stories as the basis for their interviews. Ask students to generate questions of their own, or use some of the following questions to guide their interviews:

- Do you know how were you infected with HIV?
- How has HIV/AIDS changed your life?
- Have you experienced stigmatization as a result of having HIV/AIDS? If so, what have you experienced and how do you deal with it?
- What does the future hold for you and your family?
- What help would be beneficial to you and your family?

Students should write a one-page anonymous character profile of the person they interviewed, which they will share during the process drama.

If time permits, ask students to also create a Memory Book for the family of the person they "interviewed" with HIV/AIDS. Before they die, parents with AIDS often create Memory Books or Memory Boxes for their young children to remember them by once they're gone. Memory Books and Memory Boxes contain favorite memories, family traditions, photographs, special events, journal entries, family trees, and other artifacts and information that serve to remind young children of their relationship with their parent(s) once the parents are deceased. The artifacts in the Memory Book can "help the parent and the child integrate the past and the present, and prepare the child for the future" (Pillay, 2003, p. 115). The Memory Book keeps memories alive for children who are forced to relocate or are separated from their siblings after the death of their parents, and creating one will help students better understand how AIDS truly affects not only those who suffer from the disease but also the family members and loved ones of the people.

Public Awareness Posters

One of the great challenges Africans must overcome as they tackle the HIV/AIDS pandemic ravaging their continent is awareness education. Just as the character Chanda was uneducated in the matter, so are countless other people around the world. Many people lack even basic knowledge of the disease, its transmission, and possible treatments. As seen in the novel *Chanda's Secrets* (2004), there is a stigma that also makes it difficult to prevent and treat the disease, as those with HIV face widespread public fear, scorn, and alienation. Thus, HIV/AIDS education and awareness are particularly important aspects in the battle against the disease. In preparation for the Making-A-Difference Project, ask students to create Public Awareness Posters for HIV/AIDS education. See Table 11.2 for a list of suggested requirements for the public awareness poster. For examples of Public Awareness Posters for HIV/AIDS Education, go to http://allafrica.com/photoessay/aidsawareness/photo1.html.

Making-A-Difference Project:
Process Drama on HIV/AIDS in South Africa:
"What Needs to Happen?"

Process drama is a powerful and motivating teaching tool that engages students in reading, writing, and visualizing for imaginative and functional purposes. According to Schneider and Jackson (2000), process drama "involves students in

Table 11.2. Public Awareness Poster Requirements

- Posters must be submitted on poster or illustration board.
- The overall dimensions shall be approximately 15″ X 20″.
- All artwork must be original and may be any media desired with the exception of pencil, chalk, charcoal, or glitter.
- Stenciled, traced, computer-generated, or commercially manufactured stick-on lettering or graphics are prohibited.
- Posters will be judged on both the clarity of the educational message and the quality of the art.
- Posters with misspelled words will be eliminated.

imaginary, unscripted, and spontaneous scenes which are framed by curricular topics, teacher objectives, and students' personal experiences" (p. 38). A process drama is composed of a series of episodes in which both teacher and students take various roles in order to provide multiple perspectives in solving a critical issue. First, the teacher prepares the materials needed for the episodes and provides any introductory background information necessary for the students' understanding of the topic. The teacher also should decide on the physical setting for the episodes, prepare questions to ask the students, and prepare a plan for debriefing the students at the end of each episode(s). The process drama takes close to two hours, depending on the depth of conversation and deliberation.

In this process drama, students will gain an empathy and appreciation of the complexity of the struggle against HIV/AIDS in sub-Saharan African countries. They will become personally engaged in this struggle for human rights in developing countries, especially in obtaining medical treatments. In preparation for this process drama, students should have completed the Cross-Curricular Activities that will become focus points during the drama. The following materials should be displayed in the room:

- Photos of African people that students have downloaded, framed, and placed in a visual display on a classroom wall
- Poster or overhead transparency with HIV/AIDS facts taken from a website such as www.avert.org
- Visual display of the students' Public Awareness Posters
- Video clip from *Pandemic: Facing Aids* (DVD) directed by Rory Kennedy (2002) or other available film to show video clips during the Talk Show
- Brainteaser photos and scenarios from the UNICEF website (www.unicef.org/voy/explore/aids/713_940.html) displayed in a Microsoft PowerPoint presentation

The following episodes of the drama can be implemented either individually or collectively, depending on time and interest.

Episode 1: Photojournalists Interview—Which Photo Did You Take?

In the role-play for this episode, the teacher becomes a representative of former U.S. President Bill Clinton's Clinton Global Initiative advisory committee. The Clinton Global Initiative is a nonpartisan catalyst for action, bringing together a community of global leaders to devise and implement innovative solutions to some of the world's most pressing challenges. As representative, the teacher will convene a group of photojournalists (the students in the class) to discuss their photography of African people. Ask them: "Which photo did you take?" and "What did you intend to portray about life in Africa?" After congratulating them on their fine photography, invite them to join a task force to advise Bill Clinton as he launches his New World HIV/AIDS Campaign. For more information about this campaign, go to www.clintonglobalinitiative.org/home.nsf/pt_home.

Episode 2: Task Force for Clinton's New World HIV/AIDS Campaign

In this episode, the teacher remains in the role of a representative to Clinton's advisory committee inviting photojournalists (students) to join a task force to prepare for the upcoming meeting in New York City. As you call the meeting together, begin by reviewing some of the HIV/AIDS facts found at www.avert.org. Given these facts, hold a meeting to discuss the impact of HIV and AIDS in Africa. Ask the photojournalists to imagine that they have just received an invitation to the meeting that was held on September 15, 2005, to aid Clinton in deciding how best to put to use the funding received from Congress and must now prepare for that meeting. Ask photojournalists how they might document the impact of HIV/AIDS in sub-Saharan Africa in order to advise President Clinton's Global Initiative. Divide photojournalists into groups of four or five to devise a proposal for a plan of action for documenting the suffering and making recommendations as to how the money could best be spent to deal with HIV/AIDS in South Africa. This could be a small-group collaborative writing activity.

Episode 3: Public Awareness Posters for HIV/AIDS

Display the posters photojournalists (students) have prepared around the room before beginning this episode. Continuing in the role as a representative of Clinton's advisory committee, provide them with sticky notes and ask them to

Figure 11.2. First Place Public Awareness Poster

IMPRISONED BY **AIDS**

EDUCATION AND UNDERSTANDING CAN SET THEM **FREE**

walk around the room, study the posters, and give feedback. They should write comments on the sticky notes and attach them to at least five posters. When they have completed the task, lead a discussion of the ideas presented in the posters. Which poster was most effective? Which poster addressed the most critical issue? Which poster used the best graphic design? Ask them to vote on the best poster and tell why they think it is best. Award a prize or bonus points to the winning poster and possibly the runners-up as well. The model that appears in Figure 11.2 was inspired by a First Place Public Awareness Poster by a local high school teacher, Judith Walker-Yeager.

Episode 4: Press Conference: Interviewing 26 African Women Living With HIV/AIDS

For this episode, divide the students into two groups. One group will role-play being reporters for major news media organizations, and the other group will role-play representing the person they interview who is living with HIV/AIDS. The teacher continues in the role of representative of Clinton's advisory committee who organizes the interviewing process and then moderates a press conference. Give reporters name tags and ask them to interview the students role-playing those living with AIDS. After the interviews are complete, moderate a press conference to discuss the commonalities and attitudes of people living with AIDS and what obstacles they face in obtaining support. Because Clinton's group is in a position to help HIV/AIDS victims, be sure to voice their concerns about the epidemic and solutions that might help them the most.

Episode 5: Talk Show Situation With Tucker Carlson—The Pandemic HIV/AIDS Issue: "What Needs to Happen?"

For this episode, the teacher either assumes the role of Tucker Carlson or invites a student to take this role. Tucker Carlson is the host of a U.S. television news program on MSNBC called *Tucker*, in which he leads fast-paced conversation about the day's developments in news, politics, world issues, and pop culture. The teacher appoints a technical director to manage the video clips. Each group of photojournalists sends a representative to join Carlson's panel on the stage. Other students, as photojournalists, stand by to be interviewed "long distance." The rest of the class becomes the audience for the show. Begin the talk show by showing a five-minute video clip from *Pandemic: Facing Aids* (Kennedy, 2002) and then invite photojournalists to respond to the issues and suggest what needs to happen. Continue the discussion by interviewing photojournalists and panel members in response to other video clips or brainteaser questions from the UNICEF website at www.unicef.org/voy/explore/aids/713_940.html. Ask the students, "What are the issues involved in these situations? What is your opinion?"

Conclude this episode and the process drama with a discussion of what needs to happen. How shall we move forward? Photojournalists begin by brainstorming ideas for HIV/AIDS education either to prevent new infections to improve the quality of life for HIV-positive people or to reduce the stigma and discrimination. The teacher asks, "How shall we get involved?" Make a real difference by implementing ideas for education from the discussion or by fundraising to make a financial contribution to research or to foundations supporting HIV/AIDS victims.

Conclusion

In this unit, students learn about the various struggles for human rights that existed in South Africa in the years of apartheid and in the post-apartheid era. Students discover personal connections associated with the global interconnectivity of the HIV/AIDS pandemic, and they gain understanding of the need for universal human rights concerning not only HIV/AIDS but other apartheid and post-apartheid issues, such as racial equality and the right to equal education for all citizens. The Cross-Curricular Activities for this unit require students to make a difference through public awareness and service projects to build tolerance, empathy, and compassion for those living with HIV/AIDS, especially the orphaned children of the world.

REFERENCES

AVERT. (2006). *HIV & AIDS in Africa*. Retrieved February 20, 2006, from http://www.avert.org/aafrica.htm

Byrnes, R.M. (ed.). (1996). *South Africa: A Country Study*. Retrieved February 18, 2007, from http://countrystudies.us/south-africa/56.htm.

Central Intelligence Agency (CIA). *The World Factbook: History of South Africa*. Retrieved February 20, 2006, from https://www.cia.gov/cia/publications/factbook/print/sf.html

Clinton, W.J. (2005). *Our mission*. Retrieved May 24, 2006, from http://www.clintonglobalinitiative.org/NETCOMMUNITY/Page.aspx?&pid=891&srcid=387

Chokshi, M., Carter, C., Gupta, D., Martin, T., & Allen, R. (1995, Spring). The history of apartheid in South Africa. In *Computers and the apartheid regime in South Africa*. Retrieved June 19, 2006, http://www-cs-students.stanford.edu/~cale/cs201/apartheid.hist.html

Clinton Global Initiative. (2005). Retrieved February 23, 2006, from http://www.clintonglobalinitiative.org/NETCOMMUNITY/Page.aspx?&pid=891&srcid=387

Fredriksson, J. & Kanabus, A. (Eds.). (2007). *HIV & Aids discrimination and stigma: The way forward*. Retrieved May 11, 2007 from http://www.avert.org/aidsstigma.htm

Harvey, S. & Goudvis, A. (2000). *Strategies that work: Teaching comprehension to enhance understanding*. Portland, ME: Stenhouse.

International Marketing Council of South Africa. (2006). *A short history of South Africa*. Retrieved March 7, 2007, from http://www.southafrica.info/ess_info/sa_glance/history/history.htm

International Reading Association & National Council of Teachers of English. (1996).

Standards for the English language arts. Newark, DE; Urbana, IL: Authors.

Keene, E.O., & Zimmermann, S. (1997). *Mosaic of thought: Teaching comprehension in a reader's workshop*. Portsmouth, NH: Heinemann.

Learning Skills Program. (2003). *Bloom's taxonomy*. Retrieved August 20, 2005, from http://www.coun.uvic.ca/learn/program/hndouts/bloom.html

Lechtman, T., & Watta, D. (1996, December). A Conversation with Sheila Gordon. *The Atlantic Online*. Retrieved August 15, 2005, from http://www.theatlantic.com/unbound/factfict/sgordon.htm

Naidoo, B. (2006). *Frequently asked questions*. Retrieved February 17, 2006, from http://www.beverleynaidoo.com/questions.html

National Council for the Social Studies. (1994). *Expectations of excellence: Curriculum standards for social studies*. Silver Spring, MD: Author.

Pillay, Y. (2003). Storytelling as a psychological intervention for AIDS orphans in Africa. In A. Singhal & W.S. Howard (Eds.), *The children of Africa confront AIDS* (pp. 105-118). Athens: Ohio University Press.

Schneider, J.J., & Jackson, S.A.W. (2000). Process drama: A special space and place for writing. *The Reading Teacher, 54*, 38–51.

Stratton, A. (n.d.). *Biography*. Retrieved February 20, 2006, from http://www.allanstratton.com/strattonbiorev.html

UNAIDS & World Health Organization. (2006, December). *AIDSEpidemic Update*. Retrieved February 17, 2007, from http://data.unaids.org/pub/EpiReport/2006/2006_EpiUpdate_en.pdf

LITERATURE CITED

Gordon, S. (1987). *Waiting for the rain: A novel of South Africa*. Danbury, CT: Orchard Books.

Naidoo, B. (1988). *Journey to Jo'burg: A South African story* (E. Velasquez, Ill.). New York: HarperTrophy.

Naidoo, B. (1989). *Chain of fire*. New York: HarperTrophy.

Stratton, A. (2004). *Chanda's secrets*. Willowdale, ON: Annick Press.

Stratton, A. (in press). *Chanda's war*. New York: HarperCollins.

FILM CITED

Kennedy, R. (Director). (2002). *Pandemic: Facing AIDS* [Motion picture] United States: Moxie

Firecracker Films and Umbrage Editions.

CHAPTER 12

Life and Literature in Botswana: Resolving Cultural Conflicts to Create a Better World

Jacqueline N. Glasgow

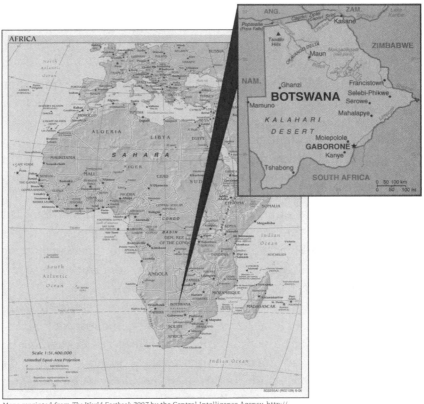

Maps reprinted from *The World Factbook 2007* by the Central Intelligence Agency, http://www.cia.gov/cia/publications/factbook.

Exploring African Life and Literature: Novel Guides to Promote Socially Responsive Learning edited by Jacqueline N. Glasgow and Linda J. Rice. © 2007 by the International Reading Association.

> "There is nothing like dream to create the future. Utopia today,
> flesh and blood tomorrow."
>
> —Victor Hugo, *Les Miserables* (1862/1976)

Botswana, the setting for the novels in this chapter, is located in south-central Africa, its borders surrounded by Namibia, Zambia, Zimbabwe, and South Africa. Most of the country is near-desert, with the Kalahari occupying the western part of the country. The eastern part is hilly, with salt lakes in the north. The country is composed of a largely roadless wilderness of savannas, deserts, wetlands, and salt pans. The population of approximately one million is sparse, with 79% being Tswana (or Setswana), 11% Kalanga, 3% Basarwa, and 7% considered "other," including white (Infoplease, 2007, ¶ 6).

While Botswana has one of the world's highest known rates of HIV/AIDS infection, it also has one of Africa's most progressive and comprehensive programs for dealing with the disease. Therefore, rather than focusing on human rights issues connected with HIV/AIDS or some of the more serious issues of struggle explored in other chapters of this book, this unit focuses on the best possibilities for life in Botswana, and the tone in the books is one that is hopeful and optimistic despite issues of struggle existing as a backdrop to the stories. In *When Rain Clouds Gather* (1969), Bessie Head, one of Africa's renowned women writers, envisions a utopian society in which there is racial harmony and peace of mind. Written against the backdrop of apartheid raging in South Africa, Bessie Head's characters find refuge in Botswana as they leave behind the cruelty and violence of their past lives and work together to increase food production. In a lighthearted series beginning with *The No. 1 Ladies' Detective Agency* (1998), Alexander McCall Smith invites readers to learn about the traditional values of Africa, especially courtesy and respect for one another. McCall Smith's sense of humor makes these stories light, engaging, and entertaining.

The Cross-Curricular Activities for these novels are designed to help students to learn more about cultural life of the people by giving One-Minute Vocabulary Reports. Students examine character development by creating Character Bulletin Boards and writing a Poem in Two Voices. The Making-A-Difference Project invites students to create zines that address social, cultural, and environmental issues of Botswana. The overview on page 253 illustrates how the Novel Guides in this chapter and their corresponding activities align with standards for the English language arts (International Reading Association [IRA] & National Council of Teachers of English [NCTE], 1996) and curriculum standards for the social studies (National Council for the Social Studies [NCSS], 1994).

NOVELS
- *When Rain Clouds Gather* (1969) by Bessie Head
- The No. 1 Ladies' Detective Agency series (1998–2004) by Alexander McCall Smith

CROSS-CURRICULAR ACTIVITIES
- One-Minute Vocabulary Reports
- Character Bulletin Boards
- Poems in Two Voices

MAKING-A-DIFFERENCE PROJECT
Create Zines to Address Social, Cultural, and Environmental Issues in Botswana

STANDARDS FOR THE ENGLISH LANGUAGE ARTS
#2 Students read a wide range of literature to understand human experience.

#7 Students conduct research on issues and interests.

#8 Students use a variety of technological and informational resources to gather and synthesize information and to create and communicate knowledge.

#12 Students use spoken, written, and visual language to accomplish their own purposes.

Adapted from IRA and NCTE. (1996). *Standards for the English Language Arts.* Newark, DE: International Reading Association; Urbana, IL: National Council of Teachers of English.

CURRICULUM STANDARDS FOR THE SOCIAL STUDIES
#1f Culture: Learners interpret patterns of behavior reflecting the traditional values and attitudes of Botswana that pose obstacles to cross-cultural understanding.

#2c Time, Continuity, & Change: Learners identify and describe significant periods and patterns of change involving post-apartheid times.

#9 Global Connections: Learners analyze causes, consequences, and possible solutions to environmental issues of food production in Botswana.

Adapted with the permission of the National Council for the Social Studies (NCSS). For the NCSS standards, see the publication *Expectations of Excellence: Curriculum Standards for Social Studies* (Washington, DC: National Council for the Social Studies, 1994). See also www.socialstudies.org.

Social and Historical Context

The political context for Bessie Head's *When Rain Clouds Gather* (1969) is set in Botswana during the 1960s. It reflects both the apartheid of South Africa from which the protagonist seeks political asylum and the more amenable social climate of Botswana (see chapter 10 for more background information on apartheid). South African apartheid formally began following the elections in 1948, and the legislation became increasingly more restrictive and repressive for blacks. During the 1960s, resistance to apartheid began building under the strong leadership of Nelson Mandela and others. For instance, there was a growing resistance to African women carrying pass books (a document similar to a passport) and to Bantu education, which provided an inferior education for blacks. To escape the violence and cruelty of this political movement, citizens such as Bessie Head found a way to flee the country.

Botswana, located directly north of South Africa, was known to harbor refugees as the native residents had been left to their own devices after achieving independence in 1966. As a British Protectorate of Bechuanaland, rather than a settler colony, the country was relatively unchanged by colonialism. The people distrusted British control, but in contrast to other surrounding countries, there were very few whites living in Botswana. Botswana was known as one of the world's poorest and most sparsely populated countries. Bessie Head was writing during the period just before independence when the internal political conflicts pitted the Pan-African socialist movement and the traditional chief system against the conservative government that had been elected to lead the country to its independence. The country is characterized by poverty, a changing political system, and drought (Central Intelligence Agency [CIA], 2006).

While Bessie Head's novel captures life in Botswana prior to its independence, Alexander McCall Smith set The No. 1 Ladies' Detective Agency series (1998–2004) in the modern city of Gaborone, Botswana. Since gaining independence in 1966, Botswana has thrived as a country. Four decades of uninterrupted civilian leadership, progressive social policies, and significant capital investment have created one of the most dynamic economies in Africa. Mineral extraction, principally diamond mining, dominates economic activity, though tourism is a growing sector due to the country's conservation practices and extensive nature preserves (CIA, 2006). Today Botswana enjoys a stable government and good health, educational, and economic standards that are reflected in Alexander McCall Smith's novels.

When Rains Clouds Gather (1969) by Bessie Head

About the Author

Bessie Head, one of Africa's most prominent writers, was born in South Africa in 1937. Head was born of an illicit union between a Scottish woman and a black stable boy at a time when interracial relationships were illegal. As punishment, Head's mother's family committed her mother to a mental asylum where the baby was born. Head was taken from her mother at birth and raised in a foster home. At age 13, she was sent to an Anglican missionary school and eventually became a teacher in 1957. After teaching for only a few years, Bessie Head began a career in journalism, first writing for the *Golden City Post* in Johannesburg and then founding her own newspaper, *The Citizen*, in Cape Town. There, she met and married Harold Head, a man interested in political journalism. In 1964, as political turmoil escalated in South Africa and emotional instability instigated by divorce ravaged her life, Bessie and her son, Howard, managed to find peace and refuge in Botswana. She remained a refugee there for 15 years before she was granted citizenship. In spite of a severe mental breakdown, she wrote three major novels—*When Rain Clouds Gather* (1969), *Maru* (1971), and *A Question of Power* (1974)—as well as other works during her exile in Botswana. After brief international recognition, Bessie Head died of hepatitis in 1986 at the age of 49. She has earned an international reputation as one of Africa's most remarkable writers (Bhana, 2000).

Summary

This novel follows an African refugee named Makhaya Maseko who, after serving time in prison in Johannesburg for sabotage, flees across the border into Botswana. He settles in the village of Golema Mmidi (named for the occupation of the village, crop growing), which seems friendly to refugees and populated by people seeking a better life. Makhaya meets an elder of the community, Dinorego, who respects his education and mentors him in the ways of the local people. Also joining the community is an Englishman by the name of Gilbert Balfour, whose interest is in establishing an agricultural project that would better the lives of the villagers. Makhaya joins Gilbert's cause to involve the villagers, particularly the women, to adopt new agricultural techniques that would increase the yield of crops. They also form a cattle cooperative, which is not popular with the local village chief who personally benefits from keeping the people poor and in his control. In order to be successful the community must overcome rigid customs, a corrupt local chief who eventually commits suicide, and the unrelenting drought. In addition, Makhaya struggles to overcome his personal bitterness and hatred that are a legacy of his life as victim of South Africa's apartheid. Eventually, Makhaya and Gilbert, along with fellow villagers, succeed in building a community based on a strong work ethic, respect for one another, and prosperity.

The No. 1 Ladies' Detective Agency series (1998–2004) by Alexander McCall Smith

About the Author

Alexander McCall Smith was born in Zimbabwe (formerly called Southern Rhodesia) and was educated there before he moved to Scotland, where he continued his studies. He became a law professor in Edinburgh, Scotland, and it was in this role that he first returned to Africa to work in Botswana, where he helped to set up a new law school at the University of Botswana. In Botswana, while visiting friends in a small town called Mochudi, he happened to see a woman cheerfully chasing a chicken around a well-kept yard and making clucking noises as she ran. She eventually caught the chicken, offered it to his friends for Botswana National Day, and inspired McCall Smith to write a story about a cheerful woman with a traditional build (Random House, n.d.). What began as a short story has evolved into a popular series that McCall Smith continues to develop.

Today McCall Smith lives in Edinburgh with his wife, Elizabeth (a doctor in Edinburgh); their two daughters, Lucy and Emily; and their cat, Gordon. In addition to writing novels, he is currently Professor of Medical Law at the University of Edinburgh, but he has been a visiting professor at a number of other universities elsewhere, including ones in Italy and the United States (where he has twice been visiting professor at the Dedman School of Law in Dallas, Texas). His hobbies include playing wind instruments with an amateur orchestra he founded called The Really Terrible Orchestra in which he plays bassoon and his wife plays the flute (Random House, n.d.).

Summary

With the proceeds from selling her father's cattle after his death, Mma Ramotswe purchases both a home on Zebra Drive and a building on a busy street at the edge of town for the No. 1 Ladies' Detective Agency. She hires a secretary, Mma Makutsi and hangs out her shingle on her shop in a small storefront. After a slow start, she finds her services very much in demand. In this novel, her cases range from exposing a freeloader posing as a father to solving the mystery of a missing husband, following an Indian girl to identify her boyfriend, returning a stolen car to its rightful owner, identifying an unfaithful husband, exposing a witch doctor using human bones in the making of *muti* (medicine), exposing a fraudulent injury claim, and revealing the real reason behind a young doctor's inconsistent performance. Using her good sense and intuition, Mma Ramotswe supplies at least some information for her clients, but when she cannot, she waives her fee, which means all her clients come away satisfied with her work. When she has questions about these cases, she telephones her friend, Mr. J.L.B. Matekoni, for advice. Rra Matekoni is a good-natured, kind, and honest man who lends his wisdom freely to her as well as repairs her little white van. They often share a cup of bush tea in his office at Tlokweng Road Speedy Motors in the heat of the afternoon. The novel ends with his proposal to marry her.

In the subsequent novels in the series, the saga continues to follow the colorful characters as Mma Ramotswe, Rra Matekoni, and Mma Makutsi resolve the problems of their own lives as well as those of the good people in Garborone,

Botswana. In *Tears of the Giraffe* (2000) amidst wedding plans, the primary mystery to be solved concerns the disappearance and possible death of a U.S. woman's son who had joined a commune of people interested in growing vegetables in the harsh environment. In *Morality for Beautiful Girls* (2001), the mystery cases involve a Government Man who is convinced his new sister-in-law is out to poison his beloved younger brother, and the director of a beauty pageant needs help in finding a "good girl" who will not bring disgrace to the pageant and to Botswana. In *The Kalahari Typing School for Men* (2002), Mma Makutsi, enterprising woman that she has become, decides to better her situation by opening the Kalahari Typing School for Men, but she gets more than she bargained for. In *The Full Cupboard of Life* (2003), Mma Ramotswe is approached by a wealthy woman, owner of a beauty salon chain, who wants Mma Ramotswe to scrutinize her suitors. She is to determine which one of the four is most interested in her and which one is just after her money. In *In the Company of Cheerful Ladies* (2004), the cases involve locating a financier from Zambia who disappears with considerable company funds, retrieving Charlie (the apprentice mechanic) from his retreat with a rich woman and discovering a Shebeen (illegal drinking establishment) in Mr. J.L.B. Matekoni's old house. The mysteries are solved, and the novel closes leaving room for yet another book in the series.

Making Connections

Making connections between text-to-self, text-to-text, and text-to-world helps students to understand what they read (Keene & Zimmermann, 1997). The following questions offer specific prompts to help students explore the novels featured in this unit, and Figure 12.1 shows a sample journal response to a text-to-text question for this Novel Guide created by preservice teacher Jami Paintiff.

Figure 12.1. Student Journal Response to a Making Connections Text-to-Text Question

Text-to-Text: "What else have I read about racial discrimination?"

The point in my life when I began to ponder what it means to be privileged was after viewing a documentary titled *Color of Fear*. This films diaries the interactions among men of different races during a given weekend; throughout the weekend, they have several discussions regarding race. During the discussions, many of the men become very angry toward a Caucasian man. Initially after my viewing it, I was very angry and defensive of the Caucasian man whom, I felt, was being unjustly attacked. I viewed the documentary in a class, and the in-class discussion afterward allowed my anger to be redirected. Instead of being angry at the men being passionate about their experiences, I became angry about my inability to see the truth—that racial discrimination is alive and well.

Making Connections Questions for *When Rain Clouds Gather* (1969) and The No. 1 Ladies' Detective Agency series (1998–2004)

	Head's *When Rain Clouds Gather* (1969)	McCall Smith's No. 1 Ladies' Detective Agency series (1998–2004)
Text-to-Self	Do I seek peace of mind? Is there anything in my past I need to forget and forgive? What components would I expect to find in a utopian community? What do I believe about the values of independence and individualism?	What in my life would I like to change? Who do I turn to for guidance in solving my problems? How does one achieve happiness? What about my country would I like to change?
Text-to-Text	What else have I read about utopian societies? What else have I read about racial discrimination? What else have I read about apartheid?	What other mysteries have I read that are alike or different from this one? What other books have I read with strong, female characters? What famous detectives have I read about?
Text-to-World	What environmental issues affect food production in my region? What do I know about recycling and other ways to preserve our natural resources? Where do I see people living together peacefully?	What is the crime rate in my city or state? How do detectives and lawyers help people? How are the moral standards changing in my society? How is my culture different from the one described in this series?

Critical Exploration of Themes

Head's novel *When Rain Clouds Gather* (1969), like one of Mma Ramotswe's cases in *The No. 1 Ladies' Detective Agency* (1998), is based on a famous agricultural project at the Bamangwato Development Farm. In Botswana, the sandy, saline soil is considered by most to be unsuitable for agriculture. Because there is little rainfall, it was considered an ideal place for an agricultural project in which many of the climatic conditions could be controlled through irrigation. In Head's novel, she invites us to imagine a more just world in the utopia she envisions as the people of a remote village in Botswana learn to cooperate with each other and the English scientist to create a better life for everyone, regardless of race, gender, or ethnicity. In both Head's novel and McCall Smith's novel, the elements of a utopian or more just world depend upon seeking peace of mind, forgiving things that happened in the past, and resolving cultural conflicts.

Seeking Peace of Mind

In the opening chapter of Head's novel, we follow Makhaya's escape from South Africa into Botswana where Makhaya expects to find freedom. Recently released from prison and unable to live any longer under the cruelties of apartheid, he sets out on a spiritual quest to find "the road of peace of mind" (Head, 1969, p. 14) as he describes it to the old man, Dinorego. In further conversation, Dinorego attests that the South Africa Makhaya has just left is "a terrible place...the Good God don't like it. This is God's country" (p. 15). Contrary to what Makhaya may have expected, he is invited to join a community in which the supernatural is accepted as inevitable. Dinorego claims, "God is everywhere about here, and it's no secret" (p. 15). While Dinorego's motives for inviting Makhaya to come home with him are also selfish, in that he seeks a husband for his daughter, Makhaya's quest is framed by the spiritual context. He has come to this pastoral setting to find an inner peace.

Other characters also come to the community to seek peace and realize their dreams. Ousted by his bourgeois family in England, Gilbert Balfour comes to Golema Mmidi to find his peace of mind. When he meets Makhaya for the first time, he says, "This is Utopia, Mack. I've the greatest dreams about it" (Head, 1969, p. 25). He continues to describe his dissatisfaction with the England that he left behind. While Gilbert's rationale is based more on disillusionment, Makhaya explains his desire for immortality: "Since I found myself so near death over the past two years, I thought I best to find a wife before I found anything else" (p. 26) because a wife could bear him a child and allow a part of him to go on living after he dies. While Gilbert is taken aback by this comment, the conversation enables them to bridge their racial differences and begin a working relationship that will lead to peace of mind for both of them.

In McCall Smith's The No. 1 Ladies' Detective Agency series (1998–2004), characters come to Mma Ramotswe seeking peace for the complexities of their personal lives. She loves Africa, loves Botswana, and loves "all the people God made, but I especially know how to love the people who live in this place. They are my people, my brothers and sisters" (McCall Smith, 1998, p. 4). She feels it is her duty to help her people "solve the mysteries in their lives. That is what I am called to do" (p. 4). Treating everyone as equals, as brothers and sisters, is the principle that guides the story, introduces readers to the lives of the remarkable characters, and sustains interest in the series that McCall Smith continues to write. With each chapter, readers get either a new situation or another piece of the puzzle, which leads to a final resolution of the mysteries or cases that Mma Ramotswe is solving. As the mysteries are resolved, the characters find the peace of mind they were seeking.

Forgetting and Forgiving the Past

In order for the characters to enter the utopian community Golema Mmidi describes in *When Rain Clouds Gather* (1969), they have to forget and forgive the violence and oppression of their past lives. However, merely moving from one geographical location to another to escape cruelty and pain does not ensure healing. Makhaya and other major characters must rid themselves of hatred and bitterness to join the utopian community. The dysfunctional and destructive social orders embodied in the corrupt tribal rulership, capitalism, and apartheid from which these characters fled serve as reminders of the real social orders that exist in the world outside of Golema Mmidi. However, Bessie Head offers some resolution to those problems in the ideal society that she envisions through the key players in the novel. As the characters learn to forgive and forget the social orders that victimized them, they are able to join the new community. Makhaya struggles longer to do this, as the evils of apartheid are deeply rooted in his soul. While he may want to "undo the complexity of hatred and humiliation that had dominated his life for so long" (Head, 1969, p. 67), Makhaya is unable to do so on his own, but he is willing to turn to the community, especially Mma-Millipede, for help. He eventually comes to the understanding that "he could run and hide no longer and would have to turn around and face all that he had run from" (p. 159). Once able to forgive his past, he enters the utopia in Golema Mmidi by marrying Paulina Sebesco and beginning the family he so desires.

In McCall Smith's novel, Mma Ramotswe must forget and forgive an abusive first marriage in order to enter into a new relationship. After her first nightmare of a marriage, Mma Ramotswe vowed never to marry again unless she met a man who could live up to the memory of her late Daddy, Obed Ramotswe, a man "everybody respected for his knowledge of cattle and for his understanding of the old Botswana ways" (McCall Smith, 2002, p. 4). In spite of her high regard for her father, Mma Ramotswe is suspicious of most men's motives and finds most of them to be dull. She says, "The trouble with men was that they went about with their eyes half closed...whether men actually wanted to see anything...whether they decided that they would notice only the things that interested them" (p. 17). Having forgiven and recovered from an abusive relationship with a cruel man, Mma Ramotswe is sympathetic to women who suffer at the hands of men. Many of her cases involve solving such injustices. Through forgetting and forgiving, she helps other women as well as herself to move beyond the pain and form better relationships.

Resolving Cultural Conflict

In Bessie Head's village of Golema Mmidi, the men attend to the cattle at remote cattle posts and help with the plowing, while the women are the agriculturists and tillers of the earth. When the women need to learn new ways of farming to preserve the land, Gilbert provides the technical know-how from his English education and Makhaya bridges the relationships with the people. By joining together and recognizing the interdependence of two members of opposing colors, they are able to their knowledge and resources to persuade the peasants in the village to cooperate with their plan and reject the primitive techniques that were ruining the land. As Gilbert has such a poor command of Tswana, Makhaya's part of the bargain with Gilbert is to teach the women agriculture. Their plan starts by teaching the women how to cultivate Turkish tobacco and how to build a curing and drying shed. With the proceeds of this cash crop, they can then afford fertilizers, seed, and equipment necessary to increase food production in Golema Mmidi. As the community adopts this plan, relationships grow stronger and members work hard to achieve a common goal as they replenish the land.

McCall Smith's series contains many references to the old Botswana morality. On the one hand, Mma Ramotswe does not want Africa to change. "She did not want her people to become like everybody else, soulless, selfish, forgetful of what it means to be African, or, worse still, ashamed of Africa" (McCall Smith, 1998, p. 215). Mma Ramotswe believes in the traditional values requiring good manners, respect, courtesy, and politeness, and customs that include proper greetings and hospitality, including serving bush tea. While Mma Ramotswe opposes change in these fundamental values, she is critical of other aspects of African culture such as abuse of women through beatings, unfaithfulness, and accusations of witchcraft. As Mma Ramotswe moves into a professional role, she herself is moving from the old morality into a newer one as an independent businesswoman.

While she believes in some of the "old Botswana ways," Mma Ramotswe counters the traditional stereotypes for women by becoming a central figure in the community and giving voice to women's issues by chasing down unfaithful husbands. She demonstrates her prowess as a hunter by shooting a crocodile, her assertiveness when she deals with the Government Man, and her courage when she confronts the witch doctor making muti (medicine) from human bones. As Mma Ramotswe looks to the future leaders of her country, she entertains the idea that a woman might one day become president of Botswana. That is, of course, on the condition "that the lady in question had the right qualities of modesty and caution" (McCall Smith, 2003, p. 5). Admittedly, these qualities of civility were not cultivated in enough women, according to Mma Ramotswe.

Teacher Talk

The open-ended questions that follow are designed to elicit higher level, critical thinking responses from students as they delve into the novels. These questions could be used to engage students in lively discussions or to write critical papers. The questions should spark meaningful connections with prior learning and personal experiences (Wiggins & McTighe, 2005).

Open-Ended Questions for *When Rain Clouds Gather* (1969) and *The No. 1 Ladies' Detective Agency* (1998)

Head's *When Rain Clouds Gather* (1969)	McCall Smith's *The No. 1 Ladies' Detective Agency* (1998)
Why do people come to Golema Mmidi to live?	What are the values that characterize the "old" and "new" Botswana morality?
On what basis do the characters reject tribalism?	What does Obed Ramotswe's life reveal about the history of South Africa?
How are the roles of the men and women changing in this village?	What differences in black and white cultures does the novel portray?
How is knowledge power in this novel?	What makes Mma Ramotswe's business succeed?
How are racial conflicts resolved in this novel?	How are peace and harmony achieved in Mma Ramotswe's world?
How does the struggle to preserve the environment affect this community?	What are the responsibilities of the individual in regard to social justice?
How would you define a utopian society?	
What are the ideals that should be honored in a utopian society?	

Cross-Curricular Activities

The Cross-Curricular Activities for this unit begin with One-Minute Vocabulary Reports to build students' background knowledge in preparation for reading Head's *When Rain Clouds Gather* (1969) or McCall Smith's *No. 1 Ladies' Detective Agency* series (1998–2004). In addition, teachers may require students to keep personal journals to capture their reader response to important quotes and passages in preparation for class discussion. The Character Bulletin Board and the Poem in Two Voices strategies are designed to help students visualize the physical, emotional, and cultural aspects of character development throughout the novels in this series. The culminating project for this unit is for students to create a zine (magazine) to research the social, cultural, or environmental issues raised in the novels for this unit.

One-Minute Vocabulary Reports

In order to provide students with the background information for reading the novels set in Botswana, ask them to prepare One-Minute Vocabulary Reports. Adapted from Glasgow (2002), this strategy is used to familiarize students with cultural concepts associated with the life and literature of Botswana mentioned in the novels. To implement this strategy, make a list of people, places, and events that students should know in order to appreciate the novels. Then, ask students to select a concept, research the meaning of it, prepare a visual, and give a one-minute presentation to the class. The activity can be done individually or collaboratively in pairs. In a one-minute presentation, students should give basic background of the concept and the phrases, places, and names they will be reading and hearing about in their discussion groups. The presentation can be read from a notecard, and a visual aid must accompany the presentation addressing the following: (1) who or what the topic is, (2) when it was important, (3) why it was important, and (4) what its impact is on society today. Ask students to take notes during the presentations and then give a quiz based on the information presented. As students read the novel, they can revise their definitions based on the context from the book. Table 12.1 offers a list of suggested concepts for One-Minute Vocabulary Reports.

Character Bulletin Boards

As students read and get to know the characters in the text, making Character Bulletin Boards gives them quick references to characters as they are developed and revealed in the text. This bulletin board becomes a visual place where they

---

Table 12.1. Suggested Concepts for One-Minute Vocabulary Reports

Acacia trees	Mafikeng
Alexander McCall Smith	HIV/AIDS
Apartheid laws	interracial marriage laws
Bamangwato Development Farm	Masarwa
Bantu education	Mma and Rra
Bishop of Anglican Cathedral	missionary schools
Bessie Head	Molepolole
Boers	Motswana
British Protectorate	Nambia
bush tea	Orange Queen
bushwalking	orphan farm
Cambridge School Certificate	Pan African Socialist Party
cattle cooperative	pumpkin
diamond mines in South Africa	Queen Elizabeth II
Gaborone	Queen of Tonga
Go-Away Bird	savannah
HIV/AIDS	Setswana
Hoopoe Bird	Sir Seretse Khama
Kalahari	Tswana
King Sobhuza II of Swaizland	Zambia
Lobatse	Zimbabwe

can give form and voice to the characters and the culture in which they live and show character development in the novel. When in small groups, students spend time brainstorming and discussing the social, emotional, and physical traits of each character. These character bulletin boards can be a work-in-progress as students read and add information as they watch characters grow and change. The bulletin is bright and cheerful and often becomes the center point for the reading of the book. Character Bulletin Boards could be made for any of the main characters in Head's *When Rain Clouds Gather* (1969) or Alexander McCall Smith's The No. 1 Ladies' Detective Agency series (1998–2004).

The procedure for the Character Bulletin Board strategy is as follows (adapted from Allison Baer's activity; see Baer, 2005). First, make a list of the main characters in the book, then divide the class into small groups and assign or have students select one character for each group. Groups should spend time creating lists of physical, emotional, and social traits for their character, preferably documenting them from the text. Ask students to create a rough draft of what the character looks like physically, using the book. From this rough draft, create a large model of the character using construction paper. Tape the model to the bulletin board and label it with the character's name. Then have students write the emotional and social traits of their character on index cards and place them around the character model. Encourage students to use quotes from the text to give authority to their ideas. As time goes on, students can place other things around the character, such as pictures of what they like, places they visit, and artifacts that show the cultural or social context of events.

Writing Poetry in Two Voices

Using the poetic structure first developed by Paul Fleischman in *Joyful Noise: Poems for Two Voices* (1988), students will write poetry in two voices for characters who hold opposing views. In writing the poems, students explore the themes of racial issues, gender roles, and environmental concerns. It will be necessary to discuss the effects of sound, rhythm, and format in constructing the poems. In a poem for two voices, there are poetic lines arranged in two columns, one side for each of the two characters. The lines are arranged on the page so that sometimes one person speaks and other times both speak at the same time (they share the same line or say different lines at the same time). For example, see Figure 12.2 for a Poem in Two Voices written by preservice teacher Diana Limo based on *When Rain Clouds Gather* (Head, 1969).

Students can write the poems individually or in pairs, with each student writing from the perspective of a different character. Students should choose characters that represent different points of view. For instance, in *When Rain Clouds Gather*, they could choose Makhaya versus Gilbert, Gilbert versus

Figure 12.2. Student's Poem in Two Voices Based on *When Rain Clouds Gather* (Head, 1969)

Makhaya	Gilbert
I have come to a	
	I have created a
Utopia.	Utopia.
Why am I here?	Why am I here?
I am running	I am running
A refugee	
Trying to escape,	
My past,	
My people	These people
	Need me.
	I can fix their land,
	Their crops,
	Their animals.
I have different ideas.	I have different ideas.
I don't believe	
In tribalism.	
In politics.	
I am just	
	I am just
One man.	One man.
Not knowing	
How my life	That my life
Would change	Would change
As I waited	
	For a time
When rain clouds gather.	When rain clouds gather.

Matenge, or Makhaya versus Joas Tsepe. In *The No. 1 Ladies' Detective Agency* (1998), students could choose Precious Ramotswe versus Note Mokoti, J.L.B. Matekoni versus Charlie, or Precious Ramotswe versus Obed Ramotswe. After choosing the characters, students should examine the text to find points of agreement and disagreement. Then using key words from the text, students begin to write the poem for each voice. After drafting the poem, students must decide which lines should be recited together and which lines should be recited alone. Once the poems are complete, ask students to choose a partner and share their poems with the rest of the class.

Making-A-Difference Project: Zines to Address Cultural and Environmental Issues

Zines (pronounced /zeens/, from fanzines or magazines) are often a righteous, radical form of creative self-expression. In the real world, there are no hard-and-fast standards for zines, but they may contain one or more of the following: feature articles, advice columns, comic strips, artwork, photography, collage, poetry, and editorials. Zines provide forums for a wide variety of people to express themselves in diverse ways; they allow ideas and stories to be told that otherwise may not be told because they have no place in more mainstream publications. Zine writing constitutes a powerful type of communication and often introduces new voices and new ideas that challenge traditional, mainstream thinking. Since zines represent uncensored, underground writing on the edge, the language is usually informal and expressive. Zine writing often breaks with conventions of punctuation, spelling, and formatting to create a more experimental form of personal expression.

The style, voice, and focus of a zine are as varied as the people who create it. For this zine project adapted for the English language arts and social studies classroom, students can collaborate and work cooperatively on composing the zine both inside and outside of the classroom, or they can work independently and create a zine of their own. While topics for zines are normally left up to the passions of the writers, they can also be focused on specific research topics determined by the teacher. In this case, the focus is on the cultural, social, or environmental issues of Botswana. See Table 12.2 for a list of suggested zine topics for this unit. Although requirements for the zine project can vary, Table 12.3 pro-

---

Table 12.2. List of Suggested Zine Topics for Unit

1. Reasons to love Botswana
2. News From the No. 1 Ladies' Detective Agency
3. Changing Gender Roles in Africa
4. Women's Access to Education in Africa
5. HIV/AIDS Epidemic
6. Confrontation of Stereotypes of Africans (*Tears*, pp. 27–30)
7. African Traditional Weddings
8. Diamond Mining
9. Subsistence Farming/Cattle Raising
10. Drought, Irrigation, and Crops: Experimental Farming (*Tears*, p. 31–34)
11. Safaris and Bushwalking Into the Game Preserves of Botswana
12. Mochudi Village Life: Mma Ramotswe's Dream
13. "It Takes a Village to Raise a Child" (*Cupboard*, p. 126)
14. Racial Equity Based on DNA (*Morality*, p. 12)

vides a list of suggested zine requirements that have proven effective (Glasgow, 2005). A student example created by preservice teacher Laura Williams is illustrated in Figure 12.3. Titled "Oh Africa," this zine deals with the environmental

---

Table 12.3. List of Zine Requirements

- Cover and title page (You need a GREAT title!)
- Table of contents
- Introduction of yourself to readers
- Zine design that appeals to the audience you specify
- Zine format—you may use a brochure format such as Microsoft Publisher, Microsoft Newsletter, or Microsoft Word. Consider the page format and the binding before you start. Use of color ink is a bonus.
- Nine creative, journalistic pieces (e.g., feature articles, letters to the editor, advice column, cartoons, sports articles, editorials, poetry, movie and book reviews, advertisements, hotlines)
- Evidence of research on the zine topic (i.e., creative incorporation of factual material)
- Notes page that distinguishes between imagination and fact for each piece
- References—correct documentation of resources used in creating the zine
- A presentation of the zine to the class through sharing graphics and excerpts
- An extra copy for me to keep
- A two–three-page self-reflection of your experience in creating the zine

Adapted from Glasgow (2005).

Figure 12.3. Student Zine Opening Page: "Oh Africa"

issues concerned with the endangered animals found on the game preserves of Botswana. The writer personified the animals to speak to their causes by naming the editor of the zine "Laura Giraffe" and naming the writer of the article "Ronnie Rhino." Her zine, composed using the Microsoft Word Newsletter Template, addresses poaching, deforestation, vegetarianism, weather alerts, and odes to the rainforest using a humorous style of writing.

Conclusion

By reading the novels by Head and McCall Smith, students have the opportunity to explore the possibility of utopian societies where people live peacefully, yet interdependently. In Head's novel, students can imagine a more just world in which the people create a better life regardless of race, gender, or ethnicity. In McCall Smith's novels, students explore social justice issues as they imagine solutions to the mysteries that Mma Ramotswe solves for her clients. By creating zines, students learn more about the social and cultural conflicts and environmental issues of Botswana.

REFERENCES

Baer, A. (2005). Character bulletin boards. In J. Glasgow (Ed.), *Strategies for engaging young adult readers: A social themes approach.* Norwood, MA: Christopher-Gordon.

Bhana, H. (2000, October 28). Bessie Head: 1937–1986. *The literary encyclopedia.* Retrieved January 21, 2006, from http://www.litencyc.com/php/speople.php?rec=true&UID=2051

Fleischman, P. (1988). *Joyful noise: Poems for two voices.* New York: Harper & Row.

Glasgow, J. (Ed.). (2002). *Using young adult literature: Thematic activities based on Gardner's multiple intelligences.* Norwood, MA: Christopher-Gordon.

Glasgow, J. (Ed.). (2005). *Strategies for engaging young adult readers: A social themes approach.* Norwood, MA: Christopher-Gordon.

Hugo, V. (1976). *Les miserables* (N. Denny, Trans.). New York: Penguin. (Original work published 1862)

Infoplease. (2007). *Botswana: Ethnicity.* Retrieved February 19, 2007, from http://www.infoplease.com/ipa/A0107353.html

International Reading Association & National Council of Teachers of English. (1996). *Standards for the English language arts.* Newark, DE; Urbana, IL: Authors.

Keene, E.O., & Zimmermann, S. (1997). *Mosaic of thought: Teaching comprehension in a reader's workshop.* Portsmouth, NH: Heinemann.

National Council for the Social Studies. (1994). *Expectations of excellence: Curriculum standards for social studies.* Silver Spring, MD: Author.

Random House. (n.d.). *Alexander McCall Smith: About the author.* Retrieved June 8, 2005, from http://www.randomhouse.com/features/mccallsmith/main/author.html

Wiggins, G.P., & McTighe, J. (2005). *Understanding by design* (2nd ed.). Alexandria, VA: Association for Supervision and Curriculum Development.

LITERATURE CITED

Head, B. (1969). *When rain clouds gather.* Oxford, England: Heinemann.

Head, B. (1971). *Maru.* Oxford, England: Heinemann.

Head, B. (1974). *A question of power.* Oxford, England: Heinemann.

McCall Smith, A. (1998). *The no. 1 ladies' detective agency.* New York: Anchor Books.

McCall Smith, A. (2001). *Morality for beautiful girls* (The No. 1 Ladies' Detective Agency series). New York: Anchor Books.

McCall Smith, A. (2002). *Tears of the giraffe* (The No. 1 Ladies' Detective Agency series). New York: Anchor Books.

McCall Smith, A. (2002). *The kalahari typing school for men* (The No. 1 Ladies' Detective Agency series). New York: Pantheon Books.

McCall Smith, A. (2003). *The full cupboard of life* (The No. 1 Ladies' Detective Agency series). New York: Pantheon Books.

McCall Smith, A. (2004). *In the company of cheerful ladies* (The No. 1 Ladies' Detective Agency series). New York: Pantheon Books.

Cultural Conflicts and Choices for Education of Young Women in Pre- and Post-Colonial Zimbabwe

Jacqueline N. Glasgow and Kara Haas

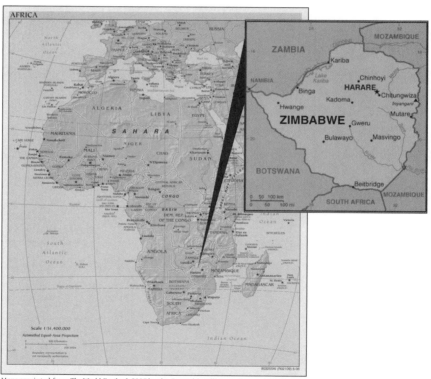

Maps reprinted from *The World Factbook 2007* by the Central Intelligence Agency, http://www.cia.gov/cia/publications/factbook.

Exploring African Life and Literature: Novel Guides to Promote Socially Responsive Learning edited by Jacqueline N. Glasgow and Linda J. Rice. © 2007 by the International Reading Association.

"The status of 'native' is a nervous condition."

—Jean-Paul Sartre, in *The Wretched of the Earth* (1963, Preface)

Zimbabwe is a landlocked country at the base of the African continent and is the home of the Shona people. The country features spectacular natural beauty. It lies on a high plateau, and its terrain consists primarily of grasslands bordered on the east by mountains. The northeastern border of the country is marked by the mighty Zambezi River, one of the world's best water adventure travel destinations, offering outstanding whitewater rafting in the Zambezi Gorges below the falls as well as excellent canoeing and kayaking above them (InterKnowledge, 1998). Zimbabwe's game reserves rank among the most abundant and beautiful on the African continent (for more information on Zimbabwe's landscape and history, see "Exploring Zimbabwe" at www.geographia.com/zimbabwe/index.html). The Zambezi River flows out of Lake Cabora Bassa from Mozambique, and this lake provides the setting for Nhamo's journey in Nancy Farmer's *A Girl Named Disaster* (1996). Before her 12th birthday Nhamo learns that she must marry a cruel man with three wives, and because her mother is dead and her father is absent, in order to escape this fate, she runs away. Nhamo takes off in a stolen boat and journeys down river encountering all manner of dangers before finding refuge and safety. The other Novel Guide for this chapter is for Tsitsi Dangarembga's *Nervous Conditions* (1988), set in Southern Rhodesia during the 1960s before the land became known as Zimbabwe. The protagonist, Tambu, is a young girl who yearns to be free of the constraints that come with living in a rural village. When her wealthy uncle offers to sponsor her schooling in his mission school, she thinks her dreams are coming true, until she discovers that education comes with a price.

The Cross-Curricular Activities for these two novels are designed to introduce students to the cultural conflicts experienced by young women in pre- and post-colonial Zimbabwe and their limited choices for education. By completing the Significant Passages activity, students will reflect on critical aspects of the culture portrayed in the novels, which address the needs and concerns of women. The Split-Open Mind activity requires students to reflect on the critical decisions made by the protagonists regarding cultural change and consequences of their educational experiences. The Unsent Letter activity provides students the opportunity to "communicate" with characters in the book by expressing their opinions and concerns about controversial issues to the character in the novel responsible for creating the issue. The Found Poem captures a critical

Novels, Activities, and Curricular Standards for English Language Arts and Social Studies

NOVELS
- *Nervous Conditions* (1988) by Tsitsi Dangarembga
- *A Girl Named Disaster* (1996) by Nancy Farmer

CROSS-CURRICULAR ACTIVITIES
- Significant Passages
- Split-Open Mind
- Unsent Letter
- Found Poem
- "Where I'm From" Poem

MAKING-A-DIFFERENCE PROJECT
I-Search Paper on Cultural Conflicts and Choices of Educated Women

STANDARDS FOR THE ENGLISH LANGUAGE ARTS
#2 Students read a wide range of literature.

#5 Students employ a wide range of strategies as they write.

#7 Students conduct research on issues and interests.

#11 Students participate as critical members of a variety of literacy communities.

#12 Students use spoken, written, and visual language to accomplish their own purposes.

Adapted from IRA and NCTE. (1996). *Standards for the English Language Arts.* Newark, DE: International Reading Association; Urbana, IL: National Council of Teachers of English.Curriculum Standards for the Social Studies

#1a Culture: Learners analyze and explain the ways the Zimbabwean culture addresses the needs and concerns of women.

#1d Culture: Learners compare and analyze Zimbabwean patterns for preserving and transmitting culture while adapting to social change such as education of women.

#1f Culture: Learners interpret patterns of behavior such as female circumcision and arranged marriages that pose obstacles for cross-cultural understanding.

Adapted with the permission of the National Council for the Social Studies (NCSS). For the NCSS standards, see the publication *Expectations of Excellence: Curriculum Standards for Social Studies* (Washington, DC: National Council for the Social Studies, 1994). See also www.socialstudies.org

moment in the text, and the "The Where I'm From" poem explores the identity of the protagonist.

The Making-A-Difference Project for this chapter is the I-Search Paper, adapted from Ken Macrorie's *The I-Search Paper* (1988), and is an alternative to the traditional research paper. This project provides students the opportunity to research both cultural and social issues that create obstacles for young girls trying to acquire an education and the other obstacles that make career opportunities limited and choices difficult even for educated women in the patriarchal cultures of Zimbabwe. The I-Search format of the paper uses conversational, informal writing and reporting of students' inquiry into issues surrounding women's educational opportunities. The overview on page 272 illustrates how the Novel Guides in this chapter and their corresponding activities align with standards for the English language arts (International Reading Association [IRA] & National Council of Teachers of English [NCTE], 1996) and curriculum standards for the social studies (National Council for the Social Studies [NCSS], 1994).

Social and Historical Context

Prior to its liberation in 1980, Zimbabwe was called Southern Rhodesia, a white-ruled British colony. Colonization began when Cecil Rhodes arrived in 1890, accompanied by his British South Africa Company, with the goal of expanding the wealth and territory of the British Empire. When the anticipated gold deposits did not materialize, employees of the British South Africa Company stayed and became farmers. Despite the natives' opposition to this invasion, the British South Africa Company's police force destroyed all resistance. Establishing themselves as victors, the ruling British named the area Southern and Northern Rhodesia (today Zimbabwe and Zambia, respectively) in honor of Cecil Rhodes. British rule lasted until 1965 when white-ruled Southern Rhodesia declared itself independent from Britain. After 14 years of guerilla-style civil war, Britain briefly reclaimed the nation and then liberated Zimbabwe on April 18, 1980 (Middleton, 1997).

Both novels discussed in this chapter reflect the cultural conflicts between the Shona culture and modernity. Dangarembga's novel reflects her experiences as a young girl coming of age during the turbulent times of the 1960s and 1970s when the country was still known as Southern Rhodesia (George & Scott, 1993). Farmer's novel is set in post-colonial times. Growing up in the dominant Shona culture (70% of the population today) where families are defined by strict paternal order or authority, the status of Shona women is determined by their husbands and sons (Saliba, 1995). To traditional Shona, good manners mean being silent and obedient to those who are higher in rank, relegating women to a voiceless and passive position (Hill, 1995). The protagonists in both coming-of-age novels must emancipate themselves from the traditional male authority and find a place and an education in modernity—the struggles and "nervous conditions" women frequently face regardless of their class.

Nervous Conditions (1988) by Tsitsi Dangarembga

About the Author

Tsitsi Dangarembga was born in Mutoko, Zimbabwe (then Rhodesia), in 1959. Although born in Africa, she spent her early childhood in Britain, where she learned English and began her schooling. At age 6, she returned to Southern Rhodesia with her family to continue her education. She learned the Shona language again, attended a mission school in Mutare, and later completed her secondary education at a U.S. convent school. In 1977, Dangarembga returned to England to attend Cambridge University and study medicine but returned to Southern Rhodesia (Zimbabwe) in 1980 just before independence was established. In 1985, Dangarembga wrote *Nervous Conditions*, which was published by Women's Press in London in 1988 after being rejected by four male-owned African presses. The book became the first novel published by a black Zimbabwean woman. The novel has won various prizes including the Commonwealth Writers Prize in 1989 (Grady, 1997).

After Dangarembga returned to Africa, she studied psychology at the University of Zimbabwe, where she also enrolled in the university's drama group. In this venue, she found a creative outlet in playwriting. She wrote several plays that were performed at the university, including her well-known *She No Longer Weeps* in 1987. She was the first Zimbabwean to write plays with major roles for black women. In addition to theater, Dangarembga also studied film production in Berlin, Germany. She wrote a documentary for German television and then produced the film *Everyone's Child* (1996), which has been shown worldwide at various festivals including the Dublin Film Festival. It follows the story of the tragic fates of four siblings after their parents die of AIDS. The soundtrack featured songs by Zimbabwe's most popular musicians (Wilkinson, 1992).

Summary

Tambudzayi (or "Tambu") Sigauke grew up on an impoverished Southern Rhodesian farm during the late 1960s. Even though Tambu aspires to an education, her responsibilities are domestic because the family has no money for her schooling. The enterprising Tambu grows maize to earn her own school fees, only to have her brother steal her produce. Babamukuru, her uncle who has taken responsibility for the extended family, comes to her rescue and takes her to town to sell her maize. There, a woman gives her enough money to pay her school fees.

In 1968, Tambu is 13 years old when her brother dies of an unidentified illness. Because the family has no other sons, Tambu is invited to attend the mission school in his place. Living with her educated uncle Babamukuru, who is the headmaster of the mission school, and his family, she befriends her cousin Nyasha, who helps her make the transformation from peasant to family member in an affluent home. Tambu takes the role of poor relative and remains the obedient, studious student who pleases her uncle and serves as a foil for the rebellious Nyasha who smokes, flirts, and talks disrespectfully to her parents. At Christmas, the family leaves their comfortable surroundings and returns to the dilapidated homestead for a celebration with the entire extended family. While there at a family "dare," in which members of the patriarchy gather to discuss serious family business, a decision is made to have a wedding of Tambu's parents as a cleansing ceremony to cure her father's sinfulness. He is "a roving and a lazy hand" (Dangarembga, 1988, p.145) who leaves his family living in poverty. In the end, Tambu refuses to attend the wedding she considers to be a farce because she knows it will not change her father's behavior, and because of this she is severely punished for defying Babamukuru. Later, Tambu is selected for one of the two seats available at Young Ladies College of the Sacred Heart. Attending this school also means a difficult separation from Nyasha, who does well at the convent school but has a mental breakdown and develops anorexia. In the end, Tambu sees that she must free herself from the Shona traditions that oppress women and enter a more modern world in which women find intellectual, emotional, and material empowerment.

A Girl Named Disaster (1996) by Nancy Farmer

About the Author

Nancy Farmer grew up in a hotel that her father managed on the border of Arizona and Mexico in the United States. She joined the Peace Corps in the 1960s and served in India for two years. When her tour of duty was finished, she spent the next 24 years living and working in Mozambique and Zimbabwe. Farmer's first experience in Africa was working as an entomologist in a lab on Lake Cabora Bassa in Mozambique. When her contract ran out, she moved to Zimbabwe, where she met and married her husband. Farmer published her first books with a Zimbabwean publisher. Back in the United States after living in Africa for 20 years, Farmer published four novels, all set in the African countries in which she lived, and the first three of which received Newbery Honor awards: *The Ear, the Eye, and the Arm* (1994), *A Girl Named Disaster* (1996), *The House of Scorpion* (2002), and *The Sea of Trolls* (2004).

A Girl Named Disaster (1996) follows a 12-year-old Shona girl named Nhamo (Disaster) through her adventures on Lake Cabora Bassa as she tries to escape an arranged marriage to a cruel, elderly man who already has three wives. In an interview with Jessica Powers (2006), Farmer said that this book is the most autobiographical story that she has written. Most of the incidents in the book are based on real experiences: "cholera epidemic, Rumpy the baboon and his troop, getting groomed by a baby baboon, hiding in a tree from a leopard, living off a leopard kill—all these things happened" (Powers, 2006, ¶ 5). Farmer lived on Lake Cabora Bassa for several years, and it was during this time that she came across a leopard's kill when the family had been eating nothing but fish for weeks. They found a dead kudu that was too heavy for the cat to drag up into a tree, so they cut off one of the legs and carried it over to their canoe before the leopard came back. She said, "as we carried the leg, blood dripped off into the lake and tiger fish, predators with long teeth, leaped out of the water and snapped at the drops" (Powers, 2006, ¶ 6). As shared in the interview with Powers (2006), this memorable image worked its way into her novel.

Summary

Eleven-year-old Nhamo (Disaster) lives as a slave with unloving maternal relatives in a traditional Shona village in Mozambique. When she was young, her mother was killed by a leopard, and her father shamefully ran away after killing another man. Because the Shona are a paternalistic tribe, Nhamo has no social standing because she lives with her mother's relatives. For the most part, the village follows the traditional ways of its ancestors. When cholera strikes the village, the people travel to a Portuguese trading post to seek counsel from a traditional healer. The healer makes Nhamo the scapegoat for deaths in the village by decreeing that she must become the junior wife of the brutal brother of her father's victim to placate the angry spirit of the murder victim. Her grandmother helps her escape this dreadful situation by giving her provisions and directions that enable her to steal a boat and set off on a journey to Zimbabwe by herself to find her father's family.

A journey that was to take two days becomes a year-long odyssey. Nhamo travels the full length of Lake Cabora Bassa, stopping at various islands to camp along the way. The book chronicles her survival against starvation, isolation, illness, and other physical and psychological dangers. At one of the larger islands where she stays the longest period of time, she replenishes her supplies, builds a treehouse, and carves a new boat to replace her damaged one. The island is also the home of a troop of baboons who become like a substitute family for her. Nhamo's survival can be attributed in part to her beliefs in the Shona spirit world. As she travels along her journey, she drifts in and out of the spirit world in dreams and visions. Nhamo draws strength from her own spirit and the spirit realm to make decisions, enabling her to continue her journey.

Eventually Nhamo sets out once again for Zimbabwe to find the Jongwes, her father's family. Upon reaching land, Nhamo abandons her boat and happens upon a science station at Efifi, where she is nursed back to health by the scientists and their staff. She is later taken to the home of her paternal uncle in Mtoroshanga. Nhamo's uncle is the wealthy manager of a chrome mine. Here, Nhamo finds her paternal relatives, but once again is barely tolerated. Her intellectual curiosity, achievements in school, and hard work earn her the respect of the Efifi scientists. They pay her for the work she does for them in the summer and help her set up a bank account. She spends her vacations back at the science station with those who embrace her into their family of scientists.

Making Connections

Most students benefit from teachers helping them make connections between their personal experiences and the protagonists' experiences in the novel (Keene & Zimmermann, 1997). The following questions provide teachers and students with a list of text-to-self, text-to-text, and text-to-world questions applicable to Tsitsi Dangarembga's *Nervous Conditions* (1988) and Nancy Farmer's *A Girl Named Disaster* (1996). See Figure 13.1 for a sample journal response to a text-to-text question for this Novel Guide written by preservice teacher Jennifer Hudak.

Figure 13.1. Student Response Journal to a Making Connections Text-to-Text Question

Text–to-Text: "What have I read with strong, female protagonists?"

The strongest female protagonists that I think of first are the women from novels like *Pride and Prejudice* and *Little Women*. I remember reading those books in high school and thinking wow, with all the inferiority, they are truly trying to break out and I found myself rooting for them to succeed. These women thrived on education and made the best of it. The outspoken nature of these women caused some trouble within their families, especially the men, because they were doing things that they weren't supposed to. But they stepped outside those lines and are very strong and memorable characters.

Making Connections Questions for *Nervous Conditions* (1988) and *A Girl Named Disaster* (1996)

	Dangarembga's *Nervous Conditions* (1988)	Farmer's *A Girl Named Disaster* (1996)
Text-to-Self	Do I experience cultural conflict due to my race, class, or gender? What do I know about the effects of poverty on people's lives? What opportunities and choices do I have as a result of my education? What do I believe about bilingual education?	How self-reliant am I? What do I believe about arranged marriages? What kind of education do I need in order to establish my career? What do I believe about the spirit world? How important do I consider my family?
Text-to-Text	What have I read in which the protagonists experience cultural conflict? What have I read that shows the consequences of people living in poverty? What have I read in which the protagonist struggles to acquire an education? What have I read in which the protagonist struggles to preserve her or his native language?	What books have I read that feature strong, female protagonists? What have I read about arranged marriages? What have I read about places where women are well educated? What have I read about the spirit world? What have I read about successful family relationships?
Text-to-World	What are the circumstances that create cultural conflict in people's lives? What is the poverty rate where I live and what are the consequences for people living in poverty? What are the inequities in the educational system in my state? What are some successful models for preserving one's language and culture?	In what cultures is self-reliance a virtue? What do I believe about choosing a marriage partner? Why are women educated in some countries and not others? What do I believe about the freedom of worship? What family configurations are successful and acceptable?

Critical Exploration of Themes

Colonialism and patriarchy play a combined role in oppressing women in both of these novels. The characters live in a state of "nervousness" because of the complex effects of colonialism, gender inequality, and poverty. Each of the four women in *Nervous Conditions* (1988) represents a type of black woman living in Southern Rhodesia (Zimbabwe) within the Shona patriarchy during colonialism. The female characters in both novels struggle to overcome these overlapping and intertwining systems that relegate them to an inferior status (Uwakweh, 1995). Thus, the female characters' struggles with the patriarchy parallel the struggles Africans felt toward their colonizers and their push toward independence through the 1960s and 1970s until the present (Hill, 1995). Each female character reflects the cultural conflicts of Shona cultural expectations, educational beliefs, and identity formation.

The Oppression of Shona Cultural Expectations of Women

In *Nervous Conditions* (1988), when Tambu is young, she is told by her mother that "this business of womanhood is a heavy burden" (Dangarembga, p. 16). Her mother, Mainini, the resident Mother of the Sigauke homestead, explains that the burden is worse these days "with the poverty of blackness on the one side and the weight of womanhood on the other" (p. 16). The weight of womanhood is defined as the bearing of children and servitude to husband and family. Mainini, trapped in poverty and uneducated, represents the essence of the oppressed, passive black female.

In *A Girl Named Disaster* (1996), Nhamo is not only deprived of an education, she is also placed into a lowly position in the community. In her village, which follows the traditional ways of its ancestors, males and females are segregated by duties and social standing. Females tend to the cooking, sewing, childcare, and making cloth and pots, while males protect the village from predators like leopards, tend to domestic animals, hunt and fish, and rule the households and the village. The Shona are a paternalistic tribe, so children are perceived as belonging to their father's family. Thus Nhamo has no social standing in the village because she lives with her mother's relatives. Her father, Proud Jongwe, came from a distant town in Zimbabwe and has not returned to claim his daughter. Nhamo is treated poorly by her relatives and made to do the most onerous chores.

The Effects of Colonialism and Patriarchy on Education

In *Nervous Conditions* (1988), the difficulty and heavy price of an education are portrayed through the experiences of Tambu (Dadzie, 1990). Tambu's placement at the mission school reveals how difficult getting an education was for African girls during this period. Education was seen as valuable only for boys and a waste for girls. These gender biases render an education for Tambu and other females in the novel nearly impossible. Even though Tambu overcomes the odds of receiving an education, she discovers that a white education comes with a heavy price. She must trade in her Shona ways for the ways of white Christians in order to advance academically and socially. Education creates tension and "nervousness" in this character. Though Tambu excels at the missionary school and pursues a higher degree at Sacred Heart Convent, she continues to struggle with the effects of a colonial education in a world run by white men.

After Tambu moves to the mission school, Maiguru (Babamukuru's wife) became the ideal role model for Tambu. Maiguru is a black woman who holds a master's degree just like her husband. She teaches at the mission school, but according to Shona tradition, even an educated woman is still subject to her husband and to domestic servitude. For instance, although she commands salary, she is not allowed to spend it without her husband's permission. She has to watch her income be siphoned off to her brother-in-law. While Maiguru enjoys the comforts of a higher standard of living, but she still is silenced and oppressed by male authority. Tambu admires Maiguru, but she eventually rejects the burden of womanhood and turns to examine the views of her cousin, Nyasha.

Nyasha's liberal education in Britain opens her eyes to other possibilities for womanhood, but at the same time, puts her at odds with life in her native land. Her experiences of living in England separate her from her family and friends at the mission school, and Nyasha's cultural conflict manifests itself through her smoking, disrespecting her parents, and dressing provocatively, all symbols of her rebellion against society's expectations for women. She behaves badly at church and other public places, embarrassing her father at every turn. Babamukuru, her father, tries to subdue her by forcing her to eat all her food and by physically assaulting her. As his behavior worsens, she reaches her limit. As a result, Nyasha, unable to cope with the demands of a patriarchal world complicated by alienations acquired through her Western education, breaks down even further as evidenced by her illness, anorexia nervosa.

In *A Girl Named Disaster* (1996), the reader learns that Nhamo is very much like her late mother—intelligent, imaginative, curious, and eager for knowledge. Life in the traditional village has developed other traits in Nhamo as well, such as independence, strength, and resourcefulness. These are qualities that enable her to survive her long journey down the lake to escape the tyrannies of the Shona patriarchy. Nhamo is searching for her heritage, and she finds it in an unexpected way. Initially, the search is an escape from an unwanted marriage. During her time alone, she comes in close contact with the Shona spirits that become the true source of strength throughout her journey into personal freedom. Under the influence of the scientists at Efifi, Nhamo is nurtured back to health, realizes her dreams for an education, and becomes fiscally independent. In addition, for the first time in her life, Nhamo is loved and accepted for her accomplishments.

The Impact of Colonialism and Patriarchy on Identity
The duality of colonialism and patriarchy affect one's sense of self. In particular, life for most Shona women and men in colonial Rhodesia is well represent-

ed by the characters of Nyasha and her father, Babamukuru, in *Nervous Conditions* (1988). In *A Girl Named Disaster* (1996), Nhamo's identity develops more fully when she escapes the Shona culture and comes to live with the Matabele scientists at Efifi.

First, Nyasha represents the alienation and unstable sense of self that results from the double oppression of colonialism and patriarchy. Though she is at home, she is alone (George & Scott, 1993). Unlike most Shona, she has a safe and comfortable environment and is surrounded by parents who have sacrificed much to give her an education. However, she feels isolated, as if she is an alien in what should be her native country. Spending many of her formative years in England while her parents pursued advanced degrees has left her with an inability to speak Shona. Nyasha is trapped between two worlds: native and colonial. She is too Anglicized to passively accept her father's insistence that she dress modestly and speak only when spoken to. And yet she is black. She can never fully assimilate into the white colonial world. Thus she is relegated to the periphery. Her identity is neither Shona nor English, and in Southern Rhodesia, there is no label for someone in between.

This struggle with identity is also apparent in the character of Babamukuru. This Anglicized Shonan is powerful, yet powerless (George & Scott, 1993). For his family, he is their savior; he is the venerable Babamukuru. He has education and wealth beyond what his extended family could ever achieve. Consequently, Babamukuru is the patriarch and everyone obeys him. And yet his power is limited and precarious. Though highly educated, he is still lower in status than any white man or woman. Just like his daughter, he is trapped between two cultures.

In addition to Babamukuru and Nyasha, Tambu fights against alienation and a lack of identity (Nair, 1995). By telling her story, she is exerting her voice, finding her place in a colonial and patriarchal world bent on silencing her, keeping her on the periphery. Unlike her foil, Nyasha, Tambu manages to maintain her pride and love of her Shona culture while seeking an education. She does not buckle under the pressure of colonialism and patriarchy. Gradually, Tambu leaves behind those parts of her family, herself, and her culture that she cannot accept. In the end, she learns to operate in the white world and still maintain a strong sense of self as she writes her story, giving voice to the heavy burden of womanhood experienced by many other African women who may be unable to write their own.

In *A Girl Named Disaster* (1996), Nhamo sheds her ties to the oppressive ways of the Shona culture and seeks a new identity while living with her uncle in Mtoroshanga. He is the wealthy manager of a chrome mine and lives in the only large house in a dust bowl of a town. For all its rich accoutrements, the house is a cold, loveless place where Nhamo is barely tolerated. This life is in direct contrast to the warm bustle of Efifi. The science station is a village in itself and is isolated from civilization by its purpose—to study disease-carrying tsetse flies. The lifestyle at Efifi provides a rich environment for Nhamo to recover her health after the long journey, acquire an education, and become a surrogate child to the scientists and their staff. Her sense of belonging enables her to realize her potential to lead a self-determining life.

Teacher Talk

Questioning is a critical strategy that helps readers make meaning of literature by promoting critical thinking about what is being read. The type of question asked to guide comprehension should be based on the information readers need to answer the question. Some questions have answers that can be found directly in the text. Other questions have answers that require students to think about information they have read in the text. They have to search for ideas that are related to one another and then put those ideas together to answer the questions. Still other questions require students to rely mainly on prior knowledge and experience. In other words, responses to these questions are more inside the reader's head than in the text itself. These questions are schema based and lead to "author and you" and "on your own" answers. "Right there," "think and search," "author and you," and "on your own" are mnemonics for questions–answer relationships described by Raphael (1986) and will be used for the novels in this unit.

Using Schema-Based Questions for *Nervous Conditions* (1988) and *A Girl Named Disaster* (1996)

	Dangarembga's *Nervous Conditions* (1988)	Farmer's *A Girl Named Disaster* (1996)
"Right there" questions (text explicit)	What are some characteristics of the Shona culture? Has Tambu's opinion of her brother always been resentful? What feelings does Tambu experience during the gathering of her relatives? In what ways is Tambu responsible? Irresponsible?	What has Nhamo learned from the Shona culture that enables her to make the journey? Why is her relationship with Aunt Chipo so difficult? What kind of relationship does Nhamo have with her mother? Who in the village is sympathetic toward Nhamo? Why is Nhamo on a quest to find her father?

"Think and search" questions (text explicit)	What is the cause of Tambu's anger toward her family? What are Tambu's family dynamics like? In what part of the novel do you think Tambu is the happiest or most intrigued?	What are some of the dangers Nhamo faces from her predators? What are some of the other physical dangers she faces? What are some of the setbacks she encounters? What makes Nhamo's emotional survival difficult?
"Author and you" questions (text implicit or experience based)	What do you think about the family roles that the men and women are supposed to play? What are some of Tambu's personality traits? How does Tambu compare and contrast with other females in the story?	How is Nhamo like her mother? What qualities enable Nhamo to survive so long a journey? How does her belief in the spirit world sustain her? Why is the relationship with her grandmother precarious? What does the symbol of the stork margarine advertisement represent? What symbol does the leopard represent? What symbol does the panga represent?
"On your own" questions (text implicit or experienced based)	What person in the story do you identify with the most and why? What job opportunities will be available to Tambu once she graduates?	How would you react to an arranged marriage? In what ways is Nhamo a heroine? What will Nhamo's future life be like?

Cross-Curricular Activities

The Cross-Curricular Activities for this chapter engage students in the life and cultural conflicts experienced by the protagonists as they overcome obstacles that oppress them. Both of the young protagonists make difficult choices as they pursue the independence that comes with education. Through the Significant Passages and Journal Entry, the Split-Open Mind, Unsent Letter, Found Poem, and "Where I'm From" Poem, students will explore these difficult choices.

Significant Passages and Journal Entry

The Significant Passages activity helps students keep track of important passages in the novel they are reading (adapted from Glasgow, 2005). As a during-reading strategy, ask students to use a sticky note to mark passages (30 words or fewer) that seem dramatic, provocative, surprising, disturbing, or important to the development of plot or protagonist. When they have completed the reading, ask them to select the 10 most important passages and then select the one "quote of the novel" that best summarizes an important point or theme in the novel. Finally, ask students to write a journal entry giving a rationale for their choices of passages and "quote of the novel." They may refer to the quotes in their discussion of key points. They should submit both the top 10 passages and the journal entry when they have finished. See Figure 13.2 for an excerpt from a journal entry written by preservice teacher Amy Channell for *Nervous Conditions* (1988).

Split-Open Mind

For this activity, students need to get into the mind of a character to explore a major decision the character faced and the options the character had to consider in order to make that decision (adapted from Glasgow, 2002). For instance, Tambu must realize the consequences of leaving her parents and siblings to go with her uncle to the mission school. Therefore, students should consider what her life was like before she left and what it was like afterward. In the spur of the moment, Nhamo must decide to stay in the village and accept the dreadful marriage offer or heed her grandmother's advice to run away. What was the difference between her life in Mozambique versus afterward in Zimbabwe? For this activity, ask students to draw a large head of a person on a piece of newsprint or poster board. Draw a line down the middle of the head and label each side with the decision that was made (see Figure 13.3 for a Split-Open Mind Template). Ask students to find examples in the text to support both sides of the

---

Figure 13.2. Excerpt From a Student's Journal Entry for *Nervous Conditions* (Dangarembga, 1988)

The quote of the book is where Tambu states that the male/female conflict "comes back to this question of femaleness. Femaleness as opposed and inferior to maleness" (p. 16). In the patriarchal Shona culture, women are confined to the home—barefoot, pregnant, and penniless. When Tambu aspires to an education, her father makes his objections quite clear, "Can you cook books and feed them to your husband? Stay at home with your mother. Learn to cook and clean. Grow vegetables" (p. 15). For her father, cooking defines womanhood, not intellectual pursuits. While Tambu rejects these cultural expectations that repress her strength and desire for an education, she still has many obstacles to overcome to become educated herself. She sells mealies to pay her school fees. She pays a great price for education at the mission school when she leaves behind those parts of her family and her culture that would relegate her to an inferior position. She rejects her mother's advice to be content with an inferior status rendered by African men and "carry [her] burdens with strength" (p. 16). She rejects Maiguru who represents an educated woman chained to her husband's authority. She also rejects her highly educated uncle, Babamukuru, who believes that Tambu's education would enable her to marry well. In the end, she refuses to accept the Shona cultural standard in which the female is considered inferior to the male.

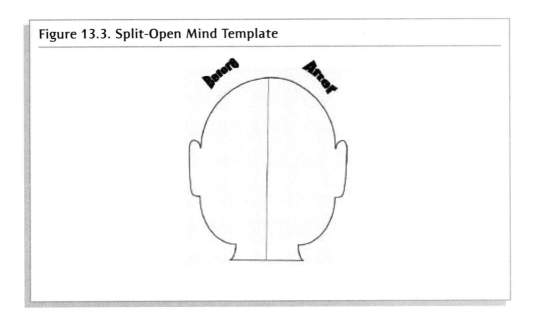
Figure 13.3. Split-Open Mind Template

dilemma. This activity helps students sort out the conflicts and consequences of decisions made. They can also reflect on the changes in lifestyle, education, and survival issues.

Unsent Letter

This strategy establishes a role-play situation in which students are asked to write letters in response to issues raised in the novel (adapted from Vacca, Vacca, & Gove, 1999). This activity requires the use of imagination and often demands that students engage in interpretive and evaluative thinking. Ask students to write an Unsent Letter for one of the following situations in Dangarembga's *Nervous Conditions* (1988) or Farmer's *A Girl Named Disaster* (1996).

1. From Tambu to her mother, father, or uncle, explaining how much she appreciates the opportunity to attend the mission school and complete her education
2. From Tambu to Nyasha, encouraging her to value and finish her education in spite of the conflict with her parents and her culture
3. From Nhamo to the Muvuki, pleading for a suitable husband or describing the cholera epidemic and pleading for mercy
4. From Nhamo to her grandmother, describing her travels to Mozambique
5. From Nhamo to her paternal uncle, pleading to return to the science station at Efifi

Found Poem

For this creative response to prose, ask students to select passages from the text with strong descriptive and figurative language. After students have selected powerful passages, ask them to pick out the best words, phrases, and lines from their passages and arrange them in poetic lines (adapted from Dunning & Stafford, 1992). See Figure 13.4 for a Found Poem written by preservice teacher Danielle Moore titled "*In Spite of Her Fear* With Thanks to Nancy Farmer."

"Where I'm From" Poem

A well-known poem by George Ella Lyons (1999) called "Where I'm From" lends itself to imitation and exploration on the topic of belonging to a family, home, and community. Using Lyons's poem as a template, ask students to write a poem from the point of view of a character in a novel. See Figure 13.5 for a "Where I'm From" poem for Nancy Farmer's Nhamo before she decides to run away, written by preservice teacher Jessica Radzik.

Making-A-Difference Project: I-Search Paper on Cultural Conflicts and Choices of Educated Women

In *Nervous Conditions* (1988), both Nyasha and Tambu face many obstacles in deciding to become educated women. While education is critical to overcoming poverty and leading independent lives, it also creates conflicts with the patriarchy of the Shona culture and remnants of colonialism. In *A Girl Named Disaster*

Figure 13.4. Student's Found Poem: *In Spite of Her Fear* With Thanks to Nancy Farmer

Clinging to Grandmother,
Ambuya smoothes her hair,
A tear drops onto her head.
"Little Pumpkin, you
can't wait any longer,
Before he beats you,
Before his wives poison you,
Go!
The journey will be the hardest."
Sick with fear and grief, she crept out,
All around stood the dark huts,
A lion roared, leaves rustled,
"Please protect me, Mai,"
An offered prayer as she tiptoes along.

Figure 13.5. "Where I'm From" Poem for Nancy Farmer's Nhamo

I'm from
A village that strongly supports tradition,
An older man and his proposition,
And a lifetime of living in a horrendous condition.

I'm from
A life of poverty where I can be sold,
A gender that is socialized to do what they're told,
And a future that I could easily trade for gold.

I'm from
A silenced voice,
A lack of choice,
And a heart that can't rejoice.

I'm from
A wedding without romance,
A celebration where I refuse to dance,
And a vow that is only about finance.

I'm from
A husband who is three times my age,
A prison where I have been put in a cage,
And years of built up despair and rage.

I'm from
A life of a child bride,
A world in which I have no one to confide,
And hundreds of nights that I have cried.

(1996), girls living in the tribal village are totally deprived of education. It is only when Nhamo makes her way to her rich uncle in Mozambique that she is given the opportunity to attend school and acquire an education. For the Making-A-Difference Project for this unit, students will research women's issues, cultural conflicts, and choices regarding education. The form for the project is an alternative to the traditional research essay—the I-Search Paper adapted from Ken Macrorie's (1988) model. (For a sample I-Search Paper developed by Pia Seagrave [2000] for the Gallaudet University English Department, go to the Gallaudet website at http://depts.gallaudet.edu/englishworks/writing/formatsheet.html.) See Table 13.1 for a list of suggested topics to use for this I-Search Paper.

Macrorie (1988) wrote that a good way to organize an I-Search Paper is to simply tell the story of the research in the order in which everything happened. Students do not need to tell everything, only the facts crucial to the hunt or

> **Table 13.1. List of Suggested Topics for I-Search Paper**
>
> Students could choose from the following list of suggested topics or choose their own dealing with gender and education in Africa.
>
> • Women and education in Africa
> • Women's access to higher education
> • Career opportunities for educated women
> • Women resisting the patriarchy
> • Arranged marriages as obstacle to acquiring an education
> • Bride price or bridewealth and early marriage as obstacles to acquiring an education
> • Comparison of the social and cultural customs of the Shona and Matabele tribes

the journey. The paper is written in first person and the discussion divided into four parts as follows:

- Part I: What I Knew (and Did Not Know About My Topic When I Started Out). Students should begin by thinking out loud on paper and tell all about their prior knowledge of the topic.

- Part II: Why I Am Writing This Paper. A real purpose should emerge here. For this part, students discuss their interest and motivation for the topic. They should end the discussion with a research questions, or questions.

- Part III: The Search. (This will be the bulk of the project.) In this part, students should complete the required readings and interviews and tell the story of their research. They should write in first person as they take the reader through the search with them. Each day that they do anything for the paper—stop at the library, read an article, try to call someone—they should note it in their paper and tell what they learned from that source. This is, in essence, the body of the paper. This section reads as a series of journal entries, not as a traditional research paper.

- Part IV: What I Learned (or Did Not Learn). This reflective part should include what students learned about their topic as well as what they learned about themselves as a learner. The paper concludes with a list of references consulted in alphabetical order by writer.

Conclusion

The Novel Guides for this unit expose students to the cultural conflicts young women experience in pre- and post-colonial Zimbabwe experience and the limited choices for education these young women have available to them. By participating in the Cross-Cultural Activities, students come to understand the restraints imposed on women by the Shona patriarchy, particularly regarding women's access to education and personal freedom. In the Making-A-Difference Project, students research women's issues that further complicate the choices for education young women have as they struggle to preserve their heritage and yet live independent lives. Students can then examine the cultural conflict inequities of the education system in their own lives and compare them to the lives of the protagonists. Students should consider how they might make a difference both at home and abroad.

REFERENCES

Dadzie, S. (1990). Books reviewed [Electronic version]. *Journal of Southern African Studies, 16*(2), 374–375.

Dunning, S., & Stafford, W. (1992). *Getting the knack: 20 poetry writing exercises.* Urbana, IL: National Council of Teachers of English.

Exploring Zimbabwe. (2005). Retrieved April 5, 2006, from http://www.geographia.com/zimbabwe/index.html

Fanon, F. (1963). *The wretched of the earth.* New York: Grove Press.

George, R.M., & Scott, H. (1993). An interview with Tsitsi Dangarembga. *Novel: A Forum on Fiction, 26*(3), 309–319.

Glasgow, J. (2002). *Using young adult literature: Thematic activities based on Gardner's multiple intelligences.* Norwood, MA: Christopher-Gordon.

Glasgow, J. (2005). *Strategies for engaging young adult readers: A social themes approach.* Norwood, MA: Christopher-Gordon.

Grady, R. (1997). *Tsitsi Dangarembga.* Retrieved April 5, 2006, from http://www.english.emory.edu/Bahri/Dangar.html

Hill, J.E. (1995). Purging a plate full of colonial history: The "nervous conditions" of silent girls. [Electronic version]. *College Literature, 22*(1), 78–91.

InterKnowledge. (1998). *Exploring Zimbabwe.* Retrieved January 17, 2007, from http://www.geographia.com/zimbabwe/index.html

International Reading Association & National Council of Teachers of English. (1996). *Standards for the English language arts.* Newark, DE; Urbana, IL: Authors.

Keene, E.O., & Zimmermann, S. (1997). *Mosaic of thought: Teaching comprehension in a reader's workshop.* Portsmouth, NH: Heinemann.

Macrorie, K. (1988). *The I-search paper* (Rev. ed. of *Searching writing.* Portsmouth, NH: Heinemann.

Middleton, J. (Ed.). (1997). *Encyclopedia of Africa: South of the Sahara* (Vol. 4). New York: Simon & Schuster.

Nair, S. (1995). Melancholic women: The Intellectual hysteric(s) in nervous conditions. *Research in African Literature, 26*(2), 130–139.

National Council for the Social Studies. (1994). *Expectations of excellence: Curriculum standards for social studies.* Silver Spring, MD: Author.

Powers, J. (2006). *An interview with Nancy Farmer.* Retrieved March 4, 2006, from http://www.suite101.com/article.cfm/african_history/97782/2

Raphael, T.E. (1986). Teaching question-answer relationships, revisited. *The Reading Teacher, 39,* 516–622.

Saliba, T. (1995). On the bodies of third world women: Cultural impurity, prostitution, and other nervous conditions. [Electronic version]. *College Literature, 22*(1), 131–147.

Seagrave, P. (2000). *I-Search paper guide.* Retrieved March 28, 2006, from Gallaudet University English Department website: http://depts.gallaudet.edu/englishworks/writing/formatsheet.html

Uwakweh, P.A. (1995). Debunking patriarchy: The liberational quality of voicing in Tsitsi Dangarembga's nervous conditions. *Research in African Literature, 26*(1), 75–85.

Vacca, R.T., Vacca, J.A.L., & Gove, M.K. (1999). *Content area reading: Literacy and learning across the curriculum* (5th ed.). New York: Longman.

Wilkinson, J. (Ed.). (1992). *Talking with African writers: Interviews with African poets, playwrights & novelists.* Portsmouth, NH: Heinemann.

LITERATURE CITED

Dangarembga, T. (1987). *She no longer weeps.* College Press.

Dangarembga, T. (1988). *Nervous conditions.* London: The Women's Press.

Dangarembga, T. (1995). *Everyone's child.* [Video recording]. J. Persey, J. Riber, & B. Zulu (Producers). Columbia, MD: Media for Development Trust.

Farmer, N. (1994). *The ear, the eye, and the arm.* New York: Puffin Books.

Farmer, N. (1996). *A girl named Disaster.* New York: Puffin Books.

Farmer, N. (2002). *The house of scorpion.* New York: Atheneum Press.

Farmer, N. (2005). *The sea of trolls.* New York: Atheneum Press.

Lyons, G.E. (1999). *Where I'm from: Where poems come from.* Spring, Texas: Absey & Co.

PART V

Resources to Explore Africa Through Film, Children's Literature, and the Oral Tradition

CHAPTER 14

Using Film Media as Visual Text for Studying the Rwandan Genocide

Ruth McClain

"Of all the products of popular culture, none is more sharply etched in our collective imagination than movies.... Cultural historians have treated movies as sociological documents that record the look and mood of particular historical settings as ideological constructs that advance particular political or moral values or myths; as psychological texts that speak to individual and social anxieties and tensions; as cultural documents that present particular images of gender, ethnicity, class, romance, and violence; as visual texts that offer complex levels of meaning and seeing."

—Steven Mintz (2003, ¶ 1–2)

Through images, music, the spoken word, and text, film is a powerful shaper of consciousness. The study of Africa can be woven into many parts of the high school and college curricula, and, because students today are so visually oriented, film is one of the best media forms teachers can use to help students truly understand the complexities of life on the African continent. By carefully selecting and using films in the classroom, teachers have the opportunity to expand students' understanding of Africa, its history, conflicts, richness, and diversity. This chapter will offer an overview of various films set in Africa that are appropriate for high school and college students and focus in depth on *Hotel Rwanda* (George, 2004) as a way of modeling how to teach using film as text.

Hotel Rwanda (George, 2004) is one film that documents the genocide in Rwanda in 1994. It is set in Kigali, Rwanda's capital city, and focuses on the

Exploring African Life and Literature: Novel Guides to Promote Socially Responsive Learning edited by Jacqueline N. Glasgow and Linda J. Rice. © 2007 by the International Reading Association.

incredible story of Paul Rusesabagina, assistant manager of the Hotel Des Milles Collines, who uses both his connections and his own ingenuity to save the lives of more than 1,200 Tutsis from genocide. Billed as a true story, the film focuses on Rusesabagina's efforts to provide sanctuary for those seeking refuge from slaughter. While other films could certainly be used to model how to teach film as "text" and help students learn about Africa, *Hotel Rwanda* has been chosen as the featured work for this chapter because among the suggested films, it is the most recent and therefore most likely to be recognized and popular for teachers and students alike.

This major motion picture has appeared on movie screens around the world, has won critical acclaim, and has educated viewers about this important event in recent Rwandan history. Because the actual events chronicled in *Hotel Rwanda* (George, 2004) occurred in the last decade of the 20th century, this film helps students see that the struggle for human rights is not something from the distant past but is, in fact, a struggle of modern times. Even common depictions in the film, from the clothes and hotel amenities to the United Nations uniforms and vehicles, will demonstrate to students that tragedies such as the Rwandan genocide are occurrences of contemporary times, allowing students to be more connected to the film and the events depicted in it. Furthermore, educating students about the genocide itself is a way to show them the importance of international awareness and involve them in resolving injustices that occur around the globe.

Exploring Various Film Portrayals of Africa

Films about Africa or set in Africa are particularly useful in helping high school and college students understand various aspects of the continent, from its history and conflicts to its landscape and traditions. While the bulk of this chapter will focus on *Hotel Rwanda* (George, 2004) and using that particular film as a model for how to teach film as "text," this portion of the chapter is intentionally more broad and general in its presentation of films that take place in various African countries. The purpose of this is to provide teachers with an overview of films that they may find useful when teaching about the diversity of the African continent, as discussing the various films in class will be an important tool to assist teachers and students in distinguishing between the various cultures, countries, and conflicts of Africa.

Three of the films in this chapter—*Ghosts of Rwanda* (Barker, 2003), *100 Days* (Hughes, 2004), and *Sometimes in April* (Peck, 2005)—relate directly to the Rwandan genocide and may be used in conjunction with *Hotel Rwanda* (George, 2004). Other films are intended to serve as an introduction, demonstrating the diversity of the continent, and to broaden students' awareness of the continent. In this way, when students view *Hotel Rwanda*—or any other film depicting a particular historical event or country in Africa—they will be able to distinguish its uniqueness and not inadvertently view one film or event as representative of all 54 nations that make up the continent.

Because we live in a visual world, students should find that films go hand in hand with the Novel Guides provided in this book. Film provides background to help readers—particularly reluctant or struggling readers—understand what they are reading and why they are reading a given text. Like novels, the content of a film is engaging, providing us with characters we care about, a narrative structure or chronological line, places we can visualize, values, and ethical and political dimensions. Film connects us to written text and more often than not provides us with a historical context within which fits the written text.

For instance, *Cry, the Beloved Country* (Singh & Roodt, 1995), one of the films described in this chapter, could be viewed in conjunction with the book by the same title in chapter 10's exploration of racial tensions, injustice, and harmony in South African literature. *I Dreamed of Africa* (Jaffe & Hudson, 2000), *Nowhere in Africa* (Bareib & Link, 2000), and *Out of Africa* (Jorgensen & Pollack, 1985) all take place in Kenya and concern effects of war, colonialism, and Christian missionaries and would therefore pair nicely with the Novel Guides in chapter 6, which feature two books by Kenyan novelist Ngugi wa Thiong'o. *Something of Value* (Berman & Brooks, 1957) tells the story of the Mau Mau uprising and would also pair well with Ngugi's *Weep Not, Child* (1964). *Lost Boys of Sudan* (Reid, Mylan, & Shenk, 2003) would work well with chapter 3 which features Mende Nazer and Francis Bok's real-life stories of living as slaves. The other films from this chapter—*African Queen* (Spiegel & Huston, 1951), *Flame Trees of Thika* (Baker, 1982), *Yesterday* (Roodt, 2004), and *Zulu* (Baker & Enfield, 1964)—could be viewed independently to expand students' awareness and ability to visualize different aspects of Africa, its culture, landscape, and history; alternately, these films could stand alone as "texts" just like *Hotel Rwanda*, provided teachers use the ideas presented here as a model for teaching film as "text."

To begin this study of Africa through film, divide students into viewing groups, and ask them to select one of the films in Table 14.1 as their focus of study. Some of the films are documentaries; others are based on well-known novels. After groups have viewed one of the films, they should exchange films until all students have viewed at least three films. Students should then complete the chart in Table 14.2 as a way of analyzing and comparing film portrayals of Africa.

Having had some exposure to films about Africa and invested critical thinking into the portrayals of the continent, students can write a comparative essay or

Table 14.1. List of Suggested Films About Africa

1. *African Queen* (Spiegel & Huston, 1951)is set in Africa during World War I. The film centers on a hard-drinking riverboat captain (Humphrey Bogart) providing passage for a Christian missionary spinster (Katherine Hepburn).
2. *Cry, the Beloved Country* (Singh & Roodt, 1995) is a film adaptation of Alan Paton's novel written in 1948 by the same name (see chapter 9 in this book for the Novel Guide). In the film, a beloved rural minister (James Earl Jones) in South Africa makes his first trip to Johannesburg in search of his son. His son's destiny has been linked with that of a doomed young white man, whose racist father (Richard Harris) is approached in the spirit of mutual understanding.
3. *The Flame Trees of Thika* (Baker, 1982) is based on the beloved autobiographical novel of the same name by Elspeth Huxley. The story brings an eventful childhood in Eastern Africa to vivid life. In 1913, 11-year-old Elspeth Grant (Holly Aird) travels with her mother, Tilly, from England to Kenya to help build a coffee plantation.
4. *Ghosts of Rwanda* (Barker, 2003) depicts the Rwandan genocide—a state sponsored massacre in which some 800,000 Rwandans were methodically hunted down and murdered by Hutu extremists.
5. *I Dreamed of Africa* (Jaffe & Hudson, 2000) is about Kuki, a divorced Italian socialite who changes her life after a serious car crash. She accepts a marriage proposal from Paulo Gallmann, a man she does not know well, and moves to Kenya with him and her young son to start a cattle ranch.
6. *Lost Boys of Sudan* (Reid, Mylan, & Shenk, 2003) is a gripping documentary about young refugees from the Sudanese conflict as well as a moving story of survival and acclimation in a strange and daunting land. The film centers around two young Dinka tribesmen who must flee a vicious civil war in their homeland and risk thirst, starvation, and animal attack to reach refugee camps thousands of miles away in Kenya and then in Ethiopia.
7. *Nowhere in Africa* (Bareib & Link, 2000) begins with a Jewish woman named Jettel Redlich fleeing Nazi Germany with her daughter Regina to join her husband (Regina's father), Walter, on a farm in Kenya. At first, Jettel refuses to adjust to her new circumstances (she brings with her a set of china dishes and an evening gown), while Regina adapts readily to this new world, forming a strong bond with her father's cook, an African named Owuor. But this is only the beginning of a series of uprootings as the surface of their lives is torn away.
8. *100 Days* (Hughes, 2004) deals with the 1994 Rwandan genocide and makes clear the crucial role of the UN.
9. *Out of Africa* (Jorgensen & Pollack, 1985) is one of the screen's great epic romances. It is the fascinating true story of Karen Blixen (Meryl Streep), a strong-willed woman who, with her philandering husband, runs a coffee plantation in Kenya, circa 1914. To her astonishment, she soon discovers herself falling in love with the land, its people, and a mysterious white hunter (Robert Redford).
10. *Something of Value* (Berman & Brooks, 1957) tells the story of the Mau Mau uprising in Kenya, Africa, in the 1950s (see the Novel Guide in chapter 6 for further discussion of the Mau Mau Revolt).
11. *Sometimes in April* (Peck, 2005) gives a clear-eyed look at the 1994 slaughter that claimed upwards of 800,000 lives in Rwanda. The film zeroes in on the U.S. government's distinction that "acts of genocide" occurred in Rwanda rather than "genocide."
12. *Zulu* (Baker & Enfield, 1964) is a rousing adventure recounting the true story of a small 18th-century regiment of British troops endlessly besieged by a seemingly unceasing number of fierce Zulu attackers.
13. *Yesterday* (Roodt, 2004) tells the story of a young mother who discovers that she has AIDS, given to her by her husband, a migrant laborer. Her ambition is to live long enough to see her daughter go to school.

Table 14.2. African Film Analysis and Comparison

	Title of Film 1	Title of Film 2	Title of Film 3
Country of emphasis			
Landscape or other notable physical features of the country as represented by the film			
Film's primary type (entertainment, documentary, literary) with an explanation of how you know			
Main conflict or issue dealt with in the film (Did the film have a noticeable agenda, if so, what was it?)			
Characterization (identify and describe major characters)			
Personal critique of the film			
Questions remaining for you after viewing the film			

discuss their findings in class prior to a whole-class study of *Hotel Rwanda* (George, 2004), the film text that is the emphasis of the remainder of this chapter.

The Genocide in Rwanda

Rwanda is one of the smallest countries in Central Africa, with just 7 million people, and, today, is composed of two main ethnic groups, the Hutu and the Tutsi (United Human Rights Council, 2006). The Tutsi are descendants of the biblical Ham and are tall—often over 7 feet (Marks, 2006). They were traditionally a nomadic people, herders of cattle. The Hutu, on the other hand, were agricultural—cultivators who were basically poor and uneducated. Although the Hutu account for 85% of the population, in the past, the Tutsi minority was considered the aristocracy of Rwanda and dominated Hutu peasants for decades, particularly when Rwanda was under Belgian colonial rule.

Under Belgian rule, the Tutsi were more favored because of their tall stature and thin noses, which made them appear more "white." The Belgians did little to bring the two ethnic groups together and forced both groups to carry ethnic identity cards in order to clearly identify each individual as a member of one of the groups (Marks, 2006). Following independence from Belgium in 1962, the Hutu majority seized power and reversed the roles, oppressing the Tutsi through systematic discrimination and acts of violence (Marks, 2006). As a result, over 200,000 Tutsi fled to neighboring countries where they formed a rebel army, the Rwandan Patriotic Front (Marks, 2006). In 1990, this rebel army invaded Rwanda and forced Hutu President Juvenal Habyarimana into signing an accord, which mandated that the Hutu and Tutsi would share power (Marks, 2006).

Ethnic tensions in Rwanda significantly heightened, and on April 6, 1994, Hutu president Juvenal Habyarimana's plane was shot down (Marks, 2006). It is generally believed by Rwandan citizens that the president's own Hutu extremist supporters orchestrated the attack in order to prevent the president from signing peace agreements, but the exact circumstances of this have not been verified. Regardless, the Tutsi were blamed. Over the next 100 days, an estimated 800,000 Rwandans, mostly Tutsis, were indiscriminately slaughtered by Hutu militia wielding clubs, machetes, guns, and grenades (Marks, 2006). The killers were mostly civilians spurred on by hate propaganda, and, in the end, an estimated 300,000 of those 800,000 killed were children. Anywhere between 90,000 and 300,000 children were left orphaned (Educational Broadcasting Corporation, n.d.). As strange as it may seem, the killing in Rwanda exceeded the daily rate of extermination in the Nazi death camps. It is also estimated that at least a quarter million women were raped during the genocide (Marks, 2006).

No effort was made to evacuate Tutsi civilians or Hutu moderates. Instead, they were left entirely at the mercy of the avenging Hutu. The United Nations (UN) Security Council responded to the worsening crisis by voting unanimously to abandon Rwanda. The remainder of UN peacekeeping troops were pulled out, leaving behind only a tiny force of about 200 soldiers for the entire country under the command of UN Colonel Oliver (United Human Rights Council, 2006).

The Hutu, now without opposition from the world community, engaged in violent acts of genocide, hacking to death with machetes the defenseless Tutsi, whom they referred to as "cockroaches" (United Human Rights Council, 2006, ¶ 1). The Rwandan state radio, controlled by Hutu extremists, further encouraged the killings by broadcasting nonstop hate propaganda and even pinpointing the locations of Tutsi in hiding. The killers were aided by members of the Hutu professional class including journalists, doctors, and educators, along with unemployed Hutu youths and peasants who killed Tutsi just to steal their property.

Many Tutsi sought refuge in churches, mission compounds, and hotels (United Human Rights Council, 2006). Finally, after being confronted with international television news reports depicting genocide, the UN Security Council voted to send up to 5,000 soldiers to Rwanda. The council, however, failed to establish any timetable and thus did not send troops in time to stop the massacre (United Human Rights Council, 2006).

The killings ended only after armed Tutsi rebels, invading from neighboring countries, managed to defeat the Hutu and halt the genocide in July 1994. By then, over one tenth of the Rwandan population had been killed (United Human Rights Council, 2006).

Objectives for Studying the Genocide in Rwanda

The legal definition of genocide as defined by the Genocide Convention is any of the following acts committed with intent to destroy, in whole or in part, a national, ethnic, racial, or religious group:

(a) Killing members of the group;

(b) Causing serious bodily or mental harm to members of the group;

(c) Deliberately inflicting on the group conditions of life calculated to bring about its physical destruction in whole or in part;

(d) Imposing measures intended to prevent births within the group;

(e) Forcibly transferring children of the group to another group. (Prevent Genocide International, 2004, ¶ 7–11)

A study of genocide through *Hotel Rwanda* (George, 2004) allows for a complex understanding of the roles played by perpetrators, victims, and bystanders in the genocide in Rwanda—and also how acts of genocide have been committed elsewhere. For many years, the term *genocide* was most commonly associated with the Holocaust of World War II, but this film has helped to expose the fact that genocide is not confined to one nation, one continent, or one ethnic group. Recent tragedies such as the Rwandan massacres have drawn the attention of the world to the idea that genocide is a political phenomenon that may be studied across time and regions.

In their study of genocide of Rwanda, students should be able to complete the following objectives:

• explain what genocide is and have a key understanding as to the events in Rwanda's history that led up to the genocide in 1994;

• explain the relationship between the Tutsi and the Hutu and understand the role of the international community in the Rwandan genocide;

• understand how *Hotel Rwanda*, in particular, depicts the atrocities and the political issues of the genocide;

• become more familiar with the cultural and political roots of human cruelty, mass violence, and genocide;

- think critically about one's own responsibility in preventing genocide;
- evaluate how the elements of film (e.g., character, plot, setting, theme, symbolism, lighting, sound, camera angles) help viewers to develop an informed appreciation of history and cinematic art; and
- transpose the analytic skills from film and apply them to any individual or collective instance of genocide or mass killing.

To reach these objectives, the remainder of this chapter includes classroom activities related to *Hotel Rwanda* designed to deepen students' understanding of the massacre in Rwanda.

Plot Synopsis for *Hotel Rwanda* (2004)

Based on a true story, *Hotel Rwanda* (George, 2004) is a cinematic experience that shines light on the courage of Paul Rusesabagina to protect his family and homeland strangers during the Rwandan genocide of 1994. The film lends a human face to an upheaval so savage it seemed beyond the realm of imagination when news of it filtered into the Western world. Rusesabagina (played by Don Cheadle in the film) is the soft-spoken Hutu manager of the Hotel Des Mille Collines in Kigali, who, with his Tutsi wife, Tatiana (played by Sophie Okonedo) and children, narrowly escapes death himself while managing to save the lives of more than 1,200 Tutsi and Hutu moderates.

At first it seems that Rusesabagina appears a bit removed from the reality about to overtake Rwanda and relies on the presence of the United Nations to quell the impending war. As the genocide escalates, however, Rusesabagina, deserted by his white superiors and made temporary manager, is transformed into the unlikely hero by turning his hotel into an impromptu refugee camp. He bribes Hutu militia for three months, managing to keep most of them outside the hotel's gates during the hundred days of slaughter.

In the end, not only do Rusesabagina and his family survive, but the 1,268 Tutsi and moderate Hutu who were sheltered in the hotel survive as well. *Hotel Rwanda* bears witness to one of Africa's greatest tragedies, and perhaps its greatest message is that it brings to light the genocide that was recognized only after the fact (*Hotel*, 2005b, ¶ 2).

Before-, During-, and After-Viewing Activities for *Hotel Rwanda*: The Structured Viewing Lesson

The activities that follow treat film as text, just as one would treat a literary work, only with visuals reinforcing the words. The activities can be conceived as a Structured Viewing Lesson, similar to the Structure Reading Lesson outlined in Glasgow (2005, pp. 9–12). The Structured Viewing Lesson helps students to maximize their readiness to view, emotionally engage with, and understand film through Before-Viewing Activities; to be active viewers who are attentive to film details both in content and form through During-Viewing Activities; and to connect more deeply with the film, examine its themes, and consider its life relevance through After-Viewing Activities.

Before-Viewing Activities

As with all texts we teach, it is important for teachers to assess students' prior knowledge before viewing *Hotel Rwanda* (George, 2004). Before-viewing strategies, like before-reading strategies, help to establish for students "a sense of purpose and motivation" for examining a text, be it literary or visual (Glasgow, 2005, p. 10). By establishing what students know in relation to the topic under investigation, teachers can help viewers "better comprehend and approach a new text" (Glasgow, 2005, p. 10). The questions in Table 14.3 will help students to explore what they already know about genocide and assess their own feelings regarding injustice.

Table 14.3. Before-Viewing Questions for *Hotel Rwanda*

- From what source do you think the word *genocide* originated? What is the definition of the word?
- Have you ever personally witnessed an injustice? What was the nature of the injustice? The circumstances? The outcome?
- If you were in the victim's shoes, what would you have wanted from an eyewitness?
- Can you name any examples of genocide in the 20th century? (Answers may include the Holocaust, the killing fields of Cambodia, Bosnia)
- Why do you think it important that there be a legal definition of genocide?
- If you were to write a definition of genocide, what might that legal definition be?
- Pass out a card to each student with the name of a group on that card. Examples might be welfare recipients, homosexuals, African Americans, Jews, gypsies, overweight persons, and so forth. Instruct students to assume the role of a person from the group written on the card. Then have students answer the following question: If you were a _____, what would you never again want to hear someone say about you? Discuss this among the group members.
- What role do media play in your life? Can you recall a film that has made you angry or caused you to take action? If so, what was the cause of your anger and the direction of your action?
- Ask students to name films that portray Africa. In small groups, discuss how the African people are depicted; who seems to be in charge; how historically accurate the films are; and what lasting images of Africa, the land, and its people are depicted in the films.

In addition to exploring the questions in Table 14.3, the following activities are helpful to establish a knowledge base and emotional context before viewing *Hotel Rwanda*.

1. Locate Rwanda on a map. Locate Kigali.

2. Read the story of Gitera Rwamuhuzi as reported by BBC News (available online at http://news.bbc.co.uk/1/hi/programmes/panorama/3582011. stm). Rwamuhuzi took part in the genocide, and in looking back, he stated, "It was as if we were taken over by Satan. When Satan is using you, you lose your mind. We were not ourselves. Beginning with me, I don't think I was normal. You wouldn't be normal if you start butchering people for no reason" (BBC News, 2004, ¶ 23–24). Ask students to discuss Rwamuhuzi's story and consider times that they became enraged or irrational with their words or actions and how they handled it.

3. Ask students to look at the website Remembering Rwanda: The Rwanda 10th Anniversary Memorial Project (available online at www.visiontv.ca/ RememberRwanda/main_pf.htm).

Some of the images in the Photo Gallery section focus directly on the Rwandan genocide while others deal more with the aftermath. In small-group discussion, have students outline how one might come to terms with the unbearable memories evoked by the images.

During-Viewing Activities

Again, treating film as text, the purpose of during-viewing strategies, like during-reading strategies, is to help the students view constructively (Glasgow, 2005). With focused questions and activities, teachers are able to draw students' attention to particular aspects of film and help them to engage in critical thinking and meaningful interpretation throughout their viewing of *Hotel Rwanda*. During-Viewing Activities include a Word Bank, Timeline, and Focused Viewing Questions.

Word Bank. One of the activities students should pursue throughout viewing the film is the creation of a Word Bank. The Word Bank is a place for students to record new vocabulary and concepts from the film. In their Word Bank for *Hotel Rwanda* (George, 2004) students might include the following: *amnesty, atrocities, colonialism, discrimination, ethnic cleansing, ethnicity, exile, gacaca* (process to hold perpetrators accountable), *genocide, Hutu, Interahamwe* (militia), *machete, majority, minority, racial classification, reconciliation, refugee,* and *Tutsi.* Completing the word bank will involve some outside resources such as a dictionary, Internet access, or a day in the library or media center. For this reason, the viewing of *Hotel*

Rwanda is probably best done over several class sessions, with a day or two between viewing sections of the film for additional research of terms and concepts, such as those recorded in the Word Bank. Days between viewing portions of the film will also be useful for creating a timeline and for class discussion.

Timeline. As students view *Hotel Rwanda* (George, 2004), have them keep a list of running events as they unfold. As students denote the key events, the class can work collaboratively to construct a timeline on a bulletin board. This can be compared with factual information regarding the genocide and incorporate pictures found in the Before-Viewing Activity in which students looked at the website Remembering Rwanda: The Rwanda 10th Anniversary Memorial Project (www.visiontv.ca/RememberRwanda/main_pf.htm).

Discussion. While students should individually record new words, concepts, and events while viewing *Hotel Rwanda* (George, 2004), class time should also be devoted to discussing the film. Providing time for students to discuss the film will help to ensure that students know key characters and places and understand crucial plot points and conflicts. Table 14.4 includes focus questions for students to respond to while viewing *Hotel Rwanda*. These become the basis for class discussion to ensure a sound base of knowledge and comprehension leading to a careful analysis of the film.

Table 14.4. Focused During-Viewing Questions for *Hotel Rwanda*

- Identify key characters in the film: Paul and Tatiana Rusesabagina, President Habyarimana, UN Colonel Oliver, George Rutaganda, General Bizimungu. How accurate, for example, is the treatment of Tatiana in the film compared to what really happened to her?

- Identify key places: Hotel de Milles Collines, Kigali. How did the Hotel change during the crisis in Rwanda?

- After viewing the actions of the reporter in the film, how far do you think a reporter should go in obtaining a story?

- Note how media were used in different ways: to spread hatred and bigotry or to provide documented evidence of genocide. What kind of language is used for both purposes?

- Note what the rest of the world was doing during the Rwandan genocide. Where is this most evident in the film?

- Note the members of the international community portrayed in the film (Red Cross, for example). How is the position of each of the members carried out? This might be done by dividing the class into as many groups as there are members of the international community and asking each group to write a position statement for that particular group.

After-Viewing Activities

Having viewed *Hotel Rwanda* (George, 2004) in its entirety, students will have a variety of After-Viewing Activities from which to choose (see Table 14.5 for a

---

Table 14.5. After-Viewing Activities for *Hotel Rwanda*

Role-Play Activities
- Convene the class into a panel with a member of each of the international communities as panelists. How effective was each group in preventing the genocide? What was the role of each group during the genocide?
- Role-play key characters responsible for rebuilding a country torn apart by war, genocide, or civil violence. Things to be considered might include urban development, education, care for refugees and orphans, food production and distribution, budget, justice, and reconciliation.
- Hold a trial based on the factual information surrounding the Rwandan genocide. Have students assume the roles of the prosecuting attorneys, defense attorneys, witnesses, officials, judge, jury, bailiff, defendant, plaintiff, court reporter, court visitors, and so forth. What will be the reparations, if any? The sentences, if any? For more information regarding mock trials, including rules of competition, visit the website of the National High School Mock Trial Championship at www.nationalmocktrial.org/fullrules.cfm.

Research Activities
- Research the improvements made in Rwanda since the 1994 genocide. What has been done to unify the people of Rwanda?
- Select a current national or international situation. Research the situation and prepare a report detailing whether or not the lessons learned from the Rwandan genocide are applicable to the current situation. If so, how? If not, why not?
- Investigate the plight of those who committed the Rwandan atrocities. Who has been held accountable? What has happened to them?

Activities With Other Films, Media, and Texts
- Compare the same news story on at least three different television stations (e.g., Fox News, CNN, NBC). How were the stories similar? Different? How does the viewer determine accuracy?
- Obtain a copy of *Witness to Genocide: The Children of Rwanda* (Salem, 2000). The drawings in the book are done by child survivors and can be obtained from Conflict Management Initiatives online at www.cmi-salem.org/witness.htm or from www.amazon.com.
- Draw parallels between *Hotel Rwanda* (George, 2004) and the HBO Entertainment presentation of *Sometimes in April* (2005).
- Draw parallels between *Hotel Rwanda* and the documentary *Ghosts of Rwanda* (Barker, 2005).

Presentations and Writing Activities
- Write a peace agreement between the Hutu and the Tutsi. What conditions must be considered? What is the timeline of the agreement?
- Conduct letter-writing campaigns to the United Nations or to the United States president or Congress encouraging leaders to support UN Secretary General Kofi Annan's establishment of a UN Committee on Preventing Genocide.
- Collect photos of the Rwandan genocide and host a display, information table, or commemorative event.
- Join the Hotel Rwanda Rusesabagina Foundation, which is dedicated to combat the horrors of genocide inflicted upon children by providing assistance and education. Ideas for a service learning project can be found at Rusesabagina's website, www.hrrfoundation.org.

---

list of suggested activities). After-viewing strategies encourage reflection and lead viewers more deeply into the film by "allowing them to probe and clarify ideas" (Glasgow, 2005, p. 11). Along with reflection, after-viewing strategies allow students to "reexperience favorite parts, to think about the story's meanings, and relate its themes to their lives" (Glasgow, 2005, p. 11). The classroom activities described in this section require students to get involved with role-play, research, outside sources, writing, presentation, and social action. Teachers should choose the ideas that work best for their classroom or divide the class into groups, having each group choose a different After-Viewing Activity from the list.

Making-A-Difference Project: Empty Bowls Fund-Raising Project to Contribute to the Hotel Rwanda Rusesabagina Foundation

The basic idea for Empty Bowls is for fundraising participants to make or decorate ceramic bowls and then serve a simple meal of soup and bread. In exchange for a meal and a bowl, the guest donates a suggested minimum of US$10. All of the funds raised for Empty Bowls are used for fighting hunger (Empty Bowls, 2002, ¶ 2). In this case, the contributions are to be sent to the Hotel Rwanda Rusesabagina Foundation (Hotel, 2005a) to provide food for hungry women and children. The 1994 genocide left anywhere between 90,000 and 300,000 children orphaned (Educational Broadcasting Corporation, n.d.), making Rwanda one of the highest per capita orphan populations in the world. Many of these children were born to women who were raped during the genocide and have subsequently grown up with no fathers and may lack access to basic food, clothing, or shelter, and they quickly fall prey to those seeking to exploit their condition (Donohoe, 2004, ¶ 1).

To get started with this project, students need to either make their own ceramic bowls or buy inexpensive ones from a local store. In either case, the bowls should be decorated as a keepsake and reminder of the hunger in the world, particularly hunger in Rwanda. Next, students should contact various organizations in the school or community to actually make and contribute bread and a large pot of soup. If they also provide the recipe for the soup, students could make fliers with these soup recipes. Next, students need to make arrangements for the luncheon to be held in the school cafeteria so that there will be tables, chairs, silverware, bowls, and dishwashing facilities. The soup should be served in cafeteria soup bowls so that guests can take home the clean, decorated ones without having to wash them first.

Next comes the publicity. Students should send out invitations for the Empty Bowls Luncheon as well as publicize it in the school and community. Then when the big day arrives, students can provide a program for the guests that may include music, dancing, a slideshow of orphans in Rwanda, or movie clips from *Hotel Rwanda* (George, 2004). At the end of the project, students should send the donations to the Hotel Rwanda Rusesabagina Foundation at the following address:

Hotel Rwanda Rusesabagina Foundation
c/o Burns & Levinson LLP
Attn: Marybeth Celorier, CFO
125 Summer Street
Boston, MA 02110
info@hrrfoundation.org

Conclusion

The films addressed in this chapter, particularly *Hotel Rwanda* (George, 2004), are powerful and moving in their portrayal of Africa, the continent, its varied nations, history, cultures, and conflicts. Film provides a merging of art and life and is possibly the most powerful medium for relating the human experience to students. Film also capitalizes on our strongest learning sense—sight. Through the varied films and structured viewing strategies presented in this chapter, teachers and students experience film as text—visual instead of written—and they realize film as a powerful tool that can draw students into the texture of other cultures; serve as a springboard for critical thinking and analysis; and prompt serious reflection, writing, research, and social action.

REFERENCES

BBC News. (2004, April 2). *Taken over by Satan*. Retrieved June 22, 2006, from http://news.bbc.co.uk/1/hi/programmes/panorama/3582011.stm

Donohoe, M. (2004). War, rape, and genocide: Never again? *Medscape*. Retrieved March 7, 2007, from http://www.medscape.com/viewarticle/491147

Educational Broadcasting Corporation. (n.d.) *Wideangle: The Offspring of War*. Retrieved March 2, 2007, from http://www.pbsorg/wnet/wideangle/printable/rwanda_handbook2_print.html

Empty Bowls. (2002). *Home*. Retrieved June 23, 2006, from http://www.emptybowls.net/

Glasgow, J.N. (Ed.). (2005). *Strategies for engaging young adult readers: A social themes approach*. Norwood, MA: Christopher-Gordon.

Hotel Rwanda Rusesabagina Foundation. (2005a). *About us*. Retrieved June 22, 2006, from http://www.hrrfoundation.org/about.html

Hotel Rwanda Rusesabagina Foundation. (2005b). *Orphans*. Retrieved June 23, 2006, from http://www.hrrfoundation.org/issues.html

Marks, Z. (2006). *Creating an enemy to destroy: Ethnic identity manipulation and the rules of competition*. Retrieved March 7, 2007, from

http://scholar.google.com/scholar?hl=en&lr=&
q=cache:Hkfh4W-keaQJ:www11.georgetown.
edu/programs/gervase/cfi/mentisvita/vi.i/Rw
anda.pdf+Z+Marks+and+Rwandan+Genocide

Mintz, S. (2003). Hollywood as history. *Digital History*. Retrieved June 21, 2006, from http://www.digitalhistory.uh.edu/historyonline/hollywood_history.cfm

National High School Mock Trial Championship. (2006). Retrieved June 23, 2006, from http://www.nationalmocktrial.org/fullrules.cfm

Prevent Genocide International. (2004). *The crime of "genocide" defined in international law.*

Retrieved June 22, 2006, from http://www.preventgenocide.org/genocide/officaltext.htm

Safdie, M.R., & Miller, D.E. (Photographers). (2006). *Photo gallery*. Retrieved June 22, 2006, from http://www.visiontv.ca/RememberRwanda/main_pf.htm

Salem, R.A. (Ed.). (2000). *Witness to genocide: The children of Rwanda: Drawings by child survivors of the Rwandan genocide of 1994*. Evanston, IL: Friendship Press.

United Human Rights Council. (2006). *Genocide in Rwanda*. Retrieved June 22, 2006, from http://www.unitedhumanrights.org/Genocide/genocide_in_rwanda.htm

LITERATURE CITED

Paton, A. (1987). *Cry, the beloved country*. New York: Macmillan. (Original work published 1948)

wa Thiong'o, N. (1964). *Weep not, child*. Portsmouth, NH: Heinemann.

FILMS CITED

Baker, R.W. (Director). (1981). *The Flame trees of Thika* [Motion picture]. United Kingdom: Euston Films.

Baker, S. (Producer), & Enfield, C. (Director). (1964). *Zulu* [Motion picture]. United States: MGM.

Bareib, A. (Producer), & Link, C. (Director). (2000). *Nowhere in Africa* [Motion picture]. United States: Sony Pictures.

Barker, G. (Producer/Director). (2003). *Ghosts of Rwanda* [Motion picture]. United States: PBS Paramount.

Berman, P.S. (Producer), & Brooks, R. (Director). (1957). *Something of value* [Motion picture]. United States: MGM/United Artists.

George, T. (Director). (2004). *Hotel Rwanda* [Motion picture]. United States: MGM Home Entertainment.

Hughes, N. (Producer & Director). (2004). *100 Days* [Motion picture]. United States: Vivid Features.

Jaffe, S.R. (Producer), & Hudson, H. (Director). (2000). *I dreamed of Africa* [Motion picture]. United States: Sony Pictures.

Jorgensen, K. (Producer), & Pollack, S. (Director). (1985). *Out of Africa* [Motion picture]. United States: Universal Pictures.

Peck, R. (Producer/Director). (2005). *Sometimes in April* [Motion picture]. United States: HBO Films.

Reid, F. (Producer), & Mylan, M., & Shenk, J. (Directors). (2003). *Lost boys of Sudan* [Motion picture]. United States: Actual Films.

Roodt, D. (Director). (2004). *Yesterday* [Motion picture]. South Africa: Videovision Entertainment.

Singh, A. (Producer), & Roodt, D. (Director). (1995). *Cry, the beloved country* [Motion picture]. United States: Miramax.

Spiegel, S. (Producer), & Huston, J. (Director). (1951). *The African queen* [Motion picture]. United States: Horizon Pictures.

CHAPTER 15

Children's Literature as a Means of Exploring African Life

Allison L. Baer

"Perhaps, it's a matter of censorship that is the difference. Otherwise, there ought to be no reason why an adult should not enjoy or be enriched by children's books. Of course, one of the best things about children's books is that they encourage physical contact—between people. You don't have to sit on the lap of somebody when reading Jane Austen—I think!"

—NIKI DALY (2001, ¶ 8)

Students are often presented with a new topic or text without benefit of any preexisting knowledge, thus making comprehension and understanding more difficult than they need to be. When using the Novel Guides to explore the literature and culture of Africa, students may have scarce, if not ill-informed, prior knowledge. However, according to Glasgow (2005), frontloading—or before-reading—activities can help activate "students' prior knowledge, preparing them for the challenge ahead with appropriate strategies, and helping them monitor their own performance" (p. 10). By utilizing the children's literature text sets presented in this chapter as a before-reading strategy, teachers will help their students develop a strong base of prior knowledge that will deepen students' comprehension of the topic at hand (Robb, 2000) and better equip them for the material that they will encounter through the Novel Guides.

The children's books in this chapter were chosen for their high-quality representations of African life and culture as they present accurate portrayals through illustration and text. Using such high-quality African literature will evoke an aesthetic response to accompany the information presented, deepening the level of engagement a learner experiences with each text. Used in con-

Exploring African Life and Literature: Novel Guides to Promote Socially Responsive Learning edited by Jacqueline N. Glasgow and Linda J. Rice. © 2007 by the International Reading Association.

junction with the young adult and classic literature discussed in previous chapters, these books can provide multiple opportunities to visualize that which few students have experienced—the lush, colorful, varied landscape of the African continent and its people.

The children's books in this chapter are organized by themes. Books grouped under the first theme, "Picture Books That Give an Overview of Africa," are general in nature and give the reader a basic understanding of the culture, people, and traditions of the continent of Africa. The theme of "Gender Issues in Children's Literature of Africa" focuses on the different expectations and issues faced by females in many African countries. The third theme, "Comparing and Contrasting City and Village Life," helps the reader visualize and understand the differences between urban and rural living, giving the reader a glimpse into various lifestyles in the continent. The final theme, "The Effects of Poverty" speaks to the daily hardships faced by all too many citizens of Africa.

One before-reading activity that can be used with any of these text sets is a simple read-aloud of a picture book accompanied by before-, during-, and after-reading discussion questions. Typically, this will take between 20 and 30 minutes depending on how much time is allowed for discussion—see Table 15.1 for a list of suggested discussion questions to use with the read-alouds created by Albright (2002). The before- and during-reading questions can be done as a teacher-led discussion, while the after-reading questions may be effectively done in small-group discussion.

Picture Books That Give an Overview of Africa

The picture books included in this section can be used with any of the Novel Guides and books discussed thus far as they will help the reader gain a basic understanding of the continent. Two alphabet books, *A Is for Africa* (Onyefulu, 1997) and *Ashanti to Zulu: African Traditions* (Musgrove, 1976), provide the reader with a general introduction to the people of Africa. The first is broader in scope as it draws from more of the continent and is accompanied by stunning illustrations of the terms discussed in the book. The second features photographs from Nigeria, but the author explains that they draw on the rich culture of the entire continent. Each book teaches about some aspect of African culture: family, community, religion, music, and government. Muriel Feelings's books *Moja Means One* (1971) and *Jambo Means Hello* (1974) introduce the reader to the East African culture through learning Swahili terms for the numbers 1 through 10 and the 24 letters in the Swahili alphabet. Once again, the reader is treated to beautiful illustrations, which create an even better understanding of each term. *Raymond Floyd Goes to Africa; or, There Are No Bears in Africa* (Murdock, 1993) is

---

Table 15.1. Discussion Questions for Read-Alouds

Questions for Discussion Prior to the Read-Aloud
- What can you tell me about (topic)?
- Who can tell me what a (___) is? Has anyone ever seen a (___)? Tell me about it.
- Why do you think I chose this book to read to you?
- Why might we want to read this book?
- What do you want to find out about (___)?

Questions for Discussion During the Read-Aloud
- Does this remind you of anything you have read in your textbook or discussed in class? How does it relate to that?
- What does (___) mean?
- Why do you think that happened the way it did?
- What do you think will happen next?
- Do you think that is important? Why?
- What did you notice in that illustration?
- How is that information different than what you are reading in (source)?

Questions for Discussion After the Read-Aloud
- What did you notice in the book?
- What does the book remind you of in your own life?
- How is this person's life like yours? How is it different from yours?
- How is this book like another you have read? How is it different?
- If you could talk to the author, what would you ask him or her?
- How do you think the author researched this book?
- What did you learn from this book that surprised you or you did not know before?
- How does this relate to what you have read in your textbook or discussed in class?
- What are three facts, theories, or incidents you thought were interesting?

Reprinted from Albright, L.K. (2002). Bringing the Ice Maiden to life: Engaging adolescents in learning through picture book read-alouds in content areas. *Journal of Adolescent & Adult Literacy, 45*(5), 418–428.

---

a quirky look at Africa through the eyes of a tiny teddy bear as he travels the continent on the hat of his owner. Raymond Floyd introduces the reader to different native animals and the Swahili language as he visits many game reserves around the continent. The Akimbo series (McCall Smith, 2005) follows a young boy who lives with his family on a game reserve someplace in Africa. The author introduces the reader to many of the laws dealing with wild animals and poaching as he tells of Akimbo's adventures.

Gender Issues in Children's Literature of Africa

Gender bias in the continent of Africa takes on many forms against females of all ages. On September 25, 2005, the Secretary of Leguru Wards Major Ferdinand Keku announced that in order to qualify for educational scholarship awards "no fewer than 100 girls in the nine wards comprising Leguru, in Odogbolu Local Government Area of Ogun State, Africa, would undergo virginity tests next month in order to 'encourage our young ladies to avoid pre-marital sex'" (Pereira, 2005, ¶1). This test, done to ensure that girls "zip-up" (Pereira, 2005, ¶ 2) until marriage, excludes all boys applying for the same scholarships. In addition, women need documentation of marriage to protect their property rights (Women, 2005). Other chapters in this book provide further detail on other extreme biases against women based on gender (see chapter 7 or chapter 13, for example).

When confronting these issues through the literature of Africa, particularly through the young adult literature discussed in the Novel Guides in this book, the reaction of the reader may be one of disbelief and incredulity. The children's picture books discussed in the following section help introduce the readers to this often harsh and unjust reality. Picture books often provide a bridge between the reader's known world in which he or she lives, and the unknown world of the text. The simple, honest stories and pictures can gently introduce the reader to the realities faced by young girls and women in the continent of Africa, giving them a basis for understanding many of the harsher realities contained in the Novel Guides. However, another issue presenting itself through children's books is that of the place of women within the family and community. Here the reader can see the strength and beauty of African women as they work hard to keep their families intact despite poverty and a lack of male figures.

Access to Education

In sub-Saharan Africa, a full 60% of the estimated 113 million out-of-school children are girls (Guttman, n.d.). Add to that the fact that the secondary school enrollment rate for girls is less than 10% (Bellamy, 2003) and the issue of access to education for girls is huge. There are many picture books that speak to this disturbing fact. In *Madoulina: A Girl Who Wanted to Go to School* (1999), Joel Bognomo tells the story of Madoulina, a poor, young girl who lives in Camaroon and dreams of going to school. Due to extreme poverty, she cannot go to school as she needs to help her mother bake and sell fritters to support the family, including her younger brother, who does get to go to school. Catherine Stock, in *Where Are You Going Manyoni?* (1993), beautifully describes the great lengths young girls go to in order to get an education. Set on the Limpopo River in Zimbabwe, Stock follows Manyoni as she walks across the veld (fields) toward an unknown destination. The colorful illustrations present the flora and fauna of the veld as well as the animals that watch Manyoni's daily two-hour trek to and from the school in a village far from her home.

Single Women as Providers and Caretakers

As unplanned urban sprawl stretches throughout the cities of Africa, the number of unmarried and poor women climbs (Bigombe & Khadiagala, n.d.). Consequently, households with female heads are overrepresented among the poor. Many books address this issue of single women as providers and caretakers. Niki Daly's Jamela books give the reader a glimpse into the city lives of Jamela and her single mother. *Jamela's Dress* (1999) shows the support and care of female friends in a mischievous story of a wayward piece of fabric. *Where's Jamela* (2004) begins with the excited mother announcing a new job, which means a new home for Jamela and her mother. They can also now afford to have Jamela's Gogo, or grandmother, move in with them, thereby completing a supportive circle of three generations of women.

A tale of a grandmother raising her grandchild, *The Dove* (Stewart, 1993) is set in the city of Natal in South Africa. When a great flood ruins all of the crops, Lindi and her grandmother make beaded jewelry to sell in the city. Unfortunately, many other women have the same idea, so sales are few. Close to despair and starvation, Lindi sees a dove, which inspires her to make a beaded dove that sells quickly. Bognomo's *Madoulina* (1999), discussed above, also portrays a worried mother desperately trying to provide for her children. Each day the mother makes fritters, and she and Madoulina sell them on the street in order to support their family. *My Great-Grandmother's Gourd* (Kessler, 2000) chronicles the installation of a water pump in a Sudanese village. Fatima's grandmother, doubting modern technology, sticks to the old ways of preparing her ancestral baobab tree for the rain. Kessler's portrayal of pride and family solidarity is filled with interesting pictures of the struggles of village life.

Other books speak to the need for a father to work in a city, leaving his wife and children behind. Hugh Lewin paints simple pictures of village life through the eyes of a young boy, Jafta. In *Jafta's Mother* (1983), it is apparent that the father is away as Jafta talks about how strong his mother is, comparing her to the African morning and sky. The accompanying book, *Jafta's Father* (1983), explains that his father must work far from his family, showing Jafta's sorrow at having his father so far from home. Rachel Isadora's book *At the Crossroads* (1991), set in a South African village, tells the story of five children as they stand at the crossroads of two dirt roads, waiting for their fathers to come home from working in the mines. Their waiting is filled with excitement as others gather to watch for the trucks with the men from the village.

One book stands apart from the rest as it speaks of South Africa's newfound freedom. *The Day Gogo Went to Vote* (Sisulu, 1996), set in Soweto in South Africa, tells the story of 100-year-old Gogo's first time voting in 1994, the first election open to black South Africans. Old and infirm, Gogo insists that she has waited a long time for this freedom and she *will* vote herself. While voting had become available to all, Sisulu's story focuses on the elderly matriarch of the family and the strength everyone sees in and gains from her.

Community Respect for Elderly Women

Although the books above present gender issues in the family, many of them also discuss community. *My Great-Grandmother's Gourd* (Kessler, 2000) illustrates the wisdom and respect afforded an elderly woman in the village as she stays with the old traditions rather than embracing the new technology—a water pump. Similarly, when septuagenarian Gogo (Sisulu, 1996) wants to vote in her first South African election, her place of honor is evident as a local businessman arranges for his car to pick her up and take her to vote. When she emerges from the voting booth, the community has gathered to applaud her strength. Stewart's *The Dove* (1993) shows the importance of the community as the grandmother relies on the help of local businesses to sell her handmade beaded jewelry and doves.

Maya Angelou's *My Painted House, My Friendly Chicken, and Me* (1994) presents the life and place of women, young and old, in a South African village. Photographs are used to follow Thandi, a young Ndebele girl, around her village as she introduces the reader to the colorful paintings on the houses, the women who paint them, and her friends and family. Greenfield's *Africa Dream* (1977) and Kroll's *Masai and I* (1992) set up interesting comparisons of life in U.S. cities and African villages. Each describes a young African American girl dreaming about or learning of her ancestral people in Africa. The illustrations and narratives skillfully compare and contrast the different lives as imagined by the main characters. Chris Van Wyk's *Ouma Ruby's Secret* (2006) has Chris, a young boy, telling the story of Ouma Ruby, his grandmother and matriarch of a strong family. Held in high regard by everyone around her, Ouma Ruby nonetheless keeps a secret from her grandson—while she supports her grandson's love of reading, she cannot read.

Comparing and Contrasting City and Village Life

Contrary to what many believe or portrayals from popular cartoons, the continent of Africa is made up of thriving metropolitan cities as well as vast savannahs and wild animal reserves. The sometimes contradicting cultures and lifestyles create a montage of color, sound, and scents. Unfortunately, this can and does frequently cause friction among the different peoples. For example, recently, the Baswara, or Bushmen, living on the Kgalagadi Game Reserve in South

Africa have been sealed off from all water and food supplies as the police try to get them to relocate to the New Xade settlement (Motseta, 2005). The Baswara, a proud people, are in the midst of a dispute with the Botswanian government over their right to live on their traditional homeland versus the desires of industry. The government wants to relocate them away from a possible diamond reserve while the Baswara want to stay on their ancestral homeland. The friction caused by the differing needs of the people highlights the reality of conflicting ways of living throughout the continent.

Engaged, strategic readers draw on their background knowledge when reading (Beers, 2000; Guthrie & Alao, 1997; Wilhelm, 1995). When reading the young adult literature of Africa, they may not have the necessary schema about the different kinds of cities as well as the savannahs in the continent on which to build. If their concept of the terrain of Africa is limited, their reading experience could be narrow and shallow. The illustrations in the picture books here discussed teem with color and images that will fill the mind of the reader with the flora and fauna of Africa, thus helping the reader create a knowledge base on which to build.

Setting up a comparison between two different ways of living is one theme found in the picture books in this section. *Somewhere in Africa* (Mennen & Daly, 1990) chronicles the life of Ashraf, a young boy living in a large city, as he reads and dreams of the other Africa, filled with wild animals and tall, golden grass. The illustrations show the tall buildings outside Ashraf's windows and the pages of his books depicting African wildlife. Four books follow children and adults on their travels from the village to the city. *Not So Fast Songololo* (Daly, 1985), *The Dove* (Stewart, 1993), and *Baba's Gift* (Naidoo & Naidoo, 2004) are all set in South Africa and document the differences in lifestyles as the main characters walk or take a bus from the village to a large city. *Where are You Going Manyoni?* (Stock, 1993) does the same for the country of Zimbabwe. In addition to books that highlight the differences within the continent, two books contrast life in Africa and life in America. *Masai and I* (Kroll, 1992) describes a young African American girl's dreams of living the life of a Masaai girl in Africa. Her reality is the streets of a huge American city while she dreams of the village life of the Masaai. *When Africa Was Home* (Williams, 1991) follows a young blonde-haired, blue-eyed, white boy born and raised in Africa as his family temporarily moves back to the United States. Again, the illustrations contrast the two different lifestyles beautifully.

Life in the Village

Deep browns and golds with rich shades of green fill the pages of the picture books set in African villages. Rachel Isadora's books *At the Crossroads* (1991) and *Over the Green Hills* (1992) both record the sights and sounds of the village as they draw attention to the lives of children in the village. *My Great-Grandmother's Gourd* (Kessler, 2000) shows possible conflict as a dry, dusty Sudanese village is updated with a working water pump. When the water pump breaks, it is Fatima's grandmother's forward thinking that saves the day. The illustrations in *One Round Moon and a Star for Me* (Mennen, 1994) are filled with descriptive detail of life in a South African Lesotho village while Angelou's book *My Painted House, My Friendly Chicken, and Me* (1994) chronicles the colorful houses and lifestyle of the Ndebele people. Hugh Lewin's Jafta books (1983, 1992) are all set in a village in South Africa and show the traditions and culture of a hardworking people.

Cristina Kessler tells the tale of a nomadic tribe, the Tuaregs, and one boy's journey to receive a turban, a sign of becoming a man, in *One Night* (1995), which follows the path of Muhamad as he learns wisdom from his family and takes on the responsibilities of manhood through caring for the family's herd of goats. The beauty and severity of the disappearing life of the nomads is told in simple, yet elegant terms. Using fanciful animals, Niki Daly depicts life in an African township in *Welcome to Zanzibar Road* (2006) as Mama Jumbo, an elephant, builds a house using scrap material and finds a home at Number 7-Up Zanzibar Street.

Life in the City

In sharp contrast to the books on life in the village, those in this section document the fast-paced life of a large African city. Stock's book, *Armien's Fishing Trip* (1991), is set in the beautiful town of Kalk Bay on the Cape in South Africa and recounts the effect of the Group Areas Act of 1967, which forced the relocation of many families from this town to the desolate Cape Flats on the outskirts of Cape Town. Niki Daly's Jamela books (1999, 2004) show the bright colors and community feeling of a city as they follow Jamela's mischievous adventures. Discussed previously, *The Day Gogo Went to Vote* (Sisulu, 1996) is set in a large township overshadowed by a nuclear power plant. *Charlie's House* (Shermbrucker, 1989) has a vivid description of houses in a township while Hartmann's *All the Magic in the World* (1993) illustrates the street life behind the buildings. *Bongani's Day* (Wulfsohn, 2002) is set in Westdene, a suburb of Johannesburg, South Africa, and follows 7-year-old Bongani throughout a typical day of school, play, and homework. The book is illustrated with photographs showing many places, people, and events of life in a large South African city.

The Effects of Poverty

In the various countries of Africa, 300 million children are chronically hungry. In sub-Saharan Africa, 64% of children under 18 do not have adequate shelter,

53% do not have clean water, and 35% have no suitable sanitation, such as running water or bathing facilities. The major cause of death for children under 5 is malaria and other preventable diseases. Currently, nearly 2 million Africans die each year because they are too poor to stay alive (Mmegi, 2005). While the figures are staggering, the reality is terrifying. Each number represents a piece of humanity—one child, one mother, one father, one person. How can educators convey the sheer enormity and severity of this kind of poverty? Once again, if we want students to have a better understanding of life in the continent of Africa, we need to help them visualize the extent of the poverty in which many of the people live. The stories, seen and told through the eyes of children, in the following picture books will help them understand and empathize with the extent of poverty in Africa.

The effects of poverty on the structure of the family are portrayed in vivid detail in *Jafta—The Homecoming* (Lewin, 1992) and *At the Crossroads* (Isadora, 1991). Both of these books tell the story of fathers leaving their families and going to the city to find work. Children wait expectantly for their return as their fathers have been gone for so long and have missed much of everyday family life. Although the children understand their fathers' reasons for being gone for so long, the effects of their absence are felt by all. Bognomo's *Madoulina* (1999) has previously gone to school but can no longer go as she has to help her mother make and sell fritters. The family's financial situation has changed, so school is no longer an option for Madoulina. *All the Magic in the World* (Hartmann, 1993) depicts children playing with what amounts to garbage in a backyard. While the story shows the "magic" contained in these everyday castaway items, it nonetheless speaks to the poverty in which the children all live. Of particular note, *Charlie's House* (Shermbrucker, 1989) describes the extreme poverty in the township of Guguletu in South Africa through stunning drawings and narrative. Charlie lives with his mother and grandmother in a shelter made of corrugated iron and scrap. As rain drips through holes in the roof, Charlie dreams of his house with an indoor bathroom, carpets on the floor, and a car in the garage. The story is accompanied by colorful illustrations showing the hardship of living in townships rampant with poverty.

Making-A-Difference Project: Creating Picture Books for Teaching and Learning

Once students have been exposed to the beauty and simplicity of the children's literature about Africa, they will have seen how the idea of story can be so eloquently portrayed in a mere 32 pages. Having them create their own picture book on a self-chosen topic will help make the learning process more meaningful (Owens & Nowell, 2001). In addition, "the visual representation approach, particularly in the form of drawings or paints, can serve as an expressive vehicle for expanding one's ideas, feelings, and perceptions of what is learned and how to go about that learning" (Chilcoat, 2000, p. 69). The book can then be shared with younger children to teach them about the African continent.

Begin by having students look through the African literature for common traits and components of a picture book. Then ask the following questions:

1. What topic will you choose? This can be an African-related topic being researched in class or something in which they are individually interested.

2. Will your book be fiction or nonfiction? The format of the book will differ depending on the genre. Nonfiction will require more research on the author's part and the language will be more informative yet still interesting to read, while fiction is read primarily for enjoyment and imagination (Harvey, 1998).

3. Who is your audience? The writing style will change depending on the characteristics of the chosen audience. Content and writing style should be age appropriate.

4. What kind of illustrations will you use? This can vary widely from original drawings, to a collage cut from magazines, to computer-generated artwork.

After brainstorming the above questions, students should follow the writing process beginning with a rough draft, followed by revision, editing, and a final copy before actually constructing the 32-page book. A storyboard should be used in planning what text and illustrations will go on each page. Be sure to include all of the components of a picture book such as title page, about the author, copyright page, and book jacket, including front and back flaps. Students can either use a word-processing program to present their text, cut it up, and glue it to the pages, or neatly write it. Illustrations should be well thought out, created with care and creativity, and match the text or extend the meaning. A complete cover page with illustration and identifying text (title, author, and illustrator) should be constructed. Final products can be bound in a variety of ways such as sewing, binding with a plastic comb, or hole punching and using metal rings. For more information on creating and binding a professional-looking picture book see *Written and Illustrated by...: A Revolutionary Two-Brain Approach for Teaching Students How to Write and Illustrate Amazing Books* (Melton, 1985).

Conclusion

As evidenced by the works presented in this chapter, children's literature is capable of deepening students' understanding of African culture by illuminating issues of gender, access to education, respect for the elderly, city life, village life, and the effects of poverty. When used before reading one of the suggested books in the Novel Guide chapters, these books can help enhance and bridge further understanding. The importance of frontloading necessary information for the reader is paramount as we want to ensure that our students are truly active readers. In addition, the Making-A-Difference Project further relays the importance of questioning and creativity as they relate to teaching and learning. As an extension to reading, creating picture books allows the students to stretch their learning as they synthesize information into this simple yet elegant genre.

REFERENCES

Albright, L.K. (2002). Bringing the Ice Maiden to life: Engaging adolescents in learning through picture book read-alouds in content areas. *Journal of Adolescent & Adult Literacy, 45*(5), 418–428.

Beers, K. (2003). *When kids can't read what teachers can do: A guide for teachers 6–12.* Portsmouth, NH: Heinemann.

Bellamy, C. (2003). *The state of the world's children, 2004.* New York: The United Nations Children's Fund.

Bigombe, B., & Khadiagala, G.M. (n.d.). *Major trends affecting families in Sub-Saharan Africa.* Retrieved October 27, 2005, from http://www.un.org/esa/socdev/family/Publications/mtbigombe.pdf

Chilcoat, G.W. (2000). Designing a children's picture book in the social studies classroom. *Southern Social Studies Journal, 26,* 69–94.

Glasgow, J. (Ed.). (2005). *Strategies for engaging young adult readers: A social themes approach.* Norwood, MA: Christopher-Gordon.

Guthrie, J.T., & Alao, S. (1997). Engagement in reading for young adolescents. *Journal of Adolescent & Adult Literacy, 40*(6), 438–446.

Guttman, C. (n.d.). *When girls go missing from the classroom.* Retrieved October 27, 2005, from http://unesco.org/courier/2001_05/uk/education.htm

Harvey, S. (1998). *Nonfiction matters: Reading, writing, and research in grades 3–8.* York, ME: Stenhouse.

Melton, D. (1985). *Written & illustrated by...: A revolutionary two-brain approach for teaching students how to write and illustrate amazing books.* Kansas City, MO: Landmark Editions.

Mmegi. (2005, October 20). *Eskom conference to target poverty in Africa.* Allafrica.com. Retrieved October 24, 2005, from http://allafrica.com/stories/printable/200510200657.html

Motseta, S. (2005, October 10). *Botswana bushmen 'starving' as police seal off reserve.* Allafrica.com. Retrieved October 11, 2005, from http://allafrica.com/stories/200510100448.html

Owens, W.T., & Nowell, L.S. (2001). More than just pictures: Using picture story books to broaden young learners' social consciousness. *The Social Studies, 92,* 33–40.

Pereira, M. (2005, October 4). On the planned virginity tests for girls in Leguru Wards. *This Day Online.* Retrieved October 9, 2005, from http://www.thisdayonline.com/nview.php?id=30013

Robb, L. (2000). *Teaching reading in middle school: A strategic approach to teaching reading that improves comprehension and thinking.* New York: Scholastic.

van der Walt, T. (2001). *Niki Daly.* Retrieved June 22, 2006, from http://www.childlit.org.za/ndaly.html

Wilhelm, J.D. (1997). *"You gotta be the book": Teaching engaged and reflective reading with adolescents.* New York: Teachers College Press.

Women should formalise their marriages. (2005, October 7). *The Southern Times.* Retrieved February 4, 2007, from http://www.newera.com.na/archives.php?id=9132&date=2005-10-07

LITERATURE CITED

Angelou, M. (1994). *My painted house, my friendly chicken, and me.* New York: Clarkson Potter.

Bognomo, J.E. (1999). *Madoulina: A girl who wanted to go to school.* Honesdale, PA: Boyds Mills.

Daly, N. (1986). *Not so fast Songololo.* New York: Atheneum.

Daly, N. (1999). *Jamela's dress.* New York: Farrar, Straus and Giroux.

Daly, N. (2004). *Where's Jamela?* New York: Farrar, Straus and Giroux.

Daly, N. (2006). *Welcome to Zanzibar road.* Johannesburg, South Africa: Giraffe Books.

Feelings, M. (1971). *Moja means one: Swahili counting book* (T. Feelings, Ill.). New York: Dial Press.

Feelings, M. (1974). *Jambo means hello: Swahili alphabet book* (T. Feelings, Ill.). New York: Dial Press.

Greenfield, E. (1977). *Africa dream* (C.M. Byard, Ill.). New York: HarperCollins.

Hartmann, W. (1993). *All the magic in the world* (N. Daly, Ill.). New York: Dutton Children's Books.

Isadora, R. (1991). *At the crossroads.* New York: Greenwillow Books.

Isadora, R. (1992). *Over the green hills.* New York: Greenwillow Books.

Kessler, C. (1995). *One night* (I. Schoenherr, Ill.). New York: Philomel Books.

Kessler, C. (2000). *My great-grandmother's gourd* (W.L. Krudop, Ill.). New York: Orchard Books.

Kroll, V.L. (1992). *Masai and I* (N. Carpenter, Ill.). New York: Four Winds Press.

Lewin, H. (1983). *Jafta* (L. Kopper, Ill.). Minneapolis, MN: Carolrhoda Books.

Lewin, H. (1981). *Jafta and the wedding* (L. Kopper, Ill.) Minneapolis, MN: Carolrhoda Books.

Lewin, H. (1981). *Jafta's father* (L. Kopper, Ill.) Minneapolis, MN: Carolrhoda Books.

Lewin, H. (1981). *Jafta's mother* (L. Kopper, Ill.). London, England: Evans Brothers.

Lewin, H. (1992). *Jafta—The homecoming* (L. Kopper, Ill.). New York: Knopf.

McCall Smith, A. (2005). *Akimbo and the elephants* (L. Pham, Ill.). New York: Bloomsbury Children's Books.

McCall Smith, A. (2005). *Akimbo and the lions* (L. Pham, Ill.). New York: Bloomsbury Children's Books.

Mennen, I. (1994). *One round moon and a star for me* (N. Daly, Ill.). New York: Orchard Books.

Mennen, I., & Daly, N. (1992). *Somewhere in Africa* (N. Maritz, Ill.). New York: Dutton Children's Books.

Murdock, C.H. (1993). *Raymond Floyd goes to Africa; or, There are no bears in Africa* (C.B. Pauley, Ill.). Trenton, NJ: Africa World Press.

Musgrove, M. (1976). *Ashanti to Zulu: African traditions* (L. & D. Dillon, Ill.). New York: Puffin.

Naidoo, M., & Naidoo, B. (2004). *Baba's gift* (K. Littlewood, Ill.). London: Puffin.

Onyefulu, I. (1993). *A is for Africa.* New York: Cobblehill Books.

Shermbrucker, R. (1991). *Charlie's house* (N. Daly, Ill.). New York: Viking.

Sisulu, E.B. (1996). *The day Gogo went to vote: South Africa, April 1994.* Boston: Little, Brown.

Stewart, D. (1993). *The dove* (J. Daly, Ill.). New York: Greenwillow Books.

Stock, C. (1990). *Armien's fishing trip.* New York: William Morrow.

Stock, C. (1993). *Where are you going Manyoni?* New York: Morrow Junior Books.

Van Wyk, C. (2006). *Ouma Ruby's secret* (A. Voigt-Peters, Ill.). Johannesburg, South Africa: Giraffe Books.

Williams, K.L. (1991). *When Africa was home* (F. Cooper, Ill.). New York: Orchard Books.

Wulfsohn, G. (2002). *Bongani's day: From dawn to dusk in a South African city.* Oxford, Great Britain: Oxfam.

CHAPTER 16

Exploring the African Oral Tradition: From Proverbs to Folk Tales

Jacqueline N. Glasgow

It is only the story that can continue beyond the war and the warrior.
It is the story that outlives the sound of war-drums and the exploits
   of brave fighters.
It is the story...that saves our progeny from blundering like blind
   beggars
Into the spikes of the cactus fence.
The story is our escort; without it, we are blind.
Does the blind man own his escort? No, neither do we the story;
Rather it is the story that owns us and directs us.

—CHINUA ACHEBE (1988)

While classroom instruction does not allow us to seat ourselves around a rural campfire or enrich our daily conversation with appropriate tales and proverbs, a study of African oral literature must begin with an introduction to its oral traditions. African cultures have long revered good stories and storytellers, as have most past and present peoples around the world. Ancient writing traditions do exist on the African continent, but most Africans today, as in the past, are still primarily oral peoples, and their art forms are largely oral rather than literary, unlike Western cultures. Oral compositions are created to be verbally and communally performed as an integral part of dance and music. The oral arts of Africa are rich and varied, developing with the beginnings of African cultures and remaining living traditions that continue to evolve and flourish today.

Exploring African Life and Literature: Novel Guides to Promote Socially Responsive Learning edited by Jacqueline N. Glasgow and Linda J. Rice. © 2007 by the International Reading Association.

While Vansina (1985) notes that oral tradition includes a wide spectrum of forms such as news, verbal art, memorized speech, stories on the origin and genesis of the tribe, epics, and historical accounts, this chapter will focus on various types of folk stories such as myths, legends, fables, and folk tales. According to Fayose (1995), oral literature in this narrowed sense includes

- verbal arts or oral literature;
- customs, beliefs, and other cultural institutions; and
- arts, including songs, dances, games, as well as the playing of musical instruments.

This chapter introduces collections of African fables, myths, legends, and folk tales to provide teachers and students opportunities to read, discuss, and perform this oral literature. Teachers can select a focus for this part of the unit depending on time constraints, interests, and availability of the folk tales, and can use these stories from the African oral tradition to enrich students' reading of the novels discussed in this book. One focus could be on the Anansi stories from West Africa. Another focus could be the traditional Zulu stories found online for those with computer accessibility. A third focus could be to study the oral literature found in collections or anthologies selected or retold by Verna Aardema (1994), Nelson Mandela (2002), Alexander McCall Smith (2004), Vincent Muli Wa Kituku (1997), or Steven Gale (1995). The Classroom Activities for this chapter include asking students to read, analyze, and write folk tales; exploring African culture through Henna hand painting; and organizing a Nigerian Iri Ji (New Yam Festival).

Introducing Students to African Oral Literature

Oral literature is meant to be performed, so the storyteller's creativity and technique are paramount to producing the drama. The storyteller performs the story as if it were a play, taking all the parts himself. He or she imitates the cries of animals and gives each character a different voice. The teller uses voice, body gestures, dress, musical instruments, and perhaps props to spin the tale. He or she also uses the stage (albeit a campfire or front porch) to sit, stand, move around, and mime parts of the story to engage the audience. According to Vansina (1985), "the performer provokes interaction by asking questions, welcoming exclamations, and turning to a song sung by all at the appropriate points of action" (p. 34). Interactive strategies, such as clapping, making noises, and repeating refrains, result in a cocreating of the tale with the teller leading the event, yet changing it according to the responses of the audience. The teller engages the listeners emotionally as she or he tries to frighten, delight, or entertain. The more familiar the listeners are with the tale, the more they can "enjoy the rendering of various episodes, appreciate the innovations, and anticipate the thrills to come" (Vansina, 1985, p. 35). Each performance is a new interpretation of a familiar tale from the culture.

An excellent way to introduce students to the performance aspect of oral literature is through Pete Seeger's storysong *Abiyoyo* (2001). Inspired by a South African folk tale, *Abiyoyo* is the story of how a father and son vanquish the giant Abiyoyo, who invades the quiet, rural town, while singing the Abiyoyo a song. This popular picture book, illustrated by Michael Hays, now comes packaged with an audio CD of Pete Seeger performing two different versions of this story: one from 1956 and one from a live performance in 1991. His dramatic performance of this tale captures the imaginations of the students and provides a strong model for them to emulate in their own storytelling.

Another great way to begin this lesson is by viewing the video *Stories From the Black Tradition* (Schindel & Deitch, 1993) based on the Caldecott Medal-winning picture book *A Story a Story*, retold and illustrated by Gail E. Haley (1970). The video is an animated story that tells how African folk tales were acquired from the Sky God, Nyame, by Anansi the Spider Man. Anansi wants to buy some stories, so he spins a web up to the sky and goes up to bargain with the Sky God. The price the Sky God asks is for Anansi to bring him Osebo, the leopard-of-the-terrible-teeth; Mmboro, the hornet-who-stings-like-fire; and Mmoatio, the fairy-whom-men-never-see. The video and story tell the clever ways Anansi pays the price so stories can abound on the earth. The story can be found at www.anansi-web.com/anansi.html. After viewing this tale, students can read other Anansi stories from West Africa. This section also highlights traditional Zulu stories and collections or anthologies that serve as ideal introductions to African oral literature.

Anansi the Spider Trickster Stories

Anansi (ah-NAHN-see) the Spider is a popular figure in the folklore of parts of West Africa, and the stories later came to the Caribbean islands through slaves. Like Br'er Rabbit in the United States, Anansi is a trickster figure—clever, cunning, sometimes mischievous—who uses his wits to make up for what he lacks in size and strength.

Divide students into literature circle groups and ask them to select one of the following stories (or ones found at the local library) as the focus of study:

- *Ananse and the Lizard: A West African Tale* (Cummings, 2002). Ananse (a variation on the spelling of Anansi) thinks he will marry the daughter of the village chief, but instead he is outsmarted by Lizard.

- *Anansi the Spider: A Tale From the Ashanti* (McDermott, 1986). Anansi had six dutiful sons. One day Anansi is swallowed by a fish., but each of his sons took part in saving his life. Anansi finds a lighted globe in the forest that he wishes to give as reward for the son saving his life, but the boys argued all night about it, so Anansi the Spider placed the globe (now the moon) in the sky for all to see.
- *Anansi Does the Impossible! An Ashanti Tale* (Aardema, 1997). Anansi and his wife outsmart the Sky God and win back the beloved folk tales of their people.
- *Anansi and the Talking Melon* (Kimmel, 1994). A clever spider tricks Elephant and some other animals into thinking the melon in which he is hiding can talk.
- *Anansi Finds a Fool: An Ashanti Tale* (Aardema, 1992). Lazy Anansi seeks to trick someone into doing the heavy work of laying his fish trap, but instead he is fooled into doing the job himself.
- *Anansi and the Moss-Covered Rock* (Kimmel, 1988). Anansi the Spider uses a strange moss-covered rock in the forest to trick all the other animals, until Little Bush Deer decides he needs to learn a lesson.
- *Anansi Goes Fishing* (Kimmel, 1992). Anansi the Spider plans to trick Turtle into catching a fish for his dinner, but Turtle proves to be smarter and ends up with a free meal. The story explains the origin of spider webs.
- *Anansi the Trickster Spider and the Witch Named "Five"* (Gore, n.d.). Rather than work to provide food for his family, Anansi takes others' food by tricking them into saying the name of a witch who strikes them dead.
- *The Adventures of Spider: West African Folk Tales* (Arkhurst, 1964). This collection presents six tales about Spider, including those which explain how he got a thin waist and a bald head and why he lives in ceilings and dark corners.

After students have finished reading the stories, they should exchange books until all students have read three to five of them. Instruct students to make a T-chart listing the strengths and weaknesses of Anansi the Spider (see Table 16.1 for a blank T-chart for Anansi's strengths and weaknesses).

As an alternative or in addition to the Anansi folk tales, students may choose to study traditional Zulu folk stories, such as the following (many stories can be found online at www.canteach.ca/elementary/africa.html).

- "Why the Cheetah's Cheeks Are Stained"
- "Where Stories Come From"
- "Jabu and the Lion"

Table 16.1. T-Chart of Anansi's Strengths and Weaknesses

Strengths	Weaknesses
1.	1.
2.	2.
3.	3.
4.	4.
5.	5.

- "Clever Jackal Gets Away"
- "The Curse of the Chameleon"
- "Honeyguide's Revenge"
- "King of the Birds"
- "Why the Warthog Goes About on His Knees"

Anthologies and Collections of Oral Literature

***Misoso: Once Upon a Time Tales From Africa* (1994) by Verna Aardema**. *Misoso* (me-SAW-saw) are the "Once upon a time" tales of Africa. The word *misoso*, which comes from the Mbundu ('m-BOON-doo) tribe of Angola, describes stories told mostly for entertainment. The folk tales in this collection were selected with this in mind. The tales were selected and retold by the widely known reteller of African folk tales for children Verna Aardema (1994), who says about them, "if they teach a lesson, or illuminate the culture of a people, that is a plus" (p. iv). She tells us that in Angola, there is the formula for telling misoso tales. The storyteller begins, "Let me tell you a story about ___" and ends with "I have told my story. It is finished" (p. iv). In this collection, Aardema includes a map showing where each misoso tale originated, a glossary of native terms used in each story, a retelling of the story, and an afterword that explains the cultural implications of the tale. A bibliography at the end of the collection carefully documents the sources for the folk tales.

Aardema (1994) chose three of the folk tales from early sources that were recorded in a native language and then translated into English. Three of the following stories are from the earliest of these books: "Toad's Trick" is from a book published in 1854, "The Cock and the Jackal" is from one published 1864, and "No Boconono!" is from one published in 1868 These tales come from early sources written first by the European traders and settlers and then later by missionaries and anthropologists who settled along the west coast of Africa.

Aardema (1994) arranged the collection according to geographical location so that the reader can take a literary journey around the perimeter of Africa south of the Sahara Desert. The journey begins with "Leelee Goro" from the Temnes of Sierra Leone. This pourquoi tale (a tale that explains how a phenomenon came to be) explains eight different phenomena in the context of a story portraying the close relationship of a mother and daughter characteristic of the Temne tribe's folklore and way of life. For the next tale, Aardema takes the reader down the west coast to find a tale from Khoikhoi of Southwest Africa. "The Cock and Jackal" is a Khoikhoi fable discovered in the 17th century by a missionary. The tale may have originated in Europe, with the jackal replacing Reynard the Fox, since there are no foxes in southern Africa. Another tale, "No Boconono!" is a Zulu story from South Africa. Boconono is a legendary dwarf sometimes called the Tom Thumb of Zulu. Both European dwarf tales, Tom Thumb and Snow White and the Seven Dwarfs, preceded the Zulu stories. Going north to the Swahilis of eastern African coast, readers encounter "Goso the Teacher," a tale told here in rhyme. However, this cumulative tale was originally told in the form of a question-and-answer session between storyteller and audience. The teller began by blaming the wind for knocking loose the calabash that fell on the teacher's head. The audience responded by pretending to punish the wind with a "beating." When wind blamed the wall, the listeners "beat" the wall, and so on, until the nine episodes were finished. Aardema's collection ends with a tale from back on the west coast in Nigeria. "Kindai and the Ape" originated with the Emo-Yo-Quaim, black Jews whose ancestors fled to northern Africa after the destruction of Jerusalem. The moral of this tale, that kindness is rewarded, reflects a Jewish ethic.

***Favorite African Folk Tales* (2002) by Nelson Mandela.** This collection consists of 32 of Africa's most cherished folk tales, selected by Nelson Mandela, a Nobel Laureate for Peace. In the foreword to the collection, Mandela (2002) wrote, "It is my wish that the voice of the storyteller may never die in Africa, that all children of the world may experience the wonder of books" (n.p.). Many of the folk tales are almost as old as Africa itself and were told around evening fires in centuries past. The ones from the San and the Khoi tell stories about these original hunter-gatherers and livestock herders in Southern Africa. For instance, there is a San tale that tells how the first animals found grazing and water and a Khoi narrative in which the first animals receive tails, horns, and hides from King Lion. Many of these stories were translated into English and other European languages in the 19th and 20th centuries from their original languages: Karanga, Nguni, Zhosa, and many others. This collection also includes some new stories from different parts of South Africa and the continent to supplement those of ancient times. The collection includes a map of Africa with red flags to give the reader some idea of the geographical spread and origin of the particular stories.

Mandela's intent was that by reading and performing these stories children would discover the variety of themes in African tales. The breaking of a curse in order for someone to be set free or take on his own form again is a popular theme in folklore. In the Xhosa tale, "The Snake With Seven Heads," the number 7 has magical qualities. When Manjuza's husband is cursed into a snake with seven heads, she breaks the curse by dancing at seven weddings. In "The Snake Chief," a young girl is promised to a snake for a basket of berries by her mother, but through her steadfastness, she breaks the curse and marries a prince. In another tale, "How Hlakanyaya Outwitted the Monster," the trickster Hlakanyaya, manages to outsmart everyone, including much bigger opponents such as the one-legged, one-armed, one-sided monster. In countless African folk tales, the hare, like the tortoise, appears as an excellent illustration of the principle that those who are not strong must be clever instead. In "The Lion, the Hare, and the Hyena" from Kenya, readers observe the ruler, the cunning trickster, and the underdog as they try to outwit one another. In "The Hare's Revenge" from Zambia, the Hare manages to outwit a far bigger animal, the Buffalo. "The Hare and the Tree Spirit" tells the tale of the cunning hare doing a good deed. In a most unusual hare tale, "The Cloud Princess" from Swaziland, the hare is magically transformed into a human being.

Other tales in this collection are didactic. In the "Mantis and the Moon," children learn the consequences of pride, while "Mmadipetsane" warns children against disobedience. Children in "Fesito Goes to Market" receive a triple reward for three good deeds, while in "Mpipide and the Motlopi Tree," a young boy receives his heart's desire, a baby sister, through singing a song.

In a more entertaining type of folk tale, riddles must be solved in order to receive one's wish. In "The Clever Snake Charmer," Sultan Jadi is bored in his palace and commands various subjects to come and entertain him, and when he gets bored with their performance, he has their heads chopped off. However, when the Sultan tires of Selham, the snake charmer, the Sultan says he will spare his life if he can solve three riddles. Likewise, the Malay-Indian story "The Sultan's Daughter" has the protagonist solving three riddles before he gets his reward. This collection also includes a Namaqualand story, "Natiki," which echoes the themes of the European Cinderella tale.

The Girl Who Married a Lion and Other Tales From Africa (2004) by **Alexander McCall Smith.** While McCall Smith does not claim to be a scholar of oral literature, all the stories in this collection from Zimbabwe and Botswana were told to him personally by young and old with the assistance of an interpreter when he visited the part of Zimbabwe known as Matabeleland. This original collection of stories published some years ago under the title of *Children of Wax: African Folktales* (McCall Smith, 1998) is expanded to include stories from people living in the Mochudi and Odi areas of Botswana. McCall Smith's collection of folk tales introduces the reader to a worldview in which the "boundaries between the animal and human worlds are indistinct and fluid" (p. xi). There are 33 stories contained in this anthology, which can also be purchased on CD by Recorded Books. Hearing them performed by various talented narrators brings fuller enjoyment and appreciation of the oral literature.

In these stories, we get a glimpse of the family and community values and morals that have made these societies what they are today. For instance, in "Guinea Fowl Child" we see the plight of the barren woman who finds redemption through adopting orphaned guinea. "A Bad Way to Treat Friends" shows devastating consequences of jealousy. Cutthroat rivalry between friends turns into a nasty revenge story in "The Sad Story of Tortoise and Snail." In "A Tree to Sing To," a selfish, greedy father is punished when he finds food during a famine and takes it for himself instead of sharing with his wife and children. Greed is also punished in "Hare Fools the Baboons" when hare comes in lion's clothing to steal the baboons' food. In another story, "Two Bad Friends," greed and deception are brought to justice. In "Beware of Friends You Cannot Trust," hyena is so hungry, he gets tricked into being caught stealing food by his supposed friend, jackal. Another such lesson learned, "Stone Hare" speaks of when lion learned that some people can never be trusted and that one of them is hare.

In another story, "An Old Man Who Saved Some Ungrateful People," readers learn about the consequences of ingratitude. "Blind Man Catches a Bird" tells the reader why men fight and then how friendship can be restored. A boy's loyalty and obedience to his father in spite of persecution is rewarded in "Strange Animal," while other family loyalties are rewarded in "The Grandmother Who Was Kind to a Smelly Girl." Pride is humbled when hare teaches lion a lesson in the story "Greater Than Lion." A tree grows out of the head of a man who did not keep his promises, similar to in the story in European folklore of Pinocchio's nose growing longer when he lied. These stories serve to introduce the Western reader to African cultures and conflicts told in a very different context that may serve to entertain, on the one hand, but traditionally serve as a primary way of transmitting native culture. Legends, beliefs, mores, and social attitudes have descended from one generation to another largely through the medium of the folk tale.

***East African Folk Tales: From the Voice of Mukamba* (1997) by Vincent Muli Wa Kituku.** Folk tales from Kituku's childhood in the Kamba Community,

Kenya, are translated and retold in this collection. The pen-and-ink washed illustrations complement the simplicity of the text, which appears in both English and Kikamba. In this collection of human and animal tales, Kituku retells the stories he remembers from his mother's telling or singing them as they were planting, cultivating, or harvesting crops. Growing up, he realized that these stories were motivational, and he has now recaptured the stories to pass them on to his own children growing up in the United States. Kituku wrote that embodied in Kamba folk tales are "morals, ethics, motivation, education, sense of belonging, natural resource conservation awareness, and mid-testing skills" (p. 11). Kituku regrets that the beauty and flavor of Kamba folk tales diminishes both in the translation into English and in modern U.S. settings. In the Preface, he stated that he misses

> the background of crying children, songs of men on their way home after a great day capped with a calabash of traditional beer, the smell of acacia branches, the bleating of sheep and goats, noises from insects and wild animals, and nearby dance rhythms from circumcision candidates that played a significant role in bringing out the wholeness of Kamba folk tales. (p. 14)

In addition to providing a proper context for the tales, he recognized that some of the morals had been lost in translation, so he included a brief explanation for each tale and described related Kamba customs and traditions.

***West African Folk Tales* (1995) by Steven Gale.** The cultures represented in West Africa are as diverse as the geography of the countries that comprise West Africa and as diverse as their attitudes toward storytelling. For instance, many tales are told by the *griot* or *gewel* (storyteller) in an interactive fashion with audience participation. Songs are included that were typically performed with drum or guitar accompaniment. While folk tales were entertaining, they were also meant to be didactic. At the time when few children attended school, folk tales were told to educate the young. According to Steven Gale (1995), "African tales interest and amuse audiences, while passing along historical and religious myths, lessons about social behavior, and practical advice related to daily activities such as hunting, farming, childrearing, governing, and so forth" (p. xiv).

Gale has 42 West African folk tales in his collection, *West African Folk Tales* (1995), which came about as a result of his time spent as a Fulbright Professor in Liberia in 1974. The tales are categorized according to the type of characters involved: human or animal. There is a whole series of Spider and Monkey tales, for example, in which Spider symbolizes greed and Monkey typifies intelligence. These Spider and Monkey parables are so popular that native teachers in rural mission or church schools often use them to illustrate points in the classroom. Gale's collection includes stories that are concerned with greed, pride, a lack of faith, and untrustworthiness and historical narratives used to explain why things are done in certain ways, how specific habits or practices evolved, or how a precise location has taken on a sacred significance. The stories were contributed by Gale's students, representing a cross-section of Liberia's major tribal units and translated into English by them.

Because folk tales are a form of performance art, they are not fully realized until they, too, are being told to a live audience. It in only then that the unique style of each storyteller's oral presentation is evident. Gale recommends taking this opportunity to have your students prepare a folk tale performance for one of the folk tales in this collection. Let them enjoy the tales and come to learn something about the West African peoples and their cultures.

Classroom Activities

This section includes three activities that lead to further exploration of the African oral tradition and literature. These activities involve students in reading and analyzing African folk tales, writing an original folk tale, and exploring African culture through henna painting.

Reading and Analyzing Folk Tales Published in Africa

Ask students to read three to five tales by Lady Kofo Ademola from Benin (1992a, 1992b, 1992c, 1992d, 1992e, 1992f) published in Africa or choose another collection of works to study. Invite students to think about the issues raised earlier in this chapter regarding audience, cultural values, spiritual implications, mystic bonds, or harmony with nature. To what extent are the tales didactic? To what extent are they intended to entertain? What aspects of the traditional culture do these tales preserve? Use a blank form like the Story Discussion Grid (Yarick, 1995) for Lady Kofo Ademola from Benin's collection of folk tales provided in Figure 16.1 as a format to scaffold students' reading and analysis of the folk tale set they choose to read. Students should be encouraged to read the folk tales from the countries they studied for the opening activity of this unit.

Writing African Folk Tales

If possible, ask students to interview an African native and retell one of her or his stories. If this is not possible, ask students to write and illustrate their own folk tale based on what they have learned about African folk tales they have read and discussed. Abrahams's *African Folk Tales* (1983) and Scheub's *The African Storyteller: Stories From African Oral Traditions* (1999) are excellent

Figure 16.1. Story Discussion Grid for Analyzing Folk Tales by Lady Kofo Ademola From Benin

Folk Tale	Ojeje Trader & the Magic Pebble	Olurombi	The Princess Corn	Tutu & the Magic Gourd	Greedy Wife & Magic Spoon
Audience	Young adults	Young adults	Young adults	Young adults	Young adults
Purpose	To instill values of hard work	To instruct about threats and promises	To challenge arranged marriages	To instruct the virtues of kindness and generosity	To instill the values of domestic chores
Cultural Aspects	Trading cloth in the market, polygamy	Trading cloth to provide for family	Arranged marriages	Chief, polygamy	Polygamy, bridewealth
Setting	Town of Ojeje	Ajele market	Maizeland	Mowari village	Bola's home
Characters	Lazy wife and daughters contrasted with hard-working wife and daughter	Oluromi, mother of Ore, daughter	Princess Corn, King and Queen of Maizeland, Skymen, Rain and Sun	Chief Dola who had many wives, Bimpe the oldest wife, Tutu the youngest wife, a Gene	rich man, Seyi, Wife, Bola, young wife, Tomi, Bui, the magician
Conflict	Industrious wife vs. lazy wife	Survival vs. prosperity	Arranged marriage vs. free choice	Selfish and greedy Bimpe abuses Tutu	Food thief was stealing food before it was served
Climax	Lazy wife pushed step-daughter into slavery	Prosperity with a price	Contest between Mr. Sun and Mr. Rain	Tutu leaves to run home, meets Genie in the woods	Spoon sticks to Tomi's mouth
Resolution	Industrious wife wins the husband	Prosperity at the cost of losing her daughter	Princess Corn marries the victor, Mr. Rain	Tutu receives blessings of the Genie; Bimpe learns her lesson the hard way	She must endure the disgrace of not learning to cook
Moral	Hard work and trading savvy are rewarded	Don't make promises you can't keep	The contest to win the princess is rewarded	Be kind and generous to everyone	Learn to cook and serve the family
Magic	Brown stone used to communicate with mother and daughter	Iroko tree can bless prosperity in the market	Skymen, Sun and Rain, are personified	Magical gourds	Magical powder on spoons to catch the thief
Songs	Daughter sings Yoruba song to communicate with her mother	Oluromi sings mourning song after losing her daughter	Princess Corn sings victory song—all sing and dance	No songs	Tomi's song of weeping for the spoon stuck to her mouth

resources for selecting a genre or style of tale to emulate: pourquoi stories, moral fables, trickster tales, rites of passage, or fertility tales. As students think about writing a story from another country, they need to reflect the culture through the plot, characters, uses of magic, and moral of the story. Students should be prepared to perform these stories in some type of culminating event such as an African planting or harvest ceremony.

In a U.S. children's literature class at Ohio University, students collected stories by interviewing native Africans who had come to the university to further their education. In addition to the interview, students conducted research of the country and provided a context for the story. If they used native language in the story, they provided a translation or glossary of terms. Students were also asked to illustrate their stories using graphic images that represented the symbols and culture of the folk tale. One student, Mary Adams, interviewed a friend she had made from Ghana, Charles Owu-ewie. Adams chose to retell and illustrate a folk tale he told to her and his children called "The Sheep and the Goat." (See Figure 16.2 for the text of Adams's retelling of Owu-ewie's folk tale from Ghana, "The Sheep and the Goat.")

Experiencing African Culture Through Henna Painting

Mehndi is the word in Hindi used to describe henna, henna painting, and the resulting designs. Henna is well known as a natural product used to color and condition the hair and to make temporary tattoos. Henna painting is an ancient cosmetic and healing art whereby the leaves of the henna plant are crushed into a powder, then made into a paste that is applied to the body to safely dye the skin. The painting is traditionally done in elaborate patterns and designs on the hands and feet and is an art practiced exclusively by women. The result is a kind of temporary tattoo, reddish in color, that lasts anywhere from several days to several weeks. The process is absolutely painless and safe for the skin. In fact, henna is said to condition the skin as it beautifies the body. According to Roome in *Mehndi: The Timeless Art of Henna Painting* (1998), henna painting "is a sacred practice intended not just to beautify the body, but to invite grace and good fortune into one's home, one's marriage, and one's family" (p. 2). She stated that it is a kind of talisman, a blessing upon the skin.

The henna plant is a flowering shrub that grows 8 to 10 feet high and was originally found in Australia and Asia and along the Mediterranean coasts of Africa. The flower of the henna plant is small, white, four-petaled, and sweet smelling; however, the part of the plant used to make henna powder is the leaves. Used as an antiseptic and an astringent, it is often applied to bruises and sprains as well as boils, burns, and open wounds. Roome (1998) stated that due to its cooling effect on the skin, a ball of henna paste is placed in the hand of a

Figure 16.2. Student's Retelling of a Folk Tale From Ghana, "The Sheep and the Goat"

Context for "The Sheep and the Goat"

Every morning the sheep in Ghana are let out of the pens. They roam about wherever they wish to go until they are called home in the evening. Sometimes, the sheep are struck by lorries, because they stand still, unafraid. The goats are rarely hit because they run away when they hear a lorry approach. This tale is the traditional explanation for the different behaviors of the sheep and the goat and the way our "tools" can help or harm us.

A Folk Tale From Ghana: "The Sheep and the Goat"

Storyteller:
"Kodi wongye nni o" (Stories are not to be accepted as true)

Children:
"Wogye sie" (We take and keep [the lesson])

Odwan (sheep) and Abirekyie (goat) were friends. They lived together in a town called Mempe Asem (I don't like trouble). Odwan and Abirekyie had a good friend, Okraman (dog), who lived many kilometers away in a town called Dwene Woho (Think about yourself).

One day, Okraman invited Odwan and Abirekyie to visit him. He said, "Do you have the fare for the lorry ride?" Abirekyie stuck his hand in his pocket, moved it around to feel the coins, and said, "Yes, I do!" Odwan pulled out his own coins, counted them, and said, "I do too!"

"Good," replied Okraman, "I'll see you both tomorrow."

The next morning, Odwan and Abirekyie began walking toward Dwene Woho to visit their friend, Okraman. They hailed the first lorry they saw and climbed aboard. They had not traveled far when the driver's mate began to collect fares. Suddenly, Abirekyie jumped off the lorry and ran quickly away. Adwan was confused, but he thought Abirekyie would meet him later at Okraman's house.

When Odwan arrived in Dwene Woho, he went to greet his friend, Okraman. "Where is Abirekyie?" asked Okraman. Odwan told him about Abirekyie's strange behavior, and said, "Perhaps he will join us soon."

Odwan and Okraman had a lovely visit. Abirekyie did not come. After dinner, Odwan thanked Okraman for the wonderful visit. They said, "da yie" (good-bye) to each other. Odwan traveled home on the next lorry.

Abirekyie was at home when Odwan arrived. "Why did you run away?" Odwan asked. Abirekyie hung his head and said sadly, "I did not have enough money to pay the fare. I did not tell the truth."

And that is why the sheep have no fear of the lorries, but the goats always run away when a lorry approaches. They are afraid the drivers will ask for their money.

Glossary of "Asem" (Words) in Twi

Kodi wongye nnio: Stories are not be to accepted as true
Wogye sie: We take and keep [the lesson]
Odwan: one sheep
Abirekyie: goat
Okraman: dog
Mempe asem: I don't like trouble
Dwene woho: Think about yourself
Da yie: good-bye

fevered child to bring the temperature down. As a cosmetic, henna is used for conditioning and revitalizing hair and skin color.

The earliest evidence of the cosmetic use of henna is from ancient Egypt. Traces of henna have been found on the hands of Egyptian mummies up to 5,000 years old, as it was common practice for Egyptian women to dye their fingernails a reddish hue with henna. Today, the art of henna painting is to decorate the hand and feet of the bride (and sometimes the groom) for the wedding ceremony in Africa and in other countries, as well. The art form of henna (Arabic) or mehndi (Hindi) varies from region to region. Varying designs have a different meaning for members of each culture, such as good health, fertility, wisdom, protection, and spiritual enlightenment. While Arabic henna designs are usually large, floral patterns on the hands and feet, Indian mehndi involves fine, thin lines for lacy, floral, and paisley patterns covering entire hands, forearms, feet and shins. African henna patterns are bold, large geometric designs (Roome, 1998).

Henna tattoos are traditionally done in a variety of elaborate patterns and shapes. There are specific symbols that henna artists use to symbolize thoughts such as peace, courage, love, and creativity. Traditional African designs are more geometric than designs from India. Some of the geometric designs were inspired by rug and carpet designs, but most are a product of the artist's imagination. Henna painting in its purest form is largely improvisational and intuitive. Then, once the design is created either in the mind's eye or in a stencil, henna powder is mixed with water and applied to the skin with a small stick or squeeze bottle. After the henna dries on the skin, it is flaked off to reveal the temporary tattoo.

Students can explore this folk art in several ways. First, you can introduce henna hand painting to the class by showing them pictures of henna art and discussing the beauty of this art form (you can visit the webpage www.hennapage.com for links to many different pictures and for information about henna). You can also brainstorm with the students what Western women wear that its society considers beautiful (fingernail polish, acrylic nails, mascara, eyeliner, rouge, lipstick, nylons, high heels, jewelry, etc.) and then compare Western ideas of beauty to African henna painting. Then, ask students to create the design for a tattoo by doodling and designing lines, shapes, and whatever else they can dream up to temporarily decorate their hands. If students are intimidated by imitating free-hand mehndi, stencils are a good alternative. If stencils are difficult to obtain, students can create a stencil by folding paper and cutting edges as in making paper snowflakes.

Students can practice henna painting by making up a little batch of baking soda and water to create a consistency of toothpaste and then put it in a desirable applicator and play with it. They can also use real toothpaste if you desire. The real henna paste will be similar to a smooth mud, at a toothpaste-like consistency. Then, you may continue this project by actually painting real henna on the skin (henna paint can be found at specialty retail stores or on the Internet).

As an alternative, this project can also be done with glue on paper if students or parents object to the activity. Understandably, students may not want to leave the henna on the skin for 12 to 24 hours before flaking it off, and they may not want the henna designs on their bodies for three weeks. To do as an art project, ask students to trace one of their hands with a pencil lightly on a piece of paper. Provide them with some type of colorful glue so they can trace over the design with it. After the glue dries, ask students to share their project by showing it to the class and discussing the meaning of their design. Ask them to share the purpose of their henna tattoo, be it to mark ethnic affiliations, mark a new stage in their lives, or to beautify their bodies.

For a writing project, ask students to write the story of their African henna hand painting and compare this concept of beauty to concepts of beauty in their culture. In addition to exploring henna painting as an art form, students need to remember that women in every country practicing the ritual offer their designs to the spirits, gods, of goddesses in an effort to appease them and win their favor. As such, they attempt to influence the events of the future. Students might consider how one would do this in their own culture.

Regardless of the means by which henna painting is explored, Roome (1998) stated that mehndi is about listening and getting to know a person. She said it is a way of learning about different ways of life, and it is a way of hearing your own voice. Because you cannot design your own hand, "you are using touch to effect changes, the least of which is a design in henna upon the skin" (p. 151). Many students use this opportunity to come together and listen to one another, as well as express their own individuality through henna painting.

Making-A-Difference Project: Nigerian Iri Ji (New Yam Festival)

Perhaps the best way to make a difference in students' understanding of another country when they are not able to actually travel there is to have them simulate a festival representing its culture. Therefore, the culminating activity for this unit is a simulation of the harvest festival, Iri Ji (New Yam Festival). It is a time for singing and dancing as well as dining on gourmet foods and listening to stories. Simulating the celebration will provide students an opportunity to create a mask, prepare appropriate food, tell an African myth or folk tale, share their research, and even dance to the beat of the drum. This festival will be a celebration of their immersion in African culture and literature.

In Nigeria, the Igbo celebrate the harvest at the New Yam Festival much like Thanksgiving Day is celebrated in the United States. It is a time for merry-making and thanking the Igbo gods for a bountiful harvest of the year's crops and hope for good yields with the next planting. Instead of the celebration falling on a specific day, the Iri Ji Festival is celebrated at various times within the Igbo communities, varying from August until October every year. Because the Igbo society is mainly agrarian, emphasis is placed on farming and the cultivation of sufficient food to last until the next harvest. The yam is the most important food crop in Igboland, so special emphasis is placed on yam cultivation. As one Igbo said, the Iri Ji Festival "is the culmination of a work cycle and the beginning of another" (Omenuwa, 1997, ¶ 3). The traditional Igbo man takes pride in showing off his yam barn neatly stacked with yam tubers from top to bottom, as it signifies wealth and success.

At the Iri Ji Festival, only traditional dishes of yam are served because the festival is symbolic of the abundance of the produce. On the last night before the festival, those who still have old yams from the previous year discard of them. This is because it is believed that the New Year must begin with tasty, fresh yams instead of the old dried-up crops of the previous year. Before the festival starts, the yams are offered to gods and ancestors first before distributing them to the villagers. The solemn rite of eating the first yam is performed by the oldest man or Eze (traditional ruler) of the community. It is believed that the oldest man serves as an intermediary between his community and the gods of the land. Most staunch elders will not taste the new yam until the day traditionally set aside for it. After the eldest has tasted the new yam, everyone else may follow suit (Omenuwa, 1997).

In addition to feasting, there is festive dancing as crowds of people gather in the market square to watch the display. During the ceremony entertainment includes ceremonial rites by the Igwe (King) and cultural dances by Igbo families as well as other Igbo contemporary shows and fashion parades. Igbo ancestral masks capture the festive mood and signify the approval of the gods in the celebration (Omenuwa, 1997).

To organize the New Yam Festival, ask students to sign up for the following areas to help prepare.

- Master of Ceremonies—One group should organize and oversee the schedule or agenda for the event depending on the time available. They should choose a block of time for the festival and also be responsible for invitations to parents, administrators, and other classes.

- African Cuisine—Another group should be responsible for selecting the menu, researching yam recipes and other food groups discussed in chapter 1. They should also be responsible for preparation of the dishes whether they do the cooking themselves or delegate it to other volunteers. Ask students to prepare an authentic Nigerian food for the festival. The following websites provide recipes and meal ideas: www.cookingwithstyle.com, www.motherlandnigeria.com/recipes.html, www.recipezaar.com/r/61, and www.elca.org/dgm/country_packet/nigeria/recipe.html.

- Music—The group responsible for the music should research performing groups and instruments for appropriate and suitable pieces for background music and for dancing.

  Suggest that they visit the following websites for seeing and hearing African musical instruments: www.doubleclick.com.sg/town4kids/kids/music4kids/world/african/naturalhorn.htm and www.coraconnection.com.

- African Masks—This group is in charge of mask-making (see chapter 2). While students may not choose to be traditional masqueraders, they might represent characters from the novels they have been reading or use their masks as a prop for storytelling.

- Storytelling—This group will organize the schedule and selection of performers for the storytelling component of the festival. Students should be encouraged to perform the folk tales they have read or created.

Conclusion

As this chapter demonstrates, the oral tradition has deep roots in Africa and is a primary means of transferring traditions and cultural values from one generation to the next. While it is very important for students to hear and see folk tales from Africa, the art of storytelling truly comes to life through the Nigerian Iri Ji. Those who participate in the New Yam Festival take part in the most important celebration of the Igbo culture that finds expression in their agriculture, intellectual reasoning, moral values, music, dressing, foods, kinship, marriages, and languages.

REFERENCES

Achebe, C. (1988). *Anthills of the savannah.* Portsmouth, NH: Heinemann.

Fayose, P.O. (1995). *Nigerian children's literature in English.* Ibadan, Nigeria: AENL

Omenuwa, O. (1997, November 24). *In honor of new yam.* Retrieved May 23, 2006, from http://emeagwali.com/nigeria/cuisine/igbo-new-yam-festival.html

Roome, L. (1998). *Mehndi: The timeless art of Henna painting.* New York: St. Martin's Griffin.

Vansina, J. (1985). *Oral tradition as history.* Madison: University of Wisconsin.

Yarick, S.J. (1995). *The write course: A writing course for community college freshmen.* Ottawa, KS: The Writing Conference.

LITERATURE CITED

Aardema, V. (1992). *Anansi finds a fool: An Ashanti tale* (B. Waldman, Ill.). New York: Dial Books for Young Readers.

Aardema, V. (1994). *Misoso: Once upon a time tales from Africa* (R. Ruffins, Ill.). New York: Apple Soup.

Aardema, V. (1997). *Anansi does the impossible! An Ashanti tale* (L. Desimini, Ill.). New York: Atheneum Books for Young Readers.

Abrahams, R.D. (1983). *African folktales: Traditional stories of the black world.* New York: Pantheon Books.

Ademola, L.K. (1992a). *Greedy wife and the magic spoon.* Lagos, Nigeria: Mudhut Books.

Ademola, L.K. (1992b). *Ojeje trader and the magic pebble.* Lagos, Nigeria: Mudhut Books.

Ademola, L.K. (1992c). *Olurombi.* Lagos, Nigeria: Mudhut Books.

Ademola, L.K. (1992d). *The princess corn.* Lagos, Nigeria: Mudhut Books.

Ademola, L.K. (1992e). *The princesses and the wood-cutter's son.* Lagos, Nigeria: Mudhut Books.

Ademola, L.K. (1992f) *Tutu and the magic gourd.* Lagos, Nigeria: Mudhut Books.

Arkhurst, J.C. (1964). *The adventures of Spider: West African folk tales.* New York: Little, Brown.

CanTeach. (n.d.). *African folk tales.* Retrieved June 21, 2006, from http://www.canteach.ca/elementary/africa.html

Cummings, P. (2002). *Ananse and the lizard: A West African tale.* New York: Henry Holt.

Gale, S.H. (1995). *West African folk tales.* Lincolnwood, IL: NTC.

Gore, B. (n.d.). *Anansi the trickster spider and the witch named "Five."* Retrieved June 21, 2006, from http://hillhouse.ckp.edu/~bobgore/story.html

Haley, G.E. (1970). *A story, a story: An African tale.* New York: Atheneum.

Kimmel, E. (1988). *Anansi and the moss-covered rock.* New York: Holiday House.

Kimmel, E. (1992). *Anansi goes fishing.* New York: Holiday House.

Kimmel, E. (1994). *Anansi and the talking melon.* New York: Holiday House.

Kituku, V.M.W. (1997). *East African folk tales: From the voice of Mukamba.* Little Rock: August House.

Mandela, N. (2002). *Favorite African folk tales.* New York: W.W. Norton.

McCall Smith, A. (1998). *Children of Wax: African Folktales.* Interlink Pub Group.

McCall Smith, A (2004). *The girl who married a lion and other tales from Africa.* New York: Pantheon.

McDermott, G. (1986). *Anasi the Spider: A tale from the Ashanti.* New York: Henry Holt. (Original work published 1972)

Scheub, H. (1999). *The African storyteller: Stories from African oral traditions.* Dubuque, IA: Kendall/Hunt.

Seeger, P. (2001). *Abiyoyo* (M. Hays, Ill.). New York: Simon & Schuster.

FILM CITED

Schindel, M. (Producer), & Deitch, G. (Director). (1993). *Stories from the black tradition* [Motion picture]. United States: Children's Circle.

AUTHOR INDEX

HODDER, B.W., 116
HOTEL RWANDA RUSESABAGINA
    FOUNDATION, 300, 305
HUDSON, H., 295–296
HUGHES, N., 294, 296
HUGO, V., 252
HUSTON, J., 295–296

I
IAFRICA.COM, 189–190
INFOPLEASE, 252
INTERKNOWLEDGE, 271
INTERNATIONAL MARKETING COUNCIL FOR
    SOUTH AFRICA, 240
INTERNATIONAL READING ASSOCIATION,
    xxi, 5, 52–53, 75–76, 96–97,
    120–121, 142–143, 165–166,
    188–189, 209–210, 231–232,
    252–253, 272–273
"IN THE GRIP," 62
ISADORA, R., 312, 314, 316

J
JACKSON, S.A.W., 245
JAFFE, S.R., 295–296
JALDESA, G.W., 122
JARCHOW, E., 4, 6–7, 9–10
JETTON, T.L., 62
JONES, T., 10
JORDAN, S., 10
JORGENSEN, K., 295–296

K
KAMBERELIS, G., 10
KANABUS, A., 241
KATER, K.J., 38
KEENE, E.O., 8, 58, 80, 125, 148, 169,
    193, 215, 238, 256, 277
KELLY, P.P., 13, 84, 86
KENNEDY, R., 249
KESSLER, C., 14, 18, 39, 122, 141–146,
    149–155, 160, 312–313, 315
KHADIAGALA, G.M., 312
KIMMEL, E., 323
KINGSLEY, C., 174
KITUKU, V.M.W., 327–328
KNIEP, W.M., 4
KOSO-THOMAS, O., 46
KOUBA, L.J., 40

KRATZ, C.A., 45
KROLL, V.L., 313–314
KULIKOWICH, J.M., 62
KURTZ, J., 14, 18, 165–166, 168–179,
    182–183

L
LAIBOW, R., 44
LANDIS, M., 208
LANE, S., 41
LEARNING SKILLS PROGRAM, 14, 241
LECHTMAN, T., 236, 240
LEITH-ROSS, S., 116
LENHART, L.A., 26, 86
LEONARD, R., 211
LEWIN, H., 312, 315–316
LEWIS, D., 13, 16, 55
LIEBER, J.W., 116
LINCOLN, A., 223
LINK, C., 295–296
LIUKKONEN, P., 99–100, 123–124, 213
LONSDALE, J., 45
LOVELL, J., 190
LYNN, S., 13, 131
LYONS, G.E., 286

M
MAATHAI, W., 3
MACRIS, D.R., 44
MACRORIE, K., 272, 287
MADIGAN, D., 10
MAHONEY, T., 10
MANDELA, N., 325–326
MARAIS, E., 211, 213
MARKS, Z., 297–298
MARSHALL, F., 45
MARTIN, F., 123
MARTIN, T., 210, 230
MATTHEE, D., 14, 18, 188–205
MAXON, R.M., 123
MCCALL SMITH, A., 14, 19, 36, 252–262,
    265–266, 310, 326–237
MCCAUGHREAN, G., 174
MCDERMOTT, G., 323
MCGINLEY, W., 10
MCKEON, C.A., 26, 86
MCLAREN, P.L., 5
MCTIGHE, J., 8, 14, 222, 262
MDA, Z., 225

WILLIAMS-GARCIA, R., 14, 18, 39, 122, 142–143, 147–150, 152–153
WOEHLER, C.A., 62
"WOMEN SHOULD FORMALISE THEIR MARRIAGES," 311
"WORLD FREE PRESS INSTITUTE," 135–136
WORLD HEALTH ORGANIZATION (WHO), 41–42, 233
WULFSOHN, G., 315

Y

YARICK, S.J., 329

Z

ZIMMERMANN, S., 8, 58, 80, 125, 148, 169, 193, 215, 238, 256, 277

SUBJECT INDEX

Note. Page numbers followed by *f* or *t* indicate *figures* or *tables*, respectively.

I-SEARCH PAPERS, 286–288, 288*t*
ISLAMIC PATRIARCHY: effects of, 81–82; resisting, 83

J

JAKARTA MISSING (KURTZ), 168–169
JOURNALS: in Arab women unit, 81*f*; in Botswana unit, 257*f*; in Ethiopia unit, 172*f*; in exploitation unit, 194*f*; in human rights unit, 238*f*; in Kenya unit, 126*f*; in Nigeria unit, 103*f*; in race relations unit, 215*f*; in rites of passage unit, 149*f*; sketchbook, 88–89, 89*f*; in Sudan unit, 59*f*; in Zimbabwe unit, 277*f*, 283–284, 284*f*
JOURNEY TO JO'BURG (NAIDOO), 234–235
THE JOYS OF MOTHERHOOD (EMECHETA), 101–102
JULY'S PEOPLE (GORDIMER), 213–214

K

KEGLER, CHRISTEN, 204
KEKU, FERDINAND, 310–311
KENNEDY, JOHN F., 137
KENYA, 119–139; culture and rituals of, 134–135, 135*t*; social and historical context of, 120–123
KENYATTA, JOMO, 120, 123
KNYSNA FOREST, 188–191
KOLA NUTS, 113*f*
K-W-L POSTERS: on African countries, 28–30, 29*f*

L

LESSARD, LACIE, 30
LETTERS: political action, 67–70, 68*f*, 70*t*; unsent, 285
LITERACY: in Ethiopia, project on, 181–182
LITERARY THEORY: and Kenya unit, 131–132
LITERATURE CIRCLES, 15–16
LOST BOYS OF SUDAN, 295, 296*t*

M

MAASAI PEOPLE, 143–144
MAATHAI, WANGARI, 3–4

MACRITCHIE, KAITLIN, 84
MAKING-A-DIFFERENCE PROJECTS, xxiii–xxiv; in Arab women unit, 89–90, 90*f*, 90*t*; in Botswana unit, 266–268, 266*t*, 267*f*, 267*t*; in children's literature unit, 316–317; in Ethiopia unit, 181–182; in exploitation unit, 205; in film unit, 305–306; in human rights unit, 245–249; in Kenya unit, 135–137; in Nigeria unit, 115–116, 116*t*–117*t*; in oral tradition unit, 334–336; in race relations unit, 224–227, 225*t*–226*t*, 227*f*; in rites of passage unit, 158–161; in Sudan unit, 67–70; in Zimbabwe unit, 286–288
MAKING CONNECTIONS: in Arab women unit, 79–80, 81*f*; in Botswana unit, 257–258, 257*f*; in Ethiopia unit, 169–175, 172*f*; in exploitation unit, 193–194, 194*f*; in human rights unit, 238–239, 238*f*; in Kenya unit, 125–126, 126*f*; in Nigeria unit, 102–104, 103*f*; in race relations unit, 214–216, 215*f*; in rites of passage, 148–150, 149*f*; in Sudan unit, 58–59, 59*f*; in Zimbabwe unit, 277–278, 277*f*
MANDELA, NELSON, 211, 234, 254
MANDELA AND DE CLERK, 223–224
MARIAM, MENGISTU HAILE, 167
MARXIST CRITICISM: and Kenya unit, 132
MASKS: for characters in novels, 35–36, 36*f*–37*f*; instructions for, Websites on, 35*t*; making, 32–36; for New Yam Festival, 336; slideshow presentation of, 33–34; Websites on, 34*t*
MAU MAU REVOLT, 122–123
McCLAIN, RUTH, 293–306
MEHNDI, 331–334
MEMORIES OF SUN (KURTZ), 168–171
MEMORY: questions on, 109
MEMORY BOOKS, 245
MENDAL, GIDEON, 244
MILLET, 32*f*
MIND'S EYE PREDICTIONS, 155, 156*t*
MOI, DANIEL ARAP, 122

PROCESS DRAMA: on HIV/AIDS, 245–249
PROGRAM FOR APPROPRIATE TECHNOLOGY IN HEALTH (PATH), 122
PROGRESS, 217–218
PROMOTIONAL BROCHURE: for Reading Feast Day, 227f
PROVERBS, AFRICAN: project on, 114, 115t
PSYCHOLOGICAL CRITICISM: and Kenya unit, 132

Q

Q-SORT: for animal rights, 155–157, 156t, 157f
QUESTIONING CIRCLES: on Arab women unit, 84–85, 86f
QUESTIONING STRATEGIES, 109; teacher-led, 13t–14t
QUESTIONS: on body image, 38; on *Hotel Rwanda,* 301t, 303t; for interviews, sample, 30f; for read-alouds, 310t; in Socratic seminar, 197–199; types of, 152, 241. *See also* Making Connections; Teacher Talk
QUOTE OF THE NOVEL, 284

R

RACE RELATIONS: social and historical context of, 210–211; in South Africa, 207–228, 232–233, 240
READ-ALOUDS, 309; discussion questions for, 310t
READER RESPONSE CRITICISM: and Kenya unit, 132
READER RESPONSE LOGS: requirements for, 12t
READERS THEATRE, 201–203, 202f–203f
READING FEAST DAY, 224–227, 225t–226t, 227f
RECONCILIATION, 218–220
REFLECTIVE DIMENSION, 222
REFLECTIVE ESSAYS: on women's cultural conflict, 89–90, 90f, 90t
RELIGIOUS CONVERSION: effects of, 127–128
REPETENDS, 161, 161f; definition of, 158
RESEARCH ACTIVITIES: on *Hotel Rwanda,* 304t

RESEARCH PAPERS: in rites of passage unit, 158–161, 159t
RESISTANCE: to colonial rule, 95–118; to patriarchy, 83
RESPONSIBILITY, 130–131
RHINO SPECIES, 144–145, 151, 160f–161f
RHODES, CECIL, 273
RICE, LINDA J., xvii–xxvi, 3–48, 119–139, 181, 187–228
RITES OF PASSAGE: in Central Africa, 140–163; and circumcision, 45; research papers on, 158–161, 159t
THE RIVER BETWEEN (WA THIONG'O), 123–125
ROLE-PLAY ACTIVITIES: on *Hotel Rwanda,* 304t
RUSESABAGINA, PAUL, *294*
RWAMUHUZI, GITERA, 302
RWANDAN GENOCIDE, 293–306; study objectives for, 299–300

S

SANDMANN, ALEXA L., 164–183
SAN PEOPLE, 190
SCHEMA-BASED QUESTIONS, 282
SCHWEICKERT, JEFF, 89
SCOTT, WALTER, 191
SEMANTIC MAPPING, 26–27
SEMINARS: Socratic, 197–199
SENEGAL, 73–92
SHONA PEOPLE, 271, 273, 279–282
SIGNIFICANT PASSAGES, 283–284
SKETCHBOOK JOURNAL, 88–89, 89f
SLAVE: MY TRUE STORY (NAZER), 54–56; setting of, 59–60
SLAVERY: and stereotypes of Africa, 28; in Sudan, 51–72
SLIDESHOW PRESENTATIONS: for exploitation unit, 205; of masks, 33–34; on Nigerian women, 115–116, 116t–117t
SOCIAL ACTION APPROACH, 11–12
SOCIALLY RESPONSIVE LEARNING, 3–24
SOCRATIC SEMINARS, 197–199
SO LONG A LETTER (BÂ), 78–79
SOMETHING OF VALUE, 295, 296t
SOMETIMES IN APRIL, 294, 296t

SONG ADAPTATIONS, 199–201, 200*f*
SOUTH AFRICA, 207–228; exploitation in, 187–206; human rights issues in, 229–250; novels of, 226*t*; social and historical context of, 188–191, 210–211, 232–234
SPENCER, AMY, 89
SPENCER, STEVEN, iii
SPLIT-OPEN MIND, 284–285, 285*f*
STEREOTYPES: of Africa, 27–28
STORYBOARD: narrative, 203–204, 204*f*
STORYBOARD ACTIVITY, 66–67, 67*f*
STORY IMPRESSIONS, 64–65; word list for, 65*f*
STRATTON, ALLAN, xv–xvi
STRUCTURED VIEWING LESSON, 300–305
STUDENTS: discussions generated by, 15, 15*t*; inquiry directed by, on Ethiopia, 179, 180*t*
SUB-SAHARAN AFRICA, 185–290
SUDAN, 51–72; human rights issues in, Websites on, 69*f*; social and historical context of, 54
SUNNA CIRCUMCISION, 41
SUTTON, BRETT, 238

T

T-CHART, 323, 324*t*
TEACHER(S): discussions led by, 13–15, 13*t*–14*t*; news article created by, 182*f*
TEACHERS WITHOUT BORDERS, 6–7
TEACHER TALK, xxiii, 8; in Arab women unit, 84–85; in Botswana unit, 261–262; in Ethiopia unit, 177–178; in exploitation unit, 197–199; in human rights unit, 241–243; in Kenya unit, 131; in Nigeria unit, 109–111; in race relations unit, 221–223; in rites of passage unit, 152–154; in Sudan unit, 62–64; in Zimbabwe unit, 282–283
TEFF, 32*f*
THEMES, CRITICAL EXPLORATION OF: in Arab woman unit, 81–83; in Botswana unit, 258–261; in Ethiopia unit, 175–177; in

exploitation unit, 195–197; in human rights unit, 240–241; in Kenya unit, 127–131; in Nigeria unit, 104–109; in race relations unit, 216–221; in rites of passage unit, 150–152; in Sudan unit, 59–62; in Zimbabwe unit, 278–282
THINGS FALL APART (ACHEBE), 98–100
TIMELINE: on *Hotel Rwanda*, 303
TUTSI, 297
TUTU, DESMOND, 208

U

UHAMIRI, 106
UNDERSTANDING, 129–130
UNITED NATIONS EDUCATIONAL, SCIENTIFIC AND CULTURAL ORGANIZATION (UNESCO), 136
UNITED STATES AGENCY FOR INTERNATIONAL DEVELOPMENT (USAID): investigative report on, 135–137
UNSENT LETTER, 285
UPJOHN FOUNDATION, 136

V

VIDEOS. *See* films
VILLAGE LIFE, 313–315
VISUAL DICTIONARY: Igbo, 112, 112*t*, 113*f*
VOCABULARY REPORTS: one-minute, 262–263, 263*t*
VOLUNTEERS FOR PROSPERITY, 137

W

WAITING FOR THE RAIN (GORDON), 235–237
"WAKING DREAMS OF JUSTICE", iii
WEBSITES: of African masks, 34*t*; on Ethiopia, 180*t*; on HIV/AIDS, 244; of mask-making instructions, 35*t*; of Nigerian photos, 117*t*; on Sudanese human rights issues, 69*f*
WEEP NOT, CHILD (WA THIONG'O), 123–125
WESTERN: term, xvii
WFPI. *See* World Free Press Institute
WHEN RAIN CLOUDS GATHER (HEAD), 254–255

WILLIAMS, LAURA, 36, 267
WILLIS, HOLLY, 172
WISDOM, 129–130
WOMEN: in Arab world, 73–92; cultural conflict of, essays on, 89–90, 90*f,* 90*t*; HIV/AIDS and, 233–234; magazines for, 145; in Nigeria, 108–109, 115–116; as providers and caretakers, 312–313; respect for, 313; rites of passage for, 140–163; self-determination of, 82; in Zimbabwe, 270–290. *See also* female genital mutilation
WORD BANK, 302–303
WORLD FREE PRESS INSTITUTE (WFPI): investigative report on, 135–137
WRITING: folk tales, 329–331, 332*f*; freewriting, about Africa, 27, 27*f*; I-search papers, 286–288, 288*t*; multigenre research papers, 158–161, 159*t*; political action letters, 67–70, 68*f*, 70*t*; reflective essays, 89–90, 90*f*, 90*t*; unsent letters, 285

Y

YAMS, 32*f*; New Yam Festival, 334–336
YESTERDAY, 295, 296*t*

Z

ZENAWI, MELES, 167
ZIMBABWE, 270–290; social and historical context of, 273
ZINES: in Botswana unit, 266–268, 266*t*, 267*f*, 267*t*
ZULU, 295, 296*t*